THE UNITED STATES IN INTERNATIONAL BANKING

THE UNITED STATES IN INTERNATIONAL BANKING

BY

Siegfried Stern

1951

COLUMBIA UNIVERSITY PRESS

New York

PUBLISHED IN GREAT BRITAIN, CANADA, AND INDIA
BY GEOFFREY CUMBERLEGE, OXFORD UNIVERSITY PRESS
LONDON, TORONTO, AND BOMBAY

MANUFACTURED IN THE UNITED STATES OF AMERICA

To

E. P. S. and J. S. S.

PREFACE

THIS VOLUME is an attempt to review the evolution of some of the overseas activities of United States banking during and between the two great wars. During the life of the present generation the face of the world has changed to such an extent that past events may not be a reliable guide in the years to come. Nevertheless, in order to see present and future problems in their right perspective, it may be useful to retrace our course and to appraise previous achievements in the light of experience.

In this chronicle I have tried to show the part played by United States banks in the advancement of our foreign commerce and hence in the promotion of national prosperity. I have sketched the occasional setbacks caused by economic reverses or political disturbances in distant countries and in some instances by lack of competent guidance or sufficient training on the part of those who at certain stages were the standard-bearers of United States financial enterprise abroad. Finally, I have made bold to suggest that even though the labors of the American banks were carried on far from the fields of combat, nonetheless many significant tasks were performed within the walls and behind the counters of the skyscrapers of downtown Manhattan and the other important financial centers of this country and abroad that indirectly but very truly contributed to the victory of the Allied nations.

The material is based on the knowledge acquired in the course of more than thirty years spent as head of the foreign departments of leading New York banks, including frequent and prolonged stays overseas. Accordingly, the study is a practical account by one who has spent the greater part of his business life within the orbit of United States foreign banking. To a large extent I have relied upon personal observations and recollection. Names and dates have been checked insofar as they are available in public documents and prints. This volume is not offered as a textbook on foreign banking. The machinery of foreign departments and the mechanics of foreign exchange and bank acceptances have been authoritatively covered in a number of able publications, for a partial list of which the reader is referred to the bibliography at the end of this book. Rather is this narrative presented as a factual compendium of notes and sketches on certain interesting phases of American international banking. Only casual reference to monetary theories and broad economic developments has been possible.

Owing to the scope of the material, it has been necessary to confine the survey to a restricted number of the more important countries where United States banks in the course of the last half century have taken root and have succeeded in playing a prominent role. Even so, most of the narration had to be compressed within the limited confines of the space available, while on the other hand certain facts and events have, for the sake of clarity, been mentioned several times in different contexts. As conditions have varied according to the economic advancement of the different nations and the cooperation of the respective governments and peoples, the pattern of treatment necessarily lacks uniformity, and the development will be found more detailed in those sections dealing with parts of the world where private American initiative and enterprise could be exerted under the most auspicious conditions. Only lack of space has prevented the inclusion of other countries where United States banking effort has been equally encouraged and has had similar scope for mutually beneficial expansion. It should be borne in mind that, excepting occasional complementary notes, this survey does not carry the record beyond the events of 1945, the last year of the Second World War.

During the past four decades the lives of United States foreign bankers have been filled with extraordinary experiences. On the whole, their course during this stirring epoch has been distinguished by bold initiative and vigorous, clear-sighted action. This narrative may, it is hoped, bring home to the younger men engaged in the calling and to students of the subject some of the vicissitudes as well as the accomplishments and the romance of American adventure in international banking.

I wish to record my great indebtedness to Dr. Benjamin Haggott Beckhart, of Columbia University, who has been kind enough to read the manuscript and has made many helpful suggestions in the course of its preparation. My thanks, too, are due to Mr. Winthrop W. Case, of the Research Department of the Federal Reserve Bank of New York, for his competent editorial help. In particular I want to express my gratitude to some of my former colleagues, who have been most helpful in checking certain facts and figures and giving me the benefit of their criticisms. In fact, all my former chiefs and associates, who by inspiring my best efforts and lightening my way throughout the years have had a part in the making of this volume.

In a special sense I must pay tribute to my wife, without whose devoted aid and constant encouragement this book would not have been written.

SIEGFRIED STERN

Stamford, Conn.
July, 1951

CONTENTS

PART ONE

HISTORICAL SURVEY

I

1914–1945

THE UNITED STATES did not enter the field of international banking as a serious participant until 1914. Any study of the evolution of the American role in world finance, therefore, must necessarily proceed from the situation existing at the beginning of the First World War. Unlike the British financial pre-eminence which emerged out of the practice of centuries and slow development, the prominence of this nation in the foreign financial sphere was largely the aftermath of a rather sudden and, on the whole, involuntary excursion into the area of overseas lending and exchange. This deviation, moreover, took place at a time when the country's banking system, only recently strengthened by the creation of the Federal Reserve organization, was still fully absorbed with the rapid expansion of the domestic economy. Inadequately prepared for the new task, United States foreign banking suffered from unavoidable improvisation until the banking machinery could be perfected for service in distant regions and could be better adapted for functioning under the upsetting conditions that marked the second quarter of the present century and subjected even more tested banking organisms to a severe strain. To provide a background for the detailed description of American endeavor and performance in the field of international monetary competition the following pages will sketch some of the chief developments since this country was first called upon to play a significant part in world financial pursuits.

THE FIRST WORLD WAR, 1914–1919

During the thirty-odd years from 1914 to 1945 the whole structure of international banking underwent profound and in certain respects revolutionary alterations. For more than a century England, as the leading creditor nation, had been the world's banker. The money market of the City of London wielded a decisive influence in every financial center. The discount rate of the Bank of England and the pound sterling were world barometers whose movements almost unfailingly indicated changes of weather in the international atmosphere.

England held the world's purse strings for many reasons. Her currency was regarded as the soundest and most stable in the world. For ninety-three consecutive years—since 1821—the Empire had been wedded to the gold standard. She was the principal importer of raw materials and foodstuffs and the leading exporter of manufactured goods. Her ships carried cargoes to and from all the ports of the globe. Through credits and loans her banks financed production, marketing, and distribution in every continent. Her insurance companies underwrote marine and war risks throughout the world. Her investors subscribed to foreign stock and bond issues for the building of railroads and public utilities in other countries. A considerable part of her purchases abroad were paid for out of these freight, insurance, brokerage, and banking earnings, as well as from the returns from overseas investments and the expenditures of tourists and businessmen visiting the British Isles. England's prosperity was thus linked closely with the smooth flow of world trade and the development of the colonies and foreign countries where during the nineteenth and fifteen years of the twentieth century British capitalists had with foresight invested their savings and British industry, banking, and trade had established their outposts. Above all, however, the extraordinary success of British enterprise was due to the energy and financial talents of the London merchants and bankers, who fostered sound principles in business and finance and established an enviable name for fair treatment of their customers. With very few exceptions the record and reputation of British banking were matchless.

This phase of British superiority ended with the outbreak of the First World War. Who among those whose memories go back to 1914 does not recall the eventful weeks that followed the Black Friday of July 31, 1914, when the Asquith government was compelled to proclaim a week's bank holiday, the bankrate was raised to 10 percent, and a moratorium was hastily declared on the payment of bank acceptances and commercial paper? To avoid wholesale bankruptcies and a panic in the City, the Bank of England, under a blanket guarantee furnished by the government and without the usual close scrutiny of the signatures, discounted all the portfolios of the merchant banking houses and other London banks that were offered it. Acting through the Chancellor of the Exchequer, Lloyd George, the cabinet assumed the responsibility for the ultimate payment of some 70 million pounds of English bankers' and commercial bills and thus saved the credit of the British banking world. Long after the end of the war the Old Lady of Threadneedle Street still carried some of the paper then discounted as part of its portfolio.

The declaration of war had profound repercussions on the foreign exchange markets everywhere. For a number of weeks the latter were completely demoralized. All belligerents suspended specie payments and hastened to mobilize their available financial resources. Dollars were heavily offered in all European capitals. Simultaneously, debtors all over the world, in order to be in a position to honor their maturing obligations, made frantic efforts to secure cable transfers and drafts payable in London, Paris, Amsterdam, and Zurich. For obvious reasons European creditors were reluctant to renew the acceptances and loans that fell due. On the other hand, owing to the German submarine menace and the consequent increased freight and insurance charges, the cost of shipping gold rose to prohibitive levels. In New York some transactions in sterling were reported to have taken place at $7.00 per pound. To provide cover for over 80 million dollars of maturing notes of the City of New York, placed in London and other European markets, a gold pool was hurriedly formed under the aegis of J. P. Morgan & Co. and Kuhn Loeb & Co., and the city's obligations were duly taken care of on the due date of January 1, 1915.

Fortunately, all these difficulties proved temporary. Within a few months Allied and neutral nations placed heavy orders in this country for foodstuffs and war material, and the dollar was again in strong demand. Later, when the dollar reserves of the buyers began to dwindle, England, France, and Italy were granted considerable credits and loans by various United States syndicates, in which leading banks and trust companies participated substantially. Unwittingly, the very forces that unleashed the war were also responsible for transforming the United States into not only an arsenal for democracy but also in the course of the following years a great creditor nation.

Notwithstanding active United States financial support, the oscillations of the pound were extreme in 1915. In order to steady the exchange, the British Government, by an order in council, was given authority to call for the deposit and sale to it of all foreign securities owned by British subjects. As a result about 1 1/2 billion dollars of

American and Canadian stocks and bonds were placed at the disposal of the War Cabinet. Finally, in January, 1916, sterling was "pegged." During the rest of the war J. P. Morgan & Co., as United States agent for the British Treasury, bought all sterling offered in the New York market at the fixed rate of $4.76 7/16 per pound.

THE TWENTIES, 1920–1930

Four months after the armistice, on March 20, 1919, the peg for the pound sterling was withdrawn, and the free market was reestablished. As expected, the London exchange then declined rapidly, reaching in February, 1920, an all-time low of $3.19, a drop of 34 percent from the former dollar parity of 4.8665 and of 54 percent from the wartime peak of about $7.00. In the summer of 1919 the United States returned to the gold standard and removed the ban on gold exports. By now it was apparent to most observers that, diluted as they were by the vast war expenditures and the heavy cost of postwar rehabilitation, not only the pound sterling but all the belligerent exchanges except the United States dollar were seriously overvalued in terms of gold.

Such was the situation when a vigorous movement set in among forward-looking United States bankers and businessmen, who urged a boldly aggressive policy for the assumption by this country of a more active role in the international financial field. During the preceding years, since 1914, the preponderant part that had been played by Great Britain in world financial and monetary affairs had slowly gravitated, by the force of circumstances, toward the Western Hemisphere. The foundation of nineteenth-century finance had been a monetary system anchored to the pound sterling. By 1921, however, the dollar appeared definitely in the ascendancy. The end of the great struggle of 1914–1918 ushered in a new spirit among industrial and financial leaders in the United States. In place of her debtor outlook, America adopted a creditor mentality.

Until 1914 only a few large banks on the Atlantic and Pacific coasts and a small number of private banking firms—the first harbingers of international finance in this country—had been equipped to handle overseas transactions through direct correspondents in London, where their principal balances were carried, as well as in Paris and a few other financial centers in Europe, South America, and the Orient. They supplied foreign exchange quotations to customers interested in sterling, francs, guilders, and other currencies. They likewise purchased "clean" ninety-day bills on London or Paris, drawn under acceptance credits that had been offered by merchant bankers across the ocean mainly to help finance the movement of cotton and grain crops.[1] Of course, in this connection it must not be overlooked that around the turn of the century some of the banks and banking firms occasionally handled special transactions of considerable magnitude, such as the short-term investment of American funds in 1896 in London to take advantage of the temporarily higher interest rates there, the payment of the twenty-million-dollar Philippine indemnity to Spain after 1898, the borrowing of money in Europe to help finance the Northern Pacific corner in 1901, and the handling of gold shipments from the Klondike and Australian gold mines during the last half of the nineteenth century.

Among the larger banks of the Middle West, some Chicago institutions realized early the advantage of furnishing foreign banking services to their depositors. Owing to the initiative of some of their first foreign managers—Fred I. Kent, John E. Gardin, and Max May—the names of the First National Bank of Chicago, the Continental National Bank and Trust Co., and others became well known in the financial capitals abroad. These men were later attracted to New York by the greater opportunities offered to those trained in international banking by the rising demand for foreign financial experts in the eastern city.

Favored by the growing interest in banking facilities for overseas commerce, other men gradually rose to prominence in this new field not only in New York but also the cities of the interior and the other seaports of the Atlantic and Pacific coasts, notably R. S. Hecht and Albert Breton, in New Orleans, John Bollinger in Boston, Dr. W. F. Gephart in St. Louis, A. P. Fraser in Detroit, Harry Salinger and Arthur Roberts in Chicago, P. A. Kinnoch and J. S. Curran in San Francisco, John G. Geddes in Cleveland, Stephen Ruth in Philadelphia, and in New York, Bernard Duys, George LeBlanc, Joseph Broderick, John F. Schmid, August Ulrich, Franz Meyer, David Penny, James Heckscher, L. F. Kiesewetter, Philip Vogel, Joseph Durell, Clarence Hunter, and many others, whom space forbids list-

[1] Indeed, the predecessors of some New York banking houses, such as J. P. Morgan & Co., Goldman Sachs & Co., Ladenburg Thalmann & Co., Lazard Frères, and J. & W. Seligman & Co., had been originally engaged in the textile and similar trades.

ing. Foreign banking interests were represented in New York by the Foreign Exchange Club, the Committee on Foreign Banking, the Foreign Remittance Club, and nationally by the Bankers Association for Foreign Trade. The latter, jointly with the American Bankers Association, the National Foreign Trade Council, and similar organizations, has throughout the years done outstanding work in promoting and fostering international banking and foreign trade. The successive presidents of the association—Joseph C. Rovensky and Wilbert Ward, among others—have been the eloquent spokesmen of the profession on many important occasions.

It soon became a matter of prestige as well as of informed business policy for leading banks in all parts of the country, even including some far-seeing savings banks, to have foreign departments attached to their institutions in order to be able to minister to local needs in the foreign field without having to use the services of correspondents in the metropolitan cities. Thus, United States commercial banks in general, through their more perfected foreign organizations, comprising in certain cases a rapidly expanding net of foreign branches, began to wield a powerful public influence in international commerce and finance. Under their vivifying impulse New York bade fair to become a serious contender for the position, so long held by London, of chief money center of the world. Business communities all over the land became more international-trade minded. Instead of using London bank acceptances to settle foreign accounts, they turned to their local banks for the financial services needed in connection with their imports and exports, which were reaching impressive totals. The dollar letter of credit and the American bank acceptance, payable in United States currency, made their bow on the international stage.

In their unaccustomed function as granters of foreign credits and lenders, the banks, as they branched out into this new and apparently profitable sphere, were faced at once with many strange and, to most of them, unfamiliar problems. The financing of a steadily growing share of European, Latin American, and Far Eastern trade was for the great majority of United States banks now reaching into foreign fields a novel but stimulating task. Rather more rapidly than had been anticipated, the dollar bill of exchange assumed a commanding place in much of the globe. United States banking facilities were more and more substituted for short-term sterling credits. Simultaneously, New York consolidated its position as an important foreign-exchange market, while a discount market was also created there for American bank acceptances, where domestic and foreign holders could buy and sell bills at attractive rates.[2]

As close neighbors, the Latin American nations were naturally the first to occupy the focus of United States foreign banking. The ink on the peace treaties was hardly dry when special banking corporations with strong backing were being formed to finance United States trade with Middle and South America, their activities being quickly extended also to the Far East. The promoters, however, although successful in the domestic sphere, failed to take into account that at that period there was not sufficient sound business available even for the European banks long established in those territories. The American emissaries went abroad with lofty hopes and full of energy and enthusiasm, although not, perhaps, always possessing the superior ability and thorough knowledge of local conditions with which some of their keenest competitors were equipped. The overhead was high. The newcomers had to operate in part in one- or two-crop countries, in many of which the war had generated short-lived speculative booms. In order to show earnings and spurred by native and foreign banking rivalry, they quoted easy interest rates for loans and low commissions for credits, and—worst of all—made excessive advances without sufficient margin to protect their branches against a fall of the wildly inflated commodity prices. Thus, there were both overexpansion and lack of sound banking judgment. Before the executive capacity of these first missionaries of United States international banking had had time to mature, the postwar depression of the early twenties overtook them. The resulting losses were so serious that most of the corporations, upon whose success so much had been staked, were forced to liquidate or were absorbed by the financial institutions that had provided the inspiration and the capital. While the crisis eventually passed, it was a disheartening experience for those who had looked forward to a sound and auspicious start of the first American efforts in international banking enterprise. One comforting thought, however, was that the setback was due in no small degree to the unfavorable world juncture and that those more seasoned in world finance had suffered equally.[3]

2 For an authoritative description of the discount market and an instructive analysis of acceptance practices the reader is referred to Beckhart, *The Discount Policy of the Federal Reserve System,* and Burgess, *The Reserve Banks and the Money Market.*

3 In a report of the Federal Reserve Committee on acceptance practice made to the

These costly lessons were soon forgotten. The memory of this dark period in the early history of United States foreign banking and its chilling frustrations receded all too quickly. The setbacks which had been suffered were not allowed long to retard accelerated activity and renewed expansion in another direction. Europe, showing remarkable recuperative powers notwithstanding the long struggle, was credit-hungry, and United States finance decided to turn its full attention to this promising area. Here was the coveted opportunity to engage in international financial affairs on a broadened scale and to attain a more prominent place in the foreign field by fostering the export of United States capital and by rendering banking service abroad in a larger way. Resolutely those who had been substantial borrowers from Europe during the last half of the nineteenth century now adjusted themselves to the new role of liberal lenders for both short and long terms. By generous bond flotations and freehanded banking accommodation the Continent was now furnished the funds necessary to purchase the war-expanded surplus production of United States factories and farms.

In an effort to pay for their mounting imports the European countries at first bent their energies to the promotion of their own foreign sales, while the acquisition of imported goods was discouraged except for urgently required articles that could be paid for from the proceeds of the foreign sales. Soon, however, it became manifest that the difference between income from abroad and the outgo of exchange could no longer be bridged. Gold shipments could not supply the answer; the depleted metallic reserves were inadequate even for the protection of the currency issues, which were steadily expanding in response

---

Board of Governors of the Federal Reserve System (*Federal Reserve Bulletin*, September 1937, p. 840) it was stated that actual losses were suffered by only 24 banks out of 156 banks that answered the committee's questionnaire as to their acceptance-credit experience during 1920–1932. Losses were written off to the extent of 10.3 million dollars, and an aggregate of 4.7 million was still in suspense in August, 1935. The indicated losses were slightly more than 0.02 of 1 percent of the total acceptance business done during 1920–1932. However, the experience with Central European standstill credits (see chapters X and XII) was not taken into account in these figures, nor were the reserves that were rendered necessary by the losses due to nonpayment of cash advances and overdrafts. From the list of commodities responsible for the 10.3 million dollar losses, the bulk of the underlying credits appear to have been for the account of domestic importers and also of customers in the Carribean region and Latin America. When weighing these figures it must be borne in mind that they do not reflect the capital losses written off by the shareholders of the banking corporations mentioned above or the capital contributions made by their banking creditors in order to permit their voluntary liquidation.

to rising budgetary deficits incurred to satisfy the still unallayed demand for additional food, clothing, and materials for reconstruction. And so, when no other alternative remained, recourse was had to constantly growing sales of local currencies in the principal foreign exchange markets. Despite the billions poured across the Atlantic, the financial disorganization abroad caused by the war had thus proved too great to be repaired by ordinary economic remedies. It was at this period that emergency trade and exchange controls made their first appearance.

The inevitable outcome of the insidious monetary tinkering came in 1921 when the continental currencies, especially those of former foes, started to slump. One after the other, German marks, Polish zlotys, and Austrian and Hungarian crowns plunged, until finally their purchasing power came to be almost nil. International exchange speculators with headquarters in Amsterdam and Zurich, operating with apparently unlimited and partly borrowed capital, accumulated unconscionable profits.

As to the United States, she failed to perceive then—as she was to do again and again during the following decades—that in order to receive payment for exports as well as for loans a creditor country must be willing to accept payment in the form of goods and services. She disregarded the fact that her increasingly favorable balance of trade was a grave obstacle to efforts of her European customers and debtors to settle their international accounts in the currencies of their creditors. For, having exhausted their reserves of gold and foreign exchange available for settlements of foreign accounts they would be compelled to reduce their purchases unless the United States either increased her imports, which at the time was against her traditional policy, or else financed most of her future sales by additional loans and credits, including the renewal of those falling due.

The demoralized exchange situation in Europe was partly brought about by the flight of "nervous" capital. The United States, because of her growing gold hoard, was regarded as the safest haven for these fugitive funds. Curiously enough, while this influx of frightened capital was raising the total of foreign deposits in United States commercial banks, there was, although to a lesser degree, an almost simultaneous outflow of dollars to European countries. Thousands of ill-advised and ignorant citizens and United States residents of Central European ancestry bought banknotes and internal bonds in German marks and other continental fast-depreciating currencies in the hope that some day they would return to their former parities. These unfortunate buyers of the discredited moneys of Central and Southeastern Europe suffered ruinous losses. Austrian crowns, for instance, declined to less than 1/1000 of a United States cent from a prewar value of more than 20 cents, and the mark, worth about 24 cents before the war, fell so low that during the final stage of the German inflation one United States dollar could be exchanged for several trillions of marks. Finally, in the autumn of 1923 the mark was stabilized, with one billion paper marks exchangeable for one *rentenmark,* worth 23.81 cents.

In turn, the French franc, which in 1914 had been pegged at 19.31 cents, had started to slide in the neutral markets during the third quarter of 1915, and at the time of the armistice it was quoted at about 18 1/4 cents despite continuing official support. By October, 1920, after the abandonment of such support, it touched a low of 6 1/2 cents. This drop did not come as a surprise in informed exchange circles. Scarcely a year after the armistice, the French balance of payments had turned decisively adverse. It continued to deteriorate at an accelerated pace during 1923 to 1925, and there was fear in some quarters that the franc might suffer the fate of the mark. The franc had fallen to two cents when, on July 24, 1926, Raymond Poincaré became Premier, and with a firm hand stabilized the nation's finances. Those numerous individuals, both foreigners and Frenchmen, who had sold the franc short, suffered severely; it was reported, not without a certain malice, that their losses exceeded all the profits that they had made in their bearish operations in other moneys.

In April, 1925, partly relying on United States credits, England returned to the gold standard. Her action ratified the market's judgment, which had carried the pound to its prewar level of $4.8665, although, as she was to discover some years later, at this price the pound was overvalued. Sweden had made the same decision some time earlier. Belgium, The Netherlands, and Switzerland soon followed by making their currencies again convertible. In 1927 Italy, Brazil, and the Argentine, and in 1928 France, likewise once more embraced the gold standard.

The action of the European nations, whose financial authorities were renowned for their financial acumen and conservative judgment, was the signal for the renewal of keen competition among the leading creditor countries in wooing the patronage of would-be borrowers in the Old and New Worlds. Economic conditions appeared favorable, and prospects for private investments seemed bright. Not only American and English but also Dutch, Swiss, Swedish, and French banks and issuing houses approached foreign states, cities, railroads, public utilities, and industrial corporations, offering them loans and credits without serious concern as to their ability to repay in the lender's currency. After a few years of such unrestrained rivalry it became apparent to careful observers that it was impossible to determine, on the basis of the statistics available, whether the aggregate indebtedness, short- and long-term, was not excessive and out of proportion to the gold and foreign exchange reserves, actual and potential, available to the borrowers. There was no way of ascertaining how much credit each individual debtor was actually using or what the aggregate outstanding short-term liabilities amounted to in each country. While the New York banks had adopted the habit of exchanging information as to the credit lines granted by them, foreign banks, as a rule, were reluctant to reveal the nature and amount of their outstanding foreign indebtedness. Accordingly there existed no central clearinghouse where there were recorded the facts as to the extent to which use had been made of foreign credits, with the result that individual creditors were in ignorance as to how far banks in the various lending countries had already satisfied the legitimate requirements of the borrowers. This absence of a central pool of reliable information and statistics was in part responsible for the overly lavish bestowal of credit and the losses that were shortly to be suffered by creditors and investors throughout the Western world.[4]

The boom on the New York Stock Exchange and the subsequent collapse in 1929 stopped temporarily the flow of United States credits and loans abroad. The attractive interest rates on call money and the tempting opportunities in equity investments beckoned United

[4] Since 1934 the Federal Reserve banks have collected statistics on international capital movements and foreign exchange transactions. Monthly statements prepared by the Federal Reserve Bank of New York reflect the aggregate short-term credits and advances extended abroad by United States banks, as well as the total sight deposits held in the United States for foreign account. Along the same lines, Wilbert Ward, a veteran student of American acceptance banking, has proposed that the International Monetary Fund supply statistics concerning the annual dollar requirements of foreign countries for the payment to the United States of interest and sinking fund on their short- and long-term indebtedness, including dollar payments due to United States Government institutions, the International Monetary Fund, and the International Bank for Reconstruction and Development.

States capital to domestic pastures, and interest in the acquisition of foreign bonds lapsed. The repercussions on the debtor countries were immediate and disastrous. Argentina was promptly forced to suspend convertibility and permit the peso to find its own level. In less than a year the financial structure of many of the European nations commenced to weaken under the load of foreign debts beginning to fall due, for which cover in the creditor's currency had to be provided. The decline in prices, reflected in the drop of the United States wholesale price index from 95 in 1929 to 65 in 1932, imposed unexpected burdens on the debtors the more so as international trade between these years had collapsed from 35.6 to 14 billion dollars. The situation was aggravated by reparations and the interallied war debts, which for almost a decade had hung unsettled over the former enemy countries. The heavy expenditures abroad of United States tourists helped for a time to support the balances of payments of the debtor nations, but proved insufficient to provide the considerable amounts needed to repay the maturing credits and loans. Sales of merchandise to United States consumers might have helped to alleviate the situation and create some of the dollars so sorely needed, but they were impeded by the onerous import duties imposed on foreign goods in 1930 under the Smoot-Hawley Tariff Act.

SUMMARY. This section presents the historical background of United States banking activities abroad. It outlines the events during and immediately after the First World War, as a result of which United States banks came to play a predominant role in world banking. The first ventures in Latin America and the Far East encountered initial difficulties, owing both to the depression of the early twenties and to the lack of experience. Later, American and foreign lenders made large-scale short- and long-term investments in Europe and Latin America, following the return of England and the other principal trading countries to the gold standard. The subsequent speculation that developed in the Central European currencies led eventually to their financial collapse and to the defaults and moratoria of the early thirties.

THE DEPRESSION, 1931–1939

In the spring of 1931 alarming rumors began to be circulated in the financial centers about an impending catastrophe menacing the whole of Central Europe. During the summer disastrous runs on prominent Vienna and Berlin banks, and the declaration of bank holidays and moratoria confirmed the worst fears of some of the foreign creditors. The difficulties were not confined to Germany. In France, the important Banque Nationale de Crédit had to be given support; the Comptoir Lyon-Allemand and the Banque Adam closed; there were heavy withdrawals of deposits from the Banque de l'Union Parisienne; while in Italy the Banca Commerciale Italiana had to be aided by Mussolini's government.

Storm warnings were posted all over the international banking world. Some creditor countries became panicky. France had been following the growing power of the Nazis with understandable apprehension. After the conclusion of the abortive German-Austrian customs union, in 1930, she had canceled part of her credits in Austria and Germany. Now she feared that the deep involvement of British finance in Germany might end by weakening the credit of the City of London and lead to a devaluation of the pound sterling; it was well known that the liquid foreign short-term assets of Great Britain were insufficient, in the event of heavy withdrawals of sterling deposits and gold, to cover her overseas demand and short-term liabilities. Accordingly French banks started to reduce their extensive London bank deposits. This led in turn to a heavy loss of gold by the Bank of England. The consequent reduction in the metallic backing of the British currency aroused apprehension among other holders of sterling balances and British securities, who became fearful lest the depletion of the Bank of England's bullion reserves should cause financial disorder in other countries. Finally, the decline of cable transfers on London to a point where it was profitable to ship gold caused anxiety among the central banks on the Continent. They had for decades kept substantial gold and exchange reserves at the Bank of England with the assurance that they would always be able to withdraw them on demand.

Early in August, 1931, in order to assist the British authorities in their plight, the Federal Reserve Bank of New York and the Bank of France jointly granted 250 million dollars in short-term loans to the Bank of England, secured, in effect, by part of the bank's commercial paper. But the flight from the pound could not be halted. A second credit, aggregating 400 million dollars, was extended during the last days of August, an operation in which a syndicate of United

States banks participated to the extent of one half, the remainder being furnished by the Paris market. The week-end prior to the fateful day of September 20 found most of the New York foreign department heads and exchange traders at their desks. Finally, on Sunday the dreaded notice came over the wires. The venerable British central bank had been forced to lower the flag; the preceding day the British Government, by the Gold Standard (Amendment) Act, had reluctantly relieved it of its age-long obligation to sell gold in unlimited quantities at the fixed price established by statute of £3 17s. 10 1/2d. per standard ounce.

Heavy losses were suffered by some banks of issue, especially the Bank of France and the Netherlands Bank, and other foreign owners of sterling; Dr. G. Vissering, governor of the Netherlands Bank and one of the most devoted adherents to sound monetary principles, assumed responsibility for not having foreseen developments and resigned his post. In brief succession, Britain's example was followed by her Dominions (except Canada and South Africa), the Scandinavian countries, Finland, Portugal, and Egypt. Only France, Belgium, the Netherlands, Switzerland, Italy, Czechoslovakia, and Poland still continued to cleave to the gold standard. For most of the rest of the world convertibility into gold, as it had existed for generations, was now a relic of the past.

By the end of September sterling was quoted at $3.84. Frightened capitalists hastily transferred their funds to those countries still prepared to exchange paper money for gold. Significantly, before the middle of 1932 more than 800 million dollars in gold was even withdrawn from the United States by scared owners of dollars. One influential depositor, the Bank of France, according to a New York *Times* report of October 20, 1931, also contemplated transferring its balances, estimated at 600 million dollars, unless a higher interest rate than the existing 1 1/2 percent per year was paid by the New York commercial banks.

In order to stabilize the day-to-day movements of the British currency and keep its oscillations within reasonable limits, in the early summer of 1932 the British Treasury proceeded to establish the Exchange Equalization Account. This account received 175 million pounds (and a year later an additional 200 million pounds) of British Treasury bills which it could sell for cash whenever it needed funds to pay for gold or foreign exchange bought in the course of its operations.[5]

Events in the monetary sphere thereupon followed each other in quick succession. The creditor-debtor relations between the great trading nations were profoundly affected by the going adrift of the many currencies hitherto firmly anchored to gold. In February, 1933, shortly before relinquishing his office, President Hoover advocated that the peoples of the world stabilize their moneys through a return to the gold standard. However, Franklin D. Roosevelt took an opposite stand, upon succeeding him, and shortly after the March nationwide bank holiday, called for the delivery to the Treasury, at the statutory price of $20.67 per ounce, of all gold held by the American public, in exchange for dollar notes. On April 19,1933, the President was authorized by Congress to alter the gold content of the dollar and regulate its value at his discretion and to reduce the quantity of gold in the dollar to a minimum of 50 cents as well as to fix the ratio of the silver dollar to gold. A day later an executive order was issued prohibiting the export of gold except by license of the Secretary of the Treasury.

The Gold Standard Act of March 14, 1900, had proclaimed the gold dollar as the standard United States unit of value and had made Treasury certificates and notes redeemable in gold coin. The repeal of this act shocked the international banking world. The justification offered was the need to equalize the position of United States export products competing with foreign countries who were benefiting from depreciated currencies. However, foreigners lacking faith in the new economic theories and distrusting the "compensated" dollar moved some of their balances to other financial centers, and even certain Americans converted part of their capital into foreign exchange.

In concern over the possibility of further steps by some governments that might encumber world trade, an international conference was called in June, 1933, at London under the auspices of the League of Nations to examine the reconstruction of international commerce by concerted action, through a general reduction of tariffs and the stabilization of the exchanges. The nations were all anxious to arrive

[5] For details of the functioning of the British Equalization Account the reader is referred to De Vegh, *The Pound Sterling;* Einzig, *World Finance 1914–1935;* Thomas, *The Principles and Arithmetic of Foreign Exchange;* Waight, *The History and Mechanism of the Exchange Equalization Account.*

at an agreement with the United States under which the relative values of their currencies could be definitely fixed. They were fearful of the fate of the currencies still moored to gold, should a solution prove impossible. Yet, President Roosevelt, by his famous "bombshell" cable of July 3, 1933, rejected stabilization on the ground that "what is to be the value of the dollar in terms of foreign currencies is and cannot be our immediate concern." [6]

Three months after the conference had come to an untimely end, the United States Treasury under an executive order of October 25, 1933, implemented its policy of lowering the value of the dollar in foreign markets. In an effort to raise commodity prices it placed orders for the purchase of gold abroad at increased prices in terms of dollars. Authority for these purchases was derived from sections 8 and 9 of the Gold Standard Act, under which the Secretary of the Treasury, with the approval of the President: "may purchase gold in any amounts, at home or abroad . . . at such rates and upon such terms and conditions as he may deem most advantageous to the public interest."

The Treasury now became a dominating factor in the gold and exchange markets. At first the Reconstruction Finance Corporation acted as its agent. The price for gold purchases abroad was initially fixed at $31.36 per ounce. It was gradually raised until it reached $34.06 on December 18, and $34.45 on January 16, 1934. Beginning January 15, 1934, the Federal Reserve Bank of New York assumed the conduct of the gold and exchange transactions, under the direction of the Treasury. The Gold Act of 1934, which became law on January 31, 1934, in effect reduced the value of the gold dollar to 59.06 cents. Simultaneously, by Presidential proclamation, the price of gold was correspondingly increased from $20.67 to $35.00 per ounce nine-tenths fine (that is, 15 5/21 grains per dollar nine-tenths fine, in place of the former 25 4/5 grains)—a reduction of 40.94 percent in the gold value of the dollar. Henceforth the Treasury offered to purchase all gold delivered in New York or at any other United States mint at $35.00 per ounce of fine gold 13 5/7 grains to the dollar less 1/4 percent and the usual mint charges. Thus, once more the adjustment of final balances between international debtors and creditors could be effected freely through gold shipments, with assurance of an unlimited market at a fixed and unchanging price.

[6] Statement of the United States delegation on July 5, 1933.

The repercussions of the devaluation of the dollar in the foreign exchange markets were immediate. By November, 1933, the pound sterling already had risen to $5.50 as a result of the gold purchase policy, and the dollar, responding to the vigorous official pressure upon it, fell to a record low as compared with the other leading foreign exchanges. One shadow remained in January, 1935, over the gold and exchange marts. On June 5, 1933, Congress had passed a joint resolution to the effect that all obligations calling for payment in gold could be discharged in any form of legal tender currency. Considerable uncertainty existed as to whether the United States Supreme Court would uphold the outlawing of the gold payment clause in public and private contracts. Banks and bullion dealers were averse to shipping gold to the United States until the court had rendered its decision. As the Treasury bought only gold in the actual possession of a United States mint or assay office, dealers preferred to temporize before placing orders for further shipments.

This cautious attitude was vindicated. When on February 18, 1935, the court upheld the law, the price of gold promptly advanced abroad to more than the equivalent of $35.00 an ounce, since the Treasury immediately put in large orders, and Continental hoarders were also competing in the market. As a result, gold was quoted considerably above the normal shipping point of $34.78 3/4 (calculated without taking interest into account). The transatlantic demand was due to renewed uncertainty as to the fate of the currencies still on the gold standard. The strain on the metallic reserves of the Netherlands Bank, for instance, had become acute, and to protect its gold stock the bank, faithful to its long tradition, had raised its official discount rate. Nonetheless, the sentiment of the market was expressed by the 300-point discount quoted for guilders to be delivered in three months. The Dutch financial authorities promptly took additional measures. Applications for gold had thereafter to be submitted several days before sailing date, and the guilder equivalent had to be available on the day the application was approved. This procedure handicapped those who lacked sufficient guilder balances to pay for the gold and who shrewdly tried to so arrange their position as to be able to purchase guilders at the last minute before sailing, when it was hoped that the market would be weaker. The Bank of France, in turn, abandoned its practice of allowing the withdrawal of applications for gold shipments before steamer sailing, and thenceforth gold earmarked for shipment had to be placed on board ship, or else the buyer had to resell it to the Bank of France at its then prevailing price. Short sellers of francs might thus be compelled to cover themselves at a loss if the Bank of France should in the meantime have reduced its purchase quotation for gold.

In the course of 1935 the growing concern about the continued deterioration of the international monetary situation and the increasing political unrest in Central Europe induced many central banks to convert their foreign exchange reserves into gold. This policy affected the deposits maintained with commercial banks in the United States. The transfer of such balances to a Federal Reserve Bank enabled a foreign central bank to require that a corresponding amount of gold be earmarked for its benefit. The loss of interest was minor compared with the protection afforded against a further depreciation of the dollar. That such precautions were not altogether ill-advised seemed to be confirmed by a spell of weakness of the dollar in February, 1936, when a bill was presented in Congress recommending the payment of a substantial bonus to the veterans of the First World War. As a consequence of this new threat to the already heavily burdened Federal budget, renewed flights of nervous capital took place to Canada, the West Indies, and South America.

In the fall of 1936, on the eve of the abandonment of the gold standard by France and the other members of the gold bloc, the Tripartite Monetary Agreement was signed by the governments of the United States, Great Britain, and France; it was subsequently adhered to by Belgium, Switzerland, and the Netherlands. The contracting parties agreed to "maintain the greatest possible equilibrium in the system of international exchanges and to avoid to the utmost extent the creation of any disturbance of that system by national monetary action." Thereafter, the stabilization funds of the different countries co-operated to minimize the variations in their respective exchanges. Transactions by a fund were offset at the end of each day by earmarking or purchase or sale of gold by the other fund concerned. In New York, the Federal Reserve Bank acted as agent for the foreign funds, thus guaranteeing the participating countries against losses suffered while supporting the currencies of their partners.

Dealings in the exchanges of all the interested nations were henceforth freed from all restrictions, although only the dollar was effectively linked to gold. London continued to maintain a free gold market without limitations as regards exports and imports. The buying price of the United States Treasury remained unchanged at $35.00 per ounce, less charges, the price holding good for whatever quantity of the metal was offered in the world's markets. Most of the newly mined or dishoarded gold found its way to the United States, the Treasury purchasing gold in bars and coins not only in London but also in Paris, Brussels, and other points where sellers were willing to part with their holdings. Among the United States commercial banks, those with well-trained staffs under expert technical management were alternately entrusted with the execution of the orders. The bullion divisions of the Federal Reserve Bank of New York and of the banks of issue in the various foreign capitals took an important part in the successful carrying out of the Treasury's operations.

Early in 1937, to counteract any possible inflationary effects of the constantly growing accumulation of gold in the United States, the Treasury initiated "sterilization" of all further bullion arrivals. Gold purchases thereafter were handled through an inactive account and were "sterilized" by being paid for with funds procured through the sale of Treasury bills in the open market rather than through the deposit of gold certificates to the credit of the Treasury account with the Federal Reserve Bank. By June, 1937, owing to the unceasing inflow of gold, the sterilized gold reserve exceeded one billion dollars and commenced to cause concern in the exchange markets as well as the security and commodity markets. According to unofficial estimates, without counting central bank and government reserves, the gold output of the world plus the dishoarding of gold in Europe was believed to exceed three billion dollars a year, all of which was moving to the United States. It began to be feared that this uninterrupted inflow of bullion and the resultant inflation in this country might ultimately cause a revaluation of the dollar. There also were rumors of a possible international agreement freezing all the existing gold reserves of the banks of issue at the rate of $35.00 an ounce, while future accretions would be subjected to a tax which would, in effect, reduce the net price obtainable for new gold to the former level of $20.67 per ounce.

Hardly had the gold "scare" faded from the market consciousness, when in November, as a result of the business recession, reports were started abroad that a devaluation of the dollar was contemplated. Accordingly all exchanges rose against the dollar. American exchange traders, however, discounted the possibility, because it seemed unlikely that the other nations would fail promptly to retaliate by readjusting their own currencies in line with a new dollar parity. Moreover, the Treasury continued to maintain its standing offer to sell gold to any buyer abroad at $35.00 an ounce plus 1/4 percent commission, equal to $35.24 delivered at European port. So long as England, France, and other countries could thus acquire unlimited quantities of the yellow metal, which could then be converted into pounds, francs, and so forth, their currencies could hardly rise very far above the prevailing levels without international arbitrage or the respective banks of issue intervening to smooth out the differences. Nevertheless, some ultra-cautious foreign owners of dollars were afraid to take any chances and converted them into gold held in custody in English and Swiss banks.

The transfer of deposits from the United States to London brought about another rise of the pound, which in February, 1938, was again quoted in New York at $5.02. Gold consequently flowed back across the Atlantic, and the inactive United States gold fund was soon completely "desterilized." There was no large-scale flight of disturbed capital from the country; however, exchange dealers watched the leading markets carefully, since with every pronounced weakness or firmness in the United States stock or commodity exchanges it was noticed that the foreign exchanges became more active abroad in one direction or the other. There were always speculators in foreign centers waiting for an opportunity or an excuse to sell the dollar short. By studying the movements of the exchanges in the foreign capitals much could therefore be learned by American exchange traders as to the nature of the operations favored at certain times by those who operated behind the scenes. For instance, if most offers of dollars were for future delivery, the presumption was that foreigners were on the selling side of the market and that the sales were likely to be of a speculative nature. On the other hand, selling for immediate or "spot" delivery might be due either to legitimate commercial or financial requirements or to sales on the part of alarmed foreign holders of dollar deposits or investments.

After the occupation of Austria by the Nazis in August, 1938, political tension in Europe rose, and gold reached 143 shillings in London, the highest price in three years (in November of that year even this record was to be broken when the quotation touched 150 shillings an ounce). Coincidently, all European currencies, led by the pound, declined sharply. As the Sudeten crisis in Czechoslovakia approached, they slumped still further, sterling ending the month of August at $4.86, francs at 2.72 cents, guilders at 54 1/2 cents, and Swiss francs at 22.83, while belgas were marked down to 16.89, and reichsmarks to 40.08.

Notwithstanding the hopes aroused by the calling of the Munich conference, United States banks with foreign commitments decided that the critical outlook called for careful scrutiny of the financial conjuncture. It was believed that in the event of war gold and other financial reserves might prove of as great value in the long run as aircraft and guns. Italy and Germany and their ally Japan, indeed, had already spent an important part of their monetary substance for essential war supplies and for the costly propaganda carried on in all parts of the globe. The French gold hoard, too, had been considerably reduced, but France appeared to be warranted in counting on the financial support of Britain and the United States. Although unquestionably precarious financially, the position of the Western nations seemed at least more favorable than that of their antagonists.

As the menace of an impending conflict became more acute, the worried investors on the Continent were forced to turn once more toward the United States as a refuge. In London, too, frightened foreign holders of bullion hastened to sell it to the Bank of England in order to use the sterling so obtained to acquire dollars. They feared that if war should break out England would take over all gold holdings in the British Isles, even though they were confident that the owners would be paid in full at the prevailing market value.

War risk insurance climbed to unprecedented heights, the premium rising as high as 20 shillings for £100 of gold, equal to 5 percent on a single trip. At the same time sterling declined in terms of dollars, and as a result it was possible to acquire gold in the London market at the equivalent of $34.20 an ounce, an all-time low. On this basis the cost, taking into account freight and insurance was $34.76 f.o.b. New York. Shippers reaped exceptional profits of 1 percent on the capital invested during the transit; as the trip on fast steamers did not take more than a week, this was equal to a theoretical return of 50 percent per annum. Such a windfall was unique in the memory of the oldest and most seasoned foreign exchange dealers. It was not surprising that by midsummer 1938 United States gold stocks reached a total of

14 billion dollars and represented more than 55 per cent of the world's known gold stocks.

The extensive shifting of funds from Europe to the United States was reflected in the unusually large number of new dollar accounts opened in this country by aliens during the fateful month of September, 1938. The United States deposits of European commercial banks also attained record figures, while the growth of such deposits in certain New York banks must have amounted to as much as 50 percent. From the weekly figures published by the Federal Reserve banks showing the total foreign deposits in member banks, it was clearly perceivable that Europe now lost its stores of gold at a rapid pace. An almost hysterical flight of capital took place not only from potentially belligerent nations but also from those countries which it was believed would remain neutral in the struggle which was about to sweep over the Continent, such as the Netherlands, Switzerland, and the Scandinavian countries. In New York sterling sank to $4.62, the lowest quotation since October, 1933.[7]

When at 10.28 A.M. on September 28 the news was flashed over the ticker that the Munich conference had been called, the pound rallied to $4.75 within a few minutes and the British Equalization Account had to buy dollars in order to prevent too wild a recovery of London exchange. Nonetheless, the weekly statements issued by the two central banks most directly affected showed clearly the tremendous tension in the London and Paris money markets during the exciting week that had just elapsed; the reserve ratio of the Bank of England had fallen to 13.8 percent, and the note cover of the Bank of France to 38 percent, while the advances of the latter to the French Government had risen to 50 billion francs, the note circulation to 120 billion, and the rediscounts of commercial bills to 20 billion.

Simultaneously with these developments the demand from Continental banks for dollar notes increased. These notes found their way, as they had often before during hectic times, to the strongboxes, mattresses, and stockings of frightened Europeans. Substantial amounts of dollar currency were shipped during these critical weeks to Holland, Switzerland, France, Belgium, and even Soviet Russia;

[7] According to *The United States in the World Economy* (United States Department of Commerce) there was between 1934 and 1939 an inward flow of short-term capital to the United States of 4 billion dollars. About 75 percent of this amount was believed to have been derived from foreign-owned funds transferred to this country owing to disturbed political and monetary conditions in Europe.

the reason for the remittances to the last-named were not divulged.

In spite of the agreement signed at Munich, the winter of 1938 did not bring relief to the harassed exchange markets. French francs experienced another sinking fit, the decline being arrested only after Paul Reynaud, the competent and aggressive member of the Chamber of Deputies and former Minister of Justice, had accepted the post of Minister of Finance in the Daladier Government and had submitted to the French Chamber of Deputies drastic proposals for the rehabilitation of French finances. The pound, too, remained weak, the English people having lost confidence in the appeasement policy of Neville Chamberlain. The acute feebleness of sterling exchange, which again slumped to $4.62, caused much concern in American banking circles. It was recalled that when England abandoned the gold standard in 1931, this event was followed by long months of price deflation in the United States. At a moment when the party in power in Washington was exerting its utmost energy to maintain a stable economy at home, the possibility of another major business recession was most disturbing.

As the world entered 1939, there appeared little likelihood that the gold flow to the Western Hemisphere would soon be reversed. The trade balance remained heavily in favor of the United States. In spite of the inordinately large deposits of foreigners in the United States, the periodical statistics of the Department of Commerce revealed that the aggregate sums owed in the United States by foreign countries were greater than America's total short-term and long-term foreign debt to them. The situation would have been even more unbalanced had the Johnson Act not prevented further foreign lending to those countries which were still beholden to the United States on account of the inter-allied debts contracted during the First World War. In addition, the prospective huge expenditures abroad for armaments by the European nations were bound further to stimulate the westbound movement of capital.

To counteract the steady exodus of gold from Great Britain the British Exchange Control announced early in 1939 that part of the British gold reserves would thereafter be held in South Africa. It had been an invariable rule in the past that gold purchased by the Equalization Account had to be shipped to and delivered in London. Henceforth, foreign buyers had the privilege of having bullion earmarked at the South African bank of issue, although settlement had to be made in sterling in London. It was hoped that this new facility would calm the fears of those who were offering their gold holdings for sale because of apprehension over possible seizure in the event of war. By offering them the opportunity of obtaining gold in a far-off Dominion, presumably safe from the perils of bombing and invasion, the British authorities expected that many owners would decide to leave their holdings at least within the confines of the Empire.

Notwithstanding, that shelter even just across the Channel still was considered more secure than Belgium's own vaults was evidenced by the fact that the governor and the trustees of the National Bank of Belgium were reported to have gradually transferred nearly one third of that country's official gold stock to London to be stored away in the subterranean recesses of the Bank of England.

About this time, in order to defend the pound against speculative raids, the Bank of England requested all British banks and bullion dealers to refrain from making loans against gold and from entering into future foreign exchange transactions, only strictly commercial trading being excepted. The effect was sensational. The shorts ran to cover, and the pound rose more than six cents. Even such political developments as the fall of Barcelona to the Nationalist forces of General Franco and the resignation of Reichsbank President Hjalmar Schacht, which under normal circumstances might have troubled the market, failed to stifle the better sentiment. However, guilders then declined rather sharply on the news of a Dutch-Nazi incident at the German border and the failure of a French loan publicly launched by the Mendelssohn syndicate of banks.

Despite the better feeling in the sterling market it was appreciated in London that the Equalization Account, established to prevent excessive fluctuations of the currency, needed strengthening in order to be fully able to discharge its task in the event of a further aggravation in the political situation. Accordingly, the Bank of England sold the Account 200 million predevaluation pounds in gold, equivalent to 350 million pounds at current market quotations. This step was warmly applauded by the English public and financial press alike, for the loss of gold since Munich was a bloodletting which, if not stopped in time, was bound to weaken irreparably the financial and economic structure of the nation. The move was supplemented by the raising of the private discount rate in Lombard Street from 5/8 percent to 1 1/4 percent.

In the United States, too, public uneasiness about the condition of the London market was growing. It was asked how long England could afford to suffer the persistent drainage of her wealth and substance. The doubts in the business community were reflected in an unusual discount of 2 percent per annum in the spread of future sterling. The opinion gained ground that England, in order to finance her probable requirements of dollars would have to resort, in case of war, to a mobilization of foreign securities not unlike that of twenty-five years earlier.

Another symptom of the feverish concern in Britain about a possible conflict was the interest taken by the Bank of England in the financial condition of some private banking houses. The bank made an urgent request that certain discount houses merge as soon as possible, since in its opinion the minimum capital at the disposal of any such concern should not be less than £500,000. It also intimated that the borrowings of discount companies—very large under normal conditions—should be severely curtailed. The bank, in making these requests, was undoubtedly mindful of the condition with which it was confronted at the outbreak of the First World War, when, as already noted, it had been obliged to come to the support of a number of acceptance houses and banks doing a large overseas business.

As the flight of gold to the United States assumed larger and larger proportions, criticism inside and outside the United States Congress, extending not merely to the gold and silver policy but also to the entire monetary philosophy of the administration, became exceedingly pointed. Insistent questions were raised as to the ultimate effect on United States economy of the unlimited acceptance of gold at $35.00 an ounce. Between January, 1938, and the end of 1939 gold imports reached a total of 5 1/2 billion dollars, equal to the value of the entire gold shipments received between 1921 and the end of 1937. By October, 1939, the United States gold stock exceeded 17 billion dollars. Foreign banks continued to consign shipments to this country; however, the total amount of gold under earmark for foreign account at the Federal Reserve Bank of New York was believed to amount only to about 1,250 million dollars.

SUMMARY. This section first takes up the financial disturbances following the banking troubles in Austria, Germany, France, and Italy in 1931, which forced England off the gold standard and led to heavy withdrawals of dollar deposits and gold from the United States. During this period Germany's short-term creditors were forced to enter into standstill agreements with their debtors, and Austria and Hungary resorted to a temporary suspension of payments. Lack of adequate information both as to the total amount of accumulated indebtedness and as to the abuses that had crept into the use of the short-term credits cost the foreign creditors heavily. Meanwhile developments in this country led to the devaluation of the dollar, heavy purchases of gold and silver by the Treasury, and the creation of the Stabilization Fund, as well as abrogation of the gold clause. At about this time began the successive migrations of capital from the countries whose currencies had become suspect, and the renewed flow of foreign funds and gold to the United States, followed by a partial return movement after Belgium, France, Holland, and Switzerland had also been forced off the metallic standard and their currencies devalued. Various exchange operations were undertaken pursuant to the Tripartite Agreement between the British Equalization Account and the United States and French Stabilization Funds. Later, American foreign bankers were compelled to give increasing consideration to the conditions with which they would be confronted in the event of a European war.

THE SECOND WORLD WAR, 1939–1945

In Europe and the rest of the world the political horizon seemed somewhat more serene in the early summer of 1939. The barometer of the exchanges predicted fair weather. Guilders, Swiss francs, and belgas registered sizable advances. Rates for future sterling and French francs showed improvement, offers for forward delivery apparently bearing less heavily on the market. Then came the fateful events of the end of August, followed by the invasion of Poland by Germany and the USSR and the declaration of war on Germany by France and Great Britain.

The subject of major concern which now arose for United States foreign bankers was the extent of the financial resources upon which the two Allies could draw to pay for their expected large purchases of war materials and foodstuffs from North and South America. Great Britain and France had available for immediate use the dollar deposits maintained by their governments, banks of issue, and stabilization funds in this country, Canada, and, to a lesser degree, Brazil and the Argentine Republic. In addition, the gold earmarked at the Federal Reserve Banks could be converted into cash without delay. Considerable holdings of American and Canadian securities owned by British and French nationals could be sold, or used as collateral for credits and loans. Moreover, short-term advances by commercial banks and United States Government agencies would certainly be granted to bridge the intervals between the inflow of dollars and the delivery by suppliers and manufacturing plants of raw materials and finished products. In case of absolute need, gold stocks at home could be drawn upon and shipped across the Atlantic by battleship or submarine. Finally, if the Johnson Act were repealed, long-term bond issues might be launched in the Western world for sale to investors and Allied sympathizers. In short, at first there seemed to be in sight abundant direct and indirect resources for the future armament and provisioning of the British and French military forces and civil populations. Besides, the "cash and carry" plan approved by Congress in November, 1939, also offered distinct advantages to the Allies. While it prohibited credits to all belligerents, without distinction, because of their naval supremacy, England and France were in a privileged position. After having paid cash for their purchases and having furnished armed escorts for the merchant vessels, they were able to have cargoes transported in safety to their home ports.

After the outbreak of war strict control over all exchange transactions was introduced everywhere. Thereafter, except under official license, no movement of gold or capital abroad was permitted, while exchange rates were rigorously pegged. The Tripartite Agreement was suspended for the duration of the war. A week before the beginning of hostilities England had wisely decided to let the pound find its own level, and when the war actually broke out it had already declined to well below its mint parity. France marked her closer ties with her neighbor across the Channel by linking the franc to sterling at the ratio of 176.50 francs to the pound and thus *de facto* adhering to the sterling bloc.

The sterling bloc was a remarkable product of prewar British financial ingenuity. This adroit arrangement had been devised so that Great Britain's dominions, colonies, and possessions, as well as the other countries maintaining close political or trade relations with the Empire, might derive advantage from the tying of their exchanges closely to a strong currency such as the pound sterling had been for generations.[8]

During the war the members of the group, by placing the proceeds of goods sold for dollars to the credit of the British Equalization Account made a significant contribution to Britain's war effort. The sterling equivalent of their shipments, those invoiced both in sterling and in dollars, was credited to them in blocked account, whose balances could be used only for the acquisition of British goods. As the war lengthened, however, Britain because of her own growing requirements, found it impossible to satisfy all the demands for manufactured products on the part of her associates in the sterling area and other suppliers, with the result that enormous frozen balances accumulated in their favor.

What was the situation of the exchanges in other parts of the world as the war got under way? In the Western Hemisphere the dollar was the dominating currency. However, besides the Western Hemisphere countries usually included in the dollar area,[9] some of the European currencies were on occasion and for variable periods also linked to the dollar through the operations of their stabilization funds. Thus, the guilder was supported at a certain period at 53.09 cents, and the Swiss franc at 22.42 cents. For a time even the Japanese yen was anchored to the dollar at the ratio of 23 7/16 cents to the yen.

All the South American republics had inconvertible paper money, the Argentine peso being tied during one period to sterling. In the Far East the Hong Kong dollar, through the operation of the local exchange board, moved with the pound. The Shanghai dollar oscillated during 1939 between 17 1/2 and 6 1/2 cents. Although the

[8] The following countries were generally considered to be part of the sterling bloc or area: the entire British Empire (with the exception of Canada, Newfoundland, and South Africa) Eire, Egypt, Palestine, Sudan, Iraq, Burma, and Iceland. During the Second World War these countries were joined by the Belgian Congo, and the Dutch and French colonial possessions. (In his annual report to the stockholders of Barclays Bank Sir William Goodenough stated on February 8, 1951, that "something like half the world's international payments are made in sterling.") At one time or another during the prewar era the currencies of Sweden, Norway, Denmark, Finland, Estonia, Spain, Portugal, Greece, Turkey, Iran and Thailand were also closely allied with the pound following its movements more or less faithfully up or down.

[9] Bolivia, Colombia, Costa Rica, Cuba, Dominican Republic, Ecuador, Guatemala, Haiti, Honduras, Mexico, Nicaragua, Panama including Canal Zone, Puerto Rico, El Salvador, Venezuela, the Virgin Islands, as well as the Republic of the Philippines and Canada.

Indian rupee was officially linked to sterling at 1 shilling 6 pence, the Reserve Bank of India published a special rupee-dollar rate based on the London quotation and authorized no transactions in dollars against rupees except at this official rate.

During the war the control exercised over all exchange transactions was the most serious factor with which foreign exchange traders had to contend throughout the world. In the first three months of the hostilities cable transfers on London payable in free sterling fluctuated between $3.68 and $4.04 1/2, free sterling being one of the two different kinds of sterling exchange existing during the initial years of the struggle. Free sterling was derived from the sale within the British Empire of foreign-owned securities and other assets, as well as from the proceeds of goods shipped under special import license to England for which the British Exchange Control had not paid in dollars. Such sterling could be applied to the payment of British goods shipped to the United States. All other sterling settlements had to be made in "official" or "registered" sterling, whose price was pegged by the British Equalization Account at $4.02 bid, $4.04 offered. Dollars obtained from the sale of assets owned by British citizens or residents had to be turned over to the Equalization Account, where all dollar movements had been centralized. The principal drain on its dollar holdings was the payment for essential imports into the British Isles, for which the American or other sellers insisted upon United States currency.

The early months of 1940 found the foreign departments of United States banks actively canvassing the possible effects on their overseas commitments of a further spread of the European war. The more conservative members of the foreign banking fraternity, half a year earlier, had started to curtail their outstanding future exchange contracts. By September the major part of such deals then pending in the United States or abroad had been either settled or offset.

The reduction of foreign loans and acceptance credits was naturally a more delicate and more time-consuming task. Great care was exercised thenceforth not to open new commercial letters of credit except for clearly self-liquidating mercantile transactions. To counterbalance the general slow-down in current banking operations there was fortunately a constant stream of new accounts opened by foreign nationals intent upon placing some of their capital out of the reach of the enemy and the tax collector.

On three different occasions during 1940 Great Britain published long lists of dollar securities that she called upon her nationals to turn over to designated institutions in the United States against reimbursement in pounds at their prevailing market value. Yet this was unable to arrest the downward course of the pound. While the official quotation remained fixed at $4.03, free pounds were offered in March at as low as $3.51.

When the Nazis invaded Norway and Denmark, in April, the United States Treasury promptly froze the balances and other assets in the United States of all Norwegian and Danish nationals and residents. This measure was followed in May and June by similar decrees applying to the property of Belgian, Dutch, and Luxembourg nationals, and to that of all countries that were occupied by or came under the domination of Germany and Italy. At the same moment all trading in the currencies and securities of these nations was prohibited.

The next important event affecting the foreign exchange markets was the decision of the British authorities to eliminate trading in free sterling, on the ground that the turnover in free sterling had gradually dwindled to negligible proportions. To all intents and purposes British foreign trade was now practically monopolized by government agencies settling for their purchases through the offices of the Equalization Account. Accordingly, special agreements were entered into with a number of foreign countries, including the United States, under whose terms only official sterling was to be quoted thereafter or was to be dealt in on the respective foreign exchange markets. By that time trading in the other currencies—belgas, guilders, and Scandinavian crowns—had almost come to a standstill. The turnover in sterling, French francs, Canadian exchange, reichsmarks, and lire also represented only a minor fraction of the volume that the market had handled in the past. Finally, the signing by President Roosevelt of the Lend-Lease Act, on March 11, 1941, reduced still further the occasions for the Allied nations to enter the market to cover their dollar needs.

From this digression into the annals of the foreign exchanges during the pre-Pearl Harbor period of the war we return to the vicissitudes to which American foreign banking was exposed in 1941. At the end of July the Treasury decreed the blocking of all Japanese and Chinese assets in the United States in the same manner as those of European nations that had previously been placed under the control of the Foreign Funds Administration. Chinese property was included solely as a protection for the citizens and natives living in the unoccupied part of China. Thus, all the possessions in the United States of nationals and residents of countries either invaded or threatened by Germany, Italy, or Japan were put into the custody of the United States Government.

After the events of December 7, 1941, had embroiled the United States in the war, American foreign exchange dealers were confronted with a new situation. As soon as the German declaration of war was received, trading in French francs payable in the German-occupied part of France was prohibited. However, under Treasury license support remittances to the unoccupied French Zone were permitted. These Francs were supplied by the Bank of France in Vichy at the official rate of 2.29 cents per franc. In order to prevent the enemy from cashing stolen or confiscated bank notes through neutral confederates, incoming shipments of United States currency were the object of particularly scrupulous examination. Because of the stiffened attitude of the Treasury, the dollar was offered abroad at a heavy discount. Banks in Europe and elsewhere became reluctant to purchase dollar notes of unknown origin, especially when after October 31, 1942, the amount of currency that could be brought into the United States from foreign countries (except by residents of Great Britain, Canada, Newfoundland, and Bermuda) was limited to $50.00 per person.

In November, 1942, shortly after the landing of the United States and British forces in North Africa, the Germans moved into the hitherto unoccupied parts of Southern France, and thenceforth all trade in Metropolitan French francs was discontinued. However, it was necessary to fix a rate for the conversion of dollar notes spent by the United States Army and the United States Government officials in North Africa or exchanged into franc notes acceptable and circulating there. This rate was set at 75 francs to the dollar, or 1 1/3 cents per franc. In the United States, orders for cable and mail transfers payable in North Africa were licensed at a tentative rate of 65 francs per dollar or 1.5384 cents per franc plus bank charges. In regard to such transfers a divergence of opinion arose between French and American banks, since for any payments effected by the French banks in their territory they claimed to be entitled to free dollars, while their

United States correspondent banks, under binding Treasury regulations, could give them credit only in blocked dollars.

In February, 1943, after experience had proved that the North African franc had been undervalued from the outset, the rate for both North and West African francs was raised to 50 francs per dollar, or 2 cents per franc. The franc in Metropolitan France, however, was reported to be worth only 1 cent, sellers, and 4/5 cent, buyers. Transfers of francs from the United States for commercial transactions in Africa remained prohibited, all purchases and sales of merchandise in that territory being handled and financed by the United States Commercial Company, a government agency.

At this time the slow but gradual restoration of business connections with neutral countries led to an increase in the turnover of the currencies of certain countries not taking part in the war. Since the beginning of 1941 two different quotations had been current in the United States exchange market for both Swiss francs and Swedish kronor. In the case of Swiss francs, one rate was applied to francs bought for commercial, charitable, and so-called support payments (personal remittances for the maintenance of relatives and other individuals); this rate fluctuated between 23.35 and 23.45 cents per franc, while the quotation for noncommercial "free" francs ranged considerably higher—at one time as high as 44 cents. Like the dollar, Swiss money was a "hard" currency, even commanding during certain periods of the war, a high premium over the dollar. The free rate often vibrated violently, on one occasion dipping to 28 cents. When the National Bank of Switzerland required that support payments be effected for the most part in free francs instead of in commercial francs as theretofore, the free rate jumped back to more than 30 cents. The national bank also became much stricter as regards authorizations concerning settlement of commercial transactions at the preferential rate of 23.45 and required documents of the buyers evidencing that the exchange was needed for bona fide commercial business. These papers were subjected to a minute time-consuming examination, with irritating delays for the American importers. As the months passed, the national bank tightened still more its regulations for the certification of commercial payments, calling for the presentation of customs receipts to prove that shipment had actually been effected. The number of pending orders and nonexecuted payments consequently kept growing. Customers in the United States protested strenuously, but without avail, and, rather than incur further ill-will, the foreign departments of United States banks decided to limit the acceptance of new remittance orders.

By October, 1941, the delay in carrying out payment orders reached one month or more. By putting obstacles in the way of United States importers the Swiss authorities hoped that the former would cease calling for the cheaper commercial francs. Their expectation that their attitude would in the end promote the sale of the more expensive free francs was fully realized. Many merchants came to the conclusion, as one expressed it, that "life was too short," and started to place orders at prices computed in free francs. The success of the central bank's policy is shown by the fact that during 1939 United States importers of Swiss watches purchased slightly more than 50 million francs' worth, while in 1943 more than 140 million francs were transferred to the Swiss manufacturers of timepieces distributed in the Western Hemisphere. Finally, an agreement was reached in November, 1941, between the United States and the Swiss governments taking care of some of the grievances of the United States importing concerns. The Swiss National Bank consented to accept commercial francs up to not more than 8 1/2 million francs per month. However, Swiss exporters, as to their shipments to the United States and other Western Hemisphere countries, were limited to the ratios that their individual exports during 1937, 1938, and 1940 had borne to the total Swiss exports for that period. It was provided, in addition, that the quota could be exceeded whenever the foreign buyer was willing to settle in free francs. Thereafter, remittances in payment of invoices for merchandise shipped under the new arrangement suffered no delays. However, the rate for free francs registered a sharp advance to more than 40 cents—a rise that was, of course, wholly to the advantage of the Swiss economy.

As soon as most Swiss shippers had exhausted their quotas, the exchange situation once more became alarming. In January, 1944, free Swiss francs reached an all-time peak of 44 cents. The National Bank of Switzerland, realizing that the goose that laid the golden egg was about to be killed, placed hurried orders with the Federal Reserve Bank of New York to sell francs freely for its account, with the result that within two months the quotation had fallen back to 27 cents. A new increased quota of 16 million francs per month was established, and in addition the United States Foreign Funds Control assumed control requiring a prior special license for all new transfers of free francs in payment of Swiss watches.

The Swedish exchange was, on the whole, less exposed to spectacular dislocations and maintained a more even trend. Transfers to Sweden for commercial transactions were controlled by General License 49 of the United States Treasury and by General Licenses 32 and 33 in the case of support payments. The rate for commercial payments, as approved by the Swedish Financial Attaché in New York, was variously 23.84 1/2 and 23.90 cents, and for charitable and other personal remittances 23.95 cents. Certifications for authorized Swedish transfers were issued without delay, and payments were made in Sweden with equal promptitude.

Our Latin American neighbors were bound to suffer from the abnormal exchange and monetary developments in the rest of the world. In April, 1943, the Argentine Government was compelled to initiate strict exchange control measures throughout the republic. Argentine commercial banks were ordered to file applications for licenses with the newly appointed Control Board and to supply it with full details regarding their foreign exchange operations. After one month, however, the regulations were modified, dollars for delivery in up to ten days being freed from the requirement of a prior authorization by the board. A novel directive required that pesos received in connection with the sale of dollars in amounts exceeding 1,000 pesos be entered to the credit of a special account, and prohibited their withdrawal without special permission from the board. On the other hand, the Banco Central de la Republica Argentina was granted the privilege of converting into foreign currency, after a preliminary fifteen-day notice, all balances remaining in the special peso accounts for more than ninety days.

After the United States entered the war the Latin American exchange situation was gradually reversed. United States purchases on a large scale resulted in an unusual accumulation of dollar deposits and gold holdings, a situation that was intensified by the considerable slowing down of United States exports to the southern republics. Indeed, in 1944, the foreign exchange holdings in the United States of all Latin American nations were reported to have risen to more than 2 billion dollars.

Meanwhile certain other significant developments took place during 1943 that have to be recorded. In order to bring about a closer supervision of the sources of all incoming gold, the United States Treasury came to an understanding with the Mexican Government, which provided that the Banco de Mexico thereafter would assume full control of Mexican gold imports and exports. To prevent enemy-controlled bullion from being illegally imported and disposed of in the United States it had become imperative to scrutinize all shipments arriving in United States ports or border cities most carefully before sending them on to their consignees. Thus the Mexican agreement closed one loophole.

At the end of April, 1943, the life of the 2 billion dollar United States Stabilization Fund was extended for another two years, but the authority of the President to devalue the dollar further from 59.06 to 50 cents was abrogated.

What was the situation of British exchange in 1944 as the war entered its decisive phase and the end came in sight? Registered pounds were still quoted at $4.02, buyers, and $4.04, sellers. In New York sterling transactions consisted mainly of sales to commercial houses and banks and to correspondents and business firms in Latin America, offset as a rule by purchases from merchants and commercial concerns and out-of-town banks. Balances not covered during any day were generally obtained from the British Equalization Account. On the whole the turnover had materially shrunk from its prewar norm. Britain's blocked overseas debt was now estimated to have reached 2 1/2 billion to 3 billion pounds, although it is true that much of this formidable indebtedness was owed to British colonies and dominions. These debts were already casting their shadow over the postwar outlook. After the war reliable London observers estimated that the United Kingdom would in any event have to export 300 million pounds more of goods than in prewar times in order to pay for necessary foodstuffs and raw materials. On top of this increase, however, was the further increase that would be required to cover the interest and amortization on the enlarged foreign debt, while on the other hand England's former markets in India, Australia, and the Latin American republics were no longer as dependent upon the purchase of British manufactured goods as before the war. Thus, it was easy even then to foresee that for an indefinite period sterling exchange would be under a heavy strain and that exchange control would inevitably have to be reckoned with for some years to come.

As to the British dominions, there was some question as to the future course of the Australian and New Zealand pounds. If and as exchange restrictions could be removed, there was a possibility that these currencies might appreciate in terms of the English pound, since both dominions had amassed substantial credit balances in London during the war. On the other hand, they were indebted to English and United States investors on long-term account because of their sizable borrowings in sterling and dollars contracted before 1939. Between these opposing factors it was concluded that a rise in the Australian and New Zealand pounds was not a problem with which foreign exchange traders had to count in the nearer future.

Trading in French francs remained suspended throughout 1944. Commercial transactions by individuals and private business concerns continued to be prohibited, and only the Lend-Lease Administration, the United States Commercial Company and the French Purchasing Commission were in a position to deal with offers of a commercial nature. Not until November, 1945, were individual money transfers to certain liberated parts of continental France sanctioned. The maximum amount that could then be sent being fixed at $500.00 monthly. With the exception of five or six provinces, the whole of France was gradually opened for such remittances the conversion rate being set at 49.53 francs to the dollar, or 0.201898 cent per franc, plus bank charges. The North African Control Commission, however, continued to refrain from issuing permits for payments against franc deposits in North African banks, and persisted in asking for reimbursement in free dollars for any remittances payable in francs in its territory softening only exceptionally in the case of urgent remittances for charitable or support purposes. The Bank of England, in its turn, had fixed a rate for franc payments against sterling, including also the French territories controlled by the French Committee of National Liberation, headed by General de Gaulle, of 200 francs to the pound.

During the entire war the United States Treasury's buying and selling rates for gold remained unchanged at $35.00 per ounce. Abroad, under the impact of the great struggle, the constantly growing demand for gold lifted the price for the metal far above the official value in the United States. In the Argentine Republic gold fetched in the open market as much as $40.00 an ounce. From Turkey sales at $50.00 were reported. In the Bombay bazaars buyers were willing to pay 75 rupees per tola, equivalent to $60.00 per ounce, while in Cairo, in the midsummer of 1944, gold was quoted at a new high of 186 piastres per dirjem (1/10th of an ounce), equal to $76.00 per ounce. When rumors of an early peace spread among the traders in Alexandria, both gold and silver suffered a temporary sinking spell, since it was believed that with the ending of the hostilities the interest in gold would wane and that after peace was declared gold would enter a period of eclipse. Early in 1945, however, dealers and speculators became convinced that the war, at any rate in the East, was likely to go on longer than was generally expected, and accordingly they moved again to the buying side.[10]

What ensued in the course of the victory year 1945 is still fresh in the memory of all. The signing by President Truman on July 31 of the act providing 2,750 million dollars for the International Monetary Fund and 3.175 million for the International Bank for Reconstruction and Development marked a new milestone in the history of United States foreign financial expansion. It may be said that with the signing the curtain came down on the eventful era that has been reviewed in the preceding pages. The United States emerged from the war as the strongest industrial nation, and as she entered the postwar period she appeared to hold securely the predominant position in world finance to which her resources and contributions in peace and war seemed to have given her a legitimate claim.

For United States foreign bankers, however, the war did not end on the day the armistice was signed in the little red schoolhouse at Rheims. For them it marked the beginning of a period of extreme activity. The broken threads of their overseas connections had to be rewoven. The fate of transactions in abeyance since 1939 and 1941 had to be traced. The possibility of settling long-outstanding accounts had to be explored. An intense search for overdue foreign collections and shipping documents had to be started. Statements covering past remittances and miscellaneous business operations had to be obtained and reconciled. Finally, after a careful canvass of credit and financial conditions abroad, the resumption of banking relations with former depositors and correspondents might be contemplated.

10 In 1947, the International Monetary Fund, in an effort to halt the operations in the black markets, requested its members to check all transactions in gold above the $35 official ceiling price. As a result, the United States Treasury instituted control over sales and re-exports of imported gold.

SUMMARY. This section first discusses the various protective financial measures taken in Europe after the outbreak of hostilities. The purpose and the advantages to Britain of the sterling bloc are then touched upon, as well as the exchange situation in the Western Hemisphere and the Far East. The interruption of communications and the precautions that had to be taken by the banks' foreign divisions raised special problems. These were increased in the United States by the blocking of the accounts of the nationals of the various occupied countries. Further problems had to be met after the occupation of North Africa and the subsequent liberation of Italy, France, and the other Allied countries. Later, other complications arose in connection with the undervaluation of the dollar in the neutral markets of Switzerland and Sweden. The initial hardships suffered by the Latin American countries as a result of the war were succeeded by widespread prosperity as a result of increased purchases of war materials by the United States and Great Britain. As the war progressed, increasing consideration was given to the prospective postwar financial and economic position of the United Kingdom, while the French franc market and banking relations with the North African colonies raised other problems of considerable complexity. Finally, as the end of the war became clearly imminent, the United States banks directed their attention more and more to the comprehensive tasks that would await them in the international field after the conclusion of peace.

PART TWO

INTERNATIONAL BANKING ACTIVITIES OF THE UNITED STATES

II

SOME SPECIAL WAR AND POSTWAR PROBLEMS

GENERAL

THE WAR-RENT YEARS from 1939 to 1945 presented United States foreign bankers with their greatest challenge since the United States first became preponderant in the international financial sphere. Throughout this period the officers in charge of the foreign departments of the various banks concentrated their every thought on the protection of their own and their customers' endangered business interests in all parts of the world.

Even before the actual beginning of hostilities deposits of money and valuables were being hurriedly withdrawn from the potential danger spots, especially the countries on the Continent that might be affected by the outbreak of war and the consequent severance of communications and contact with the United States. Shipping documents, negotiable instruments, currency, and securities intended for such countries were soon being forwarded only on boats flying the flags of neutral nations. Whenever possible they were first placed in the hands of reliable correspondents or branch offices in London, whence, at the discretion of the latter, who because nearer were in a better position to appraise the situation, they could be reshipped to their ultimate destination by the safest available route.

As the clouds deepened on the political and diplomatic horizons, commercial and financial planning and preparation were rendered hazardous, if not wholly upset, by a sudden steep rise in war risk insurance rates. Before each purchase of foreign drafts the various risks had to be carefully weighed by the bank officers. At the same time the demand for United States funds increased greatly. Steamship captains, afraid lest they be stranded with their crews and cargoes unable to communicate with the owners, called for large amounts of dollar currency and cashier checks. American tourists and frightened foreigners also cabled for remittances in bank notes, which suddenly commanded a premium abroad.

Along with these external activities, much time was spent by the executive officers of the foreign departments in going over all pending commitments and investments whose safety might be jeopardized by the upheaval abroad. After the declaration of war by France and England on Germany the outlook for United States financial interests in Europe became particularly uncertain, the more so because telephone connection with London and Paris, upon which the banks often depended for their daily operations, ceased to be available for private use. Special problems beset American banks that had branches of their own in London and on the Continent; some of them are described elsewhere in detail.

From September, 1939, onward all business pending or new, in countries adjacent to the invaded regions had to be reviewed not only day by day but often hour by hour. When news was received that the British banks had called all their credits on the Continent except those on a fully secured basis, the leading New York banks discussed the desirability of taking similar measures. However, inasmuch as most institutions had already called for collateral in all doubtful cases, opinion was divided as to the need of uniform action.

Other perplexing questions came up to burden the banks. Since foreign loans were governed by the Johnson Act, the banks had to determine whether the purchase of Bank of England and Bank of France bank notes would be interpreted as equivalent to extending credits to the governments specified in the act, on the ground that the latter owned or controlled their banks of issue. Similarly, the banks to which checks of British and French consulates were presented for payment were in a quandary as to their legal right to honor them. The State Department, to the relief of everyone concerned, finally ruled that such checks could be considered as covering "normal expenses" even if the drafts were drawn on the home paying agents and even though it might take several weeks before they could actually be cashed abroad. Because of the heavy penalties involved for infractions of the law, bank officers in these and other instances were hesitant to take any chances, whereas under different circumstances their personal sympathies might have controlled their decisions.

The loss of business in Europe was compensated at least partly by the banking and credit facilities extended to the purchasing missions and trade delegations of both belligerents and neutrals that were gradually established in the United States, although the actual handling of their dollar disbursements for war and other supplies was mainly entrusted to the Federal Reserve Bank of New York. Moreover, the relations of the commercial banks with the different United States Government agencies assumed progressively larger proportions as the war went on. The special foreign missions and United States agencies were created in part for the purpose of centralizing procurement by the various governments, thus effecting both economy and secrecy of operations. Although as a result the purchase of strategic and other materials was not always handled through private concerns with long experience in the trade, the old-established import and export houses generously placed their knowledge and foreign connections at the disposal of the responsible United States and foreign procurement officials.

In consequence of these changes, the European Continent, with the exception of the neutral countries, became practically a closed area to private American banks and traders, at the cost of the years of effort spent in building up United States commerce across the Atlantic. Moreover, after Pearl Harbor the whole of East Asia, apart from the unoccupied parts of China and India, was also shut off from business intercourse with the West. The opportunities for operating in Australia, New Zealand, and the British colonies likewise were reduced, in this case because of the need for the British Exchange Control to husband scarce dollar exchange both by direct restriction and by promoting British trade with the sterling area.

The beginning of open warfare against Germany, Italy, and Japan found most banks' foreign departments amply prepared for possible contingencies. One final step was suggested. Some credits and loans remained outstanding in areas likely to be drawn into the conflict. In the majority of cases the debtors had sufficient balances in their current accounts to cover the amounts due from them as and when the credits or overdrafts became due. Accordingly, in certain cases the policy was adopted of segregating the required sums from the customers' regular working balances and placing them to the credit of a special cash collateral account. Thus, the funds needed to pay for fixed maturing liabilities were tentatively set aside on the banks' ledgers, and after the necessary license had been procured prior to the due dates they could easily and automatically be employed for the settlement of the maturing obligations of the foreign debtor, the interests of both the banks and the customer being satisfactorily protected by this simple device.

With the spread of hostilities many offices of United States banks and commercial enterprises in the Far East had to be closed. Whereas during the First World War American banks had been able to increase their foreign branch activities, this time the reverse was true. With foreign exchange transactions drastically restricted everywhere and international commerce largely monopolized by government bodies, little scope, indeed, was left during 1941 to 1945 for an expansion of private banking and trade abroad.

Only in Central and South America—and there only to the degree warranted by the financial condition in the various republics—were favorable prospects offered United States bankers and businessmen. Because of the intimate ties that had always existed between the United States and its sister republics to the south, most banks' foreign departments now redirected their attention and energies toward the cultivation of closer relations with these lands, some of which were in certain respects still virgin territory bankingwise.

Toward the end of 1943 the war situation in Russia, Africa, and Italy at last began to point to a victorious end of the struggle within a measurable future. United States banks accordingly began to formulate tentative plans for the resumption of former activities in the Allied and neutral countries after the advent of peace and the expected easing of the wartime restrictions with which they had to contend during the preceding four years. It was hoped that once the hostilities had ended, concerted efforts would be made by the Allied nations to restore normal conditions throughout the Continent. There appeared to be no doubt that our country would have to provide generous public and private support in order to get the wheels of international trade revolving once more and would have to furnish not only food, clothing, and shelter but also the raw materials and the loans required for the reconstruction and rehabilitation of the shattered economies.

It was already clear that for many years to come the world would consist of two classes of nations. Sweden and Switzerland on the Continent and the United States, Canada, and the Argentine Republic in the Western Hemisphere would probably be in a position to make loans and grant credits or other financial support in one form or another. However, England, Belgium, France, Holland, Norway, Denmark, and Italy would have to rely on outside help for a more or less prolonged convalescence from the wounds inflicted by the war. A delicate task, therefore, lay before those in charge of foreign operations of United States banks. By careful investigation on the spot wherever possible, they would have to determine to what extent the economies of the debtor countries had deteriorated, how much their industries had suffered, what effects hostilities or the occupation had had on the position of their banks of issue and their commercial financial institutions, how much their currencies had depreciated in terms of foreign purchasing power, and what steps were necessary or were being mapped for the reorganization of their public and private finances in an attempt to carry out their obligations to foreign creditors. Everything, however, would evidently depend on the length of the war and the damage that still would be inflicted.

One thing was certain: this nation clearly was destined to assume again the leading role in the rebuilding of Europe and Asia, and even more than before the war New York would have to function as the chief international banking citadel. England, it was the consensus of experienced opinion, would have to continue for a long time her controls over foreign exchange and the export of capital. Considering the enormous debt incurred to her dominions and to India, Egypt, the Argentine Republic, and other countries, it was apparent that for some years to come she would not command the foreign resources prerequisite to the world-wide resumption on the former basis of the credit and acceptance business that had long been conducted by her merchant bankers.[1] London acceptance houses in particular, because of their far-flung activities, had undoubtedly suffered losses not only in Germany and Austria but also in the Balkans, the Baltic countries, and Poland. Once before, at the beginning of the First World War, the Bank of England had been obliged to help by taking over some of the most pressing liabilities of certain acceptance houses and overseas banks. This time, however, in the summer of 1939, thanks to the foresight of the central bank's directors, some of the firms had been prevailed upon through mergers to consolidate their financial resources. Similar amalgamations had also taken place

[1] In the middle of 1949 it was estimated that the British blocked balances still exceeded £3,200 million pounds of which sterling area countries were reported to hold about £1,800 million.

among the discount companies which furnished the major part of the funds required to carry the acceptances of the private banking firms and in turn used for that purpose capital borrowed from the Bank of England and the joint stock banks.

Yet it must be emphasized that during the whole course of the war the overseas affiliates and branches of the English banks operated without interruption, even in some of the countries occupied by the enemy. Despite the new situation created by the world-wide conflict and the numerous obstacles in the way of their future operations abroad, they were not discouraged. On the contrary, they prepared resolutely for the postwar period, when they counted upon their excellent foreign organization and their long-established connections to retain, if not to increase, the business that they had commanded in the past. There was no doubt that the British Government was alive to the situation. In the winter of 1943 it relaxed some of the rules governing blocked sterling accounts, and there was every reason to believe that if conditions permitted the British banks would be given more leeway in their efforts to expand their foreign operations. But would the British Treasury after the severe wartime inroads on the country's foreign balances and the substantial decrease in the foreign-security holdings of its nationals, still be able to provide the foreign exchange to finance, at least in part, the world's trade as had been done so successfully in bygone years? In the past a stable pound sterling that rested firmly on the gold standard had attracted to the City of London sufficient foreign deposits to provide for the credits and loans granted to foreign borrowers. But the trend of foreign moneys seemed now to have definitely veered toward the Western Hemisphere; indeed, by December 31, 1943, the net movement of foreign banking funds to the United States, according to the Federal Reserve Board *Bulletin,* October 1950, p. 1404, amounted to 7,267,1 million dollars, an increase of 3,334,1 million over those reported as of January 4, 1939.

For all these reasons a large field for postwar growth seemed open to United States banks with well-equipped foreign organizations in overseas countries. Without competing with the local institutions in services for which the latter were better qualified, United States banks abroad could, even more than formerly, devote themselves to trading in foreign exchanges and the opening of sight and acceptance credits on behalf of American exporters and importers. Moreover, they might finance for account of responsible and trustworthy local customers, as permitted under the Federal Reserve Act, shipments from different parts of the world to European ports and merchandise stored in warehouses. Far from reducing the value of the aid given by United States banks to American foreign traders, these activities would permit them to render even more effective service. The latter well knew that their future success would depend in no small measure on the contributions made by the United States Government and by private agencies to the prompt revival of international commerce and to the smooth and rapid resumption by the banks of their normal functions wherever United States industry and agriculture were seeking markets for their surplus goods and raw materials. All these prospects rested, of course, on the assumption that the practice, imperative during the war, of the taking over by government agencies of the tasks of private enterprise would be relaxed or abandoned as soon as feasible after the end of hostilities in order that individual initiative and business acumen might again come into their own.

What assets would be at the disposal of United States banks after the re-establishment of peace? Not only had they large liquid resources available for foreign operations but in addition the background of experience and practice in international finance accumulated during the almost three decades since they had first ventured into the foreign field on a world-wide scale.

All in all, after several years of enforced inactivity in many of their fields, the foreign departments were eager to resume their former contacts in Allied and neutral countries and to offer again their services both at home and to selected foreign banks and business concerns of high standing. From the very beginning they could be of constructive help in unraveling the thousands of transactions whose execution had been held up when communications were cut off at the beginning of the war. There they felt that their knowledge of foreign methods and credit usages could at once be put to excellent use as the channels of world trade were again opened for peaceful intercourse.

The clerical problems with which United States foreign bankers were faced when they began to make plans for the return of peace conditions make an interesting story. Beginning with the autumn of 1944, considerable numbers of employees had to be detached to go over the tons of mail that from September, 1939, on had come from Allied and neutral countries with which under existing laws and regulations the banks were forbidden to communicate or to which the danger of American mail falling into the hands of the enemy hindered acknowledgment and response. In many of these countries collections had been made, payments had been effected, credits had been honored, merchandise had been stored and insured, and foreign exchange contracts had been executed or canceled. For from four to six years no statements of accounts had been received from or forwarded to correspondents in these countries. Preparatory to the reopening of communications it was essential to scrutinize thousands of items and draft tentative advices that would comply with the rules of the Foreign Funds Control and the censorship officials. It was a great tribute to the adroitness and efficiency of the staffs both in the United States and abroad that when peace was restored after prolonged correspondence, research, and investigation order finally emerged and accounts everywhere could be satisfactorily settled.

As has been noted elsewhere, the banks' commercial letter of credit divisions were confronted with perplexing problems. Considerable quantities of goods were stranded either in United States or in foreign ports or never reached their destinations. The United States Treasury, in order to help clear the docks and piers for war needs, had issued special licenses requiring the banks to sell the merchandise that was held by the banks for foreign account and occupied needed space. The banks generally had no other interest in the goods than that of custodians, and the local agents of the foreign buyers often not only refused to authorize the moving of the merchandise but also threatened to hold the particular banks liable for any loss suffered by their foreign clients. On the other hand, the Treasury took the position that it was acting within its constitutional rights and compelled the banks to comply with its orders. However, after representations on the part of bank counsel many of these directive licenses were withdrawn.

ACCEPTANCES

During the war, business in dollar acceptances inevitably slumped. Many countries that had been in the habit of making use of dollar credits to finance the purchases of their nationals in the United States and elsewhere were separated from all contact with their American correspondents. The banks in the invaded regions operated under enemy supervision, and intercourse with them would have been impossible even if it had not been forbidden by the United States laws.

Owing to the great plethora of funds, interest rates for short-term cash advances and commercial paper declined to such a degree that it was more profitable for merchants to borrow on their own notes at 1 1/2 percent—the rate quoted by the banks to first-class customers—than to make use of acceptance credits whose net cost, including the acceptance commission due the banks of 1 to 1 1/2 percent, worked out at about 2 percent per annum. So although the discount rate for prime dollar bank acceptances declined—for several years it ranged around 3/8 percent—the demand for acceptance facilities remained sluggish, and the operations connected with them (such as the opening of commercial letters of credit and the discounting of bills, which had been welcome sources of revenue for foreign departments) languished. Moreover, the banks, while always keen to secure attractive self-liquidating acceptance business from sound debtors, were still mindful of their unhappy experiences in Central Europe during the early thirties. They therefore determined that as a rule after the end of the present struggle acceptance credits extended abroad should provide for satisfactory evidence that the bills created under them were conditioned upon actual shipments and that at the maturity of the drafts the proceeds of the shipments should be available for their payment in dollars as originally agreed.

BANKING FOR THE ARMED FORCES

After contingents of the United States armed forces had landed abroad, payments to the families at home and remittances to family members stationed in foreign countries called for diligent service on the part of United States financial institutions, especially those with branches or correspondents in the United Kingdom, Australia, and New Zealand, and later in North Africa, Italy, and finally in all the countries that had been liberated. The bank staffs in the United States and in the branch offices in Europe were particularly alive to the value of their services in bolstering the morale of the soldiers, sailors, and airmen training or fighting in far-off lands and in fortifying the spirit of the homefolk who either depended on the financial support of their sons and husbands or who were anxious to lighten in some small way the burdens of those who were defending their country on foreign soil.

As the area where our forces were battling came to reach to the far corners of the earth, many thousands of transactions had to be handled every month. The orders came from widely divergent points. In the early months of 1942 most of them originated in England, Scotland, and Ireland, but later in such distant places as Egypt, India, the Fiji Islands, and China. The clerical work required for instructing banks scattered over the country to make these payments, ordinarily small in amount, both in busy large cities and in remote hamlets, was enormous. Addresses were misspelled, and often it was necessary to trace the beneficiaries locally, and if unsuccessful to ask for further information abroad. The pressure on the banks' staffs was greatest on the eve of Christmas and other holidays and special occasions, such as Mother's Day. Orders for the purchase and delivery of flowers and other gifts were gladly and promptly executed. All hands devoted themselves with eagerness and devotion to finding the best answers to the complications that occasionally arose.

Difficulties were sometimes encountered in transmitting funds to persons in the armed forces. This was especially true when, as often happened, the particular army unit to which the beneficiary had originally directed that the funds be sent had already moved nearer to the front. At certain periods the censor even refused to authorize the dispatch of cables for such funds fearing that the movements of the forces to other destinations might be prematurely disclosed. Similarly, the War Department often gave instructions to suspend temporarily all payments for certain designated divisions.

When calling at the branches of United States banks abroad, the service men were especially appreciative of little courtesies extended to them, such as the cashing of checks for reasonable amounts, very few of which, may it be said to the credit of the men, were not honored when presented for payment to local banks in the United States. Because of the conditions under which these contacts were made, the human relationships thus established with young Americans from far-away towns and villages gave prospect of reaching well into the time when these individuals could again resume the peaceful tenor of their lives upon their return, as one of them wrote to me, "to this blessed land of light."

FOREIGN EXCHANGE CONTRACTS

In 1938, after Hitler's occupation of Austria, the disturbed conditions throughout Europe suggested to the foreign exchange departments of American banks the advisability of clarifying the conditions under which they were prepared to carry balances in foreign currency accounts in other countries for United States business firms and individuals. After purchasing merchandise abroad, many importers, in order to avoid the inherent risk of exchange when settling with the seller in his own money, had been in the habit of acquiring the approximate amount of the foreign currency needed for payment, generally upon delivery of the shipping documents. The American seller of the sterling, francs, guilders or other currencies was instructed to deposit them with his own banking correspondent abroad until the merchandise to be imported had been placed on board ship or until warehouse receipts had been presented by the foreign seller to the United States bank's local branch or agent with the invoice, insurance policies, and so forth. In the same manner, tourists had been accustomed to take advantage of what they believed to be favorable rates of exchange by securing foreign funds for their contemplated trips abroad long before the actual journey. Their banks were requested to leave on deposit with the latters' foreign offices or correspondents the sums so bought until the tourists were ready to withdraw them or convert them into letters of credit.

In the spring of 1938 the New York banks, for their own protection, decided to inform the owners of such foreign currency deposits that if the ability of the foreign correspondent bank to make payment was affected

> by any present or future laws, acts, decrees, regulations, moratorium, levy or by any executive order of the governments of the United States or any foreign government or by any political authority asserting governmental power or if loss or damage should result from any war, revolution or confiscation, any economic disturbance, any fluctuation in exchange or by reason of the insolvency of the correspondent bank,

then the American bank would hold itself free from responsibility. The banks also reserved the right to transfer such deposit to any other foreign banks selected by them.

SECURITIES HELD IN CUSTODY FOR FOREIGNERS

With the advent to power of the Nazis the inflow of foreign capital in the form of United States and foreign securities seeking refuge in the United States assumed considerable proportions. Most bank custody accounts involving such securities were carried in the names of foreign banks, which, generally without disclosing names, advised the American depositary that the securities were the property of customers. If the foreign bank made no statement whatever as to the ownership, the practice was to assume that the deposit belonged to the bank and to act according to the latter's instructions. It was recognized that this procedure involved a business risk, for in the event of a general conflagration in Europe or in the remote contingency of the failure of the foreign bank, claims by the real owners might be made for an accounting by the depositary.

In 1937, when Nazi persecutions were becoming more common and the possibility of attacks on neighboring countries was growing more threatening, a meeting of counsel for the interested New York banks was called to consider what steps, if any, should be taken to define clearly the responsibility of the custodian banks toward their foreign clients. Having in mind the actions that were started after the Bolshevist Revolution in 1918, the banks became more and more apprehensive lest similar suits be initiated by foreigners for fantastic damage claims against them. Their position seemed to be particularly vulnerable where securities had been sold on orders received from a foreign bank and the proceeds had been credited to its account. That their fears were well founded was demonstrated when a firm of New York lawyers advised one of the local institutions that certain securities held by it for account of a Berlin bank belonged to their client, a former resident of Germany. The firm warned the trust company that should instructions be received from the Berlin bank for the sale or disposal otherwise of the stocks and bonds held for their client, they should not be executed until he had been afforded an opportunity to identify those to which he claimed title and that disregard of this warning would be at the trust company's own peril. Thereupon the bank decided to block the securities specified by the alleged alien owner, being advised by counsel that under the circumstances it should not let the securities get out of its possession until the courts had ruled on the matter.

For their common protection a group of operating officers of certain New York banks then formed a Committee on Custody Accounts to confer at regular intervals on the various problems that were likely to arise in connection with foreign custody accounts. The nature of the questions presented to the committee is best illustrated by the following examples of actual practices and proposals.

One example involved a Dutch bank that carried several accounts in a United States banking institution, each earmarked by what appeared to be an identifying test word. The custodian bank received instructions that it was to permit any one of three different individuals to dispose of the securities. At a certain moment, one of the three names was eliminated. Had one of the owners died? Were his or her heirs entitled to a share of the deposit? As the bank had never heard directly from the actual owners and moreover it was not at all certain that one of the three persons had passed away, counsel for the bank advised that it was a business risk that the bank would have to assume. Rightly or wrongly, it was believed that the eventuality of someone's claiming an interest later was remote.

Other problems concerned the wide variety of custody accounts that were conducted by the banks. There were accounts opened in the names of banks abroad marked "Customer's Account" or "Client's Depôt." Accounts were also carried marked "Account of John Doe," where one individual or two jointly retained authority to give the custodian orders to deliver or sell the securities. Other deposits were made in the name of foreign banks, but earmarked for a specified company or corporation, the company or corporation having power to issue instructions without the concurrence of the foreign bank in whose name the account was actually carried. In still other variations John Doe had authorized a third party or parties to exercise all his rights with regard to his securities. One ingenious foreign bank invented a system by means of which its numerous custody accounts were identified merely by numbers or letters, the owners evidently preferring not to have their names spread on the ledgers and records of a United States bank. In other cases confidential letters from the foreign bank contained the names of individuals or corporations who had the right to withdraw the deposit or give orders regarding it; however, it was not certain that these persons or companies were the real owners, since they might be merely acting for the owners out of friendship or because of family ties or even for a monetary compensation, so as to help conceal their identity. Finally, for some accounts the United States depositary had the power to deliver to or to receive from designated brokerage houses all securities proffered or required by them, the brokers having to pay for all securities delivered to them or being entitled to receive cash payment for stocks or bonds deposited by them at the approximate market quotations then prevailing on the New York Stock or Curb Exchange.

After careful consideration, the Committee on Custody Accounts recommended to the banks that thereafter they decline to accept accounts subject to orders of third parties irrespective of whether the securities were being held for individual or joint account. Nevertheless, the banks were deeply concerned as to their liability with respect to these accounts. What, for instance, should they do if the totalitarian rulers of a country should seek to sequester or confiscate securities held in the United States for the account of banks in such a country where the American bank—although no names were furnished—was cognizant of the fact that the securities were the property of the foreign bank's private customers?

In another case, a bank located near the Atlantic coast had the following curious experience. A foreigner walked into its banking hall, and upon being interviewed by an officer declared that the bank held for his account a number of shares of some well-known United States industrial companies. He stated that the account was actually carried in the name of a Berlin bank, whose name he mentioned, and quoted the number of the receipt that the American depositary had issued to its foreign correspondent and even the numbers of the certificates forming part of the deposit. The original receipt had been handed to him by the Berlin bank at his request as a means of identification and proof of ownership. The visitor asked that the securities be delivered to him. This the United States custodian bank refused to do, but promised to cable abroad for authorization. The claimant then cautioned the officer that under no circumstances should his institution part with his property, and on the next day he had a writ served on the bank tying up all the securities held in the Berlin bank's account. The upshot of numerous cables exchanged with Berlin was that the German bank, pushed to the wall, gave its permission for the delivery of the securities to the man whose foresight had provided him with fool-proof credentials showing that he was the bona fide owner.

In order to hide their identity and remove their property from the reach of the invader or protect it against claims by their own governments, foreign depositors proposed numerous schemes to United States banks both prior to and after the beginning of hostilities. Some of these were actually put into use; others ran into legal and practical obstacles. In the spring of 1938, for instance, certain interests on the Continent planned the formation of a corporation under the laws of the State of New York to handle various types of security transactions. Behind the project was the desire to set up an organization that would attend to the safekeeping of securities belonging to European individuals who had investments in the United States. The promoters intended to solicit the patronage of Dutch, Swiss, and other capitalists on the Continent. They asserted frankly that the commercial banks in the various neutral countries feared that if the banks directed their customers to American institutions they would lose their business, since even after conditions had changed for the better their local depositors might not wish to change back to them. This would be the more likely if in the meantime the depositors had come to appreciate the excellence of American service and the perhaps lower fees for such facilities than those customarily charged in Europe. The proposed corporation was to receive a broad power of attorney from its clients making it their sole agent in the United States. For each individual customer a separate custody account was to be opened with a United States bank, but in the name of the corporation. The custodian would have no contact with the real owners, who, it was planned, would be identified solely by distinctive numbers on the books and in the other records of the corporation.

Such a system was not an innovation, having been successfully applied in the past by some New York banking houses with a considerable following among European investors. Behind it and other kindred designs was, of course, the anxiety of a great number of foreigners to mask their identity in dealing with United States banks. Several continental banks had already formed trusts for the purpose under United States and Canadian laws, and accounts were conducted in the names of these trusts on the books of their custodian banks; the creators of the trusts were prompted not so much by the desire to avoid the payment of taxes in their lands of origin as by the fear of seizure by hostile governments and by the dread of social upheavals that might jeopardize the solvency and existence of the continental banks themselves. In banking circles on this side of the Atlantic, however, no advantage could be seen in interposing a middleman between the foreign owners of securities and the United States custodians, since the corporation would run the same hazards of a disturbed world as would its own clientele, and would be unable to do more to protect its customers than the United States banks, with their machinery already functioning, had been doing for many years.

In the summer of 1938 another plan, devised with a similar object, was presented by a bank located in a neutral country. The latter inquired whether it was possible to open custody accounts subject to sealed instructions that the American custodian would agree to follow under certain contingencies. Obviously, this would place the custodian on notice that the securities, although deposited in the bank's name, were the property of a third person. It was impossible to foresee the complications that might ensue. The custodian might make itself liable for illegal disposal and for the payment of American estate and stamp taxes. Questions might also arise as to whether sealed instructions, although in form irrevocable, could be treated by the United States bank as such when as a matter of fact the latter had accepted the mandate to carry the securities as the property of the foreign bank. An invasion might result in a new government, in which case the American custodian might face a situation in which a foreign bank, by government ukase or under the direction of new managers, might be compelled to claim title to the securities in spite of the perhaps contrary sealed instructions still outstanding. The authors of such proposals seemed to be seeking protection against disastrous possibilities that might upset the whole social order abroad. Under these conditions the United States banks elected not to stray too far away from the normal routine by which they were guided in the handling of custody accounts. Even so, they feared that they might still have to cope with perplexing incidents, should the sinister events that such inquiries seemed to forebode actually take place.

Perhaps the most troubling inquiry of all was that of a foreign bank which sought to ascertain whether the United States custodian would act upon orders, written or cabled, preceded by a secret cipher or code-word, even though the message were sent from a country other than the one where the owner had previously had his legal domicile.

Foreign owners were understandably sensitive during the discussions relating to these matters. The United States banks, not wishing to forfeit their good will, had to exercise a great deal of tact in their relations with these alien customers. Some particularly cautious depositors abroad objected to the letters which they received from the banks on the subject of their accounts being signed by different officers, evidently not wanting too many individuals in the United States to gain an insight into their private affairs. Others did not wish to receive regular monthly statements or requested that they be sent to relatives or friends in the United States or other countries. When the banks raised legitimate objections to some of the more extreme demands, the foreign owners offered to indemnify them against any loss arising from the carrying out of their special wishes.

The foregoing examples indicate the range of the problems that came before the Committee on Custody Accounts for impartial consideration and decision. In each case the determining factor was whether in the event of war or internal upheaval the question of the title to the property held by the banks would become so entangled that in advance of a judgment by the competent court it would be impossible to determine where the liabilities of the custodian ended.

SUMMARY

This chapter is concerned particularly with the efforts of United States banks to protect their interests and those of their customers during the war. Various emergency steps, of course, had to be taken to avert serious losses. However, the interference by the war with the normal business in Europe and later in the Far East was compensated in part by the banking services required by the foreign purchasing missions and trade delegations and by the increased trade activity with Latin America. By the end of 1943 the banks began to give detailed consideration to the questions that would be involved in a resumption of banking activities after the war in the Allied and neutral countries and the extent of the competition likely to be encountered thereafter in the foreign sphere. Especial attention was given to the probable position of England after her heavy sacrifices made in the fighting of the enemy, and later, to the legal and clerical obstacles to the reopening of relations with foreign customers, as well as to the problems connected with the re-establishing of a sound acceptance business throughout the world.

Much routine banking assistance was extended during the war to the members of the Armed forces in Europe, Australia, and the East. The changes necessitated by the numerous regulations and laws enacted by various governments affecting payments abroad raised special problems, while various questions arose respecting securities held in custody for foreign customers and banking correspondents.

III

ADAPTING POLICIES TO WARTIME NEEDS

THE FOREIGN EXCHANGE COMMITTEE

AT THE END OF AUGUST, 1939, George L. Harrison, then governor of the Federal Reserve Bank of New York, suggested to Secretary of the Treasury, Henry Morgenthau, Jr., that he appoint a foreign exchange committee to consult with the Treasury and the Federal Reserve Bank of New York on the numerous problems in the field of international banking with which the United States business world was likely to be faced in the event of war. A number of representatives of banks and banking houses active in foreign banking were accordingly invited to become members of such a committee. Robert F. Loree, vice president of the Guaranty Trust Company, was appointed chairman, and Joseph C. Rovensky, of the Chase National Bank, vice chairman; the other members were I. C. R. Atkin, of J. P. Morgan & Co., Inc., C. E. C. Freyvogel, of the Bankers Trust Co., B. Hwoschinsky, of the Central Hanover Bank & Trust Co., Leo N. Shaw, of the National City Bank, Knight Woolley, of Brown Bros. Harriman & Co., and C. J. Stephenson, senior agent in New York of the Canadian Bank of Commerce. In February, 1942, since J. C. Rovensky had entered government service, I replaced him as a committee member and vice chairman. Ewen C. MacVeagh of Davis, Polk, Wardwell & Reed acted as counsel.

The purpose of the Foreign Exchange Committee was to provide a small compact group with which Treasury and Federal Reserve authorities could explore questions affecting foreign exchange and through which, in case of need, they could quickly establish contact with the market. The members of the committee, thus, were at all times available for the transmission of information and for the discussion of urgent measures that might have to be taken during the critical period in world finance that seemed ahead.

The meetings of the committee were given over to thorough discussions of the matters submitted to it by the Treasury, the Federal Reserve Bank of New York, and the various local and out-of-town commercial banks. Chairman Loree was spokesman for the committee and maintained contact with the officials of the Federal Reserve Bank of New York and the Treasury. Both agencies, through frequent communication with the committee, endeavored to anticipate the probable reaction of the foreign departments of commercial banks relative to contemplated regulations and amendments to the Foreign Funds Control legislation.[1] The services of the committee were likewise enlisted for correspondence with foreign banks of issue and foreign bankers' associations. For instance, the committee was occasionally requested to inform the banks in certain neutral countries of new Treasury General Rulings affecting them. It was not always an easy task to make some of the rulings palatable, not merely to local and interior banks in the United States but also to sensitive neutrals who were expected to collaborate in applying them to the relations of their citizens with the United States.

As far as wartime conditions permitted, the committee earnestly tried to safeguard legitimate trading and the orderly settlement of foreign exchange contracts in the New York market, as well as to defend the trade against injurious operations on the part of irresponsible foreign speculators. The committee frequently communicated with the Bank of England, which acted on behalf of the London banks. As a rule, negotiations were conducted through the London managers of the United States bank branches in the City. Thus, in July, 1940, an agreement was reached regarding the establishment of a fixed official rate of $4.02 for purchases and $4.04 for sales of the pound sterling. Special registered accounts were set up in the London banks to cover all future sterling trades at these new rates. Thenceforth the Federal Reserve Bank of New York, as agent for the Bank of England, bought spot sterling from banks with registered accounts at 4.02 1/2 and sold it at 4.03 1/2.

One of the more serious problems with which the committee was asked to deal was presented to it in July, 1942. The Boston wool trade had been advised by the Central Wool Committee in Melbourne that thereafter the risk of a change in the sterling-dollar rate was to be borne by the United States buyers of Australian, New Zealand, and South African wool. Obviously, both the merchants and the Boston,

[1] See pp. 67–86.

New York, and Philadelphia banks, which for many years had issued dollar letters of credit to pay for imported Empire wool, were deeply disturbed by this new requirement. It meant that in the future the wool purchased for United States textile mills would be payable in dollars at the rate of exchange that prevailed for cable transfers on London at the time of settlement rather than at the quotation current on the date of the purchase contract. Under the former practice they were able immediately, by means of a purchase of future sterling, to fix the cost price in dollars of the wool acquired abroad. Under the procedure now proposed, however, United States buyers would have been completely at the mercy of the British Exchange Control, without any possibility of protecting themselves by hedging against an advance in the price of sterling between the date of the purchase contract and the delivery of the wool in the United States. Due to the arguments presented by the Boston Wool Trade Association and the strong support lent by the Foreign Exchange Committee the view of the United States wool interests prevailed. The rate of exchange continued to be fixed at the time of the contract, the British authorities having been persuaded that in order to price and sell their wool American importers were right in wanting to know the exact cost in United States currency.

In August, 1942, at the request of the Bank of England, the Foreign Exchange Committee approved the elimination of all remaining free sterling accounts. The primary object was to do away permanently with the need of quoting free pounds in the New York market. Indeed, transactions in registered and the so-called Central American sterling already had effectively replaced those in free sterling, the use of the latter being by now restricted to a small number of countries and being, moreover, no longer accepted in settlement of exports from the sterling area. The British Exchange Control offered to purchase any balances in free or old sterling that still remained at the official rate of 4.02 1/2, or alternatively to have the accounts converted, where feasible, into registered accounts or sterling-area accounts.

On February 2, 1943, all free sterling-area and so-called "old" accounts were converted into registered accounts. This measure had the effect of conferring upon the former accounts the privilege of convertibility into dollars at the then fixed rate of 4.03 1/2 for purchases and 4.02 1/2 for sales.[2]

[2] It is a rather remarkable fact that in 1949, six and a half years later, the British au-

In the summer of 1944 the committee members, upon invitation, conferred in Washington with Harry D. White, Assistant Secretary of the Treasury, E. M. Bernstein, Assistant Director of Monetary Research, Treasury Department, and Ansel F. Luxford, Assistant General Counsel, Treasury Department, in order to obtain a better understanding of the proposals drafted by the United Nations Monetary and Financial Conference at Bretton Woods. These officials, in reply to the committee's questions, explained during the day-long meeting the principles underlying the proposals especially the International Monetary Fund, in which the foreign banking fraternity was chiefly interested. The Treasury experts pointed to the long and painstaking studies and consultations that had preceded the formulation of the plan for the Fund and sought to justify both the objectives and the measures that the Treasury had recommended. The provisions dealing with the role that the dollar was to play in the future operations of the Fund and the possible intervention of the Fund in the foreign exchange markets were reviewed and discussed at length. While not all differences of opinion could be reconciled, the committee members at least received a convincing demonstration of the fact that the Treasury officials had an unusual command of the intricacies of the international exchange problem and that they were prepared at the impending conferences to vindicate their proposals with vigor and evident conviction.

During the fall of 1944 a subcommittee of the Foreign Exchange Committee studied a foreign credit information plan submitted by the Foreign Research Division of the Federal Reserve Bank of New York. This plan was designed to make available to those interested in exports to Latin America, statistics regarding the current experience of leading New York banks with collections sent to the various Central and South American republics, as well as their volume, the total amount of letters of credit opened by foreign importers, data about cancellation of orders, attempts to secure price reductions, and so forth. Although some of the information had been assembled before and distributed in bulletin form by several commercial banks and by the Foreign Credit Interchange Bureau, it was emphasized that the proposed service would be especially authoritative and valuable to

thorities were once more confronted with the same problem. While cut-rate transactions in pound bank notes could not be prevented, the Bank of England explored the possibility of checking the sale of "bilateral" sterling in the American market at rates ranging between 2.55 and 2.60 as against the official parity of $2.80 established in September 1949.

both banks and merchants in the postwar era. The plan finally materialized in June, 1947, when the Federal Reserve Bank of New York released for publication the first of a series of monthly reports compiled on the basis of statements furnished by twelve leading New York banks covering collections paid, collections outstanding, and confirmed letters of credit outstanding in twenty-three Latin American countries. Since then the number of reporting banks has risen to fifteen.

THE NEUTRALITY AND JOHNSON ACTS

During the decade between 1935 and 1945 the foreign departments of the United States banks devoted a great deal of study to the American and foreign legislation affecting their operations both at home and abroad. Many hours were spent in conferences with counsel in order to make sure that the various decrees, laws, and proclamations not only were correctly interpreted but also were properly applied by their staffs. Both the Neutrality Act and the Johnson Act, in their respective spheres, had an important bearing on the policies of the commercial banks and on their relations with customers in the United States and abroad.

The Neutrality Act as passed in 1935 and amended in 1937 and 1939 stipulated that whenever the President proclaimed that a state of war existed between two countries or that a state of civil strife had been declared in a foreign country it would be unlawful to export, or attempt to export, or cause to be exported arms, ammunition or implements of war from any place in the United States to any belligerent state named in such proclamation or to any neutral state for transshipment to or for the use of any belligerent state.

The section of the act that was of particular significance for the banks engaged in foreign business was that which made it unlawful for any person in the United States to purchase, sell, or exchange bonds, securities, or other obligations of any belligerent state, or of any political subdivision of any such state, or of any person acting for or in behalf of any faction or asserted government within any such state wherein civil strife existed, or to make any loan or extend any credit to any such government. However, the President was given the authority to except, at his discretion, from the operation of this section: ordinary commercial credits and short-time obligations in aid of legal transactions and of a character customarily used in normal peacetime commercial transactions.

Under the terms of the act it was the President's duty to make a suitable finding when in his opinion a state of war existed, Section I of the act providing that "whenever the President shall find that there exists a state of war between, or among two or more foreign States, the President shall proclaim such fact."

From time to time the President, under the Neutrality Act, issued or revoked proclamations to the effect that such a state of war or civil strife existed in certain countries. For instance, in 1935 the President declared that a state of war existed between Italy and Ethiopia. As a result, when the Italian Government published nationalization decrees concerning certain Italian commercial banks and industrial corporations, United States banks were confronted with the delicate question whether the nationalized banks and corporations had now become *ipso facto* "persons acting on behalf of a belligerent government." President Roosevelt revoked this proclamation on June 20, 1936. This removed the previous prohibition under the Neutrality Act, but the question of the Johnson Act still remained: whether the foreign departments of American banks were legally warranted in extending credit facilities to nationalized Italian banks under that act's proscription of loans to governments that were in default on loans made by the United States Government during and after the First World War.

The countries coming within the scope of the act were Armenia, Austria, Belgium, Czechoslovakia, Estonia, France, Germany, Great Britain, Greece, Hungary, Italy, Latvia, Lithuania, Nicaragua, Poland, Rumania, the USSR, and Yugoslavia. Counsel in the United States and Italy advised that in ordinary banking transactions the Italian commercial banks, though nationalized, could not be considered as acting for the Mussolini government. Some doubt was expressed only concerning the status of the Istituto Nazionale per i Cambi, as this institution was believed to be completely owned by the Italian Government.

On April 29, 1937, Congress passed a modified Neutrality Act which contained the celebrated "cash and carry" clause. The revised act made it unlawful to export or transport "arms, ammunition and implements of war," as prohibited by Presidential proclamation, "until all rights, title and interest therein shall have been transferred to some foreign government." Under this clause, foreign purchasers paid cash and took title to the goods before the latter's exportation from the United States. Friendly nations, although engaged in war, were thus enabled to secure in the United States needed raw materials and commodities such as cotton, wheat, oil, copper, and steel, as long as they had liquid resources with which to pay before shipment from American ports and vessels protected by their naval forces to carry them to their shores.

On May 10, 1937, forty-eight hours after the passage of the amended Neutrality Act, President Roosevelt proclaimed the existence of a state of civil strife in Spain. He enumerated the articles considered to be "arms, ammunition and implements of war," and elaborated on earlier proclamations by increasing the variety of gases, chemicals, and high explosives included in the "implements" whose export and transportation to Spain was prohibited. This proclamation not only precluded the opening of export credits by the banks' foreign departments and the financing of shipments to Spain but also prevented any banking transaction with neutral countries where there might be suspicion that their citizens were acting on behalf of Spanish nationals. Nothing in the Neutrality Act or the Proclamation gave any indication as to the degree of knowledge that was expected of the banks in determining the ultimate destination of any shipment financed by them. All the foreign departments' staffs could do was to rely upon signed declarations by responsible American exporters or by the foreign banks for whose account credits were opened in favor of United States shippers, to the effect that the merchandise would not be transshipped en route and that it was destined for consumption or use in the country to which it was consigned. In addition, the United States shipper was required to furnish a certified copy of the export declaration, filed with the Collector of the Port, confirming that no interest in the articles forwarded by him resided in citizens of the United States. The greatest difficulty encountered by the banks' commercial credit and collection departments was to determine the component elements of various chemicals, which were described in the shipping documents and invoices in technical terms different from those appearing in the text of the proclamation and with which the ordinary bank clerk was not familiar.

In February, 1942, Congress repealed Section 7 of the Neutrality Act of 1939, which had made it unlawful for persons within the United States to enter into financial transactions with a belligerent covered by a Neutrality Proclamation and had fixed as the penalty for infraction a fine of up to $50,000 and imprisonment of up to five years. The new bill provided that Section 7 was not to be operative when the

United States was at war. Accordingly, although the Johnson Act still remained in force, banks were now permitted under the Neutrality Act to make loans to the nations allied with the United States in the Second World War. Canada and some of the other British dominions, such as Australia and South Africa, were not in any case subject to the Johnson Act, but many of the Allied nations were still indebted to the United States Government on account of the interallied debts contracted during the First World War.

THE FOREIGN FUNDS CONTROL

On April 10, 1940, twenty-four hours after Germany had invaded Denmark and Norway, all Danish and Norwegian assets in the United States were frozen under Executive Order No. 8389 of the President and placed under the newly organized Treasury's Foreign Funds Control Division. The government thus took immediate steps to prevent title to property owned by nationals of the two countries from being seized by the Nazis, and thereby gave notice that it was determined to protect the interests of innocent people who had entrusted their resources to the custody of American banks. By the same token the unprecedented decree provided the latter with a legal defense should unauthorized persons seek possession of looted cash, securities, or other property of Danish and Norwegian citizens.

After Luxembourg, Belgium, Holland, and eastern and northern France were occupied by enemy forces the freezing order was amended to include the property of citizens of these countries as well. Fourteen months later, on June 14, 1941, the control was further extended to embrace Germany, Italy, Czechoslovakia, Poland, and all other states of Continental Europe that had come under enemy domination. Finally, on July 26, 1941, China and Japan (the former at her own request) were brought within the scope of the blocking arrangements. Except in individual cases, only the property of citizens of the British Commonwealth and of the Central and South American republics remained outside the authority of the Foreign Funds Control.

What were the ultimate aims of the Control? In the spring of 1942, in a brief submitted to the Court of Appeals of the State of New York, they were concisely stated to be as follows:

(1) To protect property in the United States belonging to persons in occupied countries by preventing the transfer of any right or interest in such property in any manner whatsoever unless licensed;

(2) to prevent the Axis from acquiring any benefit from the blocked assets;
(3) to render the blocked assets available for the war effort of the United States and permit the bailee or depositary bank to disregard the instructions of the owner if the transaction was not licensed, and with impunity to follow some contrary instructions if licensed;
(4) to keep the blocked funds available for application to debts owing to American creditors; and
(5) to give the United States Government power to control and seize these blocked funds after the war.

The transactions prohibited under Executive Order No. 8389 were specified as: transfers of credit, payments by or to any bank, transactions in foreign exchange and withdrawals, transfers, or exportation of, or dealing in any evidences of indebtedness or of ownership of property. Special and general licenses were issued to cover various transactions. As time went on, it became necessary to issue additional regulations, general rulings, public circulars, and public interpretations and press releases to discuss special problems in detail and to explain the objectives as well as the nature of the prohibitions and their applicability and enforcement.

As soon as the different executive orders and general licenses were made known to the banks, special divisions were created in their foreign departments to apply the rulings and conform all future bank operations to both the text and intent of the new legislation. The banks welcomed the initiative that had been taken by the government. Long before the government's official attitude toward the Axis turned from formal neutrality to implicit but still unofficial hostility, the personal sympathy of the banks for the victims of Nazi aggression had been manifest. They were conscious, indeed, that despite the burdens imposed upon them in the execution of the intricate regulations that were now decreed, the best interests of the civilized world were being served by the policy to which they were asked to address themselves.

The functions assigned to the commercial banks of the country were complex. Henceforward it was their duty to police all the transactions coming within their purview. In a sense, they were ordered to take their positions in the front line of economic warfare, and the necessity for strict compliance with all the phases of the blocking procedure thereupon became unquestionable. Accordingly, the accounts of all persons and corporations believed to be domiciled in the countries designated in the executive orders were immediately blocked. It was no mean task to ascertain the citizenship of foreign depositors, with most of whom the only contact in the past had been by way of correspondence. With the help of the credit departments many thousands of files and records were reviewed, and if no indication as to nationality was available or if a doubt existed as to the customer's citizenship, inquiries were made through the usual sources of information or if possible through reliable agencies abroad. Because of the increased clerical work involved, it became necessary to expand the staffs that handled the incoming and outgoing mail and examined the mass of foreign and domestic items passing daily through the machinery of large city banks, not to mention the preparation and filing of applications for licenses and the drafting and typing of the reports called for by the various government agencies.

In order fully to inform all the departments concerned in the head offices and at the domestic and foreign branches, if any, the banks soon found it essential to circulate daily directives elucidating such parts of the regulations as seemed to require additional explanation and outlining the steps to be taken in certain contingencies. Not only the United States Government but gradually also the governments of all the belligerents and neutral nations as well as the governments-in-exile issued a steadily growing mass of decrees and restrictions that had to be observed in the business of their nationals. In due course the rules that had to be kept in mind were augmented by others promulgated by the Director of Censorship and the Alien Property Custodian. Moreover, some of the banks of issue sent out extensive material whose terms had to be carefully studied and complied with. The task of following all these directives and seeing that nothing bearing on the operations of the foreign departments and the other services of the banks would be overlooked taxed the vigilance of the officers and department heads practically every hour of the day.

Yet after the initial period of experimentation rapid progress was made. The work of the banks' license divisions became systematized. In some institutions the staff was aided by groups of officers and senior clerks who made a special study of all the more obscure aspects of the freezing problems and by constantly keeping abreast of the regulations sought to grasp their implications so as to be able to assist both employees and customers in complying with them. Owing in great part to their continual vigilance, the multiple ramifications of the property control were put into effect without serious omission, while the loopholes through which the enemy nations might profit were plugged with vigor and determination.

Considering the delicate work with which they were confronted, the Federal Reserve banks and the Treasury Department did a most thorough and creditable job. The technical carrying into effect of the blocking measures and the successful conduct of the financial contest with the Axis powers and their sympathizers in neutral areas were arduous assignments that called for unusual ingenuity, patience, and at times unrelenting persistence in enforcing the regulations. Since the staffs had to be recruited in haste, it was particularly difficult to find a sufficient number of men trained and able to deal, without too long a course of study and preparation, with the special problems that came under the Treasury and Federal Reserve Bank control divisions' activities.

As principal agent of the Treasury Department, the Federal Reserve Bank of New York was obliged to assume supervision over American foreign banking operations, the major part of which was concentrated within the New York financial district. Accordingly, the main mass of applications for licenses flocked into the imposing sandstone building at 33 Liberty Street. No checks could be paid, no foreign exchange purchase or sale could be settled, no security transaction, if for alien blocked depositors, could be cleared, and no frozen account could be charged for loans or acceptances falling due, without the coveted signature at the bottom of a Federal Reserve Bank license. During the early weeks of the control doubts were unavoidable even within the minds of those in charge of the bank's license division as to the practicability of certain provisions. As with other pieces of novel and as yet untried war legislation, these problems were to be expected, but in the end they caused no insoluble difficulties.

Later, after almost the whole of western Europe had come under the Control, the license division was flooded by such a mass of applications that although it worked overtime it fell steadily behind in the examination and issue of licenses. This plight, although involuntary and at the time inevitable, interfered with the routine of the banks and in some instances caused prejudice to those seemingly entitled to licenses. In September, 1940, the New York banks suggested that either the issue of the most urgently required licenses be accelerated or for some current types of transactions the Funds Control be authorized to provide appropriate general licenses in order to bring relief to both the Federal Reserve banks and the commercial banks as well. The latter alternative was adopted soon afterwards, and it promptly corrected the situation.

In numerous instances, it must be conceded, valid reasons existed for delay in granting permission. For example, at times the payment of checks drawn in neutral European or Latin American countries had to be deferred because the needed information as to the underlying transactions could not be readily furnished by the drawees. To alleviate such conditions special licenses were granted certain banks in neutral countries entitling them to withdraw up to 25 percent of their dollar deposits. On the other hand, the accounts of several South American institutions suspected of close relations with enemy interests were wholly frozen, and all entries passing over these accounts were subjected to close scrutiny.

Puzzling questions of a different order arose when after the invasion of countries in eastern Europe the United States correspondents of banks located in the occupied regions received instructions from them, over apparently authentic and authorized official signatures, to pay to the Federal Reserve Bank of New York the balances standing to their credit for the free disposal of the central bank of the invading power. After consultation with the State Department it was decided by the United States banks to retain possession of the dollar deposits in all such cases until such time as the legal title to them could be determined by the courts.

The blocking of foreign deposits caused considerable commotion among the numerous alien residents living in the United States. When the morning papers of Sunday, June 19, 1941, contained the news that a decree was ready for the signature of the President calling for the freezing of all foreign deposits except those belonging to British subjects and South American citizens, the refugees who had been arriving in the United States in growing numbers since the spread of Hitlerism became greatly alarmed. Fearing that they would lose free control over their savings, some hurriedly withdrew their balances in the downtown New York banks and opened accounts in the uptown offices, in the mistaken belief that their holdings would not be subject to governmental restrictions in branches where their origin and former domiciles were unknown. Other foreigners, for similar reasons, converted their dollars posthaste into Swiss francs and Argentine pesos (then considered a "hard" currency), which the banks were directed to transfer by cable to their correspondents abroad. Certain alarmed Latin Americans asked that their funds be sent to the lands of their birth, especially Mexico and Cuba. Some foreigners, at that time, started to object to the legend "Foreign Department" appearing at the top of their check forms and monthly statements of account. A few wealthy individuals removed their securities from their safe deposit boxes and hid them in secret spots, where they stayed until it became evident that no harm would come to the property of friendly aliens in this country. Nevertheless, some of the foreign depositors could not rid themselves of the suspicion that at some time in the future their assets would be impounded by the United States Government. Accordingly they investigated the possibility of creating irrevocable trusts, asking in particular whether the donor of such trusts would be considered legally to have divested himself of all rights to the property placed in trust and whether such a trust would be unfailingly exempt from future freezing orders. Altogether, a great deal of thought was thus directed by foreign men of means toward discovering the best legal methods to protect and preserve the funds that at the cost of so much exertion and sacrifice they had succeeded in caching in the New World. Several prosperous merchants even enlisted the help of the late Wendell Willkie and engaged the services of his law firm to represent their interests before Congress and the United States Treasury, but his untimely death put an end to his generous intervention on their behalf.

As the war progressed and as the need grew for more drastic measures by this country, the Treasury extended to hitherto unexplored fields its controls and its attack on the enemy's economic and financial power. On July 17, 1941, it published the *Proclaimed List of Certain Blocked Nationals,* a roll of alleged unfriendly Latin American businesses with German or Italian affiliations to whom export and fund-freeing licenses were ordinarily to be refused. By the end of 1943 this list, including the so-called "special blocked nationals," had grown to a total of 19,500 firms and corporations domiciled in all parts of the globe.

Approval by the banks of any transaction that came under the freezing legislation required prior consultation of the Proclaimed List. In addition, the thousands of individuals who received payments from foreign sources were recorded alphabetically by the banks for the benefit of the Funds Control if needed. The banks also had to watch the British Statutory List, since the account or business of anyone whose name appeared on this list was also unofficially subject to the United States Executive Orders. Moreover, the Belgian, Norwegian, Luxembourg, and Czechoslovakian governments-in-exile also issued separate orders, requiring constant close study and attention. For transactions concerning the accounts of Dutch citizens resident in Holland or of corporations with offices in that country, releases from its freezing regulations had to be secured from the Dutch diplomatic representatives before they could be completed.

Administrative directives by foreign nations affecting international trade and finance, it is true, were not actually a recent development. Ever since the First World War restrictions on export and import, as well as foreign exchange, had been impeding the work of the banks' foreign departments in many parts of the world, although only after the beginning of the Second World War did the tendency to promulgate stringent limitations and rules for foreign traders and bankers become general. The conditions under which import and export licenses and exchange permits could be secured, as well as other local usages, had varied in different countries. In most cases foreign exchange control had been under the jurisdiction of special boards, the central banks, or other authorized agencies, the sterling area adhering to the British Defense (Finance) Regulations of 1939.

The countries of the Western Hemisphere did not lag behind in taking precautionary measures, especially when after Pearl Harbor the war clouds seemed suddenly to be drawing nearer the American continent. Cuba issued a decree restricting the exportation of capital or its transfer to countries at war with her or to countries having placed restrictions upon funds belonging to her or to her residents. The same decree prohibited the withdrawal of funds, securities, and other evidences of ownership from the custody of Cuban banks if they belonged to nationals of countries at war with Cuba.

Similarly, the Republic of Panama published a decree-law blocking all assets belonging to German, Italian, and Japanese nationals and to corporations in which such nationals were interested, denying access to their safe deposit boxes.

In the United States, new postal regulations were put into force. The shipment of articles of value, such as shipping documents, securities, interest coupons, and dividend checks, to neutral countries was prohibited unless the title thereto had previously been transferred to foreign ownership. Hence all such items that were the property of United States holders, prior to being placed in the United States mails, had to be sold to buyers in the neutral countries where they were payable.

In the discharge of its heavy responsibilities the Treasury enlisted the collaboration of the commercial banks in many directions. In order to discourage the hoarding of bank notes of large denominations, the banks were requested to report substantial currency withdrawals to their local Federal Reserve Banks. Likewise, a strict control was instituted over the importation of United States currency and securities, which had to be delivered to the Federal Reserve banks for examination and identification as to nonenemy ownership.

The last-named measure caused great consternation in certain Central and South American republics. Workers in the Canal Zone had been in the habit of sending part of their wages to their families in Colombia, Ecuador, and other neighboring countries. These laborers had for many years had the practice of remitting the funds by slipping five or ten dollar bills into their letters to their wives and relatives, thereby saving the fifty-cents charge of the Panama banks for drafts or mail transfers, a similar small fee also being due when the drafts were cashed at the other end. Total commissions of a dollar for remittances as small as five dollars were rightly considered excessive. After the new regulations went into effect the banks in Central and South America experienced unexpected difficulties when shipping all this currency back to the United States for their credit. The money was seized by the United States Customs authorities or the censor and was released only after lengthy discussions. As a rule it was impossible to trace the origin of the soiled bills, which had passed through many rough hands before being finally exchanged into local currency at the foreign tellers' cages. Fortunately, the Colombian and Ecuadorean delegates to the Pan American conference held some time later in Washington succeeded in inducing their local banks to reduce their charges by fifty percent, while the United States banks established in Panama lessened their own small fee in the same spirit of good neighborliness.

Another incident in connection with the control exercised over the bringing in of dollar currency from abroad is worth recounting at this point, showing as it does that the sometimes drab atmosphere of the banking rooms is occasionally brightened by a touch of humor, although in the instance here related it had all the aspects of a domestic drama. The episode recited here occurred shortly after the currency regulations had been promulgated in this country. A Hollander on his way to an assignment in Central America called at the foreign department of a New York bank to which he carried a letter of introduction. In the course of an interview with one of the bank's officers he asked for advice as to how to proceed in order to obtain from the United States Treasury the replacement of dollar bank notes that he had owned and which had been destroyed. They represented, he said, almost all his many years' savings.

Questioned for details, he revealed the following tragic accident. When the German armies approached Paris, he had decided to hide his precious holdings in the fireplace of his country home in the suburbs of Paris—the last place, he was sure, where the Germans or thieves would look for concealed valuables. Fearing lest his wife be tempted to betray his secret, he had not taken her into his confidence. One late autumn afternoon, when returning from work, upon entering the house, he smelled smoke. Hurrying to the living-room, he noticed his wife kneeling before the hearth where she had started a fire. Frantic, he pushed her away and succeeded in extinguishing the flame with his coat. Some of the notes had already been irreparably destroyed but others were merely charred. Distractedly he gathered the ashes and collected the bits of scorched and stained remnants of his treasured stock of "hard" currency. He had now brought them to the United States carefully secreted on his person. According to his estimate they still represented about $1,500, which he wanted to attempt to recover by petitioning the competent authorities. He then unwrapped a small package in which the officer, to his surprise, discovered that the stranger had not only the fragments of the burned notes but also a few practically new twenty- and fifty-dollar bills. When the visitor was informed that he should have declared his holdings upon entering the port of New York and that he was subject not only to a heavy fine but even to imprisonment, he was bewildered and panic-stricken. He was immediately escorted to the Federal Reserve Bank, where he again explained his pathetic experience and convincingly pleaded complete ignorance of United States laws. A few days later, after having filed an application for the issuance to him of new notes in place of those scorched and singed in France, he left for his destination. Whether he received, as he sought, crisp fresh currency for the bills ruined in the chimney of his distant home, the bank's officials never learned, although they fervently hoped he did.

Just fourteen months after the first blocking order had been issued, the Treasury Department, under an order dated June 14, 1941, called for the long-contemplated inventory of all foreign-owned property held in the United States, whether held by nationals of blocked countries or not. Form T.F.R. 300, explaining the requirements, was the most comprehensive document that had been published since the government undertook to control blocked assets. The scope of the survey went beyond anything that had been attempted anywhere. What particularly concerned the various banks' foreign departments was the requirement that the names of the drawers of all outstanding bank acceptances, as well as the names of all the beneficiaries of unused commercial letters of credit, had to be submitted if they were nationals of foreign countries.[3]

Somewhat less exhaustive was the report called for March 31, 1943, on Form T.F.R. 500. To complete its records, the Treasury Department directed every person subject to the jurisdiction of the United States to file a statement as of December 31, 1942, showing any interest, direct or indirect, in any property located in any foreign country. Such property as was held in domestic trusts or estates created under the laws of the United States had also to be reported by the fiduciary. Bonds and stocks issued abroad, whether held in the United States or in foreign countries, likewise had to be listed.

Apart from Form T.F.R. 500 a new series of measures had followed the entry of the United States into the war, whose terms had to be digested and applied by the foreign departments. In the first place, they were informed that the provisions of the Trading with the Enemy Act, which was originally passed on October 6, 1917, and had already been resorted to in connection with the Foreign Funds Control, would henceforth govern again all contacts with foreign

3 The results of the inventory appeared in the Census of Foreign-Owned Assets in the United States, published by the Treasury Department in 1945. The total value of United States assets reported by foreign persons as of June 14, 1941, was reported at $12,738,700,000. British assets headed the list with $3,239,000,000, followed by Canada with $1,709,000,000, Switzerland with $1,210,000,000, France with $1,040,000,000, and the Netherlands with $977,000,000; the totals for other countries were appreciably smaller.

countries. However, a general license was issued by the President under Section 3(A) of the act, permitting trade authorized by the Secretary of the Treasury through regulations issued pursuant to Executive Order 8389 (the original freezing control order) as amended. A week after Pearl Harbor the President signed the First War Powers Act of 1941, which formally ratified all actions that had been taken under the Trading with the Enemy Act and the various executive orders since April 10, 1940. Other ordinances that had to be assimilated and obeyed by banks and foreign traders followed early in 1942, especially when Leo Crowley, Alien Property Custodian, and Byron Price, Director of Censorship, published, jointly with the Secretary of the Treasury, detailed rules regarding trade and communication with the enemy countries to be observed in connection with the restrictions imposed in the Trading with the Enemy Act.

In the autumn of 1941 several leading New York banks decided that in order to handle more efficiently the numerous enquiries that were constantly being received regarding the foreign property control legislation it would be advisable to form a subcommittee of the Foreign Exchange Committee. This subcommittee was charged with the task of maintaining close contact with the officials of the Foreign Funds Control Division at the Treasury and with the officers of the Federal Reserve Bank of New York presiding over the licensing and control activities. It was hoped that uncertainty about the interpretation of some of the decrees and rulings would be eliminated if a forum were provided where Treasury and bank officials could cooperate in the common interest through friendly discussion across the table and a frank exchange of views. The subcommittee, composed of experienced representatives prominent in foreign banking, was headed by Wilbert Ward, Vice President of the National City Bank of New York. The members met at regular intervals to pass on all phases of the control legislation from a practical angle. Obstacles encountered were candidly revealed to the Treasury agents, and the necessary solutions were often suggested by men who had been for years on the firing line at their banks. Moreover, by giving full aid in uncovering enemy-controlled assets and by reporting operations that appeared to be suspicious, the members of the subcommittee made a valuable contribution to the successful implementation of the Foreign Funds Control.

Whenever divergences of opinion arose as to the applicability of certain provisions—even among those who had made themselves experts in the interpretation of the various aspects of the rulings—such differences were brought to the notice of the subcommittee and presented to it for definite elucidation. One demand with which the banks found it almost impossible to comply was the proposal of certain Treasury assistants that the banks guarantee that the endorsements on all items received by them for collection, from both domestic and foreign depositors and correspondents, conformed to the requirements of the official freezing regulations. It was pointed out by the members of the subcommittee that during every working day literally hundreds of thousands of checks, drafts, and bills of exchange of one sort or another passed through the cages of the tellers of the great metropolitan banks. Whatever the care and vigilance exercised, how could the banks, it was asked, be held accountable when in a large number of cases no indication of the domicile of the endorser was affixed on the items and in many other instances the endorsements of individuals were completely illegible? It was clear—and the Treasury finally acquiesced—that this requirement was beyond the ability of the banks to carry out, however anxious they were to facilitate the task of the Treasury.

It was inevitable that certain constructions placed upon the freezing rules by Treasury officials should unwittingly cause the commercial banks embarrassment. As an illustration, licenses were required before the banks could charge the accounts of foreign nationals for maturing loans and credits. Often the funds for the discharge of such obligations had been provided by the debtors well in advance of the due dates. By virtue of their acceptance or of loan agreements signed by the foreign customer, the banks had acquired legitimate title to any balances or securities in their possession. Therefore, contended bank counsel, the banks should not be prevented from exercising their bankers' lien, the priority of which had been recognized by the United States courts as effective under all circumstances. The Treasury authorities agreed that the banks could not be expected to suffer because of prevailing extraordinary circumstances, but maintained that their prior consent was required under the rulings. In the end, a *modus vivendi* was agreed upon, and a more expeditious handling of the licenses was secured.

In October, 1943, the members of the Senior Committee were called upon to use their good offices to pacify and secure the friendly consent of their Swiss *confrères* to abide by the terms of General Ruling 17. This ruling directed that thereafter no order for the purchase or sale of securities or the collection of dividends or interest could be executed for banks located in blocked countries, of which Switzerland was one, unless it was certified that the owner was not a blocked national and unless his name and address were disclosed. Furthermore, the neutral banks under the new rule were obliged to keep records of all transactions and send periodical reports or abstracts of such records to the United States Treasury. At the same time, the Treasury reserved the right, in consideration of the granting of the required licenses, to ask the foreign banks to submit a complete list of all the dollar accounts maintained by their customers in the United States, together with their addresses. The Swiss banks were bound by their local time-honored laws to strict secrecy as regards their business relations with both their local and their foreign clients. In fact, these ancient laws, together with the strength and the financial solidity of the Swiss financial institutions, were among the main factors why so much foreign capital had streamed into the small Helvetian republic, especially since the old-time prestige of the neighboring capitalist countries had begun to ebb before the onslaughts of the Bolsheviks in the East and the Nazis and Fascists in Central Europe and the South. As had been expected by the United States banks, the publication of the ruling raised a storm of protests in Swiss banking circles. Prolonged conferences took place in New York with delegates of the Swiss banks, and an extended exchange of cables and wireless messages stirred the habitual serenity of the international banking atmosphere. It took a great deal of patience and persuasion to induce the Swiss authorities to submit to what they believed to be unwarranted interference with their age-old rights as an independent neutral commonwealth.

However, perhaps the most determined effort of the Foreign Exchange Committee and of the subcommittee was made in the latter part of 1941. At that time there was considerable concern in exporting and financial circles when it was learned that some shippers in South America had refused to accept United States dollar letters of credit without an irrevocable confirmation on the part of their local banks that without recourse to them the banks would purchase or discount drafts issued by them under dollar letters of credit. What was the reason for this sudden alarm which subsequently even spread as far as North Africa and the East Indies? In order to further trade with Latin America, the Treasury had published General License 53, according to which all transactions ordinarily incidental to the import and export of goods between the United States and any members of the so-called generally licensed trade area (comprising all Central and South America) were permitted, even though they were for or on behalf of or for account of a blocked national domiciled within the general-license area. Precluded were only transactions on behalf of or pursuant to the direction of individuals or concerns whose names were contained in the *Proclaimed List of Certain Blocked Nationals,* to which from time to time new names had been added by the State Department. Consequently, if the shipper or some other party to the purchase abroad was suddenly blacklisted after drafts under an irrevocable banker's letter of credit had been negotiated by the local bank, the United States drawee was forced to default on his promise to honor the drafts, although they had been drawn in accordance with the terms of the credit and had been accompanied by all the stipulated shipping documents. Unless the Treasury, in its discretion, issued a special license authorizing the acceptance or payment of such drafts, they could not be honored even though notification of the changed status of the beneficiary of the credit or of anyone else concerned in the shipment had not been received abroad at the time the drafts were negotiated.

As soon as the reluctance of foreign shippers to accept irrevocable dollar credits without the guarantee of a local bank became known, a delegation of members of the Foreign Exchange Committee and of the subcomittee went to Washington to confer with the competent Treasury officials. The delegation pointed out the disrupting effect that the issuance of General License 53 had already had on the standing and prestige of the dollar acceptance in certain foreign markets. The members emphasized that more than ever before the dollar had become the principal medium of exchange in the financing of international commerce and that through the course of events the United States had become the principal banking center of the world. Any stain on the dollar letter of credit at this crucial period would cause incalculable harm to the international position of United States banking and export trade and might undo many years of pioneer work to make the dollar the favored currency in Western Hemisphere trade. Attention was further called to the decisions of the United States courts which had upheld the binding nature of the commitment made in a bank acceptance to pay its face amount without reservation upon tender of the documents specified in the credit. For these various reasons the bankers sought at the conference to impress upon the government the fundamental importance to the financial institutions of the country that nothing be done to reflect on the instruments carrying the signature of an American bank or to impair its good will in the foreign business world. Damage had already been suffered by some banks due to their inability to meet their obligations under their letters of credit. For this situation delays in obtaining action on urgent applications for the required special licenses were mostly responsible. At the conclusion of the conference assurance was given that as far as possible the Treasury would strive not to interfere with the legitimate operations of the banks and foreign traders in this respect.

Despite such occasional incidents, however, it would be unfair to infer that the chief object of the bankers' efforts was to seek release from some of the burdens imposed on them by the blocking legislation. On the contrary, the most valuable contribution of the committees consisted in the submission of useful suggestions to the men charged with the effective implementation of the Control. Among other subjects of direct interest to the commercial banks that were raised and elucidated at the joint meetings were questions such as the following: Could an individual in the United States holding a power of attorney to operate the account of a blocked alien continue to act for the latter? Might payments be made abroad for the preservation of American patent rights in occupied areas? Was it permissible for American banks to send monthly statements to United States agents of blocked nationals? Were transfers permitted between several accounts maintained by such an individual in the same American bank? Other topics that were discussed and acted upon included: the payment of stale checks that suddenly made their appearance at the bank tellers' cages, the desirability of clarifying the censorship position as to certain foreign communications, inquiries as to the settlement of certain foreign exchange transactions, and the Treasury's policy in licensing communications under Section 3(C) of the Trading with the Enemy Act. As a result of the patient and constructive efforts of the members of the two committees in most cases, worth-while progress was made that redounded to the benefit of the whole banking fraternity.

That it was no easy task to administer the freezing control Secretary of the Treasury Morgenthau was frank enough to admit. He acknowledged that a grave responsibility had been placed on the banks of the country and that the supervision over the movement of foreign funds had raised many crucial problems for them. In an effort to lighten their work a special staff was organized at the Federal Reserve Bank of New York to confer with inquirers and applicants for licenses. By the end of 1941 the Treasury further decided to carry on a nation-wide campaign to acquaint also the banks operating in the smaller cities and towns of the country with the extent of their duties under the various orders and economic war legislation. With the co-operation of the American Bankers Association, foreign fund clinics were organized in many states where Treasury agents and members of the association's committees explained the mechanics of the Foreign Funds Control and the part that the banks were expected to play in the important field of financial warfare. On these occasions it was brought out that apart from complying with the rules and general regulations, the banks were expected to inform the Treasury whenever they were asked to finance the export of certain metals useful for strategic purposes or when they noticed suspicious movements in any of their accounts. They were relied upon to open their credit files and other records to the agents of the Federal Bureau of Information and other branches of the Department of Justice and to the Naval Intelligence, as the case might be. Moreover, the Treasury might request that payments of certain drafts or other negotiable bills be stopped when the bearers or holders were nationals or were believed to act as cloaks for individuals on the Proclaimed List.

As V-Day approached, the conviction gained ground among foreign bankers that for certain purposes the gradual resumption of business intercourse with some of the hitherto blocked countries might not be far off. In fact, after the liberation of Italy communications with that country along certain specified lines were authorized. Not long afterward cables and wires were also reopened for limited individual contacts with France and Belgium, As to the ultimate unfreezing of blocked balances, Treasury officials let it be understood that it would be some time before that bridge could be crossed. Nonetheless, in due course it saw its way clear to relax some of the restrictions that hampered financial dealings with Allied countries.

For the foreign departments of the various banks the thawing process promised to be fraught with serious legal complications. As was mentioned earlier, an enormous volume of mail had piled up in United States and foreign postoffices awaiting the reinstatement of international postal facilities at the end of the war in order that it could be dispatched to the addressees, while it was also certain that a great deal of correspondence had been lost or destroyed. Pending release from the interdictions of the Trading with the Enemy Act, tons of letters were held in the mail divisions of the larger banks before being forwarded to their destinations abroad, while foreign mail, even after it had been finally delivered to the United States banks, could not be handled in a routine way. The registered pieces might contain currency, bills of exchange, or securities, whose origin would have to be carefully traced in order to make sure that those who now requested that they receive credit for these valuable assets were the rightful owners. Before a license could be secured for the delivery of the property to them the reputed owners had to produce certificates from their governments confirming that they were recognized by them as the legitimate owners.

Another serious problem faced the banks after the final lifting of the controls. During the state of war the banks had enjoyed the official protection of the United States Government when not carrying out orders received from blocked countries. Now they would have to execute the instructions that had been held in abeyance or assume legal responsibility for their failure to do so. Conflicting orders accompanied by powers of attorney and assignments made under duress by the bona fide owners might be received from neutral countries. In such cases the banks were exposed to suits brought by one or the other of the contending parties. For these various reasons the banks, while in principle favoring the return of the *status quo ante,* welcomed the decision of the Treasury to go slowly with the "defrosting" of the blocked funds. However, as the countries of western and central Europe were liberated, the requirement of specific licenses was gradually waived.

On April 13, 1945, normal commercial and banking transactions with France were completely restored, special licenses being no longer required. Goods exported from France had still to be paid in dollars prior to their shipment to the United States and the payment placed to the credit of the French seller in his account in an American bank. These dollars could only be used for payments in the United

States, the British Commonwealth, the USSR, or Latin America. Old French balances, however, and other French prewar assets in the United States remained blocked.

Not all foreign owners of assets blocked in the United States were eager to see the controls relaxed and their deposits released. Many Europeans feared that if their dollars were freed their countries might take steps to force their conversion at the prevailing official rates of exchange for dollars into the grossly overvalued local currencies. The repatriation of blocked holdings was opposed by some foreign nationals for reasons that the various foreign governments considered selfish and unpatriotic. The holders, on the other hand, felt that they would rather own frozen dollars than liquid depreciated francs or lire. Yet, in view of the overpowering need for prompt reconstruction and rehabilitation, it was pardonable for foreign governments to look with jaundiced eyes at the substantial deposits of the badly needed dollars held by their nationals in the United States.[4]

To the banks' foreign departments any measures taken that might jeopardize the balances and investments of their foreign depositors appeared to be fraught with serious consequences. It was certain that these customers would seek the protection of the United States courts and redress there for anything to their prejudice that they might suffer. Thus, assuredly numerous injunctions were going to be served on the American banks, and costly lawsuits might be started against them. Their foreign depositors had considered the United States as the last haven for their working capital or savings. They had placed faith in the assurances given by the Treasury that the freezing measures had been taken to protect the assets of innocent holders from seizure by the enemy. Where no predominant national interest was involved, the banks, solicitous of the good will so requisite for maintaining their future position in international finance, earnestly hoped that the rights of private investors would continue to be safeguarded.

Allowing for the scope of the work and of the responsibilities with which they were burdened, the officials of the Foreign Funds Control and of the Federal Reserve Bank of New York who were charged with the technical enforcement of the freezing legislation,

[4] But the National Advisory Council in Washington was reported in February, 1948, to have expressed doubts whether under ordinary conditions the United States ought to assist foreign governments in enforcing their laws with respect to the control of assets of their own citizens that were blocked in this country.

did a painstaking and efficient job. Deserving a special tribute are John W. Pehle, the first Director of Foreign Funds Control and later Assistant Secretary of the Treasury; Orvis A. Schmidt, his successor; Edward H. Foley, Jr., General Counsel, whose place was subsequently taken by Randolph Paul; Bernard Bernstein, Assistant General Counsel of the Treasury; and Ansel F. Luxford, legal adviser at the Treasury Department. The following figures for the value of blocked property will indicate the extent of the functions exercised by these men and their various auxiliaries. These details were first disclosed in December, 1942, at the hearings before the Subcommittee of the Committee on Appropriations of the House of Representatives, 78th Congress (First Session on the Treasury Department Appropriation Bill for 1944). On that occasion the government revealed that the total value of blocked property, all of which was subject to regulation by the Foreign Funds Control, was about 8 1/2 billion dollars, as of the date of blocking, divided as follows:

Blocked nationals resident abroad	
Short-term funds, including earmarked gold	$4,000,000,000
Securities	2,000,000,000
Direct investments and miscellaneous	2,000,000,000
Blocked nationals resident in United States	
(except business enterprises abroad)	500,000,000
Total	$8,500,000,000

By owner nationality the distribution of the blocked property was as follows:

Blocked nationals resident abroad	
Netherlands, including Netherlands East Indies	$1,800,000,000
Switzerland	1,500,000,000
France and Monaco	1,400,000,000
Belgium	400,000,000
Sweden	600,000,000
China	300,000,000
Norway	100,000,000
Japan	150,000,000
Germany	150,000,000
Italy	100,000,000
All others	750,000,000
Blocked nationals resident in the United States	
(other than business enterprises abroad)	500,000,000
Holdings of American citizens in blocked enterprises	750,000,000
Total	$8,500,000,000

By June, 1945, the framework that supported the wartime property controls, and within the various parts of which the Federal Reserve banks and the commercial banks exercised their assigned functions, was composed of some 230 executive orders and a large number of administrative and explanatory documents. It has been estimated that during the first three years of the existence of the Control some of the larger New York institutions filed, on the average, about two thousand applications every month for the licensing of their own and their customers' business.

Yet, complex as was the blocking apparatus, the commercial banks —realizing how much the government leaned upon them for the exercise of the control and for frustrating all attempts to evade the regulations—co-operated wholeheartedly and steadfastly in making the Treasury effort in this field a remarkable success. Operating during the war with a reduced staff and with only minor errors or violations of the regulations in their record, and these committed inadvertently in the rush of the work, not through lack of good faith, the banks of the country could point with just satisfaction, as the war drew to its end, to the material and generally excellent aid that they had given to their government on the economic and financial front in one of the most decisive facets of the struggle against the Axis.[5] In February, 1948, the National Advisory Council made known that 1,100 million dollars of blocked private assets would be released forthwith. Simultaneously it declared that it would not be the policy of the Federal government, as a condition for Marshall Plan aid, to force liquidation of the 4,300 million dollars of "free assets" in the United States belonging to foreign nationals.

SUMMARY. The Foreign Exchange Committee was formed in August, 1939, composed of representatives of large New York banks, to advise with and assist the United States Treasury and the Federal Reserve Bank of New York in formulating policies to deal with the wartime foreign-exchange situation and financial and property controls. It was able to make useful suggestions regarding the pound sterling market and specific aspects of the Foreign Funds Control administration. Through it the banks in the interior and in neutral

[5] On February 2, 1948, Secretary of the Treasury John W. Snyder announced that: public notice will shortly be given that at the end of three months assets remaining blocked, including assets not certified by the appropriate foreign government as free of enemy taint, will be transferred to the Alien Property Custodian.

countries were made acquainted with the procedures governing the freezing of foreign accounts, and other aspects of economic warfare. The application of the provisions of the Johnson and Neutrality Acts involved special complications for the banks' foreign departments.

Under the guidance of the committee, the banks perfected an extensive technique for complying with the various wartime regulations controlling foreign-exchange transactions, the freezing of enemy assets, and the blocking of accounts and property of nationals of occupied countries. Many changes of banking methods were made necessary by the need for painstakingly scrutinizing all transactions for account of the affected countries, as a result of the rulings concerning the importation of currency and securities, the preparation of applications for special licenses, and the census of foreign assets in the United States and American property holdings overseas. Although the banks encountered many obstacles in discharging the duties assigned to them, they, as well as the government authorities and Federal Reserve Bank officials, displayed competency and skill in their extremely intricate and delicate work.

BANKING FOR THE DISPLACED PERSONS OF EUROPE

In previous chapters reference has been made to the flight of capital that started in Europe soon after the end of the First World War, in 1918, and reached its climax during the Nazi regime in the thirties.

The first exodus of wealth and movable property had taken place during the German inflation after that war, the westward tide of frightened savings spreading later to Austria, Hungary, Czechoslovakia, and the Balkans, as well as the Baltic countries. After the advent of Hitler, in 1933, a new feeling of insecurity and concern swept over many businessmen and investors throughout central Europe. According to Gresham's law, bad money drives out the good. It was now demonstrated that hostile or weak governments produce a similar effect. If capital is frightened, it rushes across national boundaries to seek safety elsewhere.

The so-called "hot money" first sought shelter in Holland and Switzerland; later, in its desire for security, it fled to the Scandinavian countries, England, the United States, and Latin America. Anxiously watching each new development, the alarmed owners transferred their funds restlessly from one center to another, always in search of a sanctuary where they would find a final unmolested resting place. At times these nervous movements of capital disrupted the fabric of the exchanges, but for the owners any incidental losses and expenses did not count; the safety of their principal outweighed all other considerations.

Neutral Switzerland, because of the internationally guaranteed inviolability of her soil and the traditional policy of her financial institutions of shielding their confidential relations with their depositors from governmental intrusion, was long the favored asylum for restive money. Frenchmen, averse to opening large foreign-currency accounts under the eye of their government at home were prominent among the regular customers of the Swiss banks. Immediately following the coach reservations in the Paris-Calais-Dover Express was the place held by reserved tickets for the Basle-Zurich trains in the regular stock-in-trade of many French rentiers and businessmen. Finally, however, doubts were raised even as to the protection accorded by Swiss legislation and growing amounts of refugee capital were transferred to banking institutions in the United States. Two leading Zurich banks, the Swiss Bank Corporation and the Crédit Suisse, in order to offer their customers the same guarantees as to the security of their funds and valuables as those furnished by United States banks, opened their own branch offices in New York.

The constant inflow of nomadic European money was regarded by some observers with unconcealed dislike, and the steady accumulation of gold in the United States that it entailed was deprecated. A considerable part of the capital sent to the United States came here in disguise. Taught by bitter experience, the owners sought to hide their foreign-exchange holdings from prying eyes and seemed ever to discover new ways of concealing their status and nationality. To cover their tracks, they often sent cash and securities through different channels, while remittances came from French, Swiss, Dutch, and other foreign banks and business houses with instructions that they be placed to the credit of the immediate senders, the identity of those who had actual title to the funds not being disclosed.

Some of the transfers came cloaked behind a corporate name, such as a Luxembourg, Liechtenstein, Monaco, or Panama holding corporation. These small countries specialized in attracting foreign companies, their favorable laws making it easy to form corporate bodies, while no publication was required of financial statements, lists of directors, and so forth. Even deposits maintained by English, Canadian, or United States banks or citizens masked, on occasion, sums belonging to German or Austrian nationals, and many emigrants, even though temporarily or permanently domiciled in Latin America or elsewhere outside the United States, still opened dollar accounts in this country, following the time-honored principle of the geographical distribution of risks.

It is difficult to conjecture the ingenuity with which some European businesses had to conduct their financial affairs during the interwar years. Ever since the early twenties farsighted merchants had proceeded to form foreign affiliates and had supplied them with the necessary working capital, while funds could still be legally exported. Others opened branches in neighboring countries. Then, when conditions became threatening in one corner of the Continent, it was relatively easy, by telephone or cable, to remove balances and securities to another center, where for the time being they seemed safe. It was essential to be constantly on the alert in order that assets in distrusted regions might be promptly moved to areas where they were less exposed to arbitrary treatment or seizure. Gold, so long as it commanded a ready market in almost every country, was the favored medium for hoarding.

Some of those who emigrated to America were men of means, and they succeeded in taking up here the industrial and commercial activities in which they had prospered abroad. After the invasion of Belgium and the Low Countries and following the occupation of France, a few prominent industrialists and heads of commercial enterprises formerly established in Western Europe made their headquarters in the United States. Some joined affiliates or branches of their own companies already operating on this side of the Atlantic. Others purchased partnerships in local firms, where their long contact with world commerce could be used to advantage.

Certain European concerns, intent upon removing their affairs from the reach of a possible enemy and also in order to be in a position to operate free of hindering domestic restrictions, formed special corporations in the United States, controlled by American citizens by reason of the latter's holdings of common stock. In exchange for the assets transferred to the United States company, preferred stock was issued to the former alien owners, although in some instances they instead received promissory notes of the company, payable over a period of years.

The initiation of Foreign Property Control during the Second World War created delicate problems for the United States commercial banks that were carrying accounts for foreign depositors. The handling of these accounts and uncertainty whether or not they were subject to the freezing legislation presented many arduous practical problems. Precise information as to the nationality of the customers was required by various government agencies. Some of the depositors were recently naturalized Dutch, Swiss, French, British, Italian, and Spanish citizens; others had hastily acquired Cuban or Haitian allegiance. In addition, the great majority had taken out first naturalization papers, expecting to become American citizens after the required five years of residence. The blocking of their accounts in this country came as a distressing surprise, and it was not easy to convince strangers to United States laws and institutions that the foreign funds legislation was introduced and applied, at least in part, for the purpose of safeguarding their possessions and those of their countrymen.

The various ventures in which the newcomers engaged and the methods employed by them in investing their savings and experience in the Western Hemisphere make a remarkable tale of human ingenuity and perseverance. A few examples illustrative of their courage and willingness to adapt themselves to their new way of life are given below.

The partners of many old continental banking firms and a number of former bank managers came to the United States for the duration of the war and sought use here for their knowledge of finance and of the European bourses. Some formed their own firms or joined houses with whom they had entertained business relations in the past. Others bought membership on the exchanges or specialized in dealing in blocked currencies and European securities.

One of the earliest of these arrivals in this country was one of the former owners of a large German business firm, who fortunately salvaged part of the family fortune and brought it over from his native land. It is significant that even as early as 1936, when he made this move, he was concerned about the fate of his assets should the United States again be at war with Germany.

A French citizen, scion of a well-known family, placed a substantial portion of his fortune in trust in England, but provided that for greater safety the securities of the trust be held in custody in the United States. However, his holdings thus became subject to the laws and regulations not only of his own country but also of the United Kingdom and the United States.

One enterprising central European set up a Swiss holding company whose cash and securities were held in safekeeping in the United States. The majority of the board of directors of the Swiss company were Swiss citizens, the legal domicile of the company being in the Zurich office of the lawyer handling its affairs.

A prominent film director, with many successful plays to his credit, who was forced to leave the scene of his former triumphs, went to Hollywood, where he found his experience and talents welcome.

Some investors made considerable purchases of American bonds that were payable in gold dollars. After the devaluation of the dollar and the repudiation of the gold clause in United States Government and private obligations in 1934, these various holders claimed payment of interest and principal in gold of the former legal tender or its equivalent in sterling, francs, or guilders; pending decision by the United States and European courts, they refrained from presenting for payment the coupons attached to the bonds. In this case, however, both the Supreme Court and the British House of Lords ruled against the owners, holding that the debtors were liable for settlement only in dollars at the prevailing new legal standard.

Taking advantage of the wide opportunities offered by this country, a group of continental traders and capitalists made investments in real estate and entered the merchant shipping business. Another group, long familiar with arbitrage in securities, were attracted by the opportunities offered by the reorganization of United States railroads and industrial companies; by purchasing the old securities and by selling the new securities for delivery "when issued," they profited by the differences between the market quotations of the respective issues.

Certain merchants with intimate contacts in the Southern States engaged in the purchase and export of raw cotton. Several former produce merchants shipped meat products to eastern Europe and imported leather and fine slippers in exchange. A few bought acreage in Florida to cultivate tobacco; some went into the raising of tung nuts and citrous fruits, while still others invested in sugar and flour mills in Canada. The list of newcomers in this country whose record in their past lines of endeavor was outstanding included a number of distinguished lawyers, doctors, writers, and the former heads of well-known textile and chemical companies, public utilities, shoe factories, automobile and truck manufacturers, distillers, and dealers in metals and ores. The connections and skill of some of these persons were later to be of distinct value to the Board of Economic Warfare and other wartime government agencies. Corporations founded here by exiles engaged in important war work, while other emigrés carrying on mining operations in distant parts of the globe, made valuable contributions to the Allied victory by selling their products to the Army and Navy. Similar worth-while help was extended by those who, because of their prewar relations in the Far East, were in a position to assist with the urgently needed importation of rubber, casein, vegetable oils, rapeseed, sunflower oil, and starches.

Prior to 1940 the headquarters of the Sumatra tobacco trade were located in Amsterdam, where United States buyers came each spring for the annual auctions. After the invasion of Holland, enterprising Dutch citizens transferred the business to this country, buying and importing the leaf tobacco and storing it in specially equipped warehouses in the New York Port Free Zone, whence it was sold to domestic cigar manufacturers.

The operations of certain world-renowned companies whose headquarters were moved to New York prior to or during the war deserve special mention. Their business interests circled the globe; they had branches and agents not only in North and South America but also in the British Dominions and the Near and Far East. They controlled public utilities, grain elevators, chain stores, groceries, bakeries, warehouses, freighters, grain lands, and organizations dealing in coffee, sugar, wool, jute, and even manufactured pasteurized milk. Everywhere their affairs were conducted on a considerable scale. In certain cases they dominated the exportation of cereals and produce, such as linseed and cattle feed. They were among the leading suppliers of these products for the various British, French, Swiss, and Portuguese purchasing commissions, as well as the United States Commodity Credit Corporation.

Among these concerns was the N. V. Philips Gloelampen Fabrieken (Philips Incandescent Lamp Company), one of the most important foreign enterprises located in the United States during the war. Its head office was in Eindhoven, Holland, and it had large factories in

England, France, Belgium, Germany, Sweden, Denmark, Norway, Switzerland, Australia, and South America; its stock was quoted on many European stock exchanges. Soon after the Munich conference the prescient heads of the corporation decided to transfer the control of a major part of their assets to a trust formed under the laws of Connecticut. The veteran Anton Fredrik Philips became chairman of the new company; Herman F. van Walsam and P. F. S. Otten were the senior executives, having offices in New York, while J. W. Beyen, former president of the Bank for International Settlements, and Crena de Jongh, former president of the Netherlands Trading Society, were members of the board of directors. When the Germans attacked Holland, plans long prepared by the company were promptly carried out. Only empty factories and laboratory buildings greeted the invaders; most of the raw material and merchandise in process of manufacture had been shipped to safety, and the transfer of operations was effected with smoothness and absence of confusion. The organization was equally ready financially, since for a number of years it had followed the practice of converting its reserves into gold or stable currencies deposited safely in centers far from the reach of any enemy.

Another company of world-wide repute that sought refuge in the United States was the Nestlé and Anglo-Swiss Holding Company, leading manufacturer of condensed and evaporated milk, chocolate, and coffee powder. Its American head office was established in Stamford, Connecticut, as a branch of a Panamanian corporation named Unilac, Inc., and there the president and moving spirit of the cluster of affiliates operating all over the globe, the resolute broad-shouldered Edouard Muller, since deceased, made his headquarters. Unilac was the holding company for the subsidiaries located in North, Central, and South America. Muller who had earned his first spurs in a Zurich bank, succeeded another ex-banker, the late Louis Dapples, former general manager of the Banque Française et Italienne, who was called in to reorganize the Nestle group during the 1921 depression. Muller was surrounded by able assistants in the persons of Gustave Huguenin, vice president, D. F. Norton, president of Nestlé's Milk Products, Inc., and Alphonse Perren, at one time in charge of finances.

The list of members of the banking fraternity who fled from Paris before the Nazi hordes, embraced the partners of the various Rothschild banking firms, among whom were the Barons Edouard and Louis de Rothschild. The latter, who had been senior partner of the family's former Austrian house and at one time chairman of the ill-fated Austrian Credit Anstalt, was once described as the wealthiest man of Austria; he had been confined for eighteen months in a German concentration camp and was reported to have purchased his freedom by turning over to the Nazis all his properties in Austria and an additional estimated two million pounds sterling. He had then been allowed to go to the Argentine, whence he finally arrived in the United States.

SUMMARY. During the thirties and forties the banking needs of the European refugees occupied an important place in the work of many foreign departments of United States banks. A succession of waves of mistrust and fear followed the inflation in central and eastern Europe after the First World War, and subsequently the rise of Hitler. As the gold standard was abandoned first by England and then by the western European countries, the flight of frightened capital spread over the Continent. With the increasing threat of war whole industries with their executive staff emigrated to the United States, where the latter, along with other prominent foreign businessmen who had already settled here, made in some instances a valuable contribution to the war effort.

IV

UNITED STATES GOVERNMENT CORPORATIONS

Before 1939 international trade had been the prerogative mainly of private industry. During the war the direction and control of foreign commerce in most countries, neutral as well as belligerent, passed into the hands of the national governments. The large amounts of capital and credit required in manufacturing and procuring armaments, war equipment, and food for the armies in the field and the civil populations, as well as the world-wide restrictions on shipping and exchange—all these factors were sufficient warrant for official incursion into what had been the traditional realm of private enterprise.

In the United States, likewise, the objections that militated against the subordination of private business to government agencies had to be cast aside. In the interest of unity and in order to co-operate in the "all out" effort necessary to win the war, foreign trade and banking circles were prepared and eager to make the necessary sacrifices, even though the temporary invasion of their traditional spheres of activity carried with it the threat that the functioning of the various government organizations, if continued in the peace era, might jeopardize the business relationships built up by private enterprise for more than a generation. In the national interest the commercial banks immediately proceeded to tender their experience and services to the various government corporations, new and old, even though these, in the performance of their tasks, were led gradually and in an ever-increasing degree to encroach upon the domain of commercial banking. Yet these government corporations, it should be admitted, made an inestimable contribution to the war effort, and considering the pressure under which they had to work they deserve high credit for having discharged their complex duties with great skill and competency.

The business entrusted to the commercial banks by the government agencies was substantial. In some banking institutions the foreign credits and routine transactions handled for the account of the various government corporations very likely represented a considerable portion of the total foreign business that passed through their foreign departments in the course of the war. It may therefore be opportune at this point to present some observations on this feature of foreign banking during the decade of the thirties and the years of the Second World War.

EXPORT-IMPORT BANK OF WASHINGTON

In the late twenties and early thirties United States banks were frequently approached by exporters to discount or make advances against bills of exchange or contracts of sale payable nine months, a year, or even two or three years after the merchandise had been delivered to the buyer abroad. In some instances it was also suggested that for a special consideration the banks should assume part or all of the credit risk. The guaranteeing of the payment of medium- and long-term foreign obligations and the discounting of bills with distant maturities had not been within the scope of normal United States banking practice in the past. To keep the good will of a valued client some institutions might have been willing occasionally to make an exception, but on the whole this special type of financing had no appeal for the average bank. There existed, it is true, one or two credit companies of moderate size that were prepared to write credit insurance; however, their operations were on a limited scale compared with the need for facilities of this nature.

Two attempts to form special organizations for the large-scale financing of United States foreign trade had proved abortive. In 1921 a Committee on Organization for the creation of a Foreign Trade Financing Corporation worked diligently for many months under the chairmanship of the late John McHugh only to see its sponsors become discouraged when as a result of the postwar depression those specialized American banks which had operated in Latin America and the Far East had to be wound up with serious losses for their stockholders and banking creditors. In 1928 another organization committee was created under the chairmanship of Franklin D. Roosevelt, then a partner of Roosevelt & O'Connor, who acted as general counsel to the committee, to develop plans for the formation, under the provisions of the Edge Act amendment to the Federal

Reserve Bank Act, of a concern to be known as the Federal International Banking Company. The principal purpose of the company was to serve as an international credit bank. Members of the organization committee included, among others, Frederic A. Delano, former vice governor of the Federal Reserve Board, and James G. Harbord, president of the Radio Corporation of America. The organizers pointed to the lack of facilities for foreign commercial credits of a longer term than six months. A survey was made of existing financial facilities in the United States at the disposal of local exporters and foreign importers, who stressed that there was a field for a corporation that would finance notes and drafts maturing in from six months to five years. Under the committee's plan the foreign banks of the importers either would guarantee fully the credits extended by the proposed institution or would themselves finance 50 percent thereof. The American exporter was to be released from recourse after acceptance of the goods by the importer, while a similar release was contemplated where a foreign bank guarantee or credit insurance by a responsible United States indemnity company was provided. John McHugh and E. R. Kemmerer, as well as the officers of the American Manufacturers Export Association, expressed their interest in the project. Unfortunately, after the Wall Street debacle of September, 1929, the zest of those who were expected to furnish the capital of the new concern waned, and the project had to be abandoned.

Because of the insistent demand for such a service on the part of United States exporters, American foreign bankers studied with keen interest the progress of credit insurance in England, which was reported to have met with a fair measure of success. In 1935 the Export Credit Department which had been formed by the British Government announced that it would receive applications from English exporters for the insurance of the exchange risk on sales to Germany and other continental countries. The British shipper was to be protected against loss if on the due date sterling cover should not be received in payment of the invoice, that is, should the buyer be unable to procure London exchange. In other words, on condition that all British exchange regulations had been fully complied with, the exporter of British goods sold to a solvent customer across the Channel was assured that six months after the due date he would receive from the Export Credit Department 75 percent of the sterling value of the merchandise. In addition to the government department and competing with it to a moderate extent, some smaller English insurance companies also catered to this special line of underwriting. Prior to the last war their losses were believed to have been moderate. Being naturally careful in the selection of risks, these concerns accepted the business only of customers who had the reputation of being conservative in their choice of foreign buyers. Prompted by the desire to increase further the ability of British industry to compete for international trade, the Cabinet, in December, 1938, introduced a bill in Parliament to enlarge the activities of the Export Credit Guarantee Department. As a first step, the government recommended that the limit of the department's liability be raised from 50 to 75 million pounds sterling, stating that the department had already received applications exceeding the proposed figure by a large amount.

In the United States the next development took place in January, 1934, in the form of a meeting called at the invitation of Fred I. Kent, then a vice president of the Bankers Trust Company and to this day, although no longer active in this field, the respected dean of the foreign banking community. Officers of the Guaranty Trust Company, the Chase National Bank, the National City Bank, and the Irving Trust Company met with him at the offices of the Federal Reserve Bank of New York to reappraise the attitude of the New York banks toward facilities such as those of the British for United States exporters. The group reviewed a plan that had been drafted with the assistance of the National Foreign Trade Council and the National Manufacturers Association to found an institution dedicated primarily to the long-term financing of United States foreign trade. The banks represented at the meeting were of the opinion that any institution created to provide long-term credit to United States exporters would be dependent mainly on the capital placed at its disposal and on the official support it could count on receiving from the administration in Washington. It was emphasized that to satisfy the large demand for long-term accommodation by countries such as China, South America, and the USSR, the institution, if it was to be privately organized, would have to rely to a considerable extent on what credit it could command from commercial banks that already were financing the greater part of the short-term credit sales of local exporters.

The project to establish an organization for the long-term financing of United States foreign trade thus was conceived and discussed by leading trade associations and foreign bankers some time before Washington announced, in February, 1934, the formation of a new bank under the name Export-Import Bank. The working capital of the bank was to be supplied by the Reconstruction Finance Corporation, and its original purpose was to finance trade with the Soviet Union. Unofficial estimates mentioned 300 million dollars as the proposed capitalization. At various times previously, tentative plans for the formation of an institution to supply long-term credit for the United States export trade had been submitted to the government by various interests. However, the credit for incorporating into the new bank's charter the salient features of the different proposals goes to the late George W. Peek, then Special Adviser to the President on Foreign Trade and his assistants.

When the details of the first draft of the charter were examined, a number of points was raised by both exporters and bank officials. It was clear that before the new organization could function proper legislation would have to be passed to give it the necessary authority and legal powers. The act under which the Reconstruction Finance Corporation operated limited the maximum life of its loans to one year and called for adequate security for any funds loaned. A special law, therefore, had to be passed to permit three- to five-year credits without recourse to the shipper, as contemplated in the charter. Another question was whether the officers were to be unrestricted as to the types of loans that they might make or whether their operations were to be confined to the financing of employment-creating business, such as the manufacture of machinery, with only a minor part of the bank's lending facilities reserved for advances against raw materials and staples, such as cotton and copper. Soviet Ambassador Troyanovsky pointed out at once that his country could place 75 million to 100 million dollars' worth of orders in the United States if terms of from five to ten years were allowed.

The first action of the bank was to establish a Bureau of Soviet Trade Extension, whose task was to determine what transactions with the USSR would be acceptable to financing by the bank, and the conditions under which such financing should be undertaken. The maximum term for any credit was fixed at five years. The bank was prepared to discount or purchase commercial paper arising out of sales and to guarantee drafts up to an aggregate amount not exceeding 75 percent of the total principal amount of each transaction. The seller of the paper had the privilege of repurchasing it when its maturity had become such as to make it rediscountable at a commercial bank. Serial payments were to be provided for in the contract with the buyer. In the original plan there was also a provision that would have permitted the financing of importations of Soviet products approved by the management of the bank.

Shortly after the incorporation of the bank it was decided to create another corporation under the title Second Export-Import Bank of Washington, for the purpose of extending credit to other countries than the Soviet Union. The first Export-Import Bank never became active, since the anticipated development of relations justifying an increased active trade relationship between the two countries failed to materialize. The Second Export-Import Bank, on the other hand, soon succeeded in making a place for itself by lending its funds to those United States exporters who were in need of additional credit facilities, especially for the more distant terms.

One of its first large-scale operations was the opening of a credit of 4 million dollars for the Republic of Cuba for the purpose of paying for silver metal purchased by the Cuban Government in the American market for melting and coinage into local currency. In a general statement of policy the bank's board of trustees explained that commercial banks would be given the opportunity to participate in the bank's loans in consideration of their introducing business to the young institution, making credit investigations on its behalf, and undertaking collections and the handling of other routine functions for it. In those early months of its existence the bank limited itself to short-term and intermediate credit to the exclusion of long-term business and discounts without recourse. Before fully exercising its powers, the organization evidently wanted first to feel its way.

In 1935, since the original Export-Import Bank still remained inactive and without prospect of any change in Soviet-American trade relations, it was decided to merge the Second Export-Import Bank with the moribund first bank under the latter's more embracing and more distinctive title. From that time on the bank's activities expanded rapidly. A great variety of credits was given consideration and extended but only a few transactions can here be cursorily described. These will give a picture, however inadequate, of some of the manifold propositions that now came before the bank's aggressive new president, Warren Lee Pierson, who succeeded the late Charles E. Stuart, first president of the institution.

In 1937 the bank was under considerable pressure to grant a substantial loan to American cotton merchants, who had accumulated many thousands of bales of raw cotton in Bremen warehouses. The agents of Polish textile mills also approached the bank for a credit to permit purchase of United States cotton under the guarantee of Polish commercial banks. This particular business was undertaken when the Polish National Bank (Bank Polski) assumed the unconditional surety for the payment of the loan in dollars at maturity.

In support of these and similar credit applications it was adduced that the financing of United States exports by the bank—whether cotton, oil, ores, lard, or other commodities—was of benefit to other American interests as well, such as the packers, labor, the railroads, steamship lines, insurance companies, and banks. Moreover, it tended to strengthen the price level of the staples and materials purchased for sale abroad and enabled United States farmers and producers to market supplies of which they had a great surplus. Above all, it was held probable that the bank's intervention would be interpreted in central and southeastern Europe as a gesture of United States good will and an indication of the likelihood of further moral and financial support in the future. If it were instrumental in bringing about the desired improvement in economic conditions in the foreign countries, the ultimate effect of the bank's action in giving practical evidence of America's sympathy and willingness to assist, it was urged, might even ultimately influence the internal and external policies of the governments concerned. Of course, the practical hazards could not be disregarded. There existed the risk that the foreign buyers whose manufactured goods were intended to be sold abroad and converted into dollars to pay off the credits of the Export-Import Bank might be forced by their governments to divert their finished products to appease threatening neighbors. Still, this did not prevent the management of the bank from making extensive loans in Czechoslovakia, Poland, Italy, and other continental countries.

At its inception the bank, as a subsidiary of the Reconstruction Finance Corporation, operated under the general direction of the chairman of its board of trustees, Jesse Jones, who was also president of the Reconstruction Finance Corporation and Federal Loan Administrator. The Assistant Federal Loan Administrator, William L. Clayton, former senior partner of Anderson Clayton & Company, of Houston, Texas, also played, because of his recognized expert knowledge of foreign trade, a decisive role in formulating policies and directing the activities of the bank into the most profitable channels. In 1939 President Roosevelt attached the bank to the Federal Loan Agency, but in 1941 Congress re-established it as a separate entity. After Jesse Jones was appointed Secretary of Commerce, in 1942, the bank so far as its place in the administrative setup was concerned was first attached to the Department of Commerce; then, in July, 1943, it became a division of the Office of Economic Warfare. Still later, it came under the wing of the Foreign Economic Administration. Yet, when Congress passed the Export-Import Bank Act of 1945, as amended, it stipulated in article 5 that "neither the Bank nor any of its functions, powers or duties shall be transferred to or consolidated with any other department of the Government unless the Congress shall otherwise by law provide."

One clause in the bank's contracts with borrowers caused occasional controversies with foreign importers and their agents in the United States. In accordance with the intent of Congress and by the terms of its charter, the goods financed by the bank's credits were required to be carried overseas in United States bottoms. This condition could not always be enforced, however, owing to lack of suitable shipping, and in certain cases the bank's officers therefore had to exercise their discretion. Faithful to the declaration made when the bank was founded and in accordance with the expressed policy of Congress, it steadfastly abstained from competing with the commercial banks in the fields for which these were well equipped to serve United States foreign and domestic trade. As the financing of imports into the United States generally called for short-term credits, the bank refrained from offering its services for this particular phase of banking. The commercial banks, owing to their broad foreign connections and the trained staffs of their commercial letter of credit and foreign exchange departments, were better qualified, the bank frankly admitted, to serve customers in the import trade than was it, with its restricted personnel and lack of technical assistants. In return for this abstinence on the part of the bank, the commercial banks placed their foreign connections and their credit departments freely at the disposal of the officers of the Export-Import Bank and assisted them, especially during the initial organization period, by lending them experienced officers and employees to help launch the bank on its career.

One of the important credits granted by the bank before the outbreak of the Second World War was extended to the Universal Trading Corporation, a concern incorporated in January, 1939, by K. P. Chen and Hsi Te Mou, two members of the Chinese Mission then in Washington and both prominent Chinese bankers, for the purpose of promoting trade between the United States and China. In order to assist the Chinese Government in its struggle against Japan, the Export-Import Bank placed a credit of 25 million dollars at the disposal of the new corporation. The credit was revolving and was good for several years. As a broad market existed in the United States for many Chinese products, such as tung oil, bristles, silk, tea, and egg yolks, the corporation became the main consignee and selling agent in the United States for these articles. The proceeds served to provide cover for the letters of credit opened by local banks in New York and other cities on behalf of and at the risk of the Export-Import Bank. These credits went to pay for the war materials and other technical equipment bought by the corporation for the account of the Chinese Government; before the corporation took over the execution of these orders, Chinese Government purchases in this country had as a rule been settled by the Central Bank of China.

The war soon placed almost insuperable obstacles in the way of the Universal Trading Corporation's import and export activities. When the Japanese occupied the principal Chinese ports, the corporation was forced to ship the machinery and other manufactured articles so badly needed by the Chinese Government via the roundabout Rangoon route, the goods being transported by truck from that port to the interior of China over the Burma Road. The appointment of Archie Lochhead, former manager of the foreign department of the Chemical Bank & Trust Co. and later Technical Assistant to the Secretary of the Treasury, as president added to the standing of the corporation. Notwithstanding the difficulties which it encountered in the Far East during the Chinese-Japanese hostilities, its business activities expanded constantly. In order further to assist the Chinese Government, additional credits were allotted to it to finance the acquisition of military equipment and the stabilization of the Chinese currency, pending the resumption of shipments of Chinese goods to the United States.

The lending authority of the Export-Import Bank became inadequate for the constantly growing scope of the bank's operations, and on March 2, 1940, it was increased from 100 million dollars to 175 million. Simultaneously the limit on loans to be outstanding to any foreign country at any one time was raised to 20 million dollars, not including loans made or authorized prior to March 2, 1940. No loans, however, were to be granted to any government that was in default in the payment of any of its obligations to the United States Government on April 13, 1934,[1] or that were in violation of international law as interpreted by the Department of State; nor might the loans be used for the purchase of war materials.

After the beginning of the Second World War the bank's activities gravitated more and more toward Latin America. Brazil, subsequently an ally of the United States, appeared to offer the most fertile field for the bank's efforts. As early as the thirties the bank had made an important loan of 19.2 million dollars to that republic to encourage her to shift her purchases from Germany to the United States. The advisers of the bank in the State Department argued correctly that if the exchange situation in Brazil and in various other Latin American countries could be eased, these nations would be under less pressure to sell their products to Germany for blocked marks, which under the Schachtian barter precepts forced Brazil and the other southern republics to buy German manufactured goods in exchange. Probably the most publicized action of the bank in South America was the financing of the creation of an iron and steel industry in Brazil to utilize the rich Brazilian ores through an initial loan of 20 million dollars for the erection of the Volta Redenda steel mill.

In June, 1945, Congress increased the capital of the bank from 175 million dollars to 1 billion. The new act contained in addition to the one mentioned earlier a provision that "the Export-Import Bank of Washington shall constitute an independent agency of the United States." The act did not repeal the Johnson Act, but provided that notwithstanding the latter, any person, firm, or corporation "may act or participate with the Bank in any operation or transaction." As emphasized by Senator Wagner when he introduced the bill, the bank assisted during the war in the development abroad of sources of strategic materials for the war industries. Its operations have at all times been self-sustaining, and it has exercised its functions with discernment and constructive judgment. Since the end of the war the bank, as pointed out in Chapter XVII, has continued to perform

1 In accordance with the intent of the Johnson Act.

a most useful part in aiding in financing the recovery of the European and Latin American economies. In its first semiannual report, for the period July to December, 1945, the bank, while not recommending governmental short-term and medium-term insurance against nonpayment, announced its willingness to relieve exporters of goods sold on medium credit terms (one to five years) to buyers in designated foreign countries, of the risk of nonpayment because of the inability of the buyer to obtain dollars.[2]

In this connection it is significant that in furtherance of the President's Point Four Program, Bill S.2197 was introduced in the United States Senate on July 6, 1949, to vest in the Export-Import Bank the power "to guarantee United States private capital invested in productive enterprises abroad which contribute to economic developments in foreign countries against risks peculiar to such investments."

The extent to which the operations of the bank have expanded during the postwar years is best illustrated by the fact, mentioned by Herbert E. Gaston, chairman of the board, that in September, 1950, the institution had outstanding commitments of almost 3 billion dollars. In many of these loans, it was stressed, the bank enjoyed the participation of private United States enterprise.

COMMODITY CREDIT CORPORATION

Among the most active corporations formed by the United States Government was the Commodity Credit Corporation, whose object was to buy and sell agricultural commodities. During the Second World War its officers included Everett R. Cook, a prominent cotton merchant of Dallas, as vice president, and Miguel Crossnay, of the Bunge North American Grain Corporation of New York, who was director of purchases in charge of the grain department. Only a few examples of the widespread activities of this corporation can here be presented.

One of the earliest large-scale operations with which it was associated was a cotton credit arranged in 1942. Although the interest rate was extremely low a number of New York and interior banks eagerly solicited the privilege of participating in the transaction. Owing to the United States Treasury guarantee, the interest rate at which the corporation borrowed from the banks was based on the rates at which the Treasury placed its own bills in the money market, namely 3/8

[2] Congressional Record of June 21, 1945, regarding S.11.

percent for 90 days' and 5/8 percent for seven months' maturities. However, the corporation was in a position, in such cases as this, to favor those banks that were willing to grant it facilities at these reduced rates by entrusting them with a share of the import credits required in connection with some of its foreign activities, a service that rated a special fee varying from 1/8 to 1/4 percent. Incidental advantages connected with these credits made them attractive to the foreign departments of United States banks. Banks in Latin America, India, and elsewhere were always eager for this type of business. Often the foreign bank notifying a local merchant of the opening of a credit in his favor would be in a preferred position when the dollar or sterling drafts were ready for negotiation, since in such cases the bank's bid for the purchase of the drafts tended to be accepted in preference to its neighbors', and the bank would consequently be able to realize a profit on the exchange. It was therefore common practice abroad for the foreign bank, in return for being selected to notify the beneficiary of the opening of a letter of credit, to direct to the American bank at least an equivalent part of its own business in the United States, such as documentary credits and collections. In banking vernacular, the foreign bank "exercised reciprocity."

On another occasion, in 1942, the Commodity Credit Corporation used the services of private banks to finance the purchase and storage of raw cotton in Peru. The transaction carried with it the usual commitment of the Treasury to pay at maturity for any advances made to the corporation, the Secretary of the Treasury having been authorized under the corporation's statute to guarantee on behalf of the United States "notes, bonds, debentures or similar obligations." The president of the corporation signed agreements by virtue of powers received through delegation from the Secretary of Agriculture who in turn had been assigned his powers by the President of the United States. The Peruvian cotton credit, too, was divided among a number of banks.

As its name implied, the Commodity Credit Corporation handled the acquisition of many different commodities. In 1943 it offered credits secured by coffee purchased and stored in Brazil. During the same year it negotiated with representatives of the Puerto Rican Sugar Producers Association for the sale of their sugar crop; the warehouse receipts were held by the San Juan office of the Reconstruction Finance Corporation for account of the Commodity Credit Corporation, and payment for the sugar was effected through the latter agency. The purchase of the Haitian and Dominican sugar crops was handled along similar lines. Reference to the corporation's outstanding efforts in connection with the financing of the storage and marketing of the Cuban sugar crop will be found in Chapter VII.[3]

DEFENSE SUPPLIES CORPORATION

The Defense Supplies Corporation, a subsidiary of the Reconstruction Finance Corporation, also maintained direct relations with United States commercial banks. Under the parent corporation's guarantee it opened credits to pay for the importation of those particular staples and commodities, such as horsehair, bristles, and certain drugs, with the acquisition of which it was primarily concerned. These articles were obtained through the intermediary of importers who were especially conversant with their markets and the best sources of supply. In India the corporation bought jute and burlap, and in Uruguay raw wool, which were paid for through bankers' letters of credit. Goatskins and cinchona bark also were bought and financed by it. In addition, for several seasons it attended to the banking operations incident to the financing of the sugar crop and molasses output of Cuba, until in February, 1943, the Commodity Credit Corporation assumed the liabilities arising from Defense Supplies Corporation advances to the sugar producers.

RUBBER RESERVE COMPANY

The Rubber Reserve Company was organized in the summer of 1940 to acquire raw rubber in the Far East in order to increase the national stockpile of this strategic material. Its original capital was 5 million dollars. Purchases were made through leading rubber importers, who acted as the agents of the company on a commission basis. Letters of credit were opened in their favor by the commercial banks under the joint guarantee of the Reconstruction Finance Corporation and the Rubber Reserve Company.

[3] The growth of Commodity Credit Corporation's operations during and since the war is best illustrated by Secretary of Agriculture Brannan's request on January 24, 1950, appearing before the Senate Agriculture Committee, for an increase in the borrowing authority of the corporation from 4,750 million dollars to 6,750 million; however, as of August 31, 1950 the Commodity Credit Corporation reported that the total amount of its purchases and loans aggregated only $3,288,738,000.

In June, 1941, the United States Government practically gave the Rubber Reserve Company a monopoly of rubber importations, the company thereafter allocating, as it considered needful, part of its purchases to the tire companies for their minimum requirements. The reason for this change of policy was that the Dutch East Indies Administration was suspected of taking advantage of the competition among American rubber merchants to hold out for higher prices. As the only United States buyer in the market, and one moreover that worked in close association with the British Government, the Rubber Reserve Company was confident of obtaining better results. The same situation prevailed in the freight market, where the company sought to charter space more advantageously than with several shippers vying with each other for shipping accommodation for the same rubber cargo. For the financing of its foreign purchases the company continued the practice of cabling credits through the commercial banks.[4]

UNITED STATES COMMERCIAL COMPANY

The United States Commercial Company was at first a subsidiary of the Reconstruction Finance Corporation, but in 1943 it was transferred to the Foreign Economic Administration. It bought and sold products in neutral countries, playing an active role during the war. Its purchases involved financing by means of commercial letters of credit and transfers of foreign exchange. The company began operations in March, 1942, under the management of Robert Ducas, who previously had been connected with the United Kingdom Commercial Corporation. The latter organization exercised in the United Kingdom and the British colonies much the same functions as its American twin.

The United States company and its British companion handled most of their countries' import and export trade that had drifted into government channels as a result of the restrictions imposed on private business in the interest of the more effective control of neutral commerce. One important aspect of the work of the United States Commercial Company was the preclusive accumulation of war material

[4] On December 28, 1950, the United States once more took over the importation and distribution of natural crude rubber according to an announcement by William H. Harrison, administrator of the National Production Authority and Jess Larson, head of the General Services Administration, which was authorized to sell the rubber to domestic processors.

in Spain, Portugal, Turkey, and South America. In this task the company was motivated by two distinct objectives: first, to frustrate Axis efforts to secure valuable war materials in neutral countries and, secondly, to extend financial support to neutral nations anxious to sell some of their surpluses. The company, with the help of the United States banks, therefore accumulated large balances in foreign exchange with which to pay for the metals and other commodities purchased in competition with and often snatched away from under the very nose of the Germans. All liabilities of the United States Commercial Company, like those of the other Reconstruction Finance Corporation affiliates, were guaranteed by the latter corporation. Reimbursement was generally received from the Federal Reserve Bank of New York.

Much of the materials paid for had to be stored abroad until after the war. For example, upon payment by the correspondent of an American commercial bank the tin warehouse receipts received would be held in custody by its foreign banking correspondent until, perhaps, the metal was ordered shipped to another country, in which case additional credits might have to be opened for the payment of export duties, ocean freight, and handling charges. In certain countries the operations of the United States Commercial Company and the Defense Supplies Corporation sometimes appeared to be overlapping.

At the end of 1942 the United States Commercial Company, to finance the purchase of tea in China, offered United States banks the opportunity of participating in an 8 million dollar credit. Drafts issued under this credit were made negotiable at the Central Bank of China. The unusual diversification of the company's operations is illustrated by the long list of countries in which it was active as buyer of local products. In Haiti it purchased cornbeans and rice; in Spain it succeeded in acquiring and storing large quantities of wolfram, a metal ardently coveted by the Germans. United States Commercial Company agents bought sisal and industrial diamonds in Venezuela; in Colombia, various metals and minerals; in Chile, Cuba, Turkey, and Madagascar, miscellaneous strategic materials, which were either shipped to the United States, and if possible from there to the theaters of war, or warehoused for future use. Many of these materials found their way into the surplus goods that were sold after the end of the war.

METALS RESERVE COMPANY

Another Reconstruction Finance Corporation affiliate was the Metals Reserve Company, which like the Rubber Reserve Company was organized in the middle of 1940, with an initial capital of 5 million dollars, and was active in many parts of the globe. Relations with commercial banks consisted in the opening by the company of letters of credit in the countries where purchases were made: Mexico, Australia, British East Africa, and Madagascar. Agents of the company also operated on an extensive scale in Chile, where banking advances were required for the substantial quantities of metals and ores acquired there, while mica and quartz were obtained in Colombia, and industrial diamonds in Venezuela. In addition, shortly after Pearl Harbor settlement had to be made in the Philippine Islands for purchases of copper, chrome, manganese, and iron ore. In connection with all credits and advances the Reconstruction Finance Corporation assumed the full and unconditional guarantee for any and all risks incurred by the banks.[5]

WAR FINANCE CORPORATION AND GRAIN STABILIZATION CORPORATION

The story of the United States Government corporations would be incomplete without a brief mention of the War Finance Corporation created in 1921 during President Harding's administration. It made substantial loans on cotton under the management of its chairman Eugene Meyer, Jr., now publisher of the *Washington Post.*

The Grain Stabilization Corporation played a prominent role during the latter part of the Hoover administration. It was formed in February, 1930, to buy surplus wheat and thereby support the tumbling grain markets hit by the convulsion of the Great Depression. Vigorous George S. Milnor was the corporation's first president, and Walker I. Beam, vice president of the Farmers National Grain Corporation, was treasurer. Theirs was an ungrateful task. As was undoubtedly expected by President Hoover, the corporation's operations resulted in ever-increasing losses. The concern made abundant use of bank credit, both in Chicago, whence its officers directed its

[5] This company, and the Rubber Reserve Company, as well as the Defense Supplies Corporation, were liquidated as of June 30, 1945, and their functions were assumed by the Reconstruction Finance Corporation.

affairs, and in New York. In five prewar years the Treasury was reported to have made good over 60 million dollars of the corporation's deficits. In retrospect, however, when compared with the cost to the taxpayers of the postwar farm price support programs, the price paid for the aid extended to the grain producers of the Middle West in the early thirties may appear to have been moderate indeed.

SUMMARY

In this chapter are described some of the functions of United States Government corporations prior and during the Second World War and the relations with them of the commercial banks. The latter, as well as the foreign traders in general, loyally lent their facilities to these various agencies, in spite of their temporary intrusion upon their accustomed fields. Aside from an occasional duplication of effort, the resulting operations of unprecedented magnitude were accomplished most efficiently and creditably. The Export-Import Bank made particularly extensive use of the services of the commercial banks, many medium and long-term credits being extended under its guarantee before and in the course of the war with the active participation of United States banks along somewhat parallel lines to the aid extended to British exporters by the British Export Credit Insurance Department.

V

THE ROLE OF SILVER IN UNITED STATES BANKING

SILVER HAS LONG LOOMED LARGE in the operations of the foreign departments of United States banks that had close connections or branch offices in the Far East. Until the early thirties three fifths of the world's population used silver as a medium of payment in their daily lives. Many years before the voice of a Detroit priest vaunted to radio listeners the virtues of the white metal as a standard of value, bankers in London, San Francisco, New York, and other great financial centers followed the price of the metal, compared it with the exchanges of silver-wedded countries, such as China and India, and imported or exported the bullion according to whether it was more profitable to ship it to or to withdraw it from the Far Eastern markets.

Following the 1929 debacle, and in line with the general slump in the prices of commodities, a serious decline in silver values took place in the early thirties. From a peak of more than $1.33 in 1920 the white metal had collapsed to a fraction more than 24 cents by December, 1932. The fall was attributed to the rise in world production and to growing agitation in the Orient for the adoption of the gold standard and the apprehended effect on the purchasing power of silver in the East.

Alarmed by the sensational decline, the United States Senate Finance Committee held hearings for the purpose of investigating the causes of the heavy depreciation of the metal, of which the United States was one of the important producers. In February, 1933, when he appeared before the committee, Winthrop W. Aldrich, president of the Chase National Bank, warned that silver could not and should not be used for the adjustment of balances in international trade, and added that it could not properly form part of central bank reserves. In contrast, the late Sir Henry Deterding, in an article published in the *Saturday Evening Post* of October 14, 1933, gave it as his carefully considered opinion that "the world would have been set on its feet again, within a very few months, if silver had been included with gold as the real standard of value."

At the World Economic Conference in London the governments represented agreed on July 20, 1933, to maintain the fineness of silver coin at no less than eight tenths, and the five silver-producing countries (United States, Canada, Mexico, Peru, and Chile) covenanted to refrain from selling during the four years beginning January 1, 1934, in excess of 25 million ounces from their total yearly mine production. The London Silver Agreement also stipulated that India's and Spain's sales of silver from their accumulated stocks should not exceed a certain fixed amount. After the ratification of the agreement, in December, 1933, the United States Treasury established a net price for its purchases of domestic silver at 641/2 cents an ounce. Purchases of up to 24,421,410 ounces, equivalent to one half of the newly mined United States production, were to be deposited with the Treasury. For the remaining half of the domestic silver production, which was reserved for coinage, the old statutory price of $1.29 an ounce was paid. Foreign bar silver by then had risen to about 43 cents an ounce in the world's markets.

On June 19, 1934, the Silver Purchase Act became law in the United States, authorizing the President to nationalize silver at his discretion and to require all silver held in the country to be turned over to the Treasury for purchase at not more than 50 cents per fine troy ounce. The act also imposed a 50 percent tax on all profits derived from dealing in silver. On August 9, at the hour of noon, the President proclaimed the nationalization order, as of the following day, and directed that all silver be delivered to the mints. Trading in silver on the New York Commodity Exchange was immediately suspended. The following day the exchange issued an order that outstanding contracts for all deliveries were to be adjusted at 49.96 cents per .999 fine ounce of silver, the actual settlement taking place at 50.01 cents. Silver held by the commercial banks was hedged either on the New York Commodity Exchange or in other future markets, and these hedges had to be undone when the silver was turned over to the United States Mint. The actual volume of silver delivered under the nationalization order apparently amounted to about 56 million ounces, according to the annual report of the Federal Reserve Board for 1934.

After the settlement of all pending transactions, the silver market at the New York Commodity Exchange was closed, since it had lost its *raison d'être*. In September, 1934, Montreal opened its own silver exchange in order that Canadian brokers might participate in the trade, which so far had been monopolized by the New York market.

No account of the effect of United States silver policies during the early thirties would be complete without taking stock of their far-reaching repercussions on the Far Eastern exchanges and the economic situation of the various countries (China, India, Mexico, and others) directly affected by the rise and fall of the metal. When it became certain that the Silver Purchase Bill would receive Congressional approval, Chinese speculators bought Shanghai dollars on a considerable scale, while Indian and other Eastern markets sent orders for the purchase of rupees in London. As to the United States Treasury, it continued its silver-acquisition policy at mounting prices. In two years it purchased more than 800 million ounces at 12 to 16 cents above the market quotations prevailing prior to the passage of the Silver Purchase Act. London silver, New York silver, Shanghai dollars, and Hong Kong dollars all experienced advances to record highs, until the Treasury decided to withdraw temporarily from the market.

When foreigners attempted to ship silver out of the United States, an embargo was placed on exports. Only the execution of sales made prior to June 30, 1934, and the export of metal owned by foreign central banks were licensed. Shipments of silver to the United States for sale by banks and brokers practically ceased. Owing to the provision in the Silver Purchase Act rendering United States citizens liable for the tax on profits made by foreign sellers, such transactions became actually prohibitive. The Treasury purchases were not subject to any tax, however, and the Treasury Department therefore had unrestricted power over the silver market without too much interference from foreign holders or speculators.

The unknown factor in the silver situation was the total amount of the white metal that the United States Government was willing to buy abroad in carrying out its official policy. Because of her large stocks of silver, China was the country most directly affected by the new situation created by the American official intervention. If the price of silver were radically raised above a certain level, it was alleged that she might find it advantageous to switch to the gold standard or even to resort to bimetallism. In fact, in September, 1934,

Sao-Ke Alfred Sze, the able and tactful Chinese Ambassador in Washington, delivered a note from his government in Nanking calling attention to the detrimental effects of the nationalization of silver on China's internal economy.

To stop the drain on its silver reserves, China, in October, 1934, placed a 10 percent export tax on all foreign silver shipments. This step seemed the only way by which the Chinese Government could defend its currency and keep control of the stocks of silver remaining within the country after the unprecedented exports that had already so harmfully depleted the national reserves. Later, the export duty was raised to 25 percent. However, when the difference between the inland price of silver in China and the world price began to favor smuggling on a large scale, the Chinese authorities were forced to reduce the duty again. At the same time, the Chinese Minister of Finance prevailed upon the Chinese banks not to take advantage of any price difference that might offer favorable opportunities for arbitrage against the United States quotations, as this might embarrass the Chinese Government.

By the end of November, 1934, a critical local shortage of cash in China induced heavy sales of dollars and sterling for immediate delivery and a correspondingly large demand for forward delivery of the same currencies. The discount on the prompt delivery amounted to as much as 15 percent per annum. In other words, those local Chinese and foreign banks established in Shanghai which had liquid temporarily unemployed funds were able to lend Shanghai dollars to local borrowers at interest rates reminiscent of pre-Federal Reserve days in the United States. These abnormal rates and a rumor that China might abandon the silver standard caused consternation among the natives, and reports of an impending serious commercial depression in China began to reach New York.

In October, 1934, Secretary of the Treasury, Henry Morgenthau, Jr., invited certain heads of foreign banking departments and others versed in Far Eastern bullion and exchange arbitrage to confer with him and his associates in order to ascertain their views on the general condition of the international silver market and the outlook for a rise in the foreign demand for the white metal. Among those attending were Herman Oliphant, general counsel of the Treasury, Archie Lochhead, technical assistant to the Secretary, and Werner Knoke, deputy governor of the Federal Reserve Bank of New York. The discussions were held in the historic room where the interallied debt-funding agreements had been signed after the First World War. Small silver tablets on the edge of the large mahogany table commemorated the earlier occasion and listed the names of the delegates, some of whom, it may be surmised, because of the incapacity of their nations to carry out the obligations assumed in these covenants, may later have wished that their identity had not been disclosed to posterity. The recommendations and views of the commercial bankers on the outlook for silver were incorporated in a memorandum addressed to the Secretary, although they had reasons to believe that their conclusions were not wholly in accordance with the monetary policies favored by the administration.

The United States Government was as fervently devoted to its silver program as ever. By the end of 1934 its holdings of the metal had risen to almost 900 million ounces. The authorities still declared that silver was preferable in payment of United States exports to the short-term or long-term promissory notes and bonds that had been received during the decade prior to 1932. And so both gold and silver continued to arrive in large volume in the holds of the ships entering New York and San Francisco harbors. At times it was impossible to secure freight carriers for additional shipments. When the facilities for safekeeping of the precious cargoes on board ship were exhausted, the underwriters were forced to decline further applications for insurance. It was not surprising that under these conditions both the Far Eastern and the European countries ardently wished for a speedy settlement of the currency tangle caused by the heavy drainage of their metallic reserves to the United States.

The Treasury's orders for the purchase of silver and gold and the execution of the foreign exchange transactions connected with it, as well as those resulting from the operations of the Stabilization Fund, were placed in the hands of the Federal Reserve Bank of New York, whose foreign activities were under the direction of its resourceful and internationally trained deputy governor, L. Werner Knoke. Silver acquired by the bank in foreign markets was acceptable only if the bars were good delivery in the country in which they were offered for sale. For instance, Bombay Mint bars, if bought by an American bank as agent for the Treasury, were received "as is," while on the other hand bars shipped on consignment—whether .999 fine or of lower fineness—had to be remelted by United States refineries at a charge of 1/4 to 1 cent per ounce, according to the degree of fineness.

One odd incident occurred in Hong Kong in 1935. A great number of boxes and bags containing silver coins had long been stored in the vault of one of the local banks. The cases had rested there for several years without being disturbed. When at last it was necessary to withdraw them, it was found upon inspection that some of the bags and boxes had been almost completely destroyed by the gnawing of innumerable colonies of white ants. How these had entered the vault remained a mystery. The sad sequel of the story was that the ants had left such heavy secretions on the coins that they were unacceptable to the Chinese natives, who could not make them ring. The whole stock had to be reminted at considerable expense to the owners of the coins.

One effect of the large silver purchases of the United States Government was the piling up of metal in the refineries in London, San Francisco, and on the Atlantic Coast. Although all worked at full blast, they were unable to cope with all the work imposed upon them, and the manufacturing-jewelry trade consequently found it difficult to cover its needs for the Christmas and normal demands except by paying a heavy premium for American-mined silver.

The Treasury, because of the extent of its operations, was in constant need of up-to-date information on the factors influencing the gold and silver markets. The managers of the United States banks stationed abroad co-operated by keeping the home offices carefully posted by cable, telephone, and mail regarding developments that might be of interest to those in charge of the Treasury operations. Many subjects had to be covered: the inflow and outgo of silver; the activities of the native and foreign banks, brokers, and speculators; the fluctuations of local stocks; the short and long positions in foreign exchange and gold bullion where known; the operations of the banks of issue; the movements in their bullion reserves; and so forth. While United States diplomatic agents were also busily engaged in canvassing the situation in their respective areas, it was probably felt that the trained staffs of the banks had channels of intelligence not so easily accessible to the representatives of the State and Commerce departments.

A new development characterized the trend of the silver markets in January, 1935. At that time Indian speculators, who had a large "long" position, started to unload. Persistent selling orders reached London from Bombay. There were rumors afloat that India would reduce its export duty on the metal (this was actually done on February 28, 1935) and that the considerable Indian silver hoards might flood the world's markets. Perceiving the situation, the Treasury (the "special buyer," as it was called in the international markets) decided to abstain from placing purchasing orders on the occasion of the official fixing of the silver price in London. Fortunately, Cuba was a buyer at that moment of 8 million ounces, which were to be delivered to the Philadelphia Mint for coinage. Other factors that caused uneasiness among silver traders were repeated reports of banking difficulties in China and the rumor that the Chinese Government contemplated reducing the silver content of the Shanghai dollar. Failing that, some trouble-makers spread the news that China would cut lose from silver entirely and adopt a paper standard. In actual fact, the Chinese Government did appoint a consultative committee to advise it on the best steps to take under the prevailing circumstances.

Nevertheless, by April, 1935, silver sold at an all-time high price, except for the abnormal period immediately after the First World War. At 81 1/2 cents per ounce it broke all records since 1921. By this time the United States Treasury had raised its bids to 77.57 cents. At this rate the Mexican silver peso had an exchange value equal to its actual silver content. Accordingly, on April 27, 1935, the Mexican Government found itself obliged to prohibit all silver exports. Simultaneously, it ordered that all subsidiary coins be exchanged for paper money and also decided on the manufacture of bronze token coins to remedy the shortage in subsidiary currency.

When April drew to a close the speculators sensed that it was time to take their profits. At once the market broke by more than 5 cents. No great damage was done, for the silver exchanges had previously risen far more: for example, instead of 37 cents, as a year earlier, the Hong Kong dollar had been quoted at around 60 cents. In the United States Senate about this time the proposal was advanced by the silver block that the silver dollar be revalued on the same basis as the gold dollar. The statutory price was to be raised to $2.58. With seigniorage of 50 percent, this would establish the domestic silver price at $1.29 and thus double automatically the nominal value of the silver stock owned by the United States Treasury. It would also reduce the quantity of silver that the Treasury still had to buy under the silver purchase program to 200 million ounces. The Treasury, since at this price it would have succeeded in arriving at the coveted 3-to-1 ratio of gold to silver, would have been out of the market until new imports of gold once more had changed the proportion. However, the proposed law was not enacted.

In May, 1935, Winthrop W. Aldrich, again appearing before a Senate subcommittee, pointed out that the boom in the price of silver had failed to accomplish what the authors of the policy had prophesied. It had failed to raise the general price level. It had caused acute crises in China and Mexico, and as to the dollar, the effects had been relatively unimportant. A few days later the Treasury prohibited the importation of foreign silver money in order to assist those countries with metallic money whose bullion content had become more valuable than the face amount of the coins themselves.

At the end of May the collapse of the American Oriental Banking Corporation in Shanghai and its affiliates was announced. While its difficulties were ascribed mainly to overextension in real estate, the failure was considered by many as another unfortunate sequel of United States silver policy. The Chinese native banks, too, showed signs of growing uneasiness owing to the tense money market situation and the fear of a general financial breakdown in Shanghai. In fact, in June the Chinese Government thought it wise to advance the native bank association 25 million Shanghai dollars in government bonds in order to assist them to meet their end-of-the-month obligations.

At about the same time the government of the Hong Kong Colony initiated further moves to prevent the export of silver from the port. An ordinance informed the trade that, thereafter, except under special license, no permission would be granted for the export of silver coins minted in China or of silver bullion other than the product of refineries located outside the colony and China. It had been learned that the Japanese were buying silver coins in that part of North China where their army was in control and were shipping the coins for refining to Kobe, whence they were re-exported to London in the form of bars. Having lost authority over that part of its domain, the Chinese Government was unable to enforce there its own interdiction of the shipment and sale abroad of Chinese coins. As a result of the Hong Kong action, Japan was henceforth forced to use a port where neither the Chinese nor the Hong Kong authorities had jurisdiction, such as Portuguese Macao. The silver was consigned to London brokers notwithstanding the higher quotations prevailing in New York, where the shippers would have been subject to the imposition of the United States silver tax. Because of its origin, United States banks refrained from bidding, so as not to play into the hands of the Japanese.

Saturday, July 6, 1935, was a red-letter day for some New York exchange traders. For several preceding weeks the United States Treasury had placed its bids in the London market to support the steadily declining silver price there. On that particular Saturday there had been very little business in the early forenoon, and the men in the foreign exchange divisions planned to close their desks as soon as possible in order to join their families at the beaches. Then a telephone call came from London to the effect that a violent break in the silver quotation was inevitable. As a rule, trading in London was listless on the eve of Sunday and the traditional week-end. However, on this exceptional occasion millions of ounces of the metal were suddenly offered without a buyer in sight. Ordinarily the fixing of the official London rate took place at 11.30 o'clock New York time, but on that day the nervous London brokers decided to delay the fixing for several hours to give New York time to intervene in the market before it was too late. The American banks in London got in touch with their New York offices. The latter relayed the unwelcome information to the Federal Reserve Bank, which in turn called the Treasury to ask for instructions. Realizing that prompt action was urgently necessary, the latter authorized the putting in of enough buying orders to soften the decline. This permitted the jittery London brokers to quote the official price at 30 11/16, which was 5/16 down from the previous day's quotation. The officers of the two banks entrusted with the orders advised the Treasury that between 10 to 15 million ounces had been allotted to them, and hurried off to seek relief from the heat wave that was enveloping downtown Manhattan. A similar incident occurred on a certain Tuesday in December, 1935, when the Treasury decided to leave the silver market to its own devices. The London brokers were buried under such an avalanche of selling orders that they were obliged to halt trading. In the absence of any demand the price declined to a fraction above the parity of 48 cents.

One fact seems worthy of mention. The foreign silver interests watched the orders coming from Washington via New York with the closest attention. When they noticed large buying orders, they were tempted to withdraw their own selling orders or even to add some buying orders of their own to those received from the United States; if they had reason to believe that Washington was temporarily out of the market, some holders might turn sellers until the Treasury decided to place new orders, when the same performance would begin all over again. For this reason, the United States banks charged with the execution of Treasury orders not only had to be extremely discreet but also had to match their wits with those of their counterparts in foreign centers and at times adapt their own tactics to those of the shrewd manipulators across the ocean. At certain periods it became a foregone conclusion that whenever United States orders failed to make their appearance, suddenly Chinese, Hong Kong, Indian, or Mexican offers of silver would be entered, apparently from nowhere, and the price of the metal would take a downward course.

The extent of the silver purchases effected by the United States Treasury was reflected in figures published early in 1936: a total of 761 million ounces had been acquired since June, 1934. The orders were distributed among a small number of American institutions known to be well equipped for operations of magnitude. A great deal of clerical work was involved both in the home offices and in the foreign branches. The confidential nature of the transactions was closely safeguarded, private ciphers and code names being used whenever it was necessary to mention the source of the orders in cables, telephone conversations, and letters.

During the fall of 1936 the strike of longshoremen interfered unpleasantly with the discharge of silver shipments consigned to United States banks. Insurance failed to offer protection against loss of interest caused by delays in the delivery of bullion to United States Assay offices. It was at this time that the following episode caused anxious hours to one foreign department executive. The scene was the port of Seattle. A steamer had arrived from China carrying a valuable cargo of silver. When informed of the strike, the crew quit work, leaving the captain in a quandary as to how to deliver the freight in San Francisco, the port to which it was consigned. He had the presence of mind to inform the New York correspondent of the prominent Chinese bank that was the shipper of the metal; the insurance brokers were notified, and on behalf of the underwriters and for their protection armed guards were stationed at the dock where the boat was anchored. Bad as was the delay, there was a more serious angle to the incident. Unless the silver were sold outside the territory of the United States, the proceeds, under the Silver Purchase Act, were subject to a 50 percent tax. It was therefore imperative to have the ship continue its voyage by sea to its destination. If the shipment had been unloaded in Seattle and forwarded by rail, the tax would have amounted to several hundred thousand dollars. Finally, after many costly exchanges of cables and telephone conversations, the troublesome cargo was transferred to a tramp steamer en route to California, and the metal was sold, in accordance with the letter of the law, outside the territorial limits of the United States.

In September, 1937, the landing of the Japanese in Shanghai caused renewed agitation in the silver markets. Silver bullion to the amount of 200 million ounces was hurriedly shipped from China to Hong Kong, and it was feared that this large quantity might flood the market. For a few days the metal was heavily offered at falling prices. Then the United States Treasury intervened, and it became known that the Chinese Government would use the silver as collateral for loans rather than offer it for sale. Prices thereupon recovered. The improvement was enhanced by the belief that Washington would do everything in its power to contain the market and not leave it without support; a contrary attitude, it was evident, would be detrimental to the hard-pressed Chinese people.

A problem that caused United States banks especial concern during this period as the possibility of war in Europe became more threatening was insurance coverage of bullion and securities while being transported on land. A similar question had already arisen in China, where there was danger that bullion might be intercepted by the enemy prior to its being loaded on trans-pacific steamers. Under the standard policies, however, no such coverage was then available, and accordingly the banks, rather than carry the risks themselves, preferred to abstain from making advances against shipments that were not fully insured against all possible contingencies.

At the end of June, 1938, the Chinese Government ordered large shipments to be effected from London to New York. As we have seen, this stock of metal had originally been deposited with various banks in the City of London to serve as security for the payment of loans contracted in sterling, guilders, and Swiss francs, but these loans had evidently been paid off. The transfer coincided with the visit of a delegation of Chinese diplomats and bankers, who in May, 1938, conferred with the Secretary of the Treasury in Washington. It was reported at this time that large amounts of Chinese silver carried by Japanese steamers had recently arrived in London and there had been sold for Japanese account. Presumably the United States Treasury gave assurances to the Chinese delegates of its firm intention to refrain from purchasing any silver that appeared to have been requisitioned by the Japanese army in China. Scarcely three months later, in August, the Treasury announced an agreement with the Central Bank of China for the purchase of 75 million ounces of silver at the world price of 77.57 cents. The principal object of this and other sales of silver by the Chinese authorities, it was stated, was to increase the gold reserves of the government and create a favorable impression on the natives.

To thwart the enemy's efforts, the Chinese Government decided to divert as much of the metal as they could lay their hands on from the interior of the country to Hong Kong, whence it was shipped to London and New York. Shipments via the Burma Road were too slow and too dangerous. To lure the metal out of hoarding places, the Chinese Government paid the natives a small premium, for the Chinese dollar was at that time quoted at 12 percent discount per annum for delivery in three months.

In the fall of 1938 the New York silver market began to question whether a favorable change in the silver policy of the Washington Administration was not within the realm of possibilities. Already, in April, the President had voided the order of August, 1934, prohibiting the exportation of silver, although the 50 percent tax on profits continued to preclude active operations on the part of the dealers. Some silver interests went so far as to predict the repeal of the Silver Purchase Act. There was also talk of measures to discourage the further inflow of gold and foreign capital. However, it soon became clear that the wish had been father to the thought. On December 31, 1938, President Roosevelt proclaimed an extension to June 30, 1939, of the Treasury authorization to purchase domestic silver at 64.64 cents an ounce. Nevertheless, several bills were before Congress at this time to repeal the silver legislation, some of the bills going so far as to provide for an embargo on the importation of silver from abroad. By this time foreign silver was being offered in New York at 43 cents an ounce.

In March, 1939, silver dealers were faced with a new discouraging development. California had just passed a 3 percent sales tax. Immediately prior to the enactment of the law a leading Chinese bank had consigned a considerable silver shipment from Manila to San Francisco. The West Coast had been selected because the eastern refineries were behind in their contracts and the proceeds of the silver if refined in California would be therefore at the shipper's disposal six months sooner than if the metal were treated in Atlantic Coast refineries. How was the Chinese institution to avoid having to shoulder a loss that it could not have foreseen when it gave the original orders to have the silver shipped to the West Coast? Lawyers for the consignee bank advised that if the silver were sold before arrival at destination the foreign shipper would not be subject to the tax. In the end a compromise was arrived at between the fiscal authorities of the state of California and the representatives of the shipper.

As the fateful date of June 30, 1939, approached, when the President's authority to buy silver was to expire, the price of the metal had another fainting spell. To be on the safe side New York dealers temporarily abstained from initiating shipments from London to New York. By the end of July silver was quoted at the lowest price in six years. In fact, in November the quotation was back at 35 cents, which was just about its pre-1933 level.

With our increasingly active participation in the war, the demands for silver on the part of United States airplane manufacturers became pressing. In addition, in April, 1942, the local refineries and metal brokers had to contend with the competition of a South American buyer whose country required the metal for coinage purposes. At that time Mexico was practically the only outside source of free silver. Mexico had been for many years the largest producer of the metal, the bullion being shipped from Vera Cruz to San Francisco, New York, London, and the Far East. American mining companies, among which the American Smelting & Refining Company and the American Metal Company were the most active, controlled many silver mines and refineries in Mexico, and much of their production was sold in the New York market.

In October, 1942, the official price for foreign silver was 44 3/4 cents. Domestic silver mined in the United States was sold at 71 5/8 cents an ounce to those "nonessential" industries which had no priority rating, namely, local factories catering to the retail jewelry and silverware trades. Although, as compared with the value of the metal in the late twenties, the cost to the manufacturers had almost doubled, under the price ceiling fixed by the Office of Price Administration they were obliged to abide by their former price schedules for finished articles.

In December, for the first time in many months, owing to heavy arrivals from Mexico, the supply of foreign silver exceeded the demand. As there were no buyers for imported silver at that time, the Metals Reserve Division of the Reconstruction Finance Corporation intervened and purchased the offered lots. Since foreign silver could not be applied to domestic needs, the purchases were stored pending the appearance of fresh demand for war production purposes.

At this time a bill sponsored by Senator Greene of Rhode Island was passed empowering the Treasury to sell silver owned by it at 50 cents an ounce. However, opponents succeeded in adding an amendment to the effect that silver thus sold could only be used for purposes connected with the prosecution of the war. Accordingly, unless a considerably increased demand should develop from the war industries there was little prospect that the Treasury would be able to dispose of the silver at the prescribed price.

In the early part of 1943 foreign silver arrivals once more exceeded the needs of the war industries, the latter being now in a position to cover their requirements out of stockpiles built up in the third quarter of 1942. Hence, the Metals Reserve Company again entered bids for foreign silver at 45 cents. At that period it was stated that a large percentage of the silver owned by the corporation—its total purchases in 1942 were believed to have amounted to 10 million ounces—had been disposed of through lend-lease and had been shipped to various parts of the British Empire in the form of bars and silver coins. The official price in New York for foreign silver was 44 3/4 cents in the middle of April; for domestic silver the quotation remained unchanged at 71.11 cents. The Mexican Government no longer shipped its silver production to the United States, since all metal mined in Mexico was needed for coinage at home to meet the demand from the agricultural and mining districts for hard money. In fact, it was reported that the natives in the interior were reluctant to accept paper money.

On July 12, 1943, the President signed a new silver bill which authorized the Treasury to make the Government's silver stocks available for both war and civilian use. According to the New York *Times* of July 13, the Treasury then had a stockpile of free silver of more than 1,250 million ounces, of which about 700 million had been loaned to the Defense Plant Corporation. In September the War Production Board called on all owners of foreign silver to submit a detailed report of their holdings. The underlying purpose of the step was to make it possible later, if necessary, to require the proprietors to sell that part of their stocks which was not urgently needed to those consumers whose requirements of the metal for war production enjoyed a priority rating. This was pre-eminently the case as regards the manufacture of electric wires for airplanes and other "must" military equipment. The nonessential industries which used domestic silver (most of which was mined in the West and manufactured in eastern plants) had to pay the higher price of 71.11 cents.

In April, 1944, Mexico was able to resume her silver shipments to the United States, but only about 20 percent of her total production found its way to New York, where it was sold at 45 cents an ounce. Under the Greene Act, the United States Treasury continued to release about 3 million ounces monthly for the use by silverware makers and industrial users, such as the photography industry. In June the influx of silver from Mexico grew in volume, and owing to the cutback in armament orders and to increased copper and lead output, the Metals Reserve Company, which now acted as agent for the Government, was obliged to absorb most of the Mexican-mined silver at 45 cents.

In India about this time the bullion market was thrown into utter confusion by the Japanese invasion of the outer provinces. Panic-stricken traders in the Bombay bazaar bid wildly for silver, pushing the price up from 100 to 140 rupees per 100 tolas and simultaneously advancing the gold quotation from 70 to 80 rupees per tola of gold. On the basis of the rate for free rupees the corresponding parities in United States currency were $1.10 per ounce of silver and $60.00 an ounce of gold. To combat the incipient inflation, the Reserve Bank of India intervened promptly and re-established more orderly trading conditions.

In the fall of 1944 the Government of India concluded an arrangement with the United States Treasury under which it obtained 100 million ounces of silver through lend-lease. The Reserve Bank of India was thus enabled to enter the market more effectively and bring about the gradual decline of the price of silver in this important market.[1]

In recent years the despoliation of silver, both as a currency and as a backing for note issues, has made appalling progress. The latest country to melt down about 80 million silver pesos is the Republic of Cuba following the example of Britain, India, and other countries that have eliminated silver from their subsidiary currencies. Yet, in the late fall of 1950 the price of silver once more registered a sizable recovery on reports of stockpiling by both governments and war industries; the former were believed to require the metal for monetary use in their mandated territories or colonial possessions. On January 8, 1951, the metal again reached a high of 90.16 cents an ounce while the United States Treasury paid 90.41 cents an ounce for newly mined domestic output.

SUMMARY

An outstanding feature of the banking history of the present era has been an attempt by the silver producing countries, under the leadership of the United States, to raise the price of the metal in the world's markets, the United States being particularly concerned to establish a ratio of one quarter of silver to three quarters of gold in the metallic monetary reserves of this country. The history of silver in the thirties has moved through successive stages: United States nationalization, embargo on exports, and taxation of profits; formidable speculation abroad; the different phases of the purchasing operations in distant markets; the acquisition by the United States of domestic production; the effect both on producing countries like Mexico and on the *de facto* or *de jure* silver-standard nations of India and China; and finally the collapse of the price in the world markets and the tacit abandonment of United States Government intervention.

1 For a circumstantial and analytical description of and commentary on the silver operations of the United States Treasury between 1932 and 1938 the reader is referred to Paris, *Monetary Policies of the United States, 1932–1938*, Johnson, *The Treasury and Monetary Policy, 1933–38*, and Everest, *Morgenthau the New Deal and Silver*.

PART THREE

UNITED STATES BANKING ABROAD

VI

LATIN AMERICA

GENERAL

DURING THE SECOND HALF of the nineteenth and the first two decades of the present century British banks occupied a preponderant place in the financing of Latin American trade. Cable transfers in pound sterling and ninety-day bills on London acceptance houses were the chief media by which trade with the principal ports of South America were settled. To avoid losses due to the depreciation of the local paper currencies, working balances, cash reserves, and a considerable part of the peoples' savings were deposited in British financial institutions or else invested in sterling bonds and common stocks. Gradually other countries, too, turned to the area, the Belgians, Canadians, Germans, Italians, Dutch, French, Portuguese, Spanish, and Swiss, and the branches or affiliates of their banks took their places alongside the various British establishments and entered into active competition with them and with each other.

United States commercial banks meanwhile maintained correspondent relationships with the important private banks and business houses operating in the leading business centers of the South American republics. As these relations widened, owing to the expansion of Latin American contacts with foreign countries, a growing volume of business began to flow to United States banks, the intercourse being considerably enhanced after the passage of the Federal Reserve Act in 1913, which empowered national banks to open foreign branches. The National City Bank of New York and the First National Bank of Boston successively established their own offices in Buenos Aires, Montevideo, Rio de Janeiro and São Paulo. After 1915 the Mercantile Bank of the Americas opened branches in Colombia, Venezuela, Ecuador, Peru, Nicaragua, and Argentina; however, during the postwar depression of the early twenties, it suffered such severe losses that its sponsors liquidated it after the creditors had been paid in full, while the Bank of Central and South America took over the remainder of its current accounts.

The Federal Reserve Act extended to United States banks generally the privileges long enjoyed by their European competitors, and it accordingly became possible for them to offer short-term dollar acceptance facilities to foreign trade interests in the Americas without enlisting the co-operation of London or continental banks. The provisions of the act, complemented by the creation of an active discount market for bankers' bills in New York and other United States business centers, supplied the banks with a welcome new instrument for the fostering of financial relations with the South American republics.

Another important contributing factor to the growth of United States financial influence in certain Latin American countries was the increasing number of United States corporations and business houses that established branch factories and assembly plants or warehouses to take advantage of the proximity to raw materials and the abundance of cheap labor. During the interwar period United States capital developed domestic industries and furnished management and industrial skill with considerable success.

With minor exceptions the Latin American states, up to the First World War, were deficient in capital resources and consequently had to lean heavily for their agricultural needs and the opening up of their mineral wealth on the direct investments and long-term loans made by the more affluent older countries of Europe and North America. During the decade following the First World War large amounts of investment capital were poured into Latin America not only by the United States but also by the other creditor countries: Britain, France, Belgium, Sweden, Switzerland, and Holland. Because of the great demand for funds to finance highways, railroads, public utilities, oil wells, and so forth, foreign investors were offered much higher interest rates than were obtainable in their home markets. The influx of capital not only caused serious inflation but in certain instances was used for unproductive ventures, some loans eventually proving to have been unwisely granted on the basis of overoptimistic expectations. However, in the great majority of cases the generosity of the lenders was not misplaced, and substantial amounts found their way into constructive enterprises and profitable undertakings. Nevertheless, when in 1930 world prices of most major export products of the Latin American continent tumbled to less than 50 percent of their previous levels new investments ceased and the effect on the foreign exchange position of the area was calamitous. Partial or total default on many issues and inability to pay private short-term obligations arising from too heavy imports were the immediate result. As the world depression deepened, it led to widespread exchange controls and excessive note issues by the hard-pressed central banks. In 1936 Colombia, Peru, and Bolivia suspended payment of interest and amortization on their foreign debt. Chile, Brazil, and Uruguay curtailed their remittances to the banks servicing their external loans. Even some Argentine provinces and municipalities became partially or completely insolvent; only the national government continued to honor its obligations.

Exchange control measures to cushion the effects of the growing currency stringency were introduced in Venezuela, Ecuador, and Paraguay besides the countries already mentioned. In the latter two countries, and also in Chile and Bolivia, the local banks suspended the remittance of foreign exchange to cover export bills received for collection from abroad, and shippers, through their banks, had to grant delays until sufficient dollars or other foreign moneys could be accumulated for the settlement of the overdue drafts. During this period, too, Brazil and some of the other east coast countries experimented, to their cost, with German and Italian barter schemes that were advanced on the ground that they relieved the buyer of securing hard currencies.

Concerned over the financial problems created by the war, the Seventh Pan American Conference at Panama set up in September, 1939, the Inter-American Financial and Economic Advisory Committee. This committee recommended to the governments of the South American republics the creation of an inter-American bank. The future development of inter-American trade was regarded as depending to no small extent on two factors: (1) the degree to which the Latin American nations would be able to sell their products in the United States and Canada and (2) the volume of short- and long-time credits that they could secure for the financing of their commercial operations. The various countries were to be invited to participate in general proportion to their commercial importance; the Argentine, Brazil, and the United States would lead, with minimum capital subscriptions of 5 million dollars each, and the bank would be chartered under an Act of Congress in the United States. One of the purposes of the bank was to help bring about more stable currency conditions in the South American countries; another was the promotion of a broader investment of funds and the extension of intermediate and long-time credits to or under the guarantee of the interested governments. Furthermore, the authors of the project sought to encourage loans in local currencies that did not command an active international market.[1] However, with the progress of the discussions for the Monetary Fund and the International Bank for Reconstruction, the plans concerning an inter-American bank gradually faded into the background.

The Second World War virtually wiped out a large number of the best markets for Latin America's agricultural and mineral production. Henceforth a greater proportion of her exports had to be diverted to the United States and Canada, a change that was soon reflected in the turnover of the dollar accounts of the local banks in the United States. The avalanche of orders pouring into the offices of United States importing houses became especially conspicuous during the fall and winter of 1939, when the former suppliers in Europe found themselves unable to fill the orders of their Latin American customers because of the British blockade of the Atlantic. On the other hand, United States importers found it difficult for the same reasons to purchase handicrafts, cutlery, and glassware formerly supplied by central Europe and thereupon proceeded to study the possibility of obtaining some of these goods in Central and South America.

Brazil, Uruguay, Chile, and Peru suffered especially from the disruption of their customary European markets, which were their main sources of foreign exchange and on which they principally relied for the necessary equilibrium in their balance of payments. Prior to 1939 Europe had taken 50 percent of Latin American exports; the United States accounted for only about 30 percent. Because of their dependence before the war on European consumption, the South American republics were particularly vulnerable to political and economic upheavals in Europe, for each time their transatlantic sales receded, their monetary situation was affected. On the other hand, when their money crops suffered from drought or other fateful dispensations of

[1] Source: Harry P. Hillen, "The proposed Inter-American Bank," New Brunswick, Graduate School of Banking, Rutgers University, 1931: a multigraphed thesis.

the elements, or when the prices of copper, rubber, or oil declined, owing to the ensuing reduction of income of the local producers and shippers, there was an immediate slump in the demand for United States automobiles and other luxury or consumption articles usually purchased from the Northern neighbor. At such times unfavorable internal economic conditions in the tropical regions of South America would be reflected in a scarcity of foreign exchange, which in turn would handicap United States industries established south of the Equator in converting their profits into dollars.

Occasionally a demand would develop on the part of United States companies and business houses operating in the Argentine, Brazil, and so forth, for three and six months' advances in pesos, cruzeiros, or other local currencies. For obvious reasons their home offices were reluctant to remit dollars because of the risk of serious losses should the exchange into which these dollars had to be converted for local pay rolls or payments for raw materials and commodities decline before the branch managers had completed the shipments with which to reimburse the parent company for its advances. In addition, there was always the threat of exchange controls or restrictions being imposed in the meantime, freezing or blocking their funds for indefinite periods. By guaranteeing the local banks that they would refund any loans made to the American subsidiaries, the United States banks played a helpful role. Not only did the native institutions charge lower interest rates than if no bank guarantee were furnished but also they were generally anxious to earn thus the good will of the American guarantor, who could reciprocate with similar facilities in dollars. Sometimes exchange conditions were favorable enough for United States banks to make these currency advances for their own account by swapping, that is, buying the currency in the foreign exchange markets and selling the equivalent for future delivery.

In the meantime, because of the growing public attention to the Hemispheric trade, many United States banks became interested in developing closer connections with their counterparts in the principal Latin American states. Toward the end of 1940 Nelson Rockefeller, the youthful and enterprising head of the Office of the Coordinator of Inter-American Affairs, sent a mission to visit the leading cities of the west and east coasts of South America to further both the trade and the cultural relations between the American republics.

The remarkable success of the efforts of United States officials, businessmen, and bankers to maintain economic stability in the South American republics during what was for them a most hazardous period was brought out during a visit of some New York bankers to the continent's main financial centers in 1941. From Ecuador south down the west coast and up the east coast increased purchases by the United States had been the prime factor in replacing the lost or shrunken outlets in Europe. One direct result was an improvement in the exchange situation in many countries. In connection with the United States defense program considerable purchases of nitrate and copper were effected. In addition, other mineral and agricultural products were shipped in considerable volume as substitutes for commodities formerly obtained elsewhere, the most valuable item in this category being raw wool, which Uruguay, Peru, and the Argentine sold to the United States in large quantities at prices considerably above prewar levels. Brazil, Colombia, and other coffee-producing countries were also materially aided during this period by the higher quotations that resulted from the coffee quota system adopted by the producing countries for the protection of the growers. However, serious problems continued to haunt some of these countries: Argentina was looking for a market for her surplus corn and wheat, while Peru and Brazil suffered the loss of the Japanese market for their cotton, which had usually been paid for in United States dollars.

In the fall of 1941, in line with its recognized policy of supporting the Allies, the United States Treasury requested all banks with branches in Central and South America to abstain thereafter "from business dealings with nationals whose names appeared on the Proclaimed List." Any loans on demand outstanding to such nationals were to be called immediately, and time loans at their maturity. No further facilities were to be extended, and any transactions in the accounts of other customers in the Central and South American branches that appeared to be for account of nationals on the proclaimed list thenceforth to be subject to license.

A little later, as evidence of our desire to assist the Latin American countries under the existing trying conditions, the Export-Import Bank informed the South American central banks that it was prepared to extend lines of credit additional to those already accorded South American private banks by United States commercial banks. These supplementary credits, the conditions of which were exceptionally favorable, were for the purpose of financing exports from the United States to the Southern continent, the Export-Import Bank under their terms insuring the arrival of the merchandise; under certain circumstances the bank was willing to maintain the credit even though the merchandise had to be stored in local warehouses pending settlement of the invoices by the buyers. These special lines of credit covered essential products that the commercial banks were not in a position to carry, the routine details being handled by the latter under the instructions and the responsibility of the Export-Import Bank. The credits were limited to "exceptional cases where neither the importer nor the exporter is agreeable, in the face of an increasing war defense economy and summary regulations, to assume the risks incidental to the delivery of the goods from plants to ports of destination." Inasmuch as the commercial banks were restricted by Federal Reserve regulations as to the character of the transactions that they might finance by means of acceptances, it was only through the helpful intervention of the Export-Import Bank that they were able to participate in these credits, as well as, for that matter, to compete with European government-sponsored guarantee schemes in supplying medium-term private credit.

After America joined the Allies, the imperative need of United States industry to concentrate on the manufacture of war material compelled the Washington administration to enforce a stricter policy as to the issuance of export licenses for the wide variety of goods and articles usually ordered by South American commission houses. The loss of valuable sources of supply, such as rubber, tin, and other raw materials made it essential that our short domestic stocks be carefully husbanded. Accordingly, even at the risk of hurting trade relations with the Latin American countries the outstanding general export licenses for agricultural implements, electrical machinery, and iron and steel manufactures using the scarce materials or employing industrial facilities needed for more pressing purposes, were reluctantly revoked.

By the spring of 1942 what remained of private export trade had become practically limited to modest shipments of consumption goods to the Caribbean islands and intermittently to Central and South America. Because of the priority of military traffic, serious congestion handicapped the movement of export freight in most United States ports. A permit system was introduced by the railroads because of the acute shortage of shipping and warehouse facilities at seaport points and the employment of freight cars as temporary storehouses at the ocean terminals. While the Coordinator of Inter-American Affairs did his utmost to obtain preferential treatment for the countries whose good will it was his task to promote, United States exports declined sharply until the Allies succeeded in coping with submarine warfare and began to benefit from the new freight carriers in course of construction at our shipyards. All these factors, together with the developing policy of concentrating all the nation's industrial power on the war, caused a general decline in the banking business conducted for Latin American banks.

Because of the shortage of exportable United States goods, Latin American dollar reserves started to accumulate in the commercial banks of New York, San Francisco, and other financial centers. Owing to the reduced shipping facilities and the wartime restrictions on United States exports, the merchants below the Rio Grande could not use their balances for urgently needed goods, while their own exports increased greatly. Consequently, their deposits in the United States and England assumed unprecedented proportions, although this was also in part the result of the migration of European funds to Latin America; from there they were generally retransferred and deposited in United States banks. Whether owing to fears of a possible devaluation of the dollar or because the totals exceeded the limits fixed by the local financial authorities for deposits with United States commercial banks, the fact is that beginning in the late thirties the banks of issue in Latin America (and also in Europe) concentrated a growing share of their dollar reserves at the Federal Reserve banks.

For the reasons described above, the volume of commercial credits opened by Central and South American banks and business houses decreased substantially during the years following our entry into the war. However, as stressed elsewhere, this loss of private trade financing was offset to some extent by the banking accommodation required by the United States Government agencies, most of which, in connection with their purchases of strategic and critical materials, increasingly had recourse to the services of United States commercial banks with overseas facilities. Moreover, during this period these agencies themselves made longer-term advances to the Latin American republics not only to assist them in obtaining needed capital goods but also in the interest of defense objectives.

By 1945 the foreign exchange resources and gold stocks of the Latin American countries had risen to nearly four billion dollars. Not only were they thus enabled to reduce their foreign short-term debts but their improved financial position also rendered easier the financing of current business and encouraged the hope that when the postwar readjustment was finally in sight some of the countries at least would have important reserves available in the form of deposits, earmarked funds, and gold to promote the exchange stability of their currencies. Moreover, the considerable holdings accumulated during the war seemed to offer several years' protection against the possible reversal in economic conditions that was predicted after the end of the war. A postwar resumption of credit relations, both short- and long-term, would also depend, it was generally agreed, on both internal political conditions and in certain states a distinctly more favorable legislative attitude toward foreign capital. Too often, exchange controls maintained beyond apparent need, restrictive labor laws, and regulations that prevented the repatriation of direct capital investments or remittances on account of earnings, were not conducive to the revival of confidence or incentives for the extension of large-scale foreign credits.

Undoubtedly, with the passage of time and the strengthening of the economic and financial structure of the South American republics and the lessening of the danger of periodic crises, the role of the dispensers of private credit in Latin America will continue to grow in importance. The Second World War has strikingly illuminated the interdependence of the countries of the Western Hemisphere and has forcibly brought home the truth to United States bankers and businessmen that in the critical times ahead the utilization and further development of the natural resources of the Latin American world should be one of their most pressing and responsible tasks.

In the spring of 1950 after a severe postwar decline the combined gold and dollar reserves of the Latin American countries had again reached the 3 1/2 billion dollar level. Economic Administration purchases, an export surplus in their trade with Europe and the United States, as well as new capital investments by foreigners notably in Uruguay—perhaps due to fears connected with the "cold war"—seem to have closed the dollar gap of the hemispheric nations as a whole. Other significant indications of a general improvement in financial conditions were reflected by a reduction in the global amount of outstanding collection items in some countries and a resumption of interest service on the defaulted bonds of certain nations owing to the carrying into effect of debt adjustment plans by Colombia, Chile, and San Salvador.

ARGENTINA

The Argentine economy in the first quarter of this century depended mainly on agriculture, and consequently the vicissitudes of the weather, and on the ability of Europe to buy and pay for the bulk of the domestic production of wheat, linseed, meat, wine, tobacco, cotton, and other commodities. The banking requirements of the local merchants, importers, exporters, and farming population were more than amply satisfied by the native and foreign banks operating in Buenos Aires and in other business centers in the provinces. In fact, in the middle thirties the country seems to have been rather overbanked. British, Canadian, and a number of European banks had offices or affiliated institutions in or near the financial district of the capital, while two prominent American banks, the National City Bank of New York and the First National Bank of Boston, maintained their own branches in spacious and impressive quarters.

Among the managers of these various banks ardent competition developed for the accounts of the important European grain firms that had their buying organizations and elevators in the republic and for the foreign and local banking operations of the wealthy owners of cattle ranches and haciendas and in general for the trade of the European and other foreign nationals who had settled in the Argentine.

With one or two exceptions the condition of the native banks prior to the Second World War was considered strong. The credit standing of the Argentine Government and the rating of its bonds also were high. Notwithstanding, there were periodic shortages of exchange, rendering it desirable to place restrictions on the sale of foreign currencies, while in 1935–1936 it became necessary to enter into clearing and barter arrangements with Germany. In 1937, because of the scarcity of capital, the Argentine banks offered to take time deposits in pesos at attractive rates or sell short-term Argentine Treasury bills. As the peso for forward delivery commanded a premium at that time, and as opportunities for employing short-term funds at equivalent rates were lacking in the United States, the interest plus the profit on the purchase and sale of the pesos were alluring enough to attract a certain amount of United States money.

The Argentine central bank exercised close control over interest rates as well as the terms of the local banks in their routine operations. Because of the large number of banks doing business in the republic and the struggle for local accounts, the Argentine Ministry of Finance frowned upon plans for the opening of additional offices on the part of foreign banks. However, the two United States banks that were established in the republic made important contributions to the mercantile progress of the country. One of them took an important part in underwriting and selling Argentine bonds and stocks, and in the forties it was said to have issued more commercial credits than all the other local banks combined. Both institutions, with their fully integrated banking services, were a credit to United States banking in overseas countries.

In July, 1940, the Export-Import Bank granted a credit of 20 million dollars to the central bank, for the purpose of facilitating the exportation to Argentina of United States agricultural commodities and manufactures. The credit was covered by three-year promissory notes of the central bank with an interest rate of 3.6 percent. Of the risk, 85 percent was guaranteed by the Export-Import Bank, while the remaining 15 percent was assumed by the participating United States commercial banks. In November, 1940, negotiations for further credits took place in Washington, with the objective of strengthening the financial and economic situation not only in the Argentine but also in Chile and Uruguay.

During the first year or two of the war Argentina lived on her exchange reserves, many of her foreign markets having been cut off. Gradually, however, her exchange position deteriorated, especially since Great Britain, because of tonnage and foreign currency deficiencies, reduced her Argentine purchases of meat and grain. Because of the closing of its chief markets in Europe, the Argentine Government considered curtailing the country's imports from the United States, a threat that naturally caused concern in United States export circles. Gradually exchange control became more stringent. Imports without prior permission of the central bank were prohibited. Permits were only issued if payment was made at the "free" exchange rate, usually 15 to 20 percent above the official quotation, American imports being thus penalized in the form of an indirect import levy.

Before the war the leading Argentine banks had had large lines of commercial credits at their disposal in the United States, available, according to custom, against delivery of full sets of shipping documents. The latter covered United States manufactured goods such as radios, refrigerators, farm machinery, and—if they were not fabricated or assembled in local United States branch factories—autos, motors, tires, and other parts of the mechanical equipment that the Argentine people preferred to those of European make. As the effects of the war spread throughout the international scene, the branches of German and Italian banks in Latin America, which before 1939 had been among the most aggressive, lost many of their depositors and customers.

The establishment of the Foreign Funds Control by the United States Treasury and the growth in the list of countries whose assets were subject to freezing and licensing regulations caused increasing apprehension in the Latin American countries. Some Argentine banks, in particular, were much concerned lest their United States balances should be blocked or free disposal of their deposits be hindered or made subject to close investigation as to actual ownership. Accordingly, it was not surprising that the Argentine dollar accounts in United States banks were substantially reduced. Upon instructions of the central bank, the Buenos Aires banks notified all foreign residents carrying United States dollar accounts with them that they would have to either convert their dollars into pesos or close their dollar accounts. Some of the dollar withdrawals at that time may also have been due to the renewed talk of a possible further devaluation of the dollar, caused by the debate in Congress on a bill authorizing the President to continue fixing the gold content of the dollar.

In the spring of 1943 the Argentine peso, which in prewar days had often been influenced by the fluctuations of the pound, advanced in the New York market to 25.25 cents, equivalent to 3.96 pesos to the dollar, compared with a rate of 23 cents in 1939. This unusual rise was apparently due in part to the conversion by fearful foreigners of some of their dollars into Argentine money, in obedience to the old rule not to put all their eggs in one basket. In addition, it was believed that the Germans were accumulating funds in the neutral republic, whence they expected to be able to finance propaganda and espionage activities in Allied countries without fear of detection or reprisal.

To the Argentine Treasury the rise in the national currency was most unwelcome. The dollar rate for the peso was the highest in four years. In order to prevent serious monetary disturbances, all movements of funds in and out of the country were placed under strict supervision. President Peron's Minister of Finance declared that this provision would remain in effect so long as the emergency lasted and until international transactions were normal again, explaining that, owing to the favorable balance of trade caused by the war, Argentina's gold and foreign exchange reserves amounted to more than 2 1/2 billion pesos, beyond which figure his country did not find it safe to invite new investment from abroad. However, the decree in question provided that new capital might enter the country if it could be shown that it was to be applied to productive purposes and that the funds did not represent floating resources that could be withdrawn at will. At the same time, the central bank issued new regulations making all noncommercial payments in pesos for foreign account subject to its authorization before they could be effected by the local banks.

In addition to the official buying rate for dollar exchange, different quotations were fixed for various kinds of exports and imports. Thus, purchases in the United States were subjected to a higher rate, depending, however, on whether they were "preferred" or "secondary" commodities or articles. Similarly, the rate for "irregular" exports differed from that for ordinary foreign shipments, while there also was a free market. As the war progressed its impact was more and more felt on the internal economy of the country. With dollars and sterling balances piling up there were steady increases in local bank deposits, note circulation, and the internal debt. Meanwhile, some of the blocked sterling assets were used to liquidate Argentine debts in England and to acquire Argentine railroad and public utilities from the British holders.

After the end of the war the huge dollar reserves were rapidly drawn down, and in consequence of its excessive swollen imports at inflated prices, the Argentine republic, along with its Latin American neighbors, was again confronted with serious foreign payment problems. Once more, although there was no concern about their ultimately surmounting their difficulties, the Argentine banks were seriously behind in the payment in foreign currencies of export bills held by them for account of United States banks, and there was a lack of available dollars to cover the commercial letters of credit opened in the United States for the payment of merchandise and equipment ordered by Argentine buyers, while the scarcity of foreign exchange was again preventing the local branches of United States corporations from obtaining dollars for the transfer to their parent concerns of the proceeds of local sales and the earnings due on the capital loaned them for their operations.

In November, 1950, the Export-Import Bank agreed to open a 3 ½ percent ten-year credit of 125 million dollars to ten Argentine banks under the guarantee of the Argentine central bank for the purpose of improving the credit position of the country by permitting the payment of the overdue collections owing to United States exporters and manufacturers. At the end of August, 1950, Argentina had devalued the peso for the second time since October, 1949, the new rate reducing the value of the peso to about 7 cents in the free exchange market. However, the special rates for imports and exports of certain essential goods were continued.

During the last part of 1950 and the first half of 1951, because of the world situation there arose a growing demand for Argentine wool, meat, grain, hides, and strategic materials with favorable effects on the republic's foreign exchange situation and the economic position of the country generally.

BRAZIL

Brazil, the largest of the South American republics, although endowed with immense natural resources, has had many financial vicissitudes during her long history. At the beginning of the First World War the Bank of Brazil had to cope with the serious conditions in the international exchange markets, which rendered it difficult and costly to cover the maturing obligations of Brazilian merchants in Europe. The latter had used substantial acceptance credits in sterling, francs, and marks, which they were now prevented from reimbursing promptly because of the interruption in shipping and the tightened credit conditions which hindered foreign importers of coffee and cocoa from paying their debts to the Brazilian shippers.

In 1931, owing to the difficulty of obtaining dollars for the settlement of their purchases from the United States, Brazilian importers again were obliged to ask for delays until sufficient dollar exchange was available for the settlement of the United States export bills held for payment by the Rio de Janeiro banks. Sir Otto Niemeyer, the adroit British Treasury expert, who had brilliantly discharged a similar task in Australia, was delegated by the London banks to study the situation. Now his mission was to counsel the Bank of Brazil, which, although a private corporation, acted as bank of issue and was the keeper of the country's gold and exchange reserves. Soon after Niemeyer's arrival, exchange control was introduced.

Two years later, in June, 1933, the Brazilian Funding Agreement was signed, under which United States exporters agreed to accept medium-term drafts in settlement of a portion of their unpaid bills. Subsequently, at the end of 1935, the Export-Import Bank, in order to assist both the United States merchants and the Brazilian Treasury, undertook to purchase without recourse the drafts held by individual United States exporters to the extent of up to 60 percent of the Brazilian promissory notes that were to be issued to them, provided that the aggregate did not exceed 17 million dollars. The Brazilian Government appointed a New York bank as its paying agent for the settlement of all the pending claims of United States shippers, and also obliged itself to deposit sufficient cash to pay in full all creditors having claims of $25,000 or less and to liquidate the remaining commercial debts by delivery of promissory notes payable monthly over a period of five years through the New York agent.

The Export-Import Bank was prepared to purchase these notes as agreed and was willing, moreover, to advance up to 100 percent against current exports, provided notes issued under the 1933 Funding Agreement were deposited as additional collateral. The National Foreign Trade Council, through a special committee, took a prominent part in implementing this settlement of a situation that for years had been a thorn in the development of United States trade with Brazil. It was estimated that about 15 million dollars of current debts covering shipments to Brazil were then overdue.

Because of the risk of depreciation in the foreign exchange value of the milreis, some American businessmen and corporations with offices in Brazil were reluctant to immobilize large amounts in plants and equipment. For the same reason their local purchases of cotton, rubber, coffee, and so forth were by preference financed through the medium of local bank overdrafts contracted under the guarantee of their banking correspondents at home. When the milreis quotations for immediate and for future delivery were about even, or when the forward contract commanded only a slight discount, the foreign exchange traders of United States banks were willing to "swap" by buying cable transfers on Rio or São Paulo with dollars and selling future contracts for the delivery of milreis to responsible United States or British counterparties.

The temptation of United States banks to open additional offices in Brazil remained checked by the growing governmental tendency to impose legal restrictions as to the nationality of the staff, amount of capital, and so forth. During the Second World War, indeed, this drift was even more in evidence: on April 9, 1941, Brazil ordained that after July 1, 1946, only those banks whose capital was wholly owned by Brazilian nationals would function in the country. However, on February 9, 1942, in response to the representations of the United States and Canadian governments, the decree was amended to exclude the North American banks. The similar exemptions granted later to other foreign institutions finally made the decree virtually a dead letter.

In 1937 Rio de Janeiro, the "Pearl City of Brazil," passed through a real estate boom. Urban real estate reached wildly inflated levels, and certain local banks engaged inordinately in the financing of buildings of various kinds.

During 1938, the servicing of Brazilian foreign bonds had to be discontinued. In February, Osvaldo Aranha, who then was Foreign Minister, conferred with high officials in Washington, and as a result of these conversations the United States Department of Commerce and the Treasury, in order to promote United States export trade, adopted a more generous policy with regard to credits not only to Brazil but to Latin American nations in general. Shortly thereafter the Export-Import Bank signed an agreement according to which eleven New York and out-of-town United States banks extended to the Bank of Brazil a credit for the creation of 19.2 million of dollar exchange. This credit was for a period of twenty-four months; it was guaranteed by the Export-Import Bank and was to be utilized by means of drafts on the participating banks at three months' sight, with renewal privileges for seven consecutive ninety-day periods. At each maturity, the Bank of Brazil engaged to make a minimum cash payment of 10 percent of the outstanding amount. The Export-Import Bank undertook to reimburse the American participants upon demand, an obligation that, moreover, was not conditioned upon a default on the part of the debtor.

In November, 1940, another loan, this time for 25 million dollars, was extended to the Bank of Brazil, available at the rate of 5 million a month. This credit was arranged by William L. Clayton, then Deputy Administrator, and was guaranteed to the extent of 80 percent by the Export-Import Bank, the balance of 20 percent being for the account and risk of the participating United States banks. The part that was not guaranteed by the Export-Import Bank carried interest at 3.60 percent.

As in other countries where foreign capital found it easy to penetrate, but sometimes difficult to withdraw from, foreign concerns desirous of operating in Brazil often canvassed the foreign exchange markets for possible ways of paying for the construction of new local plants, as by the acquisition of the cheaper "blocked" milreis. While adverse in principle to facilitating the creation of a black market for blocked bank balances, the Brazilian Government was at the same time anxious to promote the expansion of the country's manufacturing equipment. In certain cases it therefore authorized the use of frozen milreis deposits even to the extent of 100 percent of the cost of construction, if they belonged to American or British owners. Some deals were consummated at 4.50 cents per milreis, although the official quotation was in the neighborhood of 6 cents.

A number of schemes were elaborated by the foreign departments of the United States banks in an endeavor to assist United States concerns in the liquidation of their blocked assets abroad and converting them into dollars. The following example will illustrate the complex character of the transactions to which some owners resorted. A Brazilian group was known to be interested in buying sterling at a discount so that it could take over from the British owners a plant that the Brazilians wanted to bring under their national control. The Bank of England was disinclined to sell sterling for milreis converted at the official rate; on the other hand, the Bank of Brazil refused to sell sterling at the clearing rate fixed under the Anglo-Brazilian Clearing Agreement. It was an intricate situation with which various foreign exchange experts struggled until the following triangular trade was contrived. Certain United States owners of blocked sterling were eager to sell their holdings at a sacrifice, provided the approval of the Bank of England could be secured. After protracted negotiations, they were persuaded to accept payment from the Brazilian group, 50 percent in cash, payable immediately, and 50 percent in the form of long-term debentures of a Brazilian railway company. A responsible Rio de Janeiro brokerage house then agreed to purchase the debentures from the United States concern and to pay for them in dollars. In turn, the consent of the Bank of England was obtained for the British syndicate that owned the Brazilian plant to accept payment in blocked sterling. Thus, the Brazilians acquired the coveted property at a favorable price, settling for it in milreis; the United States owners disposed of their blocked sterling, collecting dollars from the Rio brokers; and the banking intermediaries were paid a well-earned commission.

The war brought great changes in the Brazilian economy. Coffee, cocoa, cotton, and the strategic materials—rubber, industrial diamonds, hides, and so forth—were the objects of an unprecedented demand. By early 1941 the immediate future was viewed with optimism; the republic was enjoying a period of internal peace, the Vargas government was apparently gaining public support, and once more there was ample foreign exchange at the disposal of the Bank of Brazil for legitimate needs. Indeed, the last Export-Import Bank credit of 25 million dollars had not even been drawn upon.

In April, 1941, the Export-Import Bank extended a credit of 20 million dollars to the National Steel Co. of Brazil to finance the purchase of material and equipment for the construction of a steel plant at Volta Redonda. The credit was secured by promissory notes of the borrower endorsed by the Bank of Brazil and guaranteed by the Brazilian Government. The notes were payable semiannually to October 1, 1955, with interest at 4 percent. According to its practice, the Export-Import Bank appointed several United States commercial banks as its agents to open letters of credit and make advances for account of the steel company under the Export-Import Bank's guarantee.

During the following period Brazil went through another of her periodic boom periods. The high prices for her raw material exports, swollen by the enormous demands of the Allies, produced a new wave of prosperity. The accumulation of dollar and sterling balances during 1942–1945, with imports severely curtailed, engendered an abnormal increase in local bank deposits and the note issue. This development in turn caused a mushrooming of small banks. Some optimists maintained that the country's foreign exchange and gold reserves were sufficient to carry it through at least ten postwar years. However, according to the information report of the Federal Reserve Bank of New York for October, 1949, the amount of Brazil's indebtedness on account of overdue export drafts amounted again to 118 million dollars.[2]

In July, 1951, plans were announced for the creation of an organization to supply private capital for the further development of the Brazilian economy under joint Brazilian–United States sponsorship.

CHILE

To the extent of about 65 to 70 percent, Chile's foreign revenues are derived from its production of copper, which for generations, together with the proceeds of the export of some other metals and minerals, has furnished this longest and narrowest of the South American republics with an abundant source of foreign exchange. Nevertheless, owing to the country's former dependence on two main exports, the periodic decline in the world's demand for its principal products has inevitably had deleterious effects on its economy.

Up to the First World War the ninety-day bill on London was the favorite means of financing Chile's international trade. At that time, however, under the leadership of the late Leopold Frederick, of the American Smelting and Refining Company, a former foreign department official of the National Bank of Commerce, the United States companies operating in Santiago and Valparaiso took the initiative in creating a market for dollar exchange, which henceforth was quoted regularly on the various South American bourses.

After the end of the First World War the Chilean peso suffered a calamitous setback, declining from 18 to about 7 pence until the influx of foreign capital in the middle twenties set in motion a new, if temporary, wave of prosperity. During the depression of the early

2 However, according to Alberto Castro Menezes, director of the Exchange Department of the Banco de Brazil, all frozen dollar obligations had been liquidated by September, 1950. Both import restrictions and the high price of coffee were believed to have been mainly responsible for the steady reduction of the short-term commercial dollar debts.

thirties copper and nitrate prices again slumped disastrously, and the Chilean economy suffered another severe check.

Like most of the other Latin American republics, Chile was forced at this moment to establish an official exchange control, which was known as Comision de Cambios Internacionales and was located in Santiago. The various United States corporations and business houses operating in Chile (particularly the West India Oil Company, the copper mining companies controlled by the Guggenheim family, Wessel Duval, and Cosach—the Anglo-Chilean Nitrate Company—which although partly British did the bulk of its trade in the United States), all were affected by the foreign exchange restrictions. Various expedients were resorted to by some United States enterprises in order to convert Chilean pesos into the dollars originally brought into and invested in the country. One construction company, for example, undertook with the money it had received in payment for its work and materials to acquire shares of a foreign mining corporation which enjoyed a market at the New York Stock Exchange. Prolonged negotiations, however, were necessary before it succeeded in inducing the Chilean exchange authorities to release the share certificates that were purchased by it and paid for in pesos, and permit their shipment to the United States where they were sold and converted into dollars.

For many years one of the most active banks in Chile was the Anglo-South American Bank, whose headquarters were located in London and whose conduct was in the hands of its experienced genral manager, Robert J. Hose, later its chairman. During more than a generation this institution financed successfully the Chilean nitrate industry. Finally, however, the demoralization of the nitrate market had disastrous repercussions on its main backer. The bank had outstanding credits and advances, which—according to an estimate then current—exceeded 6 million pounds sterling. As the deep involvement of the bank threatened to lower the standing of other British overseas and colonial institutions, a rescue syndicate, headed by the Bank of England, was organized in May, 1932, to carry for a period of three years the Anglo-South American Bank's loans to the constituent companies of Cosach. While this was not a permanent cure, it was hoped that when the nitrate situation mended an orderly liquidation might be effected.

The most prominent Chilean banks are the Banco Central de Chile

—the bank of issue—the Banco de Chile, and the Banco Espanol de Chile, all of which entertain close relations with United States banks.

The Export-Import Bank lent much financial support to Chilean undertakings, extending an initial credit of 12 million dollars to the Corporacion de Fomento de la Produccion in Santiago, primarily to finance the importation of United States industrial products. Later, the amount was increased to 17 million to foster hydro-electric development, being available against the promissory notes of the corporation repayable over four years. The contract permitted, in the event that the Chilean Government agreed to guarantee the repayment of the notes (as it later did) an extension to 1950.

By 1937 the outlook for the Chilean copper industry had improved considerably, owing to the rising demand from Japan and China, between which fighting had broken out, as well as from Europe, where rearmament was in full sway. Moreover, because of a nitrate shortage in the United States, nitrate sales increased to a more satisfactory level. Nevertheless, although general economic conditions were better the exchange situation remained precarious and the peso was offered at a discount in the black market.

In the United States the sale of Chilean nitrate was handled by the Chilean Nitrate Sales Corporation, whose New York office at this period was in charge of Kenneth Rockey, a former national bank examiner and a forceful executive. Previously, the firm of Guggenheim Brothers, then in control of the banking arrangements of the corporation, had financed the shipments by means of acceptance credits extended by New York banks under its guarantee. By reason of the excellent standing of the New York firm the business was keenly sought by the New York banks' foreign departments. Later, a syndicate credit took the place of the former private financing, secured by nitrate shipped to or stored in the United States, with a liberal margin based on the current international quotation.

For Chile the Second World War had mixed effects. Her gold and dollar reserves showed an auspicious increase, even though by comparison with those of the Argentine and Brazil they remained relatively moderate. The copper and nitrate industries again reported gratifying operating profits. In November, 1950, a free market was established in foreign exchange derived from non-commercial transactions and the inflow of foreign capital. The subsequent Export-Import Bank and International Bank loans were also encouraging factors.

SUMMARY

In the twenties European and United States capital poured into the Latin American republics for the development of their vast resources. When the worldwide depression set in many of these loans went temporarily or permanently into default, while exchange restrictions and barter were introduced. During the recent war extensive United States and British purchases brought about rapid recovery, exemplified by an accumulation of gold and foreign exchange. The latter, however, has been substantially decreased after the end of the struggle and indeed was temporarily replaced by a dollar shortage and the reappearance of controls of various kinds.

In Argentina banks of many other nations had settled even before two United States banks established branches after the First World War. Argentine credit generally stood high before the Second World War. Owing partly to the influx of refugee capital the peso before and during the war commanded a premium, especially since United States export restrictions limited the purchase by Argentina of American products needed in the United States for the war effort. After 1945 the exchange reserves were depleted, and a dollar scarcity existed.

The decline in exports to Europe during and since the Second World War has had similar repercussions in Brazil. Delays in the payment of United States exporters' invoices and drafts have been alleviated by loans of the Export-Import Bank.

Banking conditions in Chile have fluctuated with the world market for her principal exports—copper and nitrate.

VII

MIDDLE AMERICA

MEXICO

STUDENTS OF THE MONETARY HISTORY of this continent will find in the republic that borders the great State of Texas a prolific field for fruitful exploration. Indeed, Mexico has experienced successively the benefits of sound metallic money and the evils of wild currency inflation, which overtook her when, during the revolutionary period between 1912 and 1917, Huerta, Villa, and Carranza fought for the control of the country.

For centuries—ever since the Spanish conquest under Cortes—one of Mexico's most valuable sources of foreign income, next to oil, copper, lead, and the tourist industry, has been the mining and export of silver. Hence her prosperity has been dependent in no small measure on the price commanded by the white metal in the world's markets. The decline in its value in the late twenties and early thirties from 58 to 28 cents per ounce was therefore bound to have a profoundly disturbing effect on the Mexican economy. Similarly, the silver policy adopted in 1933 by the Roosevelt administration, which raised the price of newly mined United States silver first to 64 1/2 and later to 77.57 cents, caused the peso to rise so sharply as to force the Mexican Government to prohibit the exportation of Mexican silver coins. On the other hand, when, toward the end of 1935, the United States Treasury temporarily stopped its purchases of foreign silver, the Mexican silver industry suffered a severe setback, because of the decline of the world price of the metal to nearly 50 cents per ounce. Many of the smaller mining companies were forced to close until arrangements were completed by the Bank of Mexico, which as the bank of issue wields a great influence in the republic, for the sale of their output (about 25 percent of the country's production) in the London market. It was feared that the larger companies controlling the balance of 75 percent might also have to appeal for government help, and accordingly the Bank of Mexico was thereafter charged with the supervision of the sale for the benefit of all the local interests concerned.

For a number of years after the revolution Mexico found it possible to dispense with official exchange restrictions. Whenever it was necessary, the Bank of Mexico supported the peso by shipping gold—at times in the form of United States eagles—to New York or London for sale in the respective bullion markets. However, an exchange crisis broke out when, early in 1938, President Cardenas expropriated certain United States and British oil companies and the United States Treasury retaliated by canceling its orders for the purchase of silver. A few months later the Bank of Mexico requested the local banks to turn in all five-peso bills held by them or passing through their tellers' cages. According to law, these bills, which were known as "certificates," had to be backed by 12 grams of fine silver per peso, whereas the ordinary currency notes were secured by commercial rediscounts and by the country's metallic reserve in general. By withdrawing the monetary certificates from circulation and replacing them with currency notes the Mexican Treasury accomplished two objectives: they took over the silver cover back of the certificates, and by adding it to the central bank's reserves they broadened the base for the issuance of more currency notes. Because of the public commotion created by the measure, however, the local banks lost so many deposits that it was necessary to raise the rediscount limits of the member banks at the Bank of Mexico. Since the Mexican Federal government, moreover, at this time borrowed heavily from the bank of issue, the whole credit structure underwent a considerable expansion.

The sugar planters and mills, at the time of harvesting and during the grinding season, were accustomed to make heavy demands on the Mexican private banks. The financing of the crop took place through the medium of the National Union of Sugar Producers. As a rule the advances made by the banks were refinanced through rediscounts with the Bank of Mexico. In 1942, for instance, crop loans were made at the rate of 3 to 5 cents per kilo; the sugar, when sold wholesale, brought 18 to 19 cents. The banks were secured at all times by actual sugar, represented either by warehouse receipts or by bills of lading; there were no trust receipt privileges. The warehouses were considered responsible, as they were under the supervision of the National Banking Department. At retail, the sugar was then worth about 32 to 35 cents per kilo, and the banks accordingly had ample margin in the event of a drop in the price. Moreover, the large United States soft-drink manufacturers were in the market for any carry-over not absorbed by local consumers. The interest paid to the Mexican banks was in the neighborhood of 6 to 7 percent, of which they retained 3 percent after rediscount at the Bank of Mexico. The capital of the Union was relatively small compared with its current liabilities, and the Mexican banks therefore had to rely entirely on the value of the sugar.

In the fall of 1942 the Mexican Treasury took an intelligent and farseeing step by inviting the holders of Mexican external bonds in the United States, England, Spain, Portugal, Sweden, and Switzerland to register their holdings and deposit them with certain designated banks. This was done in order to obtain up-to-date reliable statistical data as to the distribution of the Mexican foreign debt, whose interest and sinking fund service had an important bearing on the country's foreign exchange situation. The Second World War had radically changed the economic outlook. The steady accumulation of gold and dollar balances suggested to the financial authorities that the time was opportune to propose a refunding arrangement to Mexico's foreign bondholders, who had been sadly neglected ever since the days of the Mexican Civil War. At about this time, too, a representative mission of engineers and bankers was delegated to Mexico, at the invitation of the President of Mexico, to study the condition of the national railways and to prepare recommendations to the Mexican Cabinet for the reorganization and modernization of the transportation system.

Because of the constant influx of capital from tourists, refugees, and foreign industry, the Bank of Mexico, early in 1943, was forced to intervene in the exchange market, but on this occasion to prevent a rise in the peso. Pegging it at 4.85 to the dollar, the bank gave orders to buy all the dollars offered at this price. During the year 1942 the resources of the bank had almost doubled, rising from 50 million dollars at the end of 1941 to almost 95 million at the end of 1942, a record high. The rise was due to greater Mexican exports, 95 percent of which went to the United States, and to lower imports because of the operation of the priority regulations. The growing resources in bullion and exchange caused rumors to circulate of a prospective revaluation of the peso, although conservative observers feared that a rise in the official value of the peso would prove detrimental to the country. They regarded the favorable balance of trade as most likely a temporary development, and thought that a reaction might set in as soon as a change in the world picture should bring about a decline in United States foreign purchases. Under the circumstances, monetary experts were inclined to favor the policy of pegging the peso to the dollar at the prevailing level and of freely selling gold to the public as recommended by Eduardo Villaseñor, former Under Secretary of Finance, who was now in charge of the destinies of the Bank of Mexico. Of middle height, with a high broad forehead and penetrating dark eyes, Villaseñor had the reputation of being one of the outstanding central bankers of Latin America. Economist, author of erudite articles and pamphlets on monetary subjects, and an eloquent speaker, he has represented his country with distinction at numerous conventions and conferences.

Whether it was his inspiration or not, the fact is that in the spring of 1943, the bank proceeded to convert some of its foreign balances into gold (part of which was purchased in Canada), which it earmarked at the Federal Reserve Bank of New York. While imports from the United States lagged, the improved economic conditions in Mexico were an incentive to more active contacts between United States and Mexican commercial banks in the field of short-term loans. Import credits were opened by United States banks to pay for various Mexican crops, such as hennequen, which was grown in Yucatan. Earlier experiences with the financing of sisal hemp back in 1921 had been deeply disappointing for the New York banks involved, but with the Defense Supply Corporation as the buyer the establishment of credits for hennequen and chick peas were transactions devoid of any risk. The hennequen was sold for distribution to United States consumers and fabricators; the peas were payable after inspection on their arrival in freight cars at the American side of the border. Like the Mexican sugar union, the Henequeneros de Yucatan concentrated the sale of their produce in their own hands, using acceptance credits of American banks, secured by the receipts of warehouses in Merida and Progreso in the state of Yucatan.

During the spring of 1943 the official rates for the dollar in Mexico continued to be held at 4.85 bid, 4.86 offered, equivalent to 20.576 cents per peso bid and 20.618 offered. At these rates the Bank of Mexico offered to absorb the daily positions of the local banks, and the market consequently fluctuated within these limits, the narrow spread often being reduced to 1/16 of a point between the buying and the selling rates.

Because of the continued transfers of funds to Mexico, arising from the flight of capital from Europe and the remittance of United States venture money for investment in Mexican enterprises and real estate, Villaseñor in public addresses and communications to American banks pointed out that the amount of liquid capital in the Mexican money market had risen to such an extent that it was causing unwelcome price rises and other deplorable disturbances in the national economy. For these reasons, he pointed out, loans by United States banks, while agreeable under different circumstances, were not welcome at this particular stage, as they were adding to the problems that the country was facing. Because of these abnormal conditions, the Mexican private banks were requested to abstain strictly from using any further United States credits.

Owing to the limitations placed upon their loaning activities, the Mexican commercial banks, notwithstanding a growth in deposits of, in certain cases as much as 50 percent, complained of their inability to make both ends meet. The decline in earnings was attributed to the increase in overhead, resulting from the higher cost of living. Still, there were new outlets for the energy and vision of Mexican banking talent. Several investment companies, some under charters of the Ministry of Finance, were formed during those halcyon years. Their object was to make fresh capital available to industrial corporations and to engage in all kinds of financial operations. Part of the capital was raised in Mexico; in some instances United States banking interests participated by subscribing to the stock of the companies and joining their boards of directors. United States cooperation was predicated on the role that it was thought the new enterprises might play in connection with the expansion of Mexican-American trade and also on the prospect of making what in the long run might prove a profitable investment.

However, in contrast to the encouragement given permanent investment capital, a plan of organizing another commercial bank in Mexico City—a project that was put forth by a group of wealthy men living in the interior of the country—was not looked upon with favor by the Secretaria de Hacienda y Credito Publico (the Ministry of Finance and Public Credit). This decision was not unexpected.

In the opinion of local United States bankers the city was overbanked. Until the large amounts of "hot money" that had found their way to Mexico had been withdrawn and more normal conditions had again been established, it was their opinion that it was best to remain on the sidelines. For the moment all the efforts of the government were directed toward preventing the inflationary symptoms from spreading still further as a result of too generous credit policies on the part of the existing local institutions. Moreover, it was pointed out that the strict labor laws and the taxes imposed on banks proved particularly burdensome in the case of United States branch offices, which were subject to double taxation. Yet American businessmen and trade emissaries, far from being discouraged, continued to arrive in the capital, keen to investigate openings for new connections and opportunities for the establishment of subsidiaries or agency offices.

The period of unprecedented prosperity enjoyed by Mexico continued without flagging throughout 1944. Contributing causes included increased production of practically all commodities except cereals and edible oils, the repatriation of Mexican capital previously invested abroad, higher prices for Mexican exports, increased government expenditures incidental to a country-wide program of public works, and the maintenance of the largest army in the history of the republic. An additional factor was the multiplication of credit-disbursing organizations, as a result of the creation in the preceding years of hundreds of small commercial banks, credit unions, finance companies, discount corporations, and investment syndicates. Consequently, real estate values had risen five to tenfold. Besides selling gold, the Bank of Mexico, in order to check further currency and credit expansion, raised the reserve requirements for member banks to 50 percent for banks in Mexico City and 30 percent for provincial banks, while interbank loans were prohibited entirely.

The note issue of the Bank of Mexico was now fully covered by gold and foreign exchange reserves of 390 million dollars. Only by official manipulation could the peso be prevented from appreciating against the dollar. The only shadow in the picture manifest to the United States visitor was the overloaned condition of some discount and finance companies, which had apparently made indiscriminate loans and investments, and which would certainly suffer sorely once deflation should set in. Many of these companies were the products of an irrational wartime optimism, and it was prophesied that in the postwar era there would be no room for them. Nevertheless, in the summer of 1950 the outlook for Mexico was again considered favorable, owing in part to the growth in gold and exchange reserves, the strengthening of the peso, and the higher export figures produced by the increased rearmament purchases of the United States. By January, 1951, the Mexican Government in order to stem the constantly growing influx of dollars, ordered that all increases in private bank deposits, except those of banks with less than 10 times their capital, be turned over to the Banco de Mexico. The rise in the world price of silver to 90 cents was expected to be reflected favorably in the country's balance of payments.

SUMMARY. Mexico's prosperity has always been largely dependent on the export of her considerable mineral and petroleum resources. In the thirties it was enhanced by the rise in the world price of silver due to the operations of the United States Treasury. It received a setback, however, when as a result of the expropriation of United States property and of other measures inimical to foreign investors, silver purchases were temporarily suspended by this country, and the price of metal slumped again. The considerable influx of United States and foreign capital during the Second World War caused severe monetary inflation, as well as a detrimental overexpansion in many directions. However, since 1949, because of increased exports in connection with expanded United States rearmament efforts the economic position has again materially improved.

CUBA

Until the outbreak of the Second World War Cuba was a typical one-crop country. As sugar went, so went Cuba. Sugar accounted for more than three fourths of the island's total exports. Tobacco was the second largest industry, but had gradually lost its importance as a substantial producer of foreign exchange. The last war greatly stimulated the mining and foreign sale of manganese and chromium, and the opening of manufacturing establishments concerned mainly with consumers' goods.

The sugar industry has had a checkered career. After 1921, during the peacetime deflation that succeeded the wild war boom, the price of raw sugar dropped spectacularly from more than 22 cents to about 3 1/2 cents. Severe losses were suffered by producers and middlemen who carried exorbitant unsold and unhedged supplies. The banks, both native and foreign, which had been overgenerous in the financing of the crop and of the raw sugar in warehouse made frantic calls for more collateral, but whatever additional thin margin was supplied was insufficient to cushion the drastic fall in the value of their security. Soon the hypothecated properties represented only a small fraction of the amounts that had been lent to the now insolvent plantations and *centrales.* There was no longer any prospect of selling in the formerly prominent sugar markets of London, Paris, and Hamburg. The control of the lands, mills, and plants of a great number of native borrowers and sugar companies owned by American investors passed into the hands of the lenders, and for many years thereafter heavy write-offs had to be reported in the annual statements of the banks involved.

Despite the disastrous experiences of the twenties, which were to be repeated though on a comparatively lesser scale during the world depression of the early thirties, the activities of the Cuban branches of United States and Canadian banks continued of necessity to be centered on the financing of the principal crops and trading activities of the island. Chastened by past experience, the banks now set up the so-called dead-season and other credits so conservatively, as a rule, that despite the low prices prevalent prior to 1939 there was seldom any difficulty in collecting the amounts advanced to the *centrales.* A pro-rata payment per bag was collected from the sugar mills, so that in practice repayment of the dead-season credits began simultaneously with the grinding of the cane. Every year, generally in the spring and early summer, lines of credit were approved by the banks' home offices covering dead-season loans for the planting of the cane and the purchase of fertilizer, burlap, and jute bags, as well as for the post-grinding advances against raw sugar and molasses. As a rule these loans were conditioned upon the prior sale or hedging of the sugar in the futures' market. Certain brokers and companies carried stocks of raw sugar during the whole year, but in most cases sugar loans were paid off during the fall.

This business was vigorously solicited by the banks that were equipped for handling its frequently complex details, and at the approach of a new crop season the Cuban sugar factors and local mills would take rightful advantage of the existing competition to bargain for lower terms. During the war, owing to shipping difficulties, the loans were outstanding for longer periods. This, however, rendered them even more attractive to the banks after the United States Government agencies had entered the field as purchasers of the crop. From then on, it was no longer necessary to fix a time limit within which the sugars had to be placed on board ship. Even though the loans were spread over as long a period as ten months the banks now had an "umbrella" that justified lower rates to those borrowers who had sold their crop to the United States Government.

A few of the soundest United States sugar companies which had successfully weathered the various crises or had undergone thorough financial and managerial reorganization were granted unsecured grinding season credits, with the understanding that upon demand the loans would be secured by sugars legally pledged on a satisfactory margin basis and also that the borrower would confine his financing to the lending institution. The funds so obtained were used for the purchase of cane from the *colonos* and for the payment of materials, supplies, and so forth. In addition to the making of raw and refined sugar, some of the borrowers made alcohol out of cane in their own distilleries, selling it to gin manufacturers and wholesalers in the United States.

There was practically no capital market in the republic. For this reason the banking functions were generally limited to routine deposit and exchange transactions. From time to time the Cuban Government was a borrower from the Clearing House banks in Havana. In 1935 the Export-Import Bank made a contract with the Cuban Treasury in which it agreed to finance the purchase of silver for coinage of 20 million Cuban pesos which had been authorized by the Cuban Congress. The Philadelphia Mint undertaking the coinage and shipment of the silver pieces to Havana, the pesos were being delivered to the Havana Agency of the Federal Reserve Bank of Atlanta (closed in 1938). The Cuban Government's seigniorage profit on the transaction amounted to roughly 270 percent, for the Export-Import Bank received payment only for the actual cost of the silver metal plus the fee charged by the Mint for its services, or $185,000 per 500,000 silver pesos, equivalent, when placed into circulation in Cuba, to $500,000. Consequently, the Cuban Treasury, whenever its cash position ran low, found it advantageous to renew the operation. The Clearing House members readily complied with the recurring demands for three months' accommodation, since they were amply secured by the incoming silver pesos which generally passed on a par with the United States dollar.

Nevertheless, as the volume of Cuban pesos circulating locally began to increase and the deficits in the Cuban budget created growing concern, the peso came to be quoted at a small discount, which gradually rose, until in the fall of 1938 it was offered at 3 percent below the dollar.

Coincident with the disheartening fall of the price of raw sugar to 1.90 cents per pound, Colonel Batista, who meanwhile had become President, had early in 1939 introduced a revalorization bill in the Cuban Congress. This proposed to set up a sliding schedule for the cutting down of old Cuban public and commercial debts. Those incurred prior to 1933 were to be reduced by 50 percent, and the balance was to be amortized over a period of 30 years; loans made after 1935 and still outstanding were to be decreased by 25 percent, the remainder being similarly repaid out of a 30-year sinking fund. As was to have been expected, this bill was strenuously opposed by the foreign banks established on the island, the trustees of Cuban loans, the chambers of commerce, and a strong committee of Cuban citizens who derived their livelihood from the sugar and tobacco industries. All argued that such a measure would ruin the internal and external credit of the country and would in the future eliminate any possibility of loans being extended by foreigners for the support of local industry. Warren L. Pierson, head of the Export-Import Bank, pointed out the harmful effect such a law would have on the friendly attitude of United States financial circles, and the Havana Clearing House also waged an energetic campaign against the bill. The Cuban cabinet had been flirting with the Export-Import Bank in an effort to obtain a credit for public works and perceived fully that the passage of the bill would preclude their government from securing additional funds from this source. The bill was finally dropped.

The atmosphere becoming more favorable after the outbreak of the war in Europe, the Export-Import Bank, in July, 1941, accorded a credit of 11.3 million dollars to the Cuban Sugar Stabilization Institute. The credit was secured by warehouse receipts for sugar and was fully guaranteed by the Cuban Government; the notes to be created under the credit were to run for five years. The United States banks with branches in Cuba participated in the credit, but because it was unconditionally guaranteed by the Export-Import Bank and could be terminated by either party upon ten days' notice, the interest rate accorded the banks was moderate. Advances were made on the basis of $4.00 per bag on sugar stored in Cuba. As a further security in addition to the sugar pledged, the proceeds of the sugar and a tax of six cents per bag were hypothecated to the lenders. Repayment was to be made in five annual installments, beginning one year from the date of the notes. The interest to be paid by the borrower was fixed at 3.6 percent per annum.

In February, 1942, the financing of the sugar crop was taken over by the United States Government Defense Supplies Corporation. Again the three United States banks—the National City Bank, the Chase National Bank, and the First National Bank of Boston—shared in the credit, which was fully guaranteed by the Reconstruction Finance Corporation. Owing to this quasi-government guarantee, the interest rate was practically identical with that for United States Treasury Bills. A commission was paid the banks for handling the warrants and other routine details on behalf of the Defense Supplies Corporation. Since it was impossible to secure war risk and cyclone insurance on the sugars and molasses which were stored in various parts of the island, these risks were assumed by the lender. The advances were made on the basis of 90 percent of the purchase price, c.i.f. United States ports. Since the shipment of currency from the United States to Cuba was rather costly, because of the high premium for war risk insurance, the United States Treasury agreed to keep adequate balances in its accounts with the Havana branches of the three banks in order to supply the cash for the substantial advances required in connection with the transaction. The larger portion of the credit was repaid by the Defense Supplies Corporation before the end of 1942; the balance was renewed for a period not exceeding six months, the obligation now being assumed by the Commodity Credit Corporation and guaranteed by the United States Treasury.

In line with the United States policy of lending effective aid to all the Allies, the Defense Supplies Corporation, in the summer of 1942, agreed to pay 90 percent of the purchase price to the Cuban sellers of sugar still awaiting shipping accommodation to the United States, this advance to be completely free of interest. Thus, the corporation to all intents and purposes took over from the United States banks and other local institutions all the sugar loans on which the borrowers had heretofore been obliged to pay interest. In order to mobilize the required funds, the Defense Supplies Corporation borrowed the equivalent from the three United States banks. The generous gesture had a most salutary effect on the Cuban economy, resulting in a large inflow of capital which would ordinarily have been spread over a number of months.

In November, 1942, the proposed purchase of the 1943 sugar crop brought a Cuban mission to Washington, headed by Garcia Montes, former Minister of Finance and prominent leader of the Havana bar. The Cuban negotiators and the representatives of the State Department, the Commodity Credit Corporation, and the Board of Economic Warfare found it a laborious task to arrive at an agreement as to the quantity to be acquired both of raw sugar and of invert and blackstrap molasses, by-products of sugar manufacture used for cattle-feed and alcohol. The price was another delicate subject, for the reason that sugar was rationed in the United States and a ceiling price had been fixed for the benefit of the United States consumer. Moreover, some members of the Washington administration had been perturbed by the earnings reported by certain Cuban companies with substantial American stock ownership. The critics, however, failed to take into account the fact that the capitalization of many Cuban corporations was disproportionately small, owing to the heavy write-offs made in the twenties and thirties, which involved disastrous losses for United States stockholders. The cost of producing the Cuban sugar crop was calculated by experts at 1.08 cents per pound. Finally, an agreement was reached on February 23, 1943, under which a United States Government agency would buy 2,700,000 short tons at 2.65 cents per pound delivered alongside ship; 300,000 tons were reserved for export, and 225,000 were allotted for Cuban consumption. The purchase was made by the Commodity Credit Corporation, as was also that of the subsequent 1944 crop. The terms for the latter were essentially the same as for the 1943 crop, the signature of the Commodity Credit Corporation being guaranteed by the United States Treasury. The 1944 agreement also covered molasses and Cuban alcohol purchased by the Defense Supplies Corporation.

Although the United States banks now had the benefit of the indirect guaranty that was furnished through the sale of raw and refined sugar to a responsible buyer, compliance with the numerous administrative requirements of the purchaser nevertheless called for the deployment of all the technical facilities at the disposal of the banks' Cuban branch offices. While the risk was considerably reduced, the earnings, too, suffered a material decline. In the past, local interest rates had ranged at times as high as 8 to 9 percent. However, for companies whose majority stock holdings were in United States hands and whose financial standing was of the highest the rate applied was as low as 2 1/2 percent, being governed by the interest charged to first-class commercial borrowers at home.

Early in 1943 the banks were confronted with a new difficulty in connection with the insurance of their collateral. At that time the Cuban Government had made it obligatory for the sugar producers to take out their insurance through a so-called Equalization Fund established by the Cuban Sugar Stabilization Institute, a contribution of 47 cents per bag having to be made to this Fund on each bag of sugar shipped. For many years, the British and United States insurance companies had enjoyed a practical monopoly of this business; the banks felt safe under the protection of policies issued by strong underwriters located in London, New York, Philadelphia, and other United States cities, for they all operated under the supervision of competent managers and directors. Henceforth, under a new law, insurance contracts arranged by Cuban brokers had to be underwritten to the extent of 20 percent by Cuban insurance companies, while 80 percent of the risk could be assumed by United States and British underwriters. Therefore, for their protection the banks required at first that the reinsurance contracts taken out with Lloyd's of London or with United States and various other English insurance companies be assigned to the Cuban Sugar Stabilization Institute in order that any losses would be payable directly to the latter. When on June 1, the Commodity Credit Corporation announced its willingness to pay 90 percent of the cost of the 1943 sugar crop, the problem lost its importance, for it was clear that the total sugar loans on the books of the banks were likely to be quickly reduced.

In April, 1943, another difficulty arose for foreign banks operating in Cuba, when Cuba passed a new tax law. Under it a tax of 0.15 percent per month was due on all deposits maintained in foreign countries by any bank established on the island in excess of 10 percent of the bank's total deposits. The law also fixed a time limit of ten days during which the owners could divest themselves of the dollars received in payment for sugar sales made in the United States and elsewhere. The United States bank managers promptly applied to the Cuban Treasury for release from this tax to the extent that their advances to the Commodity Credit Corporation were affected by the law. One local bank officer expressed the opinion that the Cuban Government appeared firmly resolved to force all Cuban and foreign corporations to repatriate any foreign exchange and investments that they held abroad. The law, moreover, created or increased certain other taxes bearing on the operations of United States branches. A tax of 3 per mil was imposed on the capital with which foreign banks were carrying on business in Cuba, as well as a tax on bills of exchange, a tax of 1 1/2 per mil on any funds or assets owned by individuals or corporations, whether Cuban or foreign, outside of Cuban territory, and finally a 15 percent tax on excess profits over and above 10 percent of the capital employed in their operations.

Because of the provisions of the new law, the United States banks were reluctant to sign an agreement with the Commodity Credit Corporation for the financing, on a demand-loan basis, of the 90 percent payment that the corporation was willing to make on account of the purchase consideration for the 1943 crop. Finally, in order to facilitate matters the corporation arranged with the United States Treasury to provide the American bank branch offices in Cuba with sufficient dollar currency to meet the demands made upon them in connection with the movement of the sugar from the interior and Cuban ports to its United States destination. On its part, in an effort to placate the banks, the Cuban Government issued a decree exempting the banks from the 2 percent export tax, which would have been levied at the moment when the United States branches in Havana, at the end of the season, were obliged to instruct their home offices to return to the United States Treasury the funds advanced by it on behalf of the Commodity Credit Corporation.

However, the decree in question did not waive the second tax of 0.15 percent per month on deposits accruing in the United States dollar accounts of the branches after the Commodity Credit Corporation had finally credited the banks for the proceeds of the sugar purchased by it during the 1942 season. Accordingly, the United States Ambassador, Spruille Braden, made urgent representations to the Cuban Prime Minister to the effect that the banks should be relieved of the payment of a retroactive tax on transactions that had redounded to the benefit of the Cuban economy and in fact had greatly contributed to the island's prosperity. In the end, another decree cleared up this difference, but not until the Cuban cabinet was informed that the United States banks had delayed extending a credit to the Defense Supplies Corporation that was intended for the settlement due Cuban sellers of molasses.

In September, 1943, the native employees of the foreign banks in Cuba sought to form a Bank Employees Syndicate. In each bank committees were formed which submitted the syndicate's demands to the managers, one of them going so far as to claim the right to be consulted with respect to the classification of the clerks concerning promotions. The demand was strongly resisted by the top executives of the banks who refused to surrender their right to select those employees whom they deemed to be entitled to advancement.

In the years prior to and during the Second World War, United States currency was legal tender in Cuba, whose circulating medium consisted to a large extent of Federal Reserve Bank notes. The Cuban peso certificates were secured by silver pesos, gold and United States currency. During the grinding season the demand for currency often drove silver pesos to a moderate premium. In June, 1944, the peso circulation was reported to amount to 198 million pesos. At that time the Cuban Treasury held as a reserve 45 million United States dollars gold deposited with the Federal Reserve Banks of a current value of 70 million dollars, and silver coins to the amount of 80 million. According to some estimates the total amount of United States bank notes then also circulating in the island must have exceeded 90 million dollars.

The inflow of money, caused by heavy United States war expenditures, as well as by the tax on assets held outside the republic, brought about a considerable growth of local deposits and cash holdings in all the foreign banks doing business in Havana. In the absence of a central bank [1] to exercise monetary control and act as repository for surplus funds, the banks became faced with an unusual situation. Because of the lack of sufficient vault space, deposits in both dollars and pesos were an actual burden instead of an asset, especially since insurance against burglary, riots, and civil commotion could be ob-

[1] On April 28, 1950, the National Bank of Cuba, which now provides the island with its own currency, was officially opened by President Carlos Prio Socarras who declared that the establishment of the bank marked the beginning of Cuba's economic independence.

tained only in relatively small amounts. Of course, however, in a prosperous Cuba there was little risk of revolution or social disorder. On the other hand, except during the few grinding months favorable opportunities were to a large extent lacking for lending money to responsible borrowers.

In September, 1944, President Grau San Martin took over office. One of the first acts of his administration was to abolish certain taxes that were considered unproductive. The tax of 3 percent per year on inactive accounts was immediately eliminated. This tax was particularly obnoxious to foreign depositors, and many accounts had been closed to escape it.[2] Since the start of the Korean crisis, with growing world demand for sugar, Cuba has entered upon a new period of prosperity and economic progress. According to a notice of the National Bank of Cuba the United States dollar ceased to be legal tender in Cuba after June 30, 1951.

PUERTO RICO

Sugar has long been the backbone of the Puerto Rican economy. Since 1942 the major part of the crop had been purchased by United States Government agencies under the terms of a contract very much like that with Cuba. In addition, the planting of sugar cane has been encouraged by the benefit checks distributed by the Agricultural Adjustment Administration. Tobacco, coffee, and rum were other important revenue producers for the island.

During the Second World War banking for the military forces played a considerable role on the island by reason of the large expenditures both by the United States Army and the Navy authorities and by the individual members of the various administrative contingents stationed in or temporarily visiting Puerto Rico. Moreover, the various defense programs absorbed large numbers of skilled and unskilled workmen who received higher than normal wages. On the other hand, the drastic decrease of transport accommodation for cargo from the United States mainland caused a marked shrinkage in insular trade, financed by the banks in the form of credits or of remittances to cover the importation of foodstuffs.

[2] In March, 1950, President Carlos Prio Socarras issued a decree reinstituting the tax on investments made abroad by Cuban citizens and foreign companies operating in Cuba, but reduced the rate from 0.15 percent per month to 0.08 percent.

There has always been keen competition for the banking business available in the island possession. In 1943, for instance, seven banks (three native, two Canadian, and two American) shared in the roughly 140 million dollars of deposits reported by the Clearing House as being at the disposal of the local merchants and the various government departments. Accordingly, each bank watched carefully the accounts of its customers and followed with equal interest the nature of the bills received for collection from the United States and elsewhere in order that by establishing personal contact with local houses and business concerns not yet on the roll of its depositors it could weld these drawees to the branch. To this end the volume received from each foreign shipper was closely scrutinized at periodic intervals, and messages of appreciation were sent when increases in the turnover were noticed, while letters of regret were directed to those whose trade seemed to be falling off. Occasionally the attention of the head office would be called to local demands for articles not then imported so that they in turn could get in touch with United States exporters likely to take advantage of the opportunity to add to their existing trade on the island or establish new connections in this territory. Contrariwise, the branch offices were constantly on the alert to discover the names of new companies or firms establishing business contacts with insular houses or contemplating the opening of factories or subsidiaries. Their addresses would be promptly forwarded to the home office, especially if the prospect was believed to be known to one of the officers, in order that the bank's new-business division could solicit the accounts or the handling of other routine banking transactions and generally offer the assistance and services of their local representatives.

Profits from collections, although modest in the aggregate, were nevertheless welcome additions to the income of the branches as they helped to defray some of the overhead expenses. For this reason and also because the number of clients that could afford to maintain several bank accounts was limited, newcomers in the banking field in islands like Puerto Rico, and generally in the small independent republics in the Carribean and Central America, were sometimes obliged, in order to recruit business for their institutions, to try hard to make inroads into the bailiwick of their neighbors. Thus, while sound banking practice frowned on the cutting of rates, a new manager might be tempted to forget the rules so that his office might secure a share of the local banking turnover and justify its existence to the head office.

In the fall of 1942 banks with branches on the island learned that an amendment to the Insular Banking Law was in course of preparation aiming at the supervision of all banking operations in Puerto Rico. The Treasurer of the island was to be invested with the power to examine the books of the banks through his department or to designate outside public accountants to make the inspection. It was also contemplated to create a Banco de Fomento—which has since been established—to act as depositary of the Insular Government and finance the Puerto Rico Development Company which had been formed to foster new industries and the expansion of existing ones.

Recent developments on the island and the new enlightened administrative policy that offers sound inducement for the entry of foreign industry and the investment of foreign capital augurs well for the future there of the United States bank branches. That the economy of the island is rapidly expanding is illustrated by the rising budgetary revenues reported by the Treasurer of Puerto Rico for the fiscal year ending June 30, 1950, and by the fact that, as of September 30, 1950, thirteen local banks, including two United States and two Canadian institutions, shared in the total deposits of $297,735,424 of which almost sixty percent represented commercial and individual account balances.

PANAMA

Since Panama is strategically located at the crossroads of the Atlantic and Pacific Oceans on the shipping lane that connects these two great tracts of water, one of the main functions of the Panama branches of United States banks has been (and still is) the payment of canal tolls. All ships transiting the canal have had to pay certain fees to the United States Collector of Revenues, large vessels, paying as much as $10,000 to $20,000. During the first twenty years after the canal was opened to international navigation in 1914, it is reported to have yielded half a billion dollars in tolls to the United States Treasury. To assure the prompt payment of the charges, shipowners, both foreign and American, were required to open revolving credits. The United States banks furnished this service in return for a commission and the payment of interest up to the dates when the resulting advances were covered by the shipping lines. On bills for dry-docking and repairs or salvage the banks likewise assumed liability for settlement of the accounts of the respective authorities and repair and towage concerns.

Another source of revenue for the United States banks whose branches operated at the two ends of the canal, in the republic as well as in the Canal Zone (the strip of territory along the canal leased in perpetuity to the United States), was interest earned on deposits carried with them by the various United States Government agencies, including the Panama Railroad. In addition, the banking offices catered to the personal banking requirements of the administrative officials and members of the United States Army and Navy forces stationed on the isthmus, and also the numerous tourists who passed through Panama on their way to or from South America. The United States military forces, in particular, played a considerable role in the operations of the United States banks by reason of the large sums of money that were spent for their upkeep and that of their families.

In Panama, as in other Latin American countries, one of the by no means minor tasks of the branch offices was to handle the collection of bills drawn by American and foreign shippers of goods to Panama, Cristobal, Balboa, and Colon. Local deposit accounts were solicited actively, especially those of importers whose purchases in the United States and other countries called for remittances in foreign exchange. The local deposits were employed in so far as the local commerce had need for them, in commercial or personal loans and in the financing of automobile purchases, the collateral for which, or the name of the borrower, seemed to offer adequate security for repayment at maturity. However, in this field the United States banks had an active competitor in the Banco Nacional de Panama.

In October, 1938, a bill was introduced in the Panamanian Assembly that contained a serious threat for the future of all foreign banking activities in the republic (at one time the Royal Bank of Canada also maintained a branch on the isthmus). Its principal aims were to compel the banks: (1) permanently to invest 20 percent of their local deposits in internal bonds of Panama, which at the time had no broad market; (2) to invest 50 percent of all local deposits within Panama; and (3) to pay a special tax of 50 cents on each draft drawn on banks not operating in Panamanian territory, a feature particularly leveled at the banks operating in the Canal Zone. Immediately the three banks affected by the bill, the National City Bank, and the Chase National Bank, and the Royal Bank of Canada, protested against its passage on the ground that the proposed legislation was equivalent to compelling the banks to subscribe to a forced loan and that its provisions, moreover, conflicted with the fundamental banking acts under which they were organized. On October 24 the bill had its third reading in the Assembly. On the same day the three banks issued a joint statement that inasmuch as they were unable to comply with the law they would immediately return all their Panamanian deposits. The statement emphasized that if the banks were obliged to carry in their portfolios unmarketable assets, it would be impossible for them to fulfill their obligations of promptly returning demand deposits to their customers and their function of satisfying the normal credit needs of their clientele.

However, notwithstanding the banks' protest, on October 25 President Juan D. Arosemena signed the act known as the "guarantee bond" law. The State Department had actively sustained the banks' position in their condemnation of the new measure. It realized that the initiative taken by the small republic was fraught with ominous possibilities if other countries decided to imitate its example.

Not only the banks but also United States public utilities and oil companies established in Panama were directly penalized by the new law, which was to become effective within thirty days. In accordance with their declaration, the foreign banks, after the law had been published in the *Official Gazette,* decided not to accept any further Panamanian deposits and to refrain from making new local loans. The repayment of deposits had to be terminated by December 7; it was rendered more arduous because under the still-existing moratorium no legal action could be started against a debtor unless interest on his loan was more than one year in arrears. Thus, while repayment of loans could not be enforced, deposits had to be refunded lest the onerous penalties stipulated in the law be incurred.

Six days before the objectionable law was to go into actual effect, the Panamanian Government proposed a compromise bill, and at the end of 1938 the law to which the banks had raised such strenuous objections was repealed.

In the autumn of 1939, with the outbreak of war in Europe and the danger of its ultimately spreading to the Western Hemisphere, a period of intense business activity started in the republic, as a result of increased defense measures by the United States for the protection of the Panama Canal. A 50 percent addition to the American garrison and the passage of a United States law authorizing a new set of locks involving an expenditure of over 250 million dollars promised a period of rising prosperity on the isthmus, apart from the considerable appreciation of real estate values that might ensue. To the banks the large amounts to be disbursed afforded hopes of increased government deposits, more steamship financing, a greater number of individual accounts with larger balances, and growing demands for commercial and personal loans.

The rise of the Nazi movement in Central Europe and the subsequent invasion of Western Europe brought one temporary benefit to Panama. Anxious to send some of their capital abroad, Europeans were attracted by the flexible and liberal Panamanian legislation, which permitted and facilitated the creation of holding corporations to mask the real ownership of the assets transferred to Panamanian companies. In the end, however, when under United States laws it became necessary for United States banks to disclose the details of any securities or property held in custody for foreign account, the Panamanian nationality of these *ad hoc* entities proved of little value.

Early in 1940 the New York newspapers were full of reports about an uprising that had taken place in the city of Panama. An armed machine gun position had been erected on the roof of the Presidential palace, which was only a block away from the business and financial district. The situation in which the manager of one of the United States banks found himself is typical of the unpredictable chances that sometimes mark foreign banking, since the office of this bank officer was in the direct line of fire. The official fervently hoped that if the machine gun ever went into action it would not be manned by someone who had a grudge against the bank for having been refused a loan. On the other hand, the insurgents might find out that the ideal way to put the pillbox on the President's palace out of action would be to put another machine gun right in the window of the manager's office. However, the latter was spared the novel and doubtless stirring experience of directing the affairs of his branch from a desk placed, as it were, in No Man's Land.

After the United States entered the war it became urgent to devise plans against the possibility of an attack on the canal. The banks had to solve the problem of getting cash and securities safely out of the possible danger zone. It was finally decided that in such an eventuality all paper money would be placed in mail sacks and loaded on an Army truck under heavy guard, to be carried to the nearest airport. From there the cash would be transported by Army plane to an undisclosed destination. The sacks were to be accompanied by a bank officer or senior employee, with authority to act in case of need. Fortunately the emergency never occurred.

To help in the war effort, the local branches of United States banks, in addition to their ordinary activities, assumed various functions for which they appeared particularly qualified. The branches established in the Canal Zone received a special citation in a radio broadcast from the Comptroller of the Panama Canal War Bond Committee for their services in furthering the sales of war bonds and stamps on the isthmus. Earlier, in a letter to the banks D. W. Bell, Under Secretary of the Treasury, expressed the appreciation of the Treasury for the manner in which the Balboa and Cristobal branches had cooperated with the government disbursing officers and other officials located in the Canal Zone.

As expected, the tremendous expansion of United States Government contracts resulted in a substantial increase in business activity and money circulation throughout the republic. The purchasing power of the population grew correspondingly, especially as wartime salaries paid to both Panamanians and foreigners were considerably in excess of those normally paid. The military and civilian personnel spent large amounts for consumption and luxury articles. In addition, the United States Government organizations bought extensively from local producers, such as the cattle industry, the soft drink manufacturers, the brewers, and the distillers. As taxes were low, only a small portion of the latter's profits were taken out of circulation. The accumulation of funds in private hands resulted in substantial liquidation of indebtedness and banking and other financial agencies suffered from an acute scarcity of applications for loans. Bank deposits expanded so rapidly that they more than doubled during the first year of United States participation in the war, while savings bank balances rose more than 40 percent.

During the postwar years a business recession took place accompanied by some unemployment and aggravated by a decline in tourist trade essential to compensate for the constant excess of imports over exports. Reduction in United States Army and Navy forces was a contributing factor. However, because of the Atlantic rearmament movement and the prospect of renewed reinforcement of the defense of the Canal, the economic outlook for the future of the Republic and the Canal Zone is considered improved.

SUMMARY. In the 1921 economic crisis heavy losses were inflicted on United States banks and investors engaged in the Cuban sugar industry. During recent years various methods have been employed in the financing of the sugar crops both in Cuba and Puerto Rico. During the war important facilities were provided by United States Government agencies to promote economic prosperity in both islands. At one time during the interwar period the Cuban Government of the day did much to hinder the operations of the foreign banks' operating branches by imposing onerous taxes and burdensome insurance regulations, partly revoked since then.

In Puerto Rico, American banking policies and the day-to-day problems of the branches have been of some importance. Recent developments on the island give promise of a continued steady growth of the local industries favoring the further expansion of United States banking activities under more propitious conditions.

United States institutions have played an important role in Panama. They have furnished various services to the American military forces and the local business community both in peace and in war, despite certain skirmishes with local politics, as well as some staff problems. Recently, as a result of increased United States military activity during the war, the small republic and the adjacent Canal Zone have known an era of relative business prosperity.

VIII

CANADA AND ENGLAND

CANADA

ACROSS 4,000 MILES of contiguous boundaries Canada and the United States have for generations entertained the closest trade and banking relations. Owing to this proximity and the advantage of a common language and the same standard monetary unit, banks on both sides of the border have long emulated each other in the promotion of intimate commercial and industrial co-operation. At an early date the enterprising chartered Canadian banks, in order to foster the economic ties of the Dominion with its southern neighbor established branch offices in New York, Chicago, and the leading ports of the West Coast. As Canadian foreign expansion developed, agencies were opened in Cuba, Puerto Rico, and certain capitals of South America, where they played an important role in advancing and facilitating trade not only with their own country but also with the whole British Commonwealth.

To aid in the exploration and exploitation of Canada's immense natural resources and the building up of her manufacturing apparatus, in the course of the first half of this century the United States invested more than 5 billion dollars in the adjacent country. Conversely, the Dominion has large assets in our own financial and industrial centers, not only in the form of cash deposits but also in investments in United States business enterprises. Like the United States, Canada, in her adolescence, was a substantial importer of foreign capital, mainly British. However, as a result of the Second World War, Canada has passed into the front rank of the world's trading nations, where she now holds third place. This has enabled her to repurchase the greater part of the Canadian securities held in Great Britain and to redeem at their maturities a not inconsiderable share of the bonds owned by United States investors. Moreover, the Dominion has extended substantial credits to the mother country and other European nations to help in the reconstruction of their productive capacity and in their economic recovery.

This support has been given notwithstanding a heavy deficit in the balance of payments with the United States, which has threatened to reduce the Dominion's dollar reserves to an abnormally low level. Canada traditionally has had a net debit excess in her trade and financial traffic with this country, as her imports from the United States were much larger than her exports. The deficit in the past was covered by transfers from London, where Canada, because of a surplus of exports, as a rule had a substantial credit balance. So long as currencies remained convertible, no barriers stood in the way of triangular settlements between debtor and creditor countries.

In this connection a special reference to the war record of the Canadian dollar may be in order. From the beginning of the hostilities strict exchange regulations governed the transfer of Canadian funds to and from the United States. Merchandise trade with the United States was financed at the officially pegged United States dollar rate of 90.9 cents per Canadian dollar. In addition, there was a market in "free" Canadian dollars, the principal sources of which can be summarized as follows: United States balances held in Canada prior to September 10, 1939; Canadian dollars collected in settlement of preregulation contracts; earnings of United States corporations doing business in Canada, repatriation of which had been approved by the Canadian Control; proceeds of securities sold in Canada with the permission of the Canadian authorities; distribution of legacies to United States heirs; cover for Canadian bank notes and currency cashed by United States banks located along the border, and for Canadian money brought into the United States by Canadian and other Allied army personnel.

Demand for Canadian dollars developed in the United States from the following sources: money orders that called for periodic purchases of Canadian exchange by the United States Post Office; miscellaneous remittances for gifts, charities, and family support; expenditures of United States tourists in Canada; purchases by United States corporations for the improvement of plants located in Canada; such purchases, however, except for companies handling war orders for the Allies, were stopped for the duration of the war.

On the whole, dealings in Canadian "free" dollars were infrequent. The market was subject to rather wide fluctuations since the margin between bids and offers depended mainly on whether sellers or buyers predominated on the particular day. Another factor that from time to time influenced the price of the Canadian dollar was the placing of loans and the sale of Canadian shares in the United States, and as it was practically a daily occurrence before the war, the purchase of United States securities by Canadian investors. Similarly, the redemption of matured Canadian dollar bonds owned in the United States served to provoke offers of Canadian exchange except when the proceeds were reinvested in Canada.

In the early thirties unwarranted criticism was leveled against the Canadian banks, coupled with a suggestion emanating from Canadian leftist quarters that the banks be nationalized. In 1933 the Canadian Royal Commission on Banking and Currency, under the chairmanship of Lord Macmillan, after examining the operations of the banks, expressed its full confidence in their management, and as in Australia at a later date the nationalization proposals were indefinitely shelved.

In 1941 United States holders of Canadian securities and dollar deposits were alarmed by speeches of Premier Hepburn in the Province of Alberta, in which he advocated an increase in the issue of paper money. The Dominion Minister of Finance promptly denied any intention on the part of the Dominion Government to embark upon currency inflation. At once the Canadian free dollar, which had dropped to a 17 percent discount against the United States dollar, rallied to a 14 1/2 percent discount.

As noted before, by a strange reversal of financial history England, which prior to 1940 had played a preponderant role in the Canadian exchange market, now paid for her vast purchases of war materials and foodstuffs by selling back to the Dominion most of the bonds and stocks that had been acquired by British investors when Canada was a debtor in need of financial assistance from the mother country. Even after doing this, however, England on balance owed large sums to the Canadian Government. According to a Bank of England study of United Kingdom overseas investments quoted by the Financial Post, Toronto, of October 21, 1950, Great Britain's capital investment in Canada dropped 61 percent in the ten years 1938–1948. Because of this debt England received with misgivings the rumor that a possible revaluation of the Canadian dollar was under discussion between the United States Treasury and Canada. In informed United

States business quarters, too, serious doubts existed as to the advisability of raising the Canadian dollar to parity with the United States dollar. It was evident that the strengthening of the Canadian exchange rate could not be defended from either the Canadian or the English point of view. It would increase British indebtedness as well as the cost of future purchases, because it would depreciate sterling in terms of the Canadian dollar. It would reduce Canadian income from United States tourist traffic, which had been favorably influenced by the cheaper Canadian dollar. It would injure Canada's export trade, which had prospered under the existing advantageous exchange rate, as a result of which Canadian merchants had been placed in a favorable competitive position abroad. Finally, the operations of Canadian gold mines would become less remunerative if the premium of 11 percent commanded by the United States dollar were to disappear, since in the past this premium had acted as an export subsidy that had been of considerable advantage not only to the gold mining companies but also to the producers of woodpulp, grain, and other Canadian commodities and raw materials.

In July, 1946, however, in order to improve her position as a buyer from the dollar area, Canada decided to raise the Canadian dollar from 90.9 United States cents to par with the United States dollar. Yet it was soon apparent that this move had been premature. Reports followed that rather than let the Canadian dollar find its own level, the Dominion Treasury contemplated stimulating the output of newly mined gold by granting a bonus to the mining companies. Actually, import restrictions were introduced and excise taxes levied in an endeavor to deal with the United States dollar shortage; an emergency credit of 300 million dollars was arranged with the Export-Import Bank, to be used only in case of need; while the suggestion that the Canadian currency should be devalued once more was rejected, dividends and interest due American investors continued to be paid at the official par of exchange. The exchange controls instituted in September, 1939, regarding the expenditures of Canadians outside the country remain virtually in force even today.[1]

Since Canada had the largest per capita trade of any nation (one third of its income was derived from exports), revival of the bilateral deals on the part of the United Kingdom and other countries was

[1] In September, 1949, after the devaluation of the pound sterling, Canada decided to devalue its dollar by 10 percent in relation to the United States dollar.

bound to produce a growing uneasiness in the country. The Canadian Foreign Exchange Control Board realized the serious effects that these agreements were likely to have on the Dominion's foreign trade and consequently authorized private barter between Canadian concerns and traders in parts of the world where payment difficulties obstructed the normal settlement in convertible currencies. Fortunately, Canada, which had conspicuously assisted England and other European countries to rehabilitate their monetary situation, was aided in turn when, with the enactment of the European Recovery Program, opportunities presented themselves for her to increase her own exchange holdings in dollars and other hard currencies.

In the summer of 1944, reflecting its then close association with its Russian allies, the Canadian Government submitted a bill creating a special corporation to finance by long-term credits the manufacture of machinery for account of the Soviets. The amount provided was 25 million Canadian dollars. Subsequently the Canadian Parliament passed an act incorporating the Exports Credit Insurance Corporation, which was authorized to make commitments totaling 300 million dollars to further Canada's export trade generally by providing financial support to Canadian industrial and banking concerns. Under the act the manufacturers were to receive in the case of contracts with Soviet agencies long-term notes carrying interest at the rate of 3 percent and maturing in from 3 to 12 years. The Canadian Government assumed full guarantee for the payment of the notes; the commercial banks had the privilege of rediscounting any notes purchased by them at the Bank of Canada. The Soviets were to deliver notes for 10 percent of the cost at the time the blueprints for machinery were ready, 80 percent in installments as manufacturing progressed, and the balance upon shipment of the equipment. A first contract for hydro-electric generators was concluded almost immediately after the passage of the law. United States manufacturers were anxious to obtain this order, but the committee at Washington that during the war had the power to allocate this type of business decided to favor their Canadian competitors, who had ample unused manufacturing capacity.

In addition to the Export Credit Insurance Corporation, the Bank of Canada formed the Industrial Development Bank with an initial capital of 25 million dollars, which under the competent direction of the former general manager of the Royal Bank of Canada, S. R.

Noble, was to perform an outstandingly useful function in the development of Canada's foreign trade.[2]

SUMMARY. Because of Canada's proximity as well as her natural affinity with the United States, the banking contacts of Canadian and United States banks, dating back to the second half of the nineteenth century, have always been of an intimate and important nature. Substantial investments made in the other country by the nationals of each, but particularly by United States enterprises, have been reflected, especially before the restrictions necessitated by the Second World War, in a considerable movement of funds across the common border, and consequently in a steady flow of exchange transactions. Canada's role during the war was of great consequence, causing her to develop into a major trading and creditor nation.

ENGLAND

In Chapter I certain factors that contributed in the past to making Great Britain the foremost nation in the world in the magnitude of her commerce and the City of London the regulator of the international money market have been briefly sketched. Among these, as was there noted, was the worldwide faith in the stability of the British pound and in the promises to pay of English banks. In addition, the policies of the Bank of England instilled universal confidence. In view of these various factors, it was not surprising that London should have become one of the most important centers of the foreign activities of United States banks. In the present chapter the main functions and operations of United States bank branches in the United Kingdom will therefore be discussed.

Until the latter part of the nineteenth century and the early years of the present century the United States commercial banks neither had nor felt the need for permanent offices of their own in Great Britain. However, about this time the close commercial and financial ties uniting the two countries suggested to certain New York trust companies the advisability of having their own branches in London's financial district. The first offices were established by the Equitable Trust Company (later merged with the Chase National

[2] To counteract the inflow of foreign capital partly of a desirable investment character but to a large extent of a speculative nature, Canada, in October, 1950, decided to let the Canadian dollar seek its own level. In international financial circles this step was greeted as a first move toward a freer exchange market.

Bank), the Guaranty Trust Company, the International Banking Corporation, and the Farmers Loan & Trust Company, which, after its absorption by the National City Bank of New York, operated under the latter's name. Later, attracted by the favorable geographical location of the City of London at the doorway of the Continent and the importance of the English bullion and exchange markets, the Bankers Trust Company, the Empire Trust Company, the Central Hanover Bank & Trust Company, and the Bank of America also opened branches in London. The Bank of the Manhattan Company, the Irving Trust Company, and certain others contented themselves with merely setting up representative offices.

As United States business gradually congregated in the modern office buildings of Bush House and Thames Embankment, additional branches were installed in the London midtown area. Finally, in order to serve American tourists as well as the United States embassy and consulate, offices were also set up in the residential sections of Whitehall and Mayfair, within easy access of hotels, clubs, and department stores. The American Express Company and Brown Shipley & Company (correspondents of Brown Bros. Harriman & Company, New York) had already preceded them in Haymarket and Pall Mall. It should also be mentioned that J. P. Morgan & Co., Lee Higginson & Co., J. & W. Seligman & Co., and August Belmont & Co. likewise had close affiliations with London houses.

All these outposts of United States finance succeeded in carving niches for themselves alongside the powerful joint stock banks, and the ancient merchant banking houses which extended acceptance credits in all parts of the globe. These British firms had had a practical monopoly of this business until French, Dutch, Belgian, Swiss, and even German banks started to rival with them even in those territories where, through their close local affiliations, they had gained a strong foothold. With the creation of the Federal Reserve banking system, United States banks were at last placed in a position where, through the medium of their own dollar acceptances, they, too, could successfully compete, with the result that they took over a growing portion of this type of financing, not only in the United States but also in many other areas of the world.

The foreign bank branches in London were not privileged to issue sterling acceptances. Therefore they devoted themselves the more actively to those lines of banking that were open to them. Every type of service was offered by the various foreign agencies, from current deposit and safekeeping accounts to the purchase and sale of securities, the issuance of travelers' letters of credit and of drafts on their parent banks and correspondents everywhere. They opened commercial letters of credit for the financing of merchandise consignments to local United States and British commercial concerns and made loans against commodities stored in warehouse or upon the security of domestic or foreign bills and securities. Their clientele was recruited not only from London but also from the numerous commission houses in Manchester, Liverpool, Glasgow, and other business centers, which either acted as purchasing or selling agents for colonial or foreign products or were themselves wholesale dealers and importers of cotton, wool, timber, pulp, and other commodities.

One of the main functions of the United States branches was to act as correspondents for their head offices and the other domestic and foreign branches of the parent institutions. In addition, every effort was made by the British branch offices to assist United States industrial and commercial concerns in the development and extension of their Anglo-American trade and their business on the Continent, by placing at the disposal of their officers or British representatives the branches' knowledge of credit conditions and by supplying them with commercial intelligence secured through the branches' intimate local connections.

United States plants and factories operating in England naturally figured prominently among the depositors and occasional borrowers of the London branches, but were by no means the latter's only source of earnings. Another important source for some of the London branch offices was the acceptance of demand and time deposits in sterling and dollars from both local and continental banks and other holders. In the days when call money commanded high rates in Wall Street, these money arbitrages (consisting in the spot purchase of dollars against sterling and the simultaneous sale of the same amount of dollars for forward delivery) assumed large proportions. Nowadays, however, dollar deposits obtained by the English branches are generally transferred to the main offices, where they are used for investment in United States Treasury bills or the purchase of dollar acceptances, or are merged with the other productive assets of the banks. Sterling deposits were directed to the purchase of bankers' acceptances and to loans on securities. To keep in constant touch with the money market and to supply the head office with up-to-date information on interest rates, the branches maintain close contacts with the leading money and bill brokers. Since the branch managers have frequently to make investments or loans, they are especially anxious to keep their fingers on the pulse of the London money market. In the past the discount houses and exchange brokers facilitated this by having their clerks call daily on the banks and prominent business houses of the City to receive bids or make offers of assorted bankers' or British Treasury bills.

A substantial portion of the sterling deposits of the branches is being invested, nowadays more so than formerly, in British short-time government bonds, not only because of the yield but also in recognition of the hospitality enjoyed by foreign banks in England and their consequent right to do business practically on a par with the British banks themselves. The amount of these holdings varies considerably as between the different United States banks, for the total strictly commercial loans that are controlled by one branch office may be larger than the similar business available to its neighbors.

Because of their close contact with the Continent, the London foreign exchange trading departments occupied a favored position. The eclipse of the pound between 1919 and 1925 failed to check the close co-operation between the continental and the London foreign-exchange markets. Not only the quicker and cheaper communications of the London banks but also their long-time familiarity with conditions in the neighboring financial centers continued to place them in a favored position although, as has been pointed out elsewhere,[3] perhaps by reason of this close proximity, they were inclined at times to take too optimistic a view of conditions across the Channel. In constant telephonic communication with the principal banking places of Paris, Amsterdam, Zurich, Brussels, Stockholm, and —before the Second World War—Berlin, Vienna, and Budapest, the United States branches gave and received orders and traded—often in considerable amounts—for both prompt and future delivery. When talking with their counterparts in the European capitals, they would at times improve on the occasion to submit bids for an increased turnover for their head offices or their other important branches.

Whenever future sterling was quoted in New York at a seemingly profitable premium, the home offices would transfer to their Lon-

[3] See p. 234.

don branches (and other banks would deposit with their London correspondents) sterling purchased in the form of cable transfer and would sell the same amount for delivery in, let us say, two or three months. In addition to the premium on the forward contract, the banks would earn whatever interest the branch or the London correspondent would allow for a time deposit due in two or three months. If the shoe was on the other foot, London might sell spot dollars for sterling and buy future dollars at a discount, the profit on the exchange and the sterling investment going in this case to the branch instead of to the home office. At certain periods these money arbitrages, commonly known in foreign exchange vernacular as "swaps," assumed large proportions; then the waning of the premium on future sterling or a rise in interest rates at home or a darkening of the political horizon abroad would render them for a time unremunerative or inadvisable.

Another type of operation that offered to London branches of United States banks attractive opportunities of earning interest, commissions, and exchange profits was arbitrage in securities, to which many London and New York banking and brokerage houses often dedicated themselves for joint account. The numerous issues of American shares and bonds quoted and dealt in on the London Stock Exchange and the British and other foreign mining and other stocks introduced on the New York Stock Exchange and Curb market were the objects of active trading between the two centers. Specialists at either end occupied themselves solely with scanning the cable and telephone reports containing the other market's latest quotations in order that advantage might be taken of any worth-while margin arising between the two markets. These operations gave rise almost daily to purchases or sales of sterling in New York and dollars in London. Furthermore, since large amounts of cash were required to finance the purchases until the securities could be delivered at the other end, loans had to be contracted by the buyer; or drafts drawn on the sellers, with the securities attached, would be sold outright to a New York or London bank as the case might be. The arbitrage in securities, which sometimes spread to Paris and Amsterdam was profitable to the banks, but it was not a clear gain, since it involved much clerical labor such as counting the securities, preparing numerical lists, insuring the shipments, and following the final liquidation at the other side. Even during periods of political tension these operations often were not interrupted, war risk insurance serving to cover possible loss of the securities in transit.

This stock draft business, although calling for a certain technical knowledge of usages here and abroad, was eagerly solicited from responsible houses and required careful supervision by officers experienced in this special type of operations. The difference of time between New York and London and the other continental financial centers often forced European exchange traders and arbitragers in securities to wait till nine or ten o'clock at night (four or five o'clock Eastern standard time) to learn how their late orders had been executed in New York. At the close of banking hours in France or the United Kingdom it would only be noon in the United States, and in New York open positions could therefore be liquidated the same day without incurring the risk of an overnight position. Vice versa, a New York trader would at critical moments receive the first quotations from Europe at his own home at 5 o'clock in the morning, and his cabled orders were carried out on the other side long before his arrival at his desk a few hours later.

The machinery of the well-equipped foreign exchange division of every London bank doing an international business included experts in the handling of consignments of precious metals—gold, silver, and platinum—that found their way to London to be sold or held in storage there. Certain private banking houses such as Samuel Montagu & Co., N. M. Rothschild & Sons, and bullion brokers such as Mocatta & Goldsmid (founded in 1684), Johnson Matthey & Co., Ltd, Pixley & Abbell, and Sharpes & Wilkins, counted among the most active dealers in the London metal market. In the days when England was on the gold standard, exchange arbitrage between London and New York included particularly lively operations in the gold bullion market whenever the dollar rate was propitious in London. Gold was bought from the Bank of England or from houses owning bullion, and paid for in pounds sterling. The shipment was dispatched, fully insured against all risks, by the quickest available steamer, and sold in New York for United States dollars in the open market or to the Federal Reserve Bank of New York. The operation, of course, took place only when it was cheaper to ship gold, paying for the cost of freight and insurance and sacrificing the interest on the capital invested during the transit to New York. Another version of the operation consisted in United States banks having their

London branches or correspondents draw dollars on them and convert the sterling so procured into bullion to be consigned to New York for sale in dollars and reconversion into sterling.

For a number of years the Soviet Union, because of the shorter distance and the reduced freight and insurance, consigned the bulk of its gold shipments to London, in preference to sending them to the United States. The bullion was routed via Murmansk, the ice-free port in the Arctic north, during the long winters when the harbor of Leningrad was frozen. The State Bank of the USSR handled all gold exports, the precious metal being carried as a rule by Russian vessels insured against all risks by British and Russian underwriters. Even when the sterling balances of the State Bank seemed abundant, gold continued to be sent. While the actual purpose of such apparently superfluous Soviet shipments was not disclosed, it was surmised that the Politbureau was accumulating foreign exchange in anticipation of possible external difficulties. In 1937, for instance, it was hinted in some quarters that Loyalist Spain had enlisted the co-operation of the Soviet Government in the disposal of Spanish gold donated to or confiscated by the Republican armies. Russian gold bars, it was believed, had been substituted for the Spanish coins, and the proceeds of their sale in London were thought to have been converted into francs and other continental currencies which then were placed to the credit of the Loyalist government at the banks—mainly in Paris—where its accounts were carried under various disguises.

As the political situation in Europe became more and more fraught with explosive possibilities, the British Chancellor of the Exchequer stated on April 20, 1939, in the House of Commons that in the judgment of the government British capital should cease to be sent abroad for investment in foreign securities, since it had become imperative that the country husband all its financial reserves. A month later the Bank of England and the London Stock Exchange brought pressure on the banks and brokerage houses in an effort to enforce this "unofficial" ban. It was emphasized that no further direct offerings of foreign securities would be countenanced in the United Kingdom, while an appeal was made to the patriotism of all British subjects to abstain from making new investments abroad.

On September 3, 1939, with the outbreak of war, the official British Defense (Finance) Regulations went into force, limiting, among other things, the foreign operations of all banks, including the United States and other foreign branches doing business in London. The purchase, sale, and loan of gold and foreign exchange and the export of gold, currency, and securities were restricted, while the British Treasury was authorized to acquire certain foreign currencies, gold coin, and bullion, and new capital issues were made subject to control. Later, the banks were prohibited from making any transfers of money abroad whatsoever except with the approval of the Bank of England. The futures' market for the pound became extremely narrow, and foreign buyers and sellers turned to New York for cover for the growing risks involved in forward-delivery contracts not only in sterling but also in many other foreign currencies. History repeated itself, for the same trend had been observed just a quarter of a century earlier. At that time the foreign banking organization in the United States was still in its early youth. Since 1914, however, it had greatly developed, and now it was well prepared in ability and equipment and financial power to acquit itself of the increased responsibilities thrust upon it when Great Britain found herself compelled to direct all her economic resources and material strength against the enemy.

Preparatory steps by the London banks did not wait on the actual beginning of hostilities, a number of City institutions, including the foreign branches, having taken the precaution some months previous to purchase or rent places outside metropolitan London to house employees and records in case of need. Immediately after the declaration of war, the understructures of some of the offices in the financial district were strengthened, the outside of the bank buildings were sandbagged, and the windows were reinforced.

As in the United States, the handling in London of foreign credits and collections and of what foreign exchange trading was left called henceforth for great discernment and care to insure the observance of the numerous regulations in effect not only in the British Isles but also in practically all other countries. These decrees and rulings applied not only to the transfer of capital but also to insurance and the issuance of bills of lading. Steamer sailings were few and far between. Cable communications were rendered difficult by the prohibition in most countries of the use of codes and private telegraphic ciphers for authenticating payment orders. Finally, all foreign drawees or beneficiaries of credits or payment orders had to be checked carefully to make sure that their names had not been placed on the British and, later, the United States blacklists.

Following the precedent of the First World War, a British Financial Mission was sent to the United States and found permanent offices in the downtown financial district of New York. In March, 1940, Mr. Gifford joined the mission as special representative of the Bank of England. Under his competent guidance the British Government embarked on the mobilization of United States securities owned in the United States by British subjects. The Bank of Montreal was appointed the main depositary, subdepositaries being designated in New York to hold the securities in custody. There was much conjecture at this time as to whether the British Government would decide to dispose of the securities in the American markets or whether United States syndicates or investment trusts would be called upon either to sell them or to use them as collateral for new British stock or bond issues to be offered to United States investors.

The outlook during the first relatively quiet year of the war took a different turn from what had been expected, the economic aspects figuring much more prominently in the conversation among United States bankers and merchants than the military prospects. At that time few dared to hazard a guess as to the immensity of the financial cost that might be necessary to bring the struggle to a victorious conclusion.

Because of the fear of bombing attacks, although the vaults were considered safe, photostats were made by the United States banks of all British bearer bonds held by them for their own or clients' account and were mailed to New York together with numerical lists of share and bond certificates.

On this side of the Atlantic the British Purchasing Mission paid for its purchases by drafts payable out of balances maintained by it or placed to its credit at the Federal Reserve Bank of New York. Concurrently, there was a flow of credits opened with American commercial banks and guaranteed by London banks, such as those opened on behalf of the British Iron and Steel Institute, the British Petroleum Pool, and the Navy Army Air Force Institute, U.K.

In October, 1940, the battle of London reached its height. The uninterrupted night attacks made it necessary for the United States bank branches to stagger their hours of work so that as many employees as possible could leave the offices early each afternoon. The increasing difficulty of traveling to and from work and the loss of sleep made it especially necessary that every member of the staff should have a chance to get as much rest as possible each night before the raids began. It was a most trying ordeal, but all stood up to it magnificently and, like all the other citizens of London and the other bombarded English towns, with unexampled courage and steadfastness. The London offices of American banks were by no means spared by the German raiders. The premises of the Guaranty Trust Company were seriously damaged, and a heavy bomb fell in the courtyard of the Chase National Bank building at 6 Lombard Street, fortunately without exploding.

The passage of the Lend-Lease Act in the United States on March 11, 1941, filled the heart of Britain with new courage. With the productive capacity of the United States now definitely ranged behind the Empire, the ultimate issue of the war was beyond doubt. The effect of the announcement, with its implication of full war aid to the Allies and its practical conversion of the United States into an "arsenal for democracy" was far-reaching, and as expected was to have a profound influence on the future course of events.

The dawn of 1942 found the bulk of foreign trade in the hands of the British Government. Government departments were importing directly most of the commodities and materials required for the economic life of the country. By this time, too, more than one third of all Britain's assets in foreign countries had been sold or pledged. Her overseas investments and dollar reserves, despite lend-lease, were now being drained rapidly.[4] In addition, most of the invisible exports—income from shipping, insurance, and banking services abroad—which formerly offset her import surplus, had been sadly reduced. For generations the yield on her foreign investments, the gold production of the Dominions and the proceeds of her commercial banking, shipping, and insurance-underwriting operations had enabled her to buy more goods abroad than she exported. Now her financial position was impaired. Not only had her overseas assets been sacrificed to a considerable extent, but in addition she had incurred heavy sterling debts to India, Egypt, the Argentine Republic and other countries from which she had purchased goods on credit. Thus

[4] In October, 1950, the Bank of England estimated that mainly to finance the war British foreign investments had declined about 45 percent between 1938 and 1948, while on the other hand income from the remaining overseas investments had been reduced by only 25 percent.

her place as a world creditor was seriously weakened. Moreover, with much of her foreign income drastically curtailed and with some of her outside markets lost, for the time being at least, if not irretrievably, the standard of living of her people promised to be seriously curbed.

In the early months of 1942, after the arrival of the first American Army and Navy contingents in the United Kingdom, the United States banks located in the neighborhood of the American embassy began to be called upon for various services to the officers and men attached to the American missions and generally to the various United States officials in charge of troop pay arrangements. G.I's and bluejackets visited the offices of the United States banks by the thousands and there dispatched or received mail orders and through the banks' head offices placed orders for the delivery of candy, flowers, and other gifts to cheer their families at home.

The American military and civilian personnel stationed in the British capital made the local branches of United States banks their headquarters for the cashing of checks and transmission of funds to and from the United States. Gradually this work assumed considerable proportions, to cope with which the staff in the West End offices had to be perceptibly strengthened. Current accounts were opened by the finance officers and disbursing officers and other governmental agencies, security in the form of United States Government bonds having to be deposited, in accordance with United States Treasury regulations, with the Federal Reserve Bank of New York for London balances of the different branches of the service.

It was natural that substantial amounts of dollar notes cashed by the British and American banks should accumulate in London. In order to save the costly marine and war risk insurance during the voyage home the banks cut the notes in half and delivered the mutilated notes to the United States embassy in London with numerical lists in quadruplicate. Little profit was derived from the numerous small private accounts conducted for the members of the armed services. Yet, although the banking staffs were overworked and at times found it difficult to satisfy all the demands made upon them, they were glad to help those who, separated from their families and homes in a strange country, were grateful for any small favors and appreciated the friendly atmosphere of what was in effect a bit of America transplanted onto British soil.

Numerous letters were received from simple soldiers and officers of high rank alike testifying to their gratitude for the cheerful assistance extended to them by the banks' officers and tellers. Moreover, directly or indirectly, the efficient and courteous treatment received in these branches was in part responsible for the opening of important account relationships with United States Government organizations, such as the War Shipping Administration, the post exchanges, the Chief Disbursing Officer of the Treasury Department, and the disbursing clerks attached to the State Department and the Navy.

While United States banks, as we have seen in the foregoing pages, have enjoyed the hospitality of the London financial community for almost half a century, English banks have not opened branch offices in the United States. Instead, the leading British institutions have appointed permanent representatives in the United States, with headquarters in New York, C. M. Parker, of the Westminster Bank, and J. H. Fea, of Lloyds Bank, and Barclays Bank's agents have long and ably cultivated relations with banks and business houses on this side of the Atlantic. They have been joined in later years by W. B. John Partridge, of the Midland Bank, Limited, and William J. H. Hyner, of the National Provincial Bank, Limited, while A. W. Beamand has recently taken over the duties of C. M. Parker, retired, and E. J. Stanley has been added to the Lloyds Bank agency.

The most significant development in British finance during the postwar period was the devaluation of the pound sterling on September 18, 1949, to $2.80. In the following year the British Treasury announced that the gold and dollar reserves of the sterling bloc had more than doubled as a result principally of the increased purchases by the United States from nations in the sterling area. Nevertheless the British authorities declared that a substantial increase in the British balance of payments was needed to enable the country to repay its debts contracted in the First World War, for financial investments abroad, and to acquire gold further to build up its reserves. Previously it had been reported that in order to strengthen the pound sterling's international position Britain had decided to grant all countries in the European Payments Union the privilege of settling in sterling—instead of in gold or dollars—any balance due to a creditor in the union. In addition, the Bank of England decided to lift practically all restrictions on the transfer within the sterling area of sterling securities and blocked sterling owned by nonresidents.

Under the ruling foreigners are allowed to convert their holdings into any sterling area securities quoted on a stock exchange anywhere in the sterling area. On December 6, 1950, Britain removed currency controls on Danish, Swedish and Norwegian kroner and Hugh Gaitskell, Chancellor of the Exchequer, announced that between 1951 and 1958 Britain would release to India and Ceylon £231,000,000 from their blocked balances.

SUMMARY. This section surveys the position of the branches of United States banks in the United Kingdom and the numerous facilities offered by them to American and British customers. The branches' activities touched especially on the London discount and foreign-exchange markets, arbitrage in money and securities, and gold and silver shipments, not to mention the operations effected formerly for account of the USSR. At the approach of the war in 1939, special precautionary financial measures had to be taken by the British Government, while the London banks, both British and foreign, faced major problems after the beginning of hostilities in their efforts to protect both their staffs and their assets. Various wartime services to the United States diplomatic and military establishment abroad were performed by the American branches. The outlook for Great Britain's future balance of payments was throughout a matter of special concern. Since the war, British joint stock banks have, for their part, been increasing their representation in New York.

IX

FRANCE

For half a century American banks have maintained offices in the French capital. At first the small staffs served primarily to cash checks and letters of credit for traveling countrymen. With the passage of time the growing number of customers called for enlarged facilities, such as the creation of special divisions for the purchase and sale of foreign exchange and securities and for discounts, loans, and collections. When war was declared in 1914, thousands of Americans were stranded in Europe in urgent need of cash and traveling accommodation for their return home. The few United States banks then established in Paris—the Equitable Trust Company (later merged with the Chase Bank), the Farmers Loan & Trust Company (later acquired by the National City Bank of New York, France, S.A.) and the Guaranty Trust Company—as well as the American Express Company and the private banking houses with New York affiliations, such as Morgan Harjes & Co. and Munroe & Co., without taking advantage of the French moratorium, honored liberally the letters of credit presented to them irrespective of whether these were payable at their own counters or not. The banks assisted many embarrassed tourists by cashing small checks on their own banks in the United States, confident that the drawers could be trusted and that the drafts would be honored. The sudden strain on their resources was considerably relieved by the establishment of a 6 million dollar credit by the Bank of France through J. P. Morgan & Co. and the arrival of 4 1/2 million in gold from the United States on the armored cruiser Tennessee.

During the period between the two wars the number of United States banks that found it worth while to open their own offices in Paris grew. Uptown branches were added in the districts of the Champs Elysées and the Etoile in the vicinity of the hotels favored by Americans and the section where many United States residents had their homes. In the meantime the main branches, too, had to broaden their services. Paris had become the center not only of

French fashion but also of important industries. American manufacturers opened branch factories and plants in the provinces. United States department stores and importers set up their own buying offices and agencies near the boulevards in order to supply their customers with the latest creation of French styles, dresses, perfumes, and luxury articles. Likewise, a number of leading Paris financial institutions gradually opened representative offices in New York; among the earliest was the Crédit Lyonnais whose authorized agent for a number of years was a middle-aged Alsatian by the name of Felsenberg. Maurice Silvester was the diligent agent of the Comptoir National d'Escompte de Paris, and Maurice Mercadier the representative of the Banque Nationale Française du Commerce Exterieur. Maurice Boyer long acted for the Banque de Paris et des Pays-Bas, while during the Second World War Robert Soliva and J. L. Morin were temporarily stationed in New York to protect the interests of the Banque de l'Indo-Chine. The French-American Banking Corporation and a branch of the Société Générale have in addition long counted among the active foreign banking agencies in this city. For longer or shorter periods officials of the Banque de France have been unofficially assigned to study and report on conditions in the United States. Finally, the private firms of J. P. Morgan & Co., Lazard Frères & Co., and J. & W. Seligman & Co. have maintained close connections over generations with their related houses in France.

The years 1920 and 1921 were prosperous in France; the boom, however, was due in no small measure to the spreading inflation. The French Government was compelled to finance by large budgetary deficits the rehabilitation and reconstruction of the devastated areas the public debt increasing, between 1918 and 1924, from 170 billion francs to 317 billion. As early as February, 1919, the franc started to decline, a deterioration that continued through the whole third decade of the century. As the downward movement gained in momentum the French *rentiers* took fright, their periodic alarms resulting in as many recurrent flights of capital into foreign exchange and international investments. The peasants hoarded gold and currency in mattresses and in the favorite refuge of French savings, the proverbial woolen stocking. To hedge against further depreciation some individuals bought common stocks in foreign currencies quoted on the Paris Bourse. Even foreign postage stamps were acquired, the collection of Junior becoming of a sudden the treasured possession of the parents. The value of the stamps fluctuated with the rates of the dollar and the pound sterling. This type of unorthodox investment was especially attractive because in addition to the exchange hedge the holder escaped the French tax collector, and a regular bourse of stamps in the Champs Elysées accordingly attracted not only numerous stamp amateurs but many investors as well.

The position of French exchange was further impaired when international speculators, after having despoiled the mark, attacked the franc. The currency was only saved when Raymond Poincaré, in July, 1926, formed the "union sacrée," the government of the National Union. The French leader inspired confidence, and the franc became steady. Formal devaluation took place on June 24, 1928, when the new official parity of the franc was fixed by law at 3.9179 cents, or 25.52 francs to the dollar, roughly one fifth of the prewar value. While the pound sterling had been stabilized at too high a figure, foreign exchange circles now considered the franc undervalued; in January, 1934, when the dollar was devalued to 59.06 cents, the gold content of the franc was not changed, and its dollar parity was thereby automatically raised to 6.6338 cents.

During the early thirties the financial strength of France, as exemplified by her vast foreign exchange and gold reserves, seemed to be at its height. French statesmen hoped to make of Paris the great financial center of European finance and to attract the banking business that heretofore had been directed to London. The Paris Bourse was one of the most influential foreign exchange markets. The wide fluctuations in the sterling-dollar cross-rate during the fall of 1934 were attributed almost entirely to the operations of French banks and exchange manipulators. The *"salle des banquiers"* at the Bourse, where the heads of the foreign departments of the French and foreign banks and the partners of private banking firms and brokers congregated between the hours of 12 and 3 o'clock, was often the scene of feverish trading. Every dealer in New York and London had arrangements by which the variations in the Paris rates were transmitted to him by urgent cable or telephone. The sterling rate in New York and the dollar quotation in London moved up or down whenever a small fraction of change in the Paris market allowed a modest margin of profit.

Much of the tremendous turnover was due to the doubts of the French investors and businessmen as to the ability of their government to maintain the franc at its official par. The tourist traffic, always an important item in the French balance of payments, had declined from 12 billion francs in 1927 to only 2 billion in 1934, while the trade balance deficit had reached 5 1/4 billion. Added to these bearish factors was the constant influx of Central European and Balkan currencies, which were sold in France and the proceeds converted through the Paris banks into sterling, Swiss francs, and dollars. Some hoarders, mistrustful of even these "hard" currencies, would convert their pounds into gold, which they deposited in London. Merchants with contracts for shipments payable at some future date in continental currencies went "long" of sterling or dollars as a protection against the possible decline of the exchange in which the buyer was to settle his purchase.

When, as happened on occasion, the franc rose above the gold import point, banks in the United States would arrange for gold shipments to France. In this they were encouraged by the French Treasury, whose high officials were anxious to conform rigorously to the rules of a gold-standard country and also wanted France to benefit from the inflow of the yellow metal. In return, France willingly authorized the export of bullion when the dollar rose in the Paris market to a point where gold exports were possible. American bank managers in Paris kept in continual close touch with the head of the foreign department of the Bank of France, Charles Carriguel, an experienced banker with international background.

By reason of the needs of the French budgetary situation the French taxes imposed on foreign banks and on industrial enterprises doing business in France were burdensome. In July, 1935, the transactions tax was raised from 17 percent to 18. Among other taxes, that on interest paid on deposits varied from 12 to 18 percent; on bank loans the tax, payable by the lender, was 18 to 24 percent, an item that had to be taken into account when fixing the rate for the borrower.

When Hitler occupied the Rhineland, on March 7, 1936, feeling about the franc became again bearish, since it was apprehended that in case of an emergency the French Government might place an embargo on the export of capital. Early in the following May, according to Paris advices, the Bank of France lost almost 2 billion francs of gold (132 million dollars) within forty-eight hours, every means of transportation being pressed into service to convey the yellow metal to London, Brussels, and New York. There were rumors of another devaluation, the pessimistic views being reflected in a discount of 36 1/2 percent per annum for delivery of francs in one month and 23 percent per annum for delivery in ninety days. Heavy withdrawals of deposits were noted in all the banks. Realizing the precarious situation in which the central bank might find itself, the United States branch banks refrained from adding to the flight from the franc even though such transactions would have been exceptionally remunerative.

As mentioned in Chapter I, in order to assist France the Tripartite Agreement was signed on September 28, 1936, by the United States, Great Britain, and France; subsequently Belgium, Holland, and Switzerland also adhered. Simultaneously the French stabilization fund, with gold resources of 10 billion francs, came into being, and started immediately to operate.

On October 2, 1936, the franc was revalued again, this time at about 28.13 percent below the previous parity. The exact gold point was not defined, but fixed limits to be maintained were set at 4.35 1/2 and 4.96 1/4 United States cents. During the rest of 1936, the franc fluctuated between 4.60 1/2 and 4.95 cents.

In 1937 the placing of a 50 million pound one-year credit in the United Kingdom for the French Railways caused a favorable impression, and it was hoped that the discount on future francs would gradually disappear. In order to frustrate the tactics of the foreign buyers of French goods who delayed their purchases of French exchange until after the arrival of the merchandise abroad, the Bank of France let the Paris banks know that it frowned upon their granting acceptance credits for this purpose. The Bank of France fixed the price of gold daily, the official limits per kilogram being 22,675 and 25,839 francs. Exports of bullion were countenanced only when for account of a foreign central bank. The October, 1936, devaluation improved the technical position of the market, but the unfavorable trade situation, the sharp decline in French rentes, and the unsettled internal conditions were not inducements for Frenchmen to repatriate the considerable amounts still on deposit abroad. Rather, what was needed, but was not achieved, was the balancing of the budget and the funding of the excessive floating debt, including the heavy overdraft of the government at the Bank of France. As such a policy could not be carried out without a reduction of military expenditures, the prospect for a return of the vagrant capital was not likely soon to improve. Moreover, the French bourgeois, before recalling their funds from abroad, wanted to be convinced that no socialistic or radical government would resort on the morrow to confiscatory capital levies and onerous inheritance taxes or impose other measures assailing private property.

That this concern about the fate of the currency was warranted was demonstrated by the decrees of June 30 and September 2, 1937, when gold reserves were once more revalued, this time on the basis of 43 milligrams 900 fine, or 38.7 milligrams fine gold, the upper and lower limits of the franc being reduced accordingly to 4.67 and 3.35 cents. In spite of this action, in October the exchange situation again became critical. In an effort to combat speculation, the government licensed only a handful of banks to deal in forward francs. In the French Chamber of Deputies, in the course of a debate on the outlook for French finance, Paul Reynaud, expressing the views of all sound observers, stated that the franc could not be saved by budgetary measures. "What is essential," he said, "is the economic recovery of the country."

The year 1938 witnessed further strenuous endeavors to relieve the heavy pressure continually exerted on the franc. Soon, owing to labor difficulties, the pound quotation climbed to 179 francs. The government of Prime Minister Daladier thereupon decided to make this rate the *de facto* limit, the rate at which the pound was thereafter pegged implying a parity of 35.80 francs to the dollar, equal to 2.79 cents for the franc. Another formal devaluation followed on November 12, when the gold reserves were so written up that the rate for the pound was reduced to 170 francs, the value of the franc now being 2.65 United States cents. The international scare of that year forced the French stabilization fund to sell part of the large resources in foreign exchange accumulated the preceding year. It was estimated that on this occasion the fund lost 5 million pounds out of the 15 million pounds it had previously been able to acquire when French holders had sold some of their foreign assets because of a temporarily improved external outlook.

Meanwhile, during the critical summer of 1938 the French authorities, because of apprehensions about the imminence of war, requested the banks to take protective measures against the event of sudden air-raids. Basements were adapted to serve as shelters for the protection of the banking staff, emergency batteries being installed for auxiliary lighting and arrangements being made for ventilation. To add to the general alarm, the Louvre and other museums were reported to be packing their art treasures for removal to places of safety. At the risk of being ultra-cautious, some of the banks rented additional vault space from French bank branches located in the south and west of France, and they also prepared duplicates of important records and ledgers and stored them in various places outside Paris.

After the Munich conference, such was the revival of confidence that, according to the estimates of exchange traders, the French stabilization fund was able to reacquire sterling to the tune of 7 million pounds. When Paul Reynaud accepted the portfolio of Minister of Finance, the discount on future francs—always the barometer of French and foreign judgment as to the economic and financial weather—improved perceptibly. The 90 days' delivery was quoted at 2 3/8 points below spot, equal to only 3 5/8 percent discount per annum. Reynaud frankly admitted that he could not balance the budget at the moment; he said that there were eight reasons militating against such a step: first, it was impossible, and that being so, the other seven reasons did not matter. Showing the inconstancy of public opinion, there were now quite a few students of the situation who asserted that the franc was undervalued; they pointed out that calculated on a gold basis the English wholesale price index stood at 71, the Belgian at 64 and that of the United States at 69, while the French index actually was as low as 54.

In January, 1939, the weather vane seemed to indicate the approach again of stormy conditions in the international atmosphere. Shrewd French investors withdrew funds from London and converted their sterling into dollars; according to reliable opinion, the French and British capital transferred from London to the United States at this time amounted to between 70 million and 100 million pounds. In New York it was noticed that purchases of raw materials and nonferrous metals, principally copper, as well as orders for airplanes, by both the French and the British governments, were assuming considerable proportions; these purchases were apparently paid out of dollar reserves, since the franc held steady around the level of 2.65 cents.

Because of the increasingly threatening international situation, the United States banks in Paris, apart from purchasing the French government's armament and defense bonds having one or two years to run, made it a point to keep in extremely liquid condition. As the air thickened, there were heavy withdrawals of deposits by frightened French and foreign customers. Matters came to a head with the declaration of war at the end of August, and a week later the export of capital was prohibited and control over all foreign exchange was decreed. In New York the franc slumped to 2.16, but recovered slightly and ended the year at 2.24.

The war had profound effects on the United States banks in France. Their staffs were depleted, between 40 and 50 percent of their French employees having to join the colors. The families of American officers and clerks were sent home, and banking hours were reduced. There were air raid alarms almost immediately, and shrapnel from anti-aircraft guns fell on some bank buildings. Buses ceased to run, and the employees were accordingly lodged in hotels near the offices. War risk insurance was impossible to obtain, except at prohibitive rates, and securities therefore were promptly removed to the vaults rented south of Paris.

In the spring of 1940 the prominent French economist Professor Charles Rist, former subgovernor of the Bank of France and one of the directors of the French stabilization fund, was delegated to Washington as economic adviser to the French Minister of Blockade. In March the gold reserve of the Bank of France underwent another revaluation to the level of 43.80 francs per dollar, equal to 2.283 cents per franc. Wild confusion followed the break-through of the German army in May. The franc declined to 1.73 cents, but recovered promptly to almost 2 cents. After the fall of Paris on June 14, trading in francs was suspended in the New York exchange market; thereafter, nominal quotations for francs, payable in unoccupied France by virtue of United States Treasury licenses, oscillated between 2.21 and 2.29 cents.

As early as April, anticipating the tragic events to follow, the governor of the Bank of France and the Paris Bankers Association had given directions as to the action to be taken in certain contingencies. All banks, both French and foreign, made active preparations for evacuation in the event of the enemy approaching the capital. The United States banks leased office space in various cities and towns in the center and south of France. Strong wooden boxes especially manufactured for the purpose were placed in all the departments, and employees were instructed as to what files and records were to be placed in them. Large trucks were rented and kept on call for an indefinite period: for several weeks prior to the fatal day when they were finally needed, some of these trucks could be seen stationed in front of the bank buildings ready for a quick get-away.

On June 10, on receipt of a telephone call from the Bank of France that its services were being moved to Chatel Guyon in southern France, whence its exchange and discount divisions were hereafter to function, both French and United States banks moved most of their staff and records to Vichy, Chateauneuf, and the other towns, where they had secured provisional quarters. Owing to the congested condition of the roads, it took several days for the staffs of the American banks to reach their destinations. The nights were spent on top of the trucks, but despite the hardships and the distressing circumstances, the men showed exemplary devotion.

After some delay the majority of the United States banks were finally installed not far from the new headquarters of the Bank of France, and from these temporary refuges henceforth tried, as best they could, to manage their French business and to maintain the accounting records covering their much-reduced operations in the southeastern corner of France that still was unoccupied.

Great difficulties attended all these various moves for the protection of the staffs and of the assets held for American and French customers. The small units that carried on from the emergency offices labored under severe handicaps as to food, heat, and clothing, and although houses were rented for them by the managements, during the troubled years that followed they, of course, missed the comfort of their own homes and the company of their families and friends. When the United States entered the war, in December, 1941, the enemy took possession of the hitherto unoccupied part of France, and the few United States citizens still on the staffs departed hurriedly.

Earlier, when the Germans invaded France and threatened Paris, meetings took place in New York at the Federal Reserve Bank to discuss the advisability of having the United States Treasury issue a general license for the operation of United States bank branches in France, since these offices had substantial deposit and acceptance liabilities both in francs and in dollars; American branch factories and sales agencies had numerous outstanding accounts receivable and securities were held in safekeeping for United States residents in France, while important dollar balances and custody accounts were conducted for French interests in national banks and trust companies in the United States. After some delay, these matters were straightened out by means of special licenses, which took care of the most urgent problems.

When, on June 22, 1940, the government of Marshall Pétain signed the armistice, the few British staff members of United States banks left hastily via Spain and Portugal lest they be placed in concentration camps. In December, 1941, the remaining Americans also became enemy nationals. Those unfortunate United States citizens who elected to stay with their French wives and children were interned in barracks near Compiègne until released by the United States Army in August, 1944.

Even before the French collapse, both French and United States banks had been encountering great difficulties in collecting bills and accounts due for merchandise sold to French buyers. After the occupation of central and northern France, however, it became practically impossible for American banks in the unoccupied part to trace the whereabouts of drawees and debtors, and franc recoveries became almost nil, although the banks, under French law, still had to honor their deposit and other liabilities when they fell due. The Bank of France and some French commercial banks had previously discounted acceptances of the United States branches aggregating many millions of francs. These acceptances represented accommodation extended affiliates and branches of United States corporations operating in France in connection with the financing of the sales of their products on the Continent of Europe; for the time being, however, the business of these companies had completely vanished, and their customers were in no position to honor their debts. Recognizing the trying situation of the American banks, the Bank of France agreed repeatedly to the renewal of the bills for further periods of ninety days. On their part the United States banks requested that before the expiration of the last ninety-day extension their debtors, the American companies, should make arrangements to unfreeze some of their accounts receivable or else have French banks with large liquid funds take them over and thus relieve the United States branches' tight position. However, not only was it difficult to find "free" francs that could be transferred to the Bank of France and the other holders of franc acceptances but also the United States Treasury was reluctant to license any transaction that might at some future time force the United States banks, in order to fulfill their contractual obligations, to remit francs to a country that might by then be entirely occupied by the Germans. For this reason the United States Foreign Property Control granted licenses for the purchase of francs payable in dollars only where these were to be credited to a blocked account in the United States. As it turned out, the Treasury was well advised not to permit fresh American capital to enter France under the conditions then prevailing.

This attitude, however, confronted the United States companies with a serious dilemma. The Bank of France firmly refused to sell francs against other than free dollars. On the other hand, the companies did not wish to incur the heavy risk of exchange by purchasing francs when they had already important franc assets of their own. Moreover, if ultimately they were to be compelled to buy French exchange, it was to their advantage to defer settlement as long as possible, for it was not unlikely that later they would be able to buy francs at a lower rate. In fact, while the Vichy official quotation for dollars continued to be fixed at 2.29 cents per franc, sales were being reported from Switzerland at 1.75 to 1.85 cents. In the United States, after the severance of diplomatic relations with France, trading in francs, of course, ceased entirely, and franc quotations were no longer available.

Long before the final tragic defection of Marshall Pétain, in June, 1940, the United States banks had trimmed their sails, contracting their staffs and reducing steadily their outstanding obligations.[1] After the occupation of southern France, small skeleton forces remained at the provisional quarters, as mentioned before, largely to take care of the liquidation of accounts which, notwithstanding the most strenuous efforts, it had been impossible to close. In recognition of the unusual hazards involved and because of the constantly increasing tension between the United States and the Laval government, the managers exercised extreme caution, fully conscious of their employers' precarious situation. That the banks should nevertheless hesitate to abandon the important place they had attained in the field of French banking was understandable in view of the generation of pioneering effort that they had devoted to promoting foreign

1 Their problems varied somewhat, for some of the United States and British banks had conducted their business in France through special affiliates organized under French law, while the others maintained branches accountable to their head offices in New York and London.

trade and furthering American financial interests in the sister republic.

Our official entrance into the war after Pearl Harbor produced a change in the attitude of the German authorities toward United States corporations and individuals in France. In Paris the premises of some of the United States banks were requisitioned, and all British and American accounts were blocked.

After the occupation of North Africa, in November, 1942, and the ensuing seizure by the Germans of the hitherto unoccupied zone, the Trading with the Enemy Act became applicable to all of Continental France. Accordingly, the United States head offices were now cut off from the few remaining representatives with whom they had still been able to keep up contact. However, long before this final interruption of relations lists of all certificates of securities held in custody in unoccupied France had been shipped to America—a step that had been the more urgent because most French bonds were in bearer form and in the absence of their numbers and dates it would have been difficult for the owners to ask that the French Government or the issuing municipalities or companies replace lost certificates or to prepare properly supported claims for damages.

On the whole, these events did not find unprepared the American banks in the formerly unoccupied zone. The major part of their tangible assets had been placed beyond enemy reach, and their liabilities had been drastically curtailed. In anticipation, the supply of blank travelers' letters of credit of the various banks and the American Express Company had been destroyed or canceled in the presence of a notary public, who drew up a signed affidavit for future submission to the interested parties. Most of the accounts still carried on their books consisted of accounts blocked in accordance with the Vichy decrees.

That these precautions were not futile was demonstrated by the reported shipping by the Germans of large amounts of French bank notes to Switzerland for sale there and conversion into gold. The scheme was uncovered when the exchange rate for French bank notes, especially for the 1000-franc and 5000-franc denominations, dropped sensationally at the Swiss bourses because of unusually large and persistent offerings. When the Swiss Government learned of these shipments, dealings in gold coins were forbidden except with the approval of the National Bank of Switzerland.

By May, 1943, the Free French of General de Gaulle were exercising the functions of a *de facto* government in the French colonies in West Africa, New Caledonia, the Cameroons, Syria, and Madagascar, and accordingly they established exchange control offices and opened dollar accounts in the United States. As the Free French could not as yet be considered a *de jure* government, there was at first some doubt as to the right of the exchange control offices to dispose of funds belonging to private individuals who later might assert their rights of ownership. The Free French Delegation in the United States was headed by Adrien Tixier, with André Istel, a former private banker of Paris and a recognized authority on French economic and financial matters, the delegation's first financial adviser.

After the liberation of Paris, on August 24, 1944, nearly all the United States business places were found to be undamaged, although some of the bank buildings had been used by Vichy and German official organizations. The head offices of United States banks were immediately flooded with hundreds of requests from customers desirous of tracing relatives and friends in France. However, the Presidential orders preventing communication with France had not been revoked or modified as yet, and the banks were therefore not in a position to establish contact with their former French offices, let alone arrange for the transaction of business. Realizing the urgency of some of the matters crying for the attention of the Paris representatives of American interests, the State Department lent its services for the transmission of messages both to and from certain French banking correspondents. United States banks were thus enabled to instruct their former French associates to extend all possible assistance to the United States Army units stationed in Paris.

The War Department, too, concluded that it would be to the advantage of the members of the armed forces if American banks were promptly invited to lend their facilities to the United States contingents that were now making their headquarters in Paris. In October, 1944, the New York banks that formerly had branches in France conferred on the matter with Major General Arthur H. Carter, Fiscal Director of the War Department and a former partner of Haskins & Sells, at his office in the Pentagon Building. Carter, who had just returned from France and Italy, already had the project so far advanced that he was awaiting only the official approval of General Army Headquarters before asking the Treasury to issue to the banks the required license permitting them to offer their services to the Army abroad; this was done soon afterward. Assistant Secretary of War John McCloy, later President of the International Bank for Reconstruction and Development was present during part of the meeting. At this meeting the bank representatives were George Whitney, Nelson D. Jay, and Henry C. Alexander, of J. P. Morgan & Co., Robert F. Loree, of the Guaranty Trust Company, and officers of the Chase National Bank, National City Bank, and the Bankers Trust Company.

On November 4 the Treasury Department announced the lifting of certain of the restrictions governing commercial communications with liberated France. Thereafter, bank statements, financial records, and business reports could be transmitted. Concerns in France and the United States could exchange information and re-establish contacts. Banks could advise their customers of the status of their accounts. New signature cards could be secured. Cable transfers not exceeding $500 per month could be made.

On October 9 the *Journal Officiel,* of France, published two decrees of General de Gaulle's provisional government relative to the holding of gold coin, foreign securities, and exchange. Every owner was to deposit his holdings within two months at the Bank of France, while all holders of foreign property or of foreign currency or drafts payable in foreign moneys were to deliver them to agencies approved by the Minister of Finance. These instructions, however, do not appear to have been heeded to any measurable degree. As will be seen later, successive French governments made similar appeals from time to time; as late as July, 1947, the French Minister of Finance, in the effort to obtain United States dollars, requisitioned all securities issued by American corporations that were then owned by French citizens.

In November, 1944, the Paris branches of United States banks were designated as general depositaries of public moneys of the United States, and thus became able to carry accounts to the official credit of disbursing officers or other agencies of the United States Army and Navy, as well as for post exchanges, the Red Cross, the USO, and so forth. In December certain officers of American banks with branches in Paris, secured visas to visit France. The group which included Robert Loree and Joseph Larkin, who had long been stationed abroad before the war, arrived in the early days of January,

1945, after a stormy voyage on a small tramp steamer, and found those of their staff who had lived through the occupation undernourished and suffering from lack of heat in their offices and homes. After the necessary licenses had been secured, food packages were dispatched regularly to alleviate the distress and help the morale of the personnel, and high cost-of-living allowances were awarded. By April any danger of internal disturbances seemed removed, transportation had become more normal, and the securities held in the south of France were accordingly sent back to Paris.

On January 19, 1945, the United States banks and business concerns, together with resident individuals, were startled when severe drastic regulations were promulgated affecting their holdings of gold, foreign exchange, and securities, both within and outside France. Even nonresidents of France, including foreign concerns, owned directly or controlled by French citizens or corporations were forbidden, except under license, to dispose of their franc holdings even when these were in the form of franc accounts or French securities. No entries in franc accounts were to be made without license except the crediting of coupons of French securities or of redeemed bonds already on deposit with French banks, and excepting also the payment from actual deposits of 1,000 francs per day to nonresidents temporarily in France, with a maximum of 20,000 francs per month. Nonresidents except if licensed likewise were forbidden to buy or sell or give or take as collateral French securities. They could not subscribe to the capital of a French company or exercise their rights in the case of an increase in the capital of companies owned by them or in which they had an interest. Going considerably further than the October 9 decrees, the new regulations required all banks to report before March 1, 1945, all gold, foreign currencies, and securities held by them for nonresidents, including instruments of all kinds representing foreign assets deposited in France for account of residents of France. Furthermore, every resident of France, including foreigners, was to declare all property, cash, securities, real estate, and so forth located outside France.

These unusually rigid requirements, of course, caused much uneasiness and resentment among foreigners living in France. Apprehension was expressed that rigorous measures of this kind, however warranted by existing needs, might ultimately lead to the elimination of foreign capital and enterprise in France. The French Ministry of Finance, realizing the commotion caused by its decrees among foreign circles, issued a statement in which it explained that the sole purpose it had in mind was to facilitate a general check-up, necessitated by the prolonged occupation of the country by the enemy. The Finance Minister denied that the government had any intention of requisitioning assets belonging to aliens or of interfering with their normal activities, and affirmed the government's wish to continue the liberal policy traditional in France with respect to foreigners whose business operations were not contrary to the national interest.

In April, 1945, a technical innovation was introduced with regard to the purchase of French Treasury bills by the local banks for the short-term investment of their franc deposits. Henceforth, all Treasury Bills were to be delivered to the Bank of France, which was designated as the future central clearinghouse for all French Treasury transactions. Special Treasury bill accounts were opened in the name of each purchaser, and all subsequent dealings were marked merely by bookkeeping entries on the ledgers of the central bank. This step was taken on the ground that it would result in substantial savings in the cost of printing, handling, and transporting Treasury paper. It also was represented as likely to improve the control of the money market and to reduce the criticism leveled by the leftist parties at the large credit institutions to the effect that these could squeeze the money market through mass redemptions of Treasury notes whenever the composition or the policies of a ministry were deemed inimical to their interests. In other quarters it was feared that the new plan was indicative of future action leading to the ultimate nationalization of the large French commercial banks. It was, indeed, not long before the great French credit establishments—the Crédit Lyonnais, the Comptoir National d'Escompte de Paris, and the Société Générale—were taken over by the French Government. In the past, private ingenuity and enterprise had played an outstanding part in making France the leading financial, banking, and investment center of the European Continent. Now no one dared to augur what the banks' evolution would be under public control and the more constrictive policies of officially inspired management.

Notwithstanding an unbalanced budget, the continued heavy deficits incurred by the nationalized industries and the burdensome military expenditures in Indo-China the economic position of France has shown conspicuous gains especially since the beginning of 1949. Owing to the considerable influx of tourist money and the contributions made by the Economic Cooperation Administration, the French franc has gradually been stabilized as evidenced by a marked decline of the dollar and of gold in the free market. In August, 1950, the Bank of France announced the revaluation of its gold reserve at the rate of 349.60 francs to the dollar instead of 119 francs which had been the basis since December, 1945. Succeeding the 1949 devaluation, the move reflected the *de facto* stabilization of the currency. Soon thereafter the French Government obtained a loan of 225 million dollars from a syndicate of United States banks headed by the Chase National Bank and J. P. Morgan & Co., Inc., 25 million being an unsecured short-term loan bearing interest at 2 1/2 percent per annum.

SUMMARY

The evolution of United States banking activities in France and of French financial representation in the United States is described. The tourist traffic and the financial requirements of American enterprises established in France have bulked large in the regular work of the United States bank offices in Paris. Foreign-exchange operations have been particularly important because of the recurrent shifting of funds to and from France in accordance with the ebb and flow of French and European politics and the changing appraisal of the monetary outlook by French investors and businessmen. The threatening international situation in the summers of 1938 and 1939 made necessary diverse provisions against possible emergencies. After the German break-through in June, 1940, the banks' staffs fled from Paris, later opening temporary quarters in the unoccupied southeastern provinces of France. The entrance of the United States into the war brought new difficulties for the American bank branches and the French subsidiaries of United States corporations, as did the assumption of control by the enemy over the Paris branches. The former managers, after their return to Paris following the liberation of the capital, had to contend at the outset with the stringent regulations affecting foreign transactions that were promulgated by the Free French Government of General de Gaulle. Meanwhile the future was clouded by the nationalization of the great French credit establishments. However, a significant improvement in the economic conditions of the country has recently resulted in the *de facto* stabilization of the franc, accomplished with the help of a United States dollar loan.

X

GERMANY

EVER SINCE THE UNITED STATES first ventured into the field of international finance American relations with German banks have been of integral importance. In the years after the Civil War German investors were among the first from overseas to acquire United States railway and industrial stocks and bonds in considerable amounts. Some of the private banking houses in Manhattan were the offspring of old Frankfort firms which continued to maintain intimate business relations with their affiliates. This chapter will seek to examine how it came about that after the First World War United States financial institutions became so deeply enmeshed in German private finance that when, in 1931, their debtors were unable to meet their obligations, it was many years before they could retrieve even a part of their sizable outstanding credits and loans.

In Chapter I reference has been made to the spectacular collapse of the German mark in 1922, when the printing presses of the young German republic were worked overtime, prices were being quoted mainly in foreign money, mark quotations had to be changed hourly, bank notes carried numerous colored stamped impressions showing their changing value, frightened depositors withdrew 75 percent of all deposits in German banks, and everybody was scrambling to convert liquid funds into foreign exchange or capital goods in order to hedge against the growing deterioration of the mark. It was not until inflation had wiped out the whole internal debt and had confiscated the savings and the working capital of the German people that the currency was finally stabilized, the old mark being established at one millionth part of the new Rentenmark.

Following the rehabilitation of the currency in 1924 and the parallel balancing of the budget of the Reich under the watchful eyes of the Reparation Commission, German bankers resumed their periodical visits to the United States. The Deutsche Bank and the Direction der Disconto Gesellschaft, the two leading Berlin banks, reopened their New York representative offices, and the Dresdner Bank, the Commerz und Privat Bank, and other banks appointed agents to cultivate their American connections. Credit began once more to flow into Germany, for the belief in German industry, scientific skill, and integrity had not been shattered by the financial debacle. In quick succession the British, French, Dutch, Swiss, and finally the United States banks succumbed to the lure of the higher interest and commission rates offered by German borrowers. Supposedly "self-liquidating" credits were granted to German banks and banking houses, and in some cases also to leading industrial concerns. Short-term cash advances likewise were extended, on a moderate scale to begin with, but gradually over the next seven or eight years many hundreds of millions of dollars in short-term credits were poured into the whole of Central Europe in one form or another. Only later was it discovered that most of this prodigious accommodation had actually been utilized, in effect, to bridge the gap in the German balance of payments by financing that part of reparations which could not be met by deliveries in kind.

Meanwhile, carried away by their desire to develop their foreign business, more and more banks in the various creditor countries rushed to participate in what appeared to be an exceptionally favorable opportunity to garner attractive earnings by helping a nation that before the Great War had enjoyed the highest credit rating, reserved for debtors of undoubted standing. The fact that many German banks had already received and used the maximum credit lines to which they were entitled by reason of their resources was either unknown or overlooked. Each lending country operated on its own without apparent regard for the loans and credits showered upon the central European borrowers by their rivals in other countries. If the excessive size of the indebtedness was evident to some observers, it was not denounced publicly. However, had the creditors had accurate information on the extent of the private loans and on the increasing difficulty of converting marks into the foreign currency for transfer abroad, they might have been spared the tragic experiences that followed in 1931.

The spectacular flow of capital overseas was attributed in the United States to some degree to the cheap money policy of the Federal Reserve Banks. In addition, the Federal Reserve Board broadened the regulations governing the acceptance by member banks of short-term drafts issued to finance the shipment of goods between foreign countries and the cost of merchandise stored abroad. The more generous rulings were interpreted by foreign drawers as permitting the use of acceptance credits even after a shipment had been delivered to the consignee and even though such bills after one renewal could no longer be considered as drawn against "actually existing values." The use of acceptances was further promoted when member banks of the Federal Reserve system were authorized to accept drafts for up to 100 percent of their capital and surplus. The German banks hastened to take advantage of the more liberal regulations, disregarding the fact that short-time credits, as a rule, carry no commitment on the part of the grantor to renew the bills at their due dates. In the absence of special stipulations to the contrary, it was assumed by the lending banks that the experienced central European bankers were familiar with this established international banking usage.

In the spring of 1931 the officers of certain American institutions sensed that German finance had seriously overextended itself. Accordingly they recommended the cancellation of open but unused lines of credit in certain cases; in others they favored immediate requests for collateral or the furnishing of satisfactory guarantees. As early as May 9, President Hoover, deeply concerned about the situation and seeking to forestall open bankruptcy, proclaimed a moratorium of the debts due the United States Government by Germany. A month later, the Reichsbank, which by then, because of heavy withdrawals of foreign credits, had lost 250 million dollars of gold and foreign exchange, received a 20-day credit of approximately 100 million dollars, supplied in equal shares by the Bank for International Settlements, the Bank of England, the Bank of France, and the Federal Reserve Bank of New York on behalf of all Federal Reserve Banks.[1]

In July the International Acceptance Bank, to further strengthen the German exchange situation, arranged a 50 million dollar credit for the benefit of the German Gold Discount Bank. This credit was secured by German trade bills, promissory notes of the German post office and railroads, and by agricultural gold mortgage bonds. After several renewals, this credit was duly paid off in July, 1933.

1 Seventeenth annual report of the Federal Reserve Bank of New York for year ending December 31, 1931.

Following the financial difficulties of the Dresdner Bank, the Allgemeine Deutsche Kreditanstalt, and the Darmstaedter Bank—which culminated in the bank holiday on July 13 and the raising of the official discount rate of the Reichsbank to 15 percent—it became evident that the time for palliatives had passed and that concerted action by creditors in the United States and Europe was imperative. At a conference held in London in the latter half of July seven interested governments (Belgium, France, Great Britain, Italy, Japan, the United States, and Germany) recommended that the governors of the respective central banks appoint an international committee to deliberate on the protective steps to be taken on behalf of the creditors of Germany. Accordingly, creditor committees were formed under the auspices of the Bank for International Settlements in London, Paris, Amsterdam, Zurich, and elsewhere for the purpose of guiding and harmonizing the policies of the banking institutions in the various interested countries. In July, Governor George Harrison of the Federal Reserve Bank of New York, at the request of the United States Treasury and State Department, appointed a committee to represent the American banks. Albert H. Wiggin, of the Chase National Bank, was elected chairman; the other original members were Charles E. Mitchell, of the National City Bank, William Potter, of the Guaranty Trust Company, George W. Davison, of the Central Hanover Bank & Trust Company, and F. Abbot Goodhue of the Bank of Manhattan. Later, Winthrop Aldrich succeeded to Albert Wiggin, and James H. Perkins to Charles E. Mitchell; Harvey D. Gibson, of the Manufacturers Trust Company, also joined the committee. From time to time other prominent bankers attended the meetings: Mortimer N. Buckner, Sloan Colt, Percy H. Johnston, Harry Ward, Amadeo P. Giannini, and Edward Delafield. The first meetings took place on July 15 and 16 at the Federal Reserve Bank of New York. There it was agreed to be in the general interest of the United States creditors to pursue a uniform course with respect to all their commitments with German debtors and for the time being to continue maintaining all acceptance lines, time deposits, advances, and loans that were actually outstanding. The preparation of a detailed programme for the future conduct of the individual banks was entrusted to a subcommittee under the chairmanship of F. Abbott Goodhue, the following bank officers being also members: Robert F. Loree, of the Guaranty Trust Company, Joseph T. Cosby, of the National City Bank, Howard J. Rogers, of the Bank of Manhattan, and the author who represented the Chase National Bank, and also functioned as secretary of the senior committee. The firm of Davis, Polk, Wardwell & Reed acted as counsel. During the first few meetings the white-haired John W. Davis, former Solicitor-General of the United States and one-time Democratic candidate for the Presidency, was present, but later he turned the problems over to his partners, Allan Wardwell and Ewen MacVeagh.

In the meantime other committees were formed in Belgium, Italy, Sweden, and Japan. A general meeting of all creditor committees met on August 8, 1931, at Basle with delegates of the Reichsbank and of the German commercial banks. Mr. Wiggin represented the American banks, assisted by James Gannon and Joseph C. Rovensky, vice presidents of the Chase National Bank, and by that bank's economist, the late Benjamin Anderson, Jr. Other banking delegates present were: Sir Walter Layton, London; P. Hofstede de Groot, Amsterdam; Emile Franqui, Brussels; Emile Moreau, Paris; Oscar Rydbeck, Stockholm; R. G. Bindschedler, Zurich; Alberto Beneduce, Rome; T. Tanaka, Tokyo; and Carl Melchior, Hamburg. At Basle a central steering committee was appointed, composed of the chairmen of the committees from the various countries; Mr. Wiggin was elected chairman.

At the meeting of the steering committee there was unanimity as to the need of maintaining a common front. It was agreed that it was imperative to continue, on a practicable and reasonable basis, the short-term facilities that had been granted to Germany, in order that she might be in a position to finance her foreign trade and thus achieve a favorable trade balance that would permit her gradually to amortize her foreign obligations. At the last meeting the first so-called standstill agreement was drafted, and on August 19 was finally initialed by the various creditor committees. As the name or its German equivalent "stillhalte" implies, the agreement proposed that foreign creditor banks should extend the due dates of their credits for a period of six months. It also recommended that foreign exchange contracts be settled as they matured and that reichsmark balances be progressively unfrozen by the German banks. After all countries had signified their approval, the agreement went officially into effect on September 17, to expire on February 29, 1932.[2]

[2] According to the report of the committee, as published by the New York *Times* of August 20, 1931, p. 12, the total short-term German credits outstanding as of August 19, 1931, were estimated at 2,450 million dollars.

During these months while the various national creditor committees were in session at Basle, the American subcommittee held almost daily meetings in New York, at which Deputy Governor Edwin Kenzel, of the Federal Reserve Bank of New York, sat as observer and consultant. The members tackled the incredible amount of detail involved in preparing necessary statistics, drawing up questionnaires to be presented to the United States banks, and providing the senior committee and the American delegates abroad with material and suggestions for consideration at the Basle meetings. The first assignment of the subcommittee was to ascertain the actual amount of short-time debt outstanding in the United States, segregated according to the different forms of liabilities due United States creditors.

From time to time the American banks received verbal reports from the delegates attending the standstill meetings abroad and were asked to pass upon suggestions for demands to be made on the German debtors. The roster of those present at the New York meetings represented practically every institution engaged in foreign banking. It was only too clear that international finance had again suffered a grave setback. This time, however, it was not so much a matter of actual insolvency of the borrowers as of their inability to find sufficient foreign exchange to honor their excessive liabilities in their creditors' currencies. The transfer problem had thrown its ominous shadow over United States banking operations abroad.

In this same historic summer of 1931 a number of German banking affiliates doing business outside Germany were forced to close their doors, calling for additional concerted efforts by American and European bank creditors to safeguard their loans and credits. First the Bank fuer Auswaertigen Handel, in Berlin, affiliate of the Austrian Credit Anstalt, in Vienna, and then the Deutsche Orientbank, of Berlin and Cairo, and the J. F. Schroeder Bank, in Bremen, were forced to invoke moratoria. Other banks, including the Internationale Bank te Amsterdam, and the Amsterdamsche Credit Maatschappij, both of Amsterdam, were next obliged to liquidate their affairs. Finally, on August 23, 1931, the firm of Aron Hirsch & Sohn, of Berlin and Halberstadt, with a long and honorable business career behind it in the metal trade, placed its affairs in the hands of its domestic and foreign creditors.

How had it happened that astute and discerning United States bankers had become so deeply entangled in what turned out to be weak and unsavory loans in Europe? The Committee on Finance of the United States Senate addressed this question to several authoritative financial leaders. The late Otto H. Kahn, partner of Kuhn Loeb & Co., whose judgment was respected in the business world, appeared before the committee on December 21, 1931. He testified that

England was living right across the street, so to speak, from Germany. She had an age-old prestige for judgment and wisdom in the matter of international financial borrowings. We were perfectly justified in following in our judgment of what was reasonable banking practice, the example of a wise old nation like England, being right there, and a wise old nation like Holland, being next door to Germany, who, in proportion to their resources, gave larger short-term credits to Germany than America did.

In answer to a question as to his estimate of short-term credits held in the United States, he said:

My estimate . . . is that it is something in excess of 600 million dollars. Which I do not consider an exorbitant amount for a great creditor nation to extend as an accommodation to an intelligent, hard-working European nation of the magnitude, ability and proven and tested capacity of Germany. It, may be locked up for a while, yes; but that is the ordinary risk of business. And the granting of credits for the purpose of facilitating trade and thereby stimulating the entire economic life of all the world, a repercussion of which is bound to redound to the advantage of America, the granting of such credits is a legitimate, natural, old-established banking function.

At the same hearings, unruffled and bland as always, Thomas W. Lamont, senior partner of J. P. Morgan & Co., asserted that there had been a great deal of exaggeration in the public mind as to the extent of the holdings of United States banks in short-term German bank credits.

What has happened . . . has been simply this, that American banks and the big banks generally over the country, from the Atlantic to the Pacific, have had German banking correspondents for years, probably for generations, and they have been in the habit of granting commercial, and sometimes other sorts of credits, to these German banks for the financing of the exports of American cotton, copper, and all sorts of things. That has been the practice that has gone on, and I am told that there are 90 of these American banks that have been engaged in this perfectly legitimate proper banking process, very necessary to the whole export trade of our country, so far as Germany is concerned. And yet the public mind has been apparently almost inflamed with the idea of large figures. I have heard statements made that certain New York banks, for instance, were loaded up with these

German short-term credits to the extent, in any individual case, of two to three hundred million dollars. Of course, that is perfectly fantastic. I have not looked at the portfolios of the banks in New York, but I happen to know that the largest amount of credit outstanding in any bank is 70 million dollars or thereabouts, and it would be in the case of a bank whose other capital resources were so large that it was not a matter of danger, or even of comment.

On January 4, 1932, Winthrop W. Aldrich, President of the Chase National Bank, appeared before the same Senate committee over which the late Senator Reed Smoot was presiding at the time. Mr. Aldrich explained the origin and use of American short-term credits, their security, liquidity, and geographical distribution. He pointed out that under the Federal Reserve Act facilities were placed at the disposal of United States banks for the granting of acceptance credits to finance imports and exports, as well as warehoused merchandise and shipments between foreign countries; and called attention to the control that the Federal Reserve Board exercised over these banking operations.

With the approach of 1932 and the impending expiration of the first standstill agreement, it was apparent that a renewal would be imperative. Two plans for the rehabilitation of the German banking situation were submitted to the United States Committee, the work respectively of the economist, author, and private banker Felix Somary, the mild-mannered but keen-minded partner of Blankart & Co., Zurich, and of the tall and forceful president of the Société Générale de Belgique and former Minister of Finance of Belgium, Émile Franqui. Both plans contemplated the freeing of the German banks from their liabilities as drawers or guarantors and the substitution of their customers' direct commitments secured by whatever collateral was then held by the German banks for the account of their debtors.

From the end of 1931 S. Parker Gilbert acted as unofficial adviser to the American committee. United States Agent General for Reparation Payments since 1924, he had later been appointed Under Secretary of the Treasury, and after his resignation from that office he had joined J. P. Morgan & Co. as a partner while still in his thirties. He had a thorough knowledge of German affairs and contributed much to the deliberations of the committee. Always tactful and modest, but possessed of determination and unusual resources, he had the ear of even the older and more seasoned bankers who comprised the United States senior committee.

In selecting the bankers who were to represent them at the successive creditor meetings, the Germans naturally put their best foot forward. During the lifetime of Gustav Schlieper, of the Deutsche Bank, their delegation was headed by him, the other members being Otto Jeidels, of the Berliner Handels Gesellschaft, and—acting for German industry—Ludwig Kastl, who, after the Hitler purge, was succeeded by Oscar Sempell, of the Steel Union. Schlieper was one of the galaxy of brilliant bankers who had been graduated from the excellent practical training provided by a long stay with the Direction der Disconto Gesellschaft. He was a frequent visitor in the United States and South America and was highly respected as a banker, although a hard trader. At one period in the middle and late twenties the account of his bank, considered to be the pick of the German business, was coveted by every foreign department head. Schlieper took shrewd advantage of the existing rivalry and contended that his institution was entitled to better rates than its neighbors. Having the interests of his own bank in mind, he succeeded for a few years in persuading his confrères on this side of the ocean that he was conferring a favor when his bank made use of the lavish credits offered to it. This independent pose, indeed, was imitated by some other German bank heads and private bankers, until finally the house of cards erected with so much ingenuity tumbled down. Gustav Schlieper, however, did not live to witness the Twilight of the Gods; he passed away in 1937.

Otto Jeidels, also since deceased, had originally been associated with a prominent Frankfort metal concern. After he joined the Berliner Handels Gesellschaft, he rose rapidly under the tutelage of the veteran banker and renowned wit Carl Fuerstenberg to a senior managing partnership. Principally in charge of the bank's large-scale issuing activities, he represented it on the boards of many prominent industrial corporations. He was endowed with incisiveness and penetration, and it was undoubtedly his well-ordered mind and amazingly quick comprehension of the details of every financial problem coming within his purview that was responsible for his rapid rise in the German financial world.

The English committee was presided over by Frank Tiarks, of the old banking firm of J. Henry Schroeder & Co., Hon. Robert H.

Brand, now Lord Brand of Eydon, of Lazard Brothers, was one of the most active members, and Edward Holland-Martin acted as secretary. Tiarks, because of his thorough mastery of the acceptance business, played a leading role during the conferences. Brand enjoyed a great reputation as a banker and economist, his expert knowledge of currency problems often bringing him to the United States, where in later years he was called upon to serve his country as chairman of the wartime Supply Commission and in other high offices in Washington.

On January 23, 1932, the final draft of the second standstill agreement was signed. It granted a one-year extension of all short-term credits to March 31, 1933. At the suggestion of the Swiss delegation the creditors were given the right to convert up to 25 percent of the unsecured advances to German banks into reichsmarks and to invest the latter in mortgages on real estate and securities, but the amounts thus invested were to remain blocked, that is, could not be withdrawn for at least five years. At the time the second standstill agreement was reached, the total amount due to foreign creditors still aggregated more than one billion dollars. Henceforth, the yearly standstill meetings were to occupy a prominent place in the banking annals of the thirties.

Scarcely six months later, the German financial situation again made front-page history. Rumors were current of the imminence of a general suspension of foreign payments. An American committee meeting was hurriedly called to discuss the measures to be taken in such a contingency. The unanimous opinion was that a moratorium would *ipso facto* terminate the standstill accords, in which event each bank should protect its interests as best it could, seizing German deposits wherever they could be found and selling whatever collateral was being held for the account of German debtors. On this occasion it was stressed that English creditors could rely on the Bank of England to continue discounting German paper, but that the Federal Reserve Banks might be prevented from doing so, since it was possible that the payment of interest, discounts, and commissions in a currency other than United States dollars would render American bank acceptances ineligible under Federal Reserve regulations. However, long before this question arose, most United States banks had decided to carry their German acceptances in their own portfolios rather than permit them to circulate in the discount market; some banks had traded their acceptances with neighbors having similar bills, and had thus secured a second endorsement which made them eligible for rediscount if needed.

During the middle of 1932 five leading German banks had to undergo a sweeping reorganization calling for total write-offs of 247 million dollars. New capital was subscribed by the German Government, which thus came to hold 90 percent of the capital stock of the Dresdner Bank, 70 percent of that of the Allgemeine Deutsche Kredit Anstalt, and 35 percent of that of the Deutsche Bank. This drastic reorganization was supposed to take care of all losses and doubtful accounts, but later many other debtors had to be helped; in many instances the German banks were obliged to waive part of their claims in exchange for promissory notes payable only as, if, and when the debtor's position permitted him to honor the notes either in whole or in part.

In view of these unpropitious internal developments, the foreign creditors uneasily asked themselves whether the Germans would not make an attempt to scale down their foreign commercial debts as well. However, reassuring messages came from the German bankers, who affirmed strongly their unanimous opposition to any devaluation of the currency or reduction of their obligations by legal fiat.

In August, James P. Warburg, who was later to become adviser to the delegation to the World Economic Conference in London, offered a plan for handling the external debts of European countries operating under exchange restrictions. He advocated that the service in foreign currency of the short-term debt be stopped and that in the case of Germany interest and amortization be settled by means of five-year German Treasury bills payable in foreign exchange and bearing interest at 3 percent or thereabouts.

By the end of November, 1932, reports were received from Berlin that sales of marks had been effected at a discount of from 16 percent to as much as 35 percent below the official exchange rate. While some of these transactions might have been privately negotiated to help fugitive capital to escape from Germany, it was believed that others had been consummated with the tacit approval of the German Ministry of Finance, since the latter was reported to be inclined to authorize deals that would permit increased foreign purchases of goods in Germany or that involved the conversion of short-term into long-time liabilities.

Along the same lines, German exporters received permission to use a percentage of the foreign exchange received for goods sold abroad for the purchase of German dollar securities offered at a discount; securities so acquired were turned over to the German companies responsible for their amortization, at prices in marks that would leave the German exporters a profit of 20 to 30 percent. This additional profit was granted them by the German authorities in consideration of their turning the bulk of the dollar proceeds over to the Reichsbank at the official rate, and permitted German manufacturers to undersell their foreign competitors and still show a sufficient return after payment of production costs and all other expenses. On the other hand, the German companies that retired their dollar bonds likewise profited by the transaction in spite of paying a premium in marks, since on the basis of the current market prices for their bonds abroad and the official selling rate for dollars in Germany—even assuming that dollars would have been made available for such a purpose—they were enabled to liquidate part of their capital debt on a basis advantageous to their stockholders.[3]

With the increasing desire of both Germans and foreigners to convert their investments in Germany into hard currencies, various propositions were presented to American banks, all designed to facilitate the partial recovery of capital immobilized in Germany in one form or another.[4]

At the bottom of all the schemes was the willingness of the holders to sell marks at the best price they would fetch irrespective of the exorbitant sacrifices that had to be made by the sellers. Under these conditions it was natural that the foreign creditors and owners of German bonds and stocks should in turn be led to re-evaluate their

[3] This practice was, of course, not confined to Germany. The Department of Commerce has estimated that between 1929 and 1939 some two to three billion dollars, par value, of United States holdings of foreign bonds were repatriated by European and Latin American countries.

[4] One of the most colorful individuals boasting of influential connections in high German circles visited New York in the autumn of 1933. Accompanied by a secretary and an "expert" in registered marks, he called on local banks known to have German credits outstanding and referred to important arrangements that, he said, had already been perfected with some western European institutions for the disposal of frozen central European credits. He left after a few weeks of expensive sojourn in one of the leading hotels, and whether he succeeded in inveigling some of the American creditors has not come to the knowledge of this chronicler. Unverified rumors, however, had it that at least one European bank that had dealings with him had asked the director responsible for the transactions to offer his resignation.

own risks and should come to the conclusion that it would be better to lose part of their assets if they could recover at least a portion of the original investment.

With the approach of the expiration date of the standstill agreement of 1932, various new ideas and suggestions for a possible solution of the short-term debt problem were advanced. One German banker inquired whether his institution's United States creditors would be willing to accept common stock of his bank in part payment of its standstill credits. An important German machine-manufacturing corporation offered to its foreign creditors the option of using the blocked marks tendered in payment of its debts for the purpose of subscribing to the capital stock created in connection with the concern's reorganization. The corporation offered to apply the blocked marks thus received from the foreign creditors to the financing of exports and to turn part of the foreign exchange proceeds of such exports over to the foreign creditor, with the approval of the Reichsbank.

Crena de Jongh, a prominent banker of Amsterdam and now Dutch member of the board of the International Bank for Reconstruction and Development, counseled the segregation of foreign credits into bona fide short-term merchandise credits and finance paper, and the transformation of the latter into mark deposits or long-time bonds payable in foreign currency.

In a statement issued in August, 1932, Robert H. Brand, chairman of the Study Committee, a subcommittee of the Steering Committee, expressed the view that each creditor should state which of his credits he was willing to continue for two or three years, which part he was prepared to fund for ten years, and which fraction he would agree to exchange for a bond of the German Government payable in gold.

However, nothing came of all these proposals. Most foreign creditors reluctantly arrived at the conclusion that their best chance of reducing their loans was to accept repayment in marks and dispose of these marks through the various channels available, as favorable opportunities presented themselves, namely, by selling them to travelers and tourists, for benevolent remittances and to purchasers of German goods, securities, real estate, works of art, and stocks in commercial or industrial German enterprises—outlets that were specifically or implicitly authorized by the standstill agreements. Admittedly, these were poor expedients at best, exposing the creditors to more or less severe losses.

Meanwhile the rehabilitation of world credit and exchange seemed more distant than ever. By now it was clear that the ultimate solution of the German debt problem was dependent upon: (*a*) the mobilization and sale of the remaining German investments and assets of various kinds in overseas countries, although they hardly lent themselves to a rapid turning into cash; (*b*) the creation of an export balance over and above the annual requirements for interest and service on the short- and long-term foreign debt. In view of the heavy tariffs and stringent import restrictions imposed in the creditor countries, including the United States, the attainment by the Reich of a favorable payments balance and consequent repayment from the proceeds of foreign sales of German goods indeed appeared discouragingly remote.

The negotiations for a new standstill agreement at a meeting called for January 30, 1933, were difficult and tedious. Upon his retirement from active business Mr. Wiggin was succeeded as chairman of the United States senior committee by F. Abbot Goodhue, the energetic young president of the Bank of Manhattan. After protracted wrangling with the Germans, a new agreement was finally signed on February 27, 1933, extending the standstill to February 28, 1934. The right for creditors to ask for repayment in reichsmarks was introduced by this agreement, the total not to exceed 5 percent of the aggregate acceptance lines granted by the foreign creditor. The marks so obtained from the debtors were deposited at the Reichsbank in a special registered account; hence these marks were thereafter known as "registered marks." They could be used for the payment of travelers' expenses in Germany and for financing "additional" exports from Germany. According to figures made available at that time, German short-term credits in the United States as of November 30, 1932, amounted to 492 million dollars extended by thirty banks and banking houses in New York and by twenty-eight interior banks. Of the total, 350 million dollars were represented by bank acceptances. About 24 percent of the total German short-term debt was held by United States banks. The following countries in order of importance accounted for the balance: England, Switzerland, Holland, and France, with a sprinkling of credits in Italy, Sweden, and Japan. By this time the gold reserves of the Reichsbank had dwindled to about 310 million marks, which provided a gold cover for the note issue of only 9 percent.

In order to relieve the German debtors and the foreign exchange position of the central bank, the foreign creditors had already twice lowered the interest rates on their outstanding loans. However, the Reichsbank was thought to be taking advantage of this leniency by tacitly allowing the remitting of funds abroad for the purchase of German bonds at the fire-sale prices that were being conceded by panicky holders in foreign markets. Had these transfers been stopped and had the interest on the long-term debt been pared to 4 or 4 1/2 percent, the banking creditors believed that the most difficult aspect of the German exchange puzzle might have been resolved.

On Saturday afternoon, May 13, 1933, a meeting was called at short notice by Governor Harrison at the Federal Reserve Bank of New York. The object of the meeting was to receive an urgent communication from Hjalmar Schacht, who had made a lecture tour through this country, and was about to return to Germany; he was accompanied by Dr. Northolf, a director of the Reichsbank. Because of the week-end, most members of the senior committee were absent from the city, but James Perkins, George Davison, F. Abbot Goodhue, and the writer, who substituted for Winthrop Aldrich, were present. The president of the Reichsbank, erect and formal, stated that because of the declining metallic reserves of the bank and in view of recent foreign-trade statistics, he proposed to request the representatives of the short-term creditors and the bondholders to discuss the situation with him in Berlin on May 25. He intimated that thereafter it might be necessary to cut down on German payments in foreign exchange, but he wished first to offer an opportunity to all concerned to become acquainted with the difficult situation with which Germany was confronted. In the ensuing discussion Schacht's attention was called to the important purchases of German long-term bonds at cut-rate prices that had been observed in the New York market and seemed to indicate that large amounts of dollars were being provided for this purpose, while at the same time ingenious arguments were being advanced for a reduction in the payment of interest and commission to short-term creditors in the United States and elsewhere. Dr. Schacht, imperturbable and frigidly polite, evaded an answer. He read a statement that he intended to give to the press, after which the conference broke up.

The Berlin meeting took place as announced, but the foreign bankers present, including the representatives of issuing houses that had sponsored German external loans, discovered that the transfer problem was not so serious as Schacht had painted it; while the country's exchange position was impaired, this condition could be ascribed in no small measure to the new policy of rearming and of conducting a costly propaganda abroad. Schacht's most difficult problem was the financing of an elaborate public works program (the "battle of production") comprising, among other things, the building of highways, and doing this without increasing the pressure on the currency. Nevertheless, on July 1, 1933, the moratorium foreshadowed during Schacht's New York visit went into effect. All payments in foreign currencies of interest, sinking fund, and debt retirement on long-term foreign loans were suspended, but the service was continued in German marks. However, the short-term standstill debt was not affected. These moves were immediately reflected in the foreign exchange markets, where the registered marks dropped to a 18 3/4 percent discount. In all fairness it should at least be held to Dr. Schacht's credit that he showed by his actions that as a former commercial banker he felt that the claims of private lenders deserved prior consideration, and the European and United States short-term creditors, in spite of the losses they suffered, were probably indebted to him for what little consideration was grudgingly shown to them by the Nazi authorities.

A little more than a month after the Berlin meeting a new ambassador was appointed by President Roosevelt to represent American interests in Germany. Prior to his departure from the United States, the members of the subcommittee met the new ambassador, William E. Dodd, in New York. Dr. Dodd, a quiet man, looked every bit the professor of philosophy. Serious and careful in his statements, he was frank to confess that he knew very little about the German debt; his chief source of information was a ninety-page monograph prepared for him by the government. The members present explained to Dr. Dodd the origin and strictly commercial character of the short-term credits and stressed that behind the individual creditor banks hundreds of thousands of American stockholders were indirectly harmed by the German default and that therefore not merely a score of prominent international bankers but also a large number of investors had a substantial stake in this situation. Dr. Dodd was sympathetic and assured the subcommittee of his interest and full future co-operation.

In August the Reichsbank let it be known with regard to the transfer moratorium on the long-term debt that it was prepared to authorize the *Konversionskasse* (the official conversion agency) to settle interest and dividends due foreign holders on the basis of 50 percent in foreign money and 50 percent in *Reichsmark* scrip. German exporters were invited to buy these scrip marks at 50 percent discount, but had at the same time to obligate themselves to sell to the Reichsbank all foreign currencies obtained by them with the aid of the additional exports thus made possible. Fearing that this new scheme might be regarded critically by Germany's foreign competitors, Dr. Schacht endeavored to make clear in an interview that there was no intention on the part of the German authorities to subsidize the German exporters beyond allowing them to sell German products at competitive prices. He was not going to enrich German exporters, he emphasized, and stated that he intended to make just enough concessions to them to enable German trade abroad to hold its own, as compared with other countries that had depreciated their currencies. Although he contended that he had a moral right to use marks at a discount up to a certain degree, he admitted that if he went beyond a reasonable limit the danger of foreign embargoes on German imports would become real. He pointed to the fact that English pounds and United States dollars had been devalued *de jure* or *de facto* by 30 to 40 percent, and he felt that he was warranted in granting German exporters a similar advantage.

When this new device became public, the United States Government decided to invoke Section 303 of the United States Tariff Act in all cases where German imported goods had been financed by the use of scrip marks. This section entitled Countervailing Duties provided that

> whenever any country shall pay or bestow directly or indirectly any bounty or grant to the manufacturer, producer or exporter of any article manufactured in such country and such article is dutiable under the provisions of the American Customs Act, then upon the importation of such article in the United States, there shall be levied and paid in all such cases, in addition to the duties otherwise imposed by this Act, an additional duty

equal to the net amount of such bounty or grant however the same be paid or bestowed.

Early in 1934 with the approaching expiration of the newest standstill agreement, the New York banks decided to re-examine the commission rate schedule generally applied by all American banks. The prevailing terms for credits guaranteed by German banks were then as follows:

	Percentage per Year
Acceptances fully secured by marketable staples	
At world market prices	1
At internal prices with proper margin	2
Genuine reimbursement credits, with evidence of shipment of staple commodities from North and South America to Germany, including re-imports from Central European ports	2
Acceptances secured by pledged collections	3 1/4
Advances secured by pledged collections	3 3/4
Miscellaneous finance bills	3 7/8

The purpose of varying rates was to encourage the debtors to take advantage of the most favorable rates by directing to United States banks self-liquidating bona fide commercial business that, because of its nature, was likely to produce the foreign currencies needed to pay off the corresponding acceptance or advance at maturity.

On March 31, 1934, the standstill was again renewed, with minor changes, until February 28, 1935. One privilege extended to foreign creditors on this occasion was the option to transfer to any other creditor that had credits outstanding to the same German debtor the right to demand repayment in registered marks. The various exchange brokers lost no time in establishing a market for the purchase and sale of these "rights." Some banks, particularly eager to reduce their credits, were willing to pay 1/4 to 3/4 percent for the right to call credits granted to certain German banks, while in the case of credits extended to private banking houses or industrial concerns as much as 1 1/2 to 2 percent ($1,500 to $2,000 for each $100,000) was readily conceded.

In the spring of 1934 the foreign creditors became seriously alarmed over the obvious policy of the Germans of constantly increasing the types of marks as an alternative to overt devaluation. According to all indications this had become a fixed feature of German financial policy. Statistics revealed that during the first quarter of 1934 registered marks created under the provisions of the standstill agreement were being steadily eliminated because of other cheaper methods of financing German exports. There were various causes for the constant pressure exerted by the ruling political faction in the German Government for higher bounties to German exporters; in addition to the competition with the depreciated pound and dollar, there were the restrictive effects of the growing volume of quotas and clearings introduced by neighboring countries and the fruitless search for new credits from America and Great Britain. Yet, open devaluation was frowned upon by German economists and financiers as certain to increase the cost of needed raw materials imported to feed the industries manufacturing goods for export. Moreover, the advantage from the lower quotations of the creditors' devalued exchanges that accrued to debtors who had borrowed when sterling and dollars commanded higher gold values, would be lost. Besides, any tampering with the currency might summon up once more before the German people the dreaded specter of inflation. Lastly, until the pound and the dollar had been definitely stabilized there existed the risk that the level selected for the devalued mark might fail to prove effective after all.

Faced with the recurrent threat of the declaration of a moratorium on the short-term German debts and the consequent termination of the standstill agreement, some United States banks, in order to protect their claims against such an emergency, explored the possibility of levying attachments against any German balances or assets free of lien that might be traced in some of the banks fortunate enough not to be implicated in the German financial difficulties. Elaborate legal documents were prepared for the purpose by counsel, asserting the rights of the claimant and setting forth details such as the names of the debtors, the amounts owing, the form of the indebtedness (whether loans or credits), their maturities, and the general terms underlying the transactions. The week-end of June 15, 1934, was particularly critical in this regard, since reports indicated an especial danger at that date of a declaration of a moratorium, lawyers, notaries, secretaries, and other employees being in attendance at the banking offices ready for immediate action if necessary. The lawyers had even gone so far as to take the precaution to ascertain where over the week-end they could locate the judge to sign the orders. Fortunately, the crucial days passed without the necessity for the banks to take the extreme steps for which they were prepared.

By August, 1934, registered marks were being offered at 39 percent discount below the value of the free mark. Nevertheless, American importers refrained from financing purchases of German merchandise by means of registered marks; the German exporters were generally willing to submit quotations in dollars or free marks, since they received a subsidy from the Gold Discount Bank equivalent to the loss suffered by selling on this basis. The price of the goods was raised correspondingly if the American importer wished to settle in registered marks. At first, the methods employed were so cleverly concealed that for a time it was not possible to apply United States Tariff Act provisions on foreign dumping.

In October the discount on registered marks reached an all-time high of 50 percent. Nevertheless, the United States banks continued, with apparently increased energy, to liquidate slowly and in orderly fashion their remaining German credits. By this time, of the amounts outstanding in 1931 more than 50 percent had been liquidated in one way or another, albeit at a heavy sacrifice. However, for all the substantial write-offs, it must be acknowledged that so far as the terms of the standstill agreements went, they were faithfully carried out. The legitimacy of the debts was never challenged, and even the critical American bank examiners were confident, when making their half-yearly reviews, that given time and patience a reasonable portion of the debts would be finally paid.

In January, 1935, American cotton merchants considered a complex plan under which the United States would sell 800,000 bales of cotton to Germany. The proposed deal would have permitted American shippers to sell the raw cotton against payment in *Reichsmarks* which were to be credited to a special account called *Ausland Sonderconto*. Of the invoice, 75 percent was to be paid in marks and 25 percent in dollars. As an inducement for agreeing to a partial payment in marks, the American cotton exporter was to be offered a premium of 22 1/2 percent over the current market price. The marks so received were to be used exclusively for the purchase of German goods. However, the project was abandoned when the American group learned that English, Dutch, French, and other businessmen had encountered many obstacles in similar clearing bargains with the Germans, having sold Germany large quantities of merchandise only to discover that unexpected restrictions on exports from Germany rendered it impossible to import German goods suitable for their home consumption and that because of lack of foreign exchange the Germans pleaded inability to perform their contracts.

The next meeting of the creditor committees was held in Berlin in February, 1935, with Harvey D. Gibson heading the American delegation. Chiefly owing to his insistence, the Reichsbank representatives were compelled to affirm that they had no intention of creating additional kinds of blocked marks competitive with registered marks or having preferential rights. According to statistics then presented, the total standstill debt had been reduced from 6,280 million *Reichsmarks* at the end of July, 1931, to 2,008 million at the end of December, 1934, a reduction of 68 percent. Between the same dates the American standstill debt alone had declined from 2,067 million marks to 529 million, a decrease of 75 percent.

In early 1935 the German Government, realizing that racial persecution had made German goods unacceptable to many people abroad and seeking to offset the consequent gradual decline of trade with America, introduced what became known as the *aski* method. Under this system American exporters were invited to ship cotton, cotton waste, oil, metals, and other commodities to Germany, the mark proceeds of which were to be credited to them in a "foreigners special account for inland payment." The account, it was proposed, would be carried in the name of the shipper's home bank. The balances in the account, with prior German approval, could be used for paying for the specific German goods simultaneously sanctioned for shipment abroad, the transaction thus being not unlike barter. The account became known as the *aski* account; the permit once obtained was good until exhausted.

German ingenuity in devising ever-fresh schemes to lure foreign buyers seemed inexhaustible. In August, 1935, it was learned that the German *Konversionskasse* intended to create a new blocked mark, to be known as the *Tilgungssperrmark,* for travel purposes. This new encroachment upon the field of the registered mark called forth an immediate protest on the part of the American committee. The German reply explained that these new marks were meant only to be used by the original owners of German securities. Brokers were quick to offer these special marks at 17 cents for benevolent remittances, while registered marks, which could be used only in conjunction with 50 percent of free marks (costing 40.40 cents per mark) would call for an expenditure of 32 cents by the sender. Coupon marks were quoted at that time at 14 1/2 cents, but as they were subject to a German tax of 55 percent, their net cost worked out at 32 1/2 cents; similarly, scrip marks, quoted at 9 1/2 cents, were liable to a tax of 70 percent, making their net cost 32 cents.

During the whole course of the standstill, travel marks played an important role. They were available in the form of travel checks very similar to American Express Company travelers' checks and were sold by most of the banks having credits frozen in Germany. Some red tape, however, was involved. The traveler had to present himself in person at the bank on which the checks were drawn or at which the letter of credit issued in the place of the travel checks was payable in order that the date on which payment was made and the amount withdrawn could be noted on his passport. Thus, this official document was transformed into a miniature travel expense ledger, a design for which it was hardly intended by the Secretary of State. The amount to which each holder was entitled was originally limited to 3,000 marks per month, but with proper German authorization larger amounts could be obtained, especially by foreign merchants desirous of buying German goods. Outward and inward steamship passages could also be secured under certain conditions by tendering registered marks, provided that no rebate was allowed and that the rules of the Atlantic conference thus were not infringed. The Passion Play in Oberammergau in 1934 and the Olympic Games in Berlin in the summer of 1936 offered a large field for the sale of travel marks.

Why were the banks so interested in the sale of travel marks? The dollar checks, after having been presented for payment abroad and cashed in marks, were sent to the issuing bank in the United States, and the face amount of the checks was placed to the credit of the account of the German bank that had honored the checks. Thus the dollar balances of the various German debtor banks grew until a sufficient amount was on deposit to pay off at least a fraction of their indebtedness.

The spring of 1936 found Germany in the same precarious economic condition as before. The unsettled international situation, owing in part to the Italian-Ethiopian conflict, clouded the outlook.

It was increasingly difficult to judge Germany's debt-paying capacity on the basis of published statistics, because it was believed that most official German data had ceased to be reliable. Meanwhile, the country's ability to make payments in foreign money remained severely impaired. Under these conditions, even though the Germans avoided a formal break with their foreign creditors, it was not surprising that some of the American adherents to the standstill agreements became restive and considered whether their interests might not be better served if they avoided joining in another binding agreement and reassumed their liberty of action.

The original need for a standstill convention grew out of an attempt to protect all the creditors in the various countries and pave the way for a gradual orderly liquidation. By mutual agreement the banks tried to prevent a precipitate scramble by the participants. To avert a fatal deterioration of their position, it was conceded that it would be in the common interest to maintain their respective positions—in the words of the official document—to "insure the maintenance of short-term banking credits to Germany . . . to assist in establishing ways and means for a more definite solution of the German indebtedness problem."

So far, the solidarity of the foreign creditors had impressed the Germans. They had hesitated to take any drastic measures that would have stamped them as defaulters. Moreover, the need for credit to finance their current requirements of raw materials and commodities to keep their industries going and their people fed and clothed was a powerful incentive for them to continue to co-operate with their foreign creditors and keep their good will. Any creditor playing a lone game would have incurred the risk of receiving a less generous deal than that accorded to the adhering creditors. Moreover, under existing German legislation he would have lacked the legal means to proceed against his debtors. Of course, one of the main reasons that any bank should wish to resign from the group of creditors was to regain freedom to cancel permanently the lines of credit that remained unused. Yet the number of United States banks that retired from the standstill was small. The motivating cause in all such cases was the fact that these banks, by various schemes, had succeeded either in being reimbursed in part or in transferring their German credits to others in the United States or abroad who, more or less as a speculation, were willing to take them over at bargain prices in the hope that with improving world conditions they might derive a profit.

A detailed study of Germany's financial situation hardly justified any optimistic views of Germany's future on the part of the creditors that assembled in Berlin, in February, 1936, when renewal of the standstill for another year was approved. The public debt had increased to tremendous proportions. The German budget was not a faithful reflection of probable revenues and expenditures, a great part of the latter being carried outside; the suspicion that an all-inclusive budget would be far out of balance gave rise to many unfavorable rumors. Still, there were also some favorable factors. Business was stimulated by the feverish armaments and the public works program. There was a decrease in unemployed, and the national income was mounting. On the other hand, Germany's territorial demands, voiced more and more insistently, and their possible international effects caused deep concern.

At the time of the February meeting there were still outstanding in the United States 136 million dollars of standstill credits and 64 million of other German short-term credits, mainly German Government notes due to the Lee Higginson group.[5] The total for all countries under the standstill arrangements was estimated to have amounted to 320 million dollars on June 30, 1936, of which the United States held 80 million, or 25 percent, England 136 million,[6] Switzerland 60 million, and Holland 30 million, the remaining 14 million being divided among a number of countries.

The list of the different kinds of marks devised by the fertile brains of the German monetary authorities became longer as the necessity of finding new sources likely to yield foreign currencies waxed more and more pressing. The various types that were created are listed below.

(1) Free *Reichsmarks*
(2) Blocked marks
(3) Registered marks
(4) Tourist marks
(5) Benevolent marks (a mixture of 50 percent registered and 50 percent free marks)

[5] See pp. 241–247.

[6] The large English total demonstrates that the English banks—be it said to their credit—even though the shadows deepened not only stood by their traditional practice of being patient with their debtors, but at times even consented to grant additional lines, although in this instance their generous attitude proved rather costly in the end.

(6) *Treuhand* marks (arising from the payment of Dawes and Young loan coupons)
(7) *Kreditsperrmarks* (blocked credit marks)
(8) Marks derived from old credit balances, similar to *Kreditsperrmarks*
(9) Emigrant marks (*Rueckwanderer* marks, similar to *Kreditsperrmarks*
(10) Blocked securities marks
(11) Coupon marks (usable for benevolent remittances, but subject to a German tax of 60 percent)
(12) Amortization marks from the repayment of German dollar bonds
(13) Scrip marks (issued by the conversion office for German external debts)
(14) *Aski* marks
(15) Barter and compensation marks (similar to *aski* marks)
(16) Silver marks
(17) British Empire *aski* marks
(18) Various clearing marks in connection with clearing agreements between Germany and foreign countries
(19) Orange marks for trade with Palestine
(20) Coffee marks used in trading with Brazil, Guatemala, etc.

The use of these different marks was surrounded by numerous and complex regulations. The Germans took a leaf out of the history of our own Civil War, when barter was resorted to in the South after the Confederate currency lost its value and civilians refused to exchange goods for depreciated Confederate money. It would go beyond the scope of this chapter to describe in detail the elaborate barter transactions in connection with which the foreign departments of United States banks were sometimes asked to assist. It need only to be noted that at times, under them, German machinery might first be exchanged for Hungarian grain, the Hungarian grain, in turn, traded for tobacco in Turkey, the Turkish tobacco later swapped for Rumanian oil, and the latter finally sold for American dollars.

On June 4, 1936, the United States Treasury issued a new ruling bearing on Section 303 of the Tariff Act of 1930. Heretofore the department had dealt mildly with minor German infringements of the act. However, certain importers evidently had prevailed upon the customs officials to have the question of German-subsidized merchandise entering United States ports referred to the Attorney General for a strict interpretation of that section of the law. The Attorney General ruled that imports from Germany, whether subsidized in that country or outside, contravened Section 303 and that countervailing duties had therefore to be levied upon such merchandise. As free marks were worth 40.40 cents per mark and registered marks 22 cents, it became incumbent upon the customs officers to charge a duty of 18.40 cents per mark in order to offset the bounty received by the exporter through the utilization of cheap registered marks, the regular duty, of course, being imposed in addition. This ruling, even though applying for the time being only to ten specific articles, such as cameras, chinaware, and toys, made any further purchase of German goods fraught with considerable risk, for according to the Treasury further articles were to be added when necessary. So far as the effect on the standstill creditors was concerned, the ruling seemed for all practical purposes to eliminate the use of registered marks in connection with German imports.

Notwithstanding the obstacles placed in the way of her exports abroad, Germany's foreign indebtedness showed a steady decrease. Not the least cause for this was the devaluation of the currencies of all her principal creditors. First, the abandonment of the gold standard by England in 1931, then the reduction of the gold contents of the dollar in 1934, and finally the disintegration of the gold bloc in 1936, when Switzerland, Holland, and Sweden found it impossible to maintain their currencies at their former parities, came as unexpected windfalls to Germany and the other central European debtor nations. Their foreign debts were thereby reduced by as much as 30 or 40 percent, and to that extent the task of the respective banks of issue was alleviated.

Early in 1937 there was a resurgence of proposals for the extension of financial assistance to Germany. One plan discussed in Washington involved a loan of 50 million dollars in the form of raw cotton, oil, lard, fruit, and other commodities. It was advocated on the ground that it would benefit the cotton planters and other producers, and the middlemen, railroads, shipping companies, and insurance underwriters. The banking fraternity felt no great enthusiasm for such a loan, since it had already been demonstrated that guarantees of the Nazi Government could not be relied upon. Based upon their experience with the German Government credit, known under the name of Lee Higginson credit (of which more later), the banks were loath to envision another important loan, regardless of its form.

The seventh standstill meeting took place in February, 1937, the agreement being extended for another year to February 28, 1938.

Some unutilized lines of credit were canceled. A new license fee was imposed of $2.50 per 100 marks to be paid by each traveler, from which it was hoped that 7–8 million dollars might be collected. The amount gathered was to be distributed twice a year among all the foreign creditors pro rata of their holdings of finance credits whose liquidation had not been possible under the standstill agreements. These creditors had resigned themselves to being thankful even for small favors. Hence the marks so collected were known as "Orphant Annie marks" after James Whitcomb Riley's famous poem.[7]

A new wrinkle was introduced into the system of blocked marks after the Austrian *Anschluss* into Greater Germany. Travel marks that were good in both Germany and Austria were issued, beginning May 1, 1938. Travel marks had thereafter to be created cocktailwise by adding to 75 percent of registered marks 25 percent of a new mark called a *dego* mark, which was sold by the Deutsche Gold Discount Bank at the same price as registered marks.

In January, 1938, the standstill agreement was renewed to February 28, 1939, but with the proviso that prior to November 15, 1938, any foreign bankers' committee or the German committee might request that the agreement be prolonged for an additional period not exceeding three months. This renewal was actually agreed upon later by all concerned.

The sale of emigrant marks (*Rueckwanderer* marks) assumed considerable proportions during the years after they were first introduced into the German exchange technique, and consequently they deserve passing mention. Their mechanics were as follows: applications of would-be emigrants were received in the United States by the five banks and agencies designated for the purpose by the German Gold Discount Bank and were forwarded by them to Germany for approval or rejection. In many respects, the sale of *Rueckwanderer* marks was similar to the trading in *Haavara* marks sold to Jewish emigrants for transfer to Palestine and the emigrant blocked marks offered for sale in the United States by those anxious to leave Germany.

The apparent success of Germany with these various pseudomarks led a number of other continental countries to imitate her example. Italy, Czechoslovakia, and Hungary, as well as Austria,

[7] Little Orphant Annie
Came to our house to stay
An' wash the cups and saucers up,
An' brush the crumbs away . . .

even before the *Anschluss,* placed at the disposal of merchants, tourists, and individuals with contacts in their countries, facilities for obtaining local money at varying discounts. Special travelers' cheques payable in blocked currencies were created, and money orders were sold to interested buyers through the intermediary of banks, foreign exchange dealers, and steamship agencies.

Meanwhile, the registered mark, the precursor of all blocked currencies, declined further and further. By August, 1938, it had tumbled to 18.40 cents, a drop of 20 percent within a year. The constant deterioration was due to a number of factors. In the first place, there was much juggling in Berlin by the German authorities in the attempt to defeat the growing efforts of foreign companies established in Germany to repatriate their investments and to operate as much as possible with marks borrowed from the local banks, in order to avoid the risk of losses in sending their dollar or sterling capital or reserves home to their parent companies.

The prevailing unrest among Germany's creditors was not alleviated when it became known that the medium-term dollar notes sold some years before in the United States to the tune of 45 million dollars by the Deutsche Bank and the Commerz und Privat Bank, of Berlin, had gone into temporary default on their respective due dates. The urgent intervention of the Reichsbank became necessary to protect the credit of these prominent German financial institutions.

Last, but not least, the Aryanization of Jewish firms caused a sustained heavy demand for foreign exchange on the part of the owners who were trying to escape from Germany. The Gold Discount Bank was reported to hold applications for the purchase of hard currencies for more than 400 million marks on the part of individuals eager to buy Swiss francs, dollars, or guilders at any sacrifice.

The Munich conference which culminated on September 30, 1938, in the dismemberment of Czechoslovakia, prompted the British and United States standstill committees to consider the advisability of combined action in line with the provisions of the standstill agreement. It was decided, in order not to lose valuable time should an emergency arise, that both committees would cable a joint notice to their Berlin representatives, which would be ready for delivery to the German committee upon receipt of a confirming telephone call or cable from New York or London. Subdivisions 1 and 2 of clause

2 of the German credit agreement of 1938 had provided that the agreement could be terminated (*a*) if a moratorium was declared in Germany affecting any obligation of German bank debtors to foreign bank creditors or (*b*) in the words of the agreement, "if in the future, international decisions or governmental action of a financial or economic character create a situation in which, in the opinion of the Foreign Bankers Committees, the carrying out of this agreement becomes seriously endangered." For the notice to be effective, it was stipulated that it was to be given in writing, specifying the date upon which the agreement was to be terminated. Such a notice required for execution that the approving foreign bankers' committees represent foreign bank creditors with short-term lines constituting at least 75 percent in face value of the short-term credit lines then outstanding.

Early in 1939 Hjalmar Schacht resigned as president of the Reichsbank and was succeeded by Walter Funk, who had already, in November, 1937, replaced Schacht as Minister of Economics.

In the spring of 1939 the standstill agreement was extended once more, subject, however, to annulment at the end of each three-month period. With the beginning of warfare between England, France, and Germany on September 3, the terms of the standstill agreement—in so far as they applied to these three countries—ceased to be in effect. In the United States, sales of registered marks were discontinued, but dealings were not yet interrupted in Belgium, Holland, and Switzerland.

The outbreak of hostilities, long expected as they had been, did not find the United States creditors unready. The credits that were still outstanding and due to a handful of banks were relatively moderate; moreover, they were amply covered by reserves. Most banks, by one method or another, had long since completely liquidated the last of their loans and in fact had withdrawn from the standstill. Those banks which maintained representative offices in Germany—the National City Bank, Chase National Bank, Guaranty Trust Company, National Shawmut Bank, of Boston, Continental Bank, of Chicago, J. Henry Schroeder Banking Corporation, and Brown Brothers Harriman & Co. either closed them or left them in charge of secretaries, while the agents themselves opened temporary offices in Amsterdam, Zurich, or London.

At the pressing request of the Germans, the American Committee agreed to send delegates to a standstill meeting called for May 15,

1940, in Rome. A technical delegation composed of J. C. Rovensky, Andrew L. Gomory, and Ewen MacVeagh, of counsel, attended. A new agreement was concluded for a period of six months as of May 1, but subject to automatic extension for a further three months if the American and German committees approved before the end of November, 1940. Of the still unutilized lines, 50 percent were subject to cancellation, and the remaining lines could be used only for the financing of shipments from the United States. Because of the interruption of transatlantic shipping this clause made the further use of such lines in practice impossible.

After Pearl Harbor the few banks that still had German credits on their books continued to remain in touch with each other on a more or less informal basis. In December, 1949, the Committee for Standstill Creditors of Germany, now headed by Andrew L. Gomory, vice president of the Manufacturers Trust Company, New York, is reported to have had discussions with Herman J. Abs, of the German Reconstruction Loan Corporation, on the subject of arrangements for the repayment of old short-term obligations still held by some United States banks. According to a dispatch to the New York *Times* dated May 20, 1950, United States creditors were said to hold about 33 million dollars, the Swiss 60 million, and the British 80 million dollars of prewar short-term standstill credits. The following day the same publication reported that the Western Allied High Commission was engaged in a consideration of a program of financial measures to alleviate the position of the standstill creditors of 1931 who were to receive a second lien on the German economy, while fresh investment capital would be granted a prior pledge. In fact, on June 15 the Commission issued a directive permitting foreign creditors to enter into voluntary agreements with their German debtors for repayment in *Deutschmarks*. Five months later, in November, 1950, Rudolf J. Ernst, of the Union Bank of Switzerland, was reported to have elaborated proposals for the liquidation of prewar foreign obligations calling for permission to be granted to Germany's foreign banking creditors to dispose freely of any *Deutschmarks* collected from German debtors with the right to convert the same within Germany without restriction into any investment of their own choice.

In fact, early in March, 1951, the Allied High Commission announced that the German State Bank was authorized to transfer

Deutschmark balances owned by persons or concerns outside Germany to other nonresidents for use in certain designated investments in Western Germany. Accordingly, trading in blocked marks was resumed at rates fluctuating between 11 and 13 cents.

The tangled experiences of the American banks with respect to their short-term commitments in Germany have been deemed worthy of being related at some length, because they throw a glaring light, on one hand, on the risks incurred and the losses suffered as a result of excessive borrowing on the part of unreliable debtors, and on the other, on the consequences of unco-ordinated overgenerous lending by banks everywhere.

As contributing to a fuller understanding of the methods employed by a borrower in compounding not only the commercial but also the government short-time debt, one further phase of the history of German finance in the thirties will be described in the pages that follow.

THE GERMAN GOVERNMENT CREDIT

Although not ranking in importance with the short-term commercial debt, the short-term German Government credit of 1930 also was conspicuous among the perplexities that harassed United States banks during the period just reviewed.

In the fall of 1930 Hjalmar Schacht toured the United States advocating a larger measure of financial support for his country lest a serious collapse overwhelm the whole European continent. At the same time he painted an optimistic picture of the ability of German industry to make an important contribution to the rehabilitation not only of German trade but also of international commerce generally. His effort bore fruit in the German Government credit of 125 million dollars granted the German Reich by an international group headed by Lee Higginson & Co. United States banks underwrote 79 million of the total, Dutch participants 10 million, Swedish banks 3 million, and England 8 million; the balance of 25 million was placed in Germany. Net interest and commission yielded to syndicate members 5 15/16 percent per year. The credit was to run for six months, with option for three renewals by the Reich; the final maturity was to be not later than November 10, 1932. The Reichsbank was to hold as collateral for the account of the participants notes of the Reich Government. A sinking fund was to be created by monthly payments in *Reichsmarks,* to be effected by the German Ministry of Finance in amounts sufficient to pay for the foreign currencies required to retire the entire loan by its expiration. At the same time the German Government agreed "to carry into effect a series of financial measures designed among other things to ensure budgetary equilibrium and the extinguishment or funding of floating debt."

Because of the financial conditions then prevailing and the reservations of the banking community regarding further credits to the German Republic, the original members of the syndicate had to keep the bulk of their participations for their own account, since despite the attractive terms offered only a few outside institutions were willing to accept sub-participations.

Sooner even than expected, the German financial crisis created serious apprehensions about the ability of the German Ministry of Finance to carry out its obligations as to the amortization of the loan. The maturity of the notes was extended to March 10, 1933, and early that year George Murnane, representing the American holders, and Lee Higginson & Co., the syndicate managers, went to Berlin to study the chances of a settlement. Under the contract the German Government had the right to "declare these payments beyond its capacity to make." Ultimately the banking syndicate consented to an extension of the notes to May 10, 1934, in consideration of the payment of interest and amortization to date as originally stipulated; however, subsequent interest payments were reduced from 5 to 4 1/2 percent.

Complications arose in 1934, when the United States passed a law abolishing the gold clause. That portion of the German Government credit which was payable in foreign exchange was specifically due in gold, but under the new legislation United States holders of the notes were prevented from insisting upon settlement in that form. In order to prevent the European participants from thereby receiving preferential treatment, it was agreed that the gold clause would be waived until the American banks had received payment in full, albeit only in dollars of the new parity.

Representation of the United States group was provided throughout the period by a small committee formed by the principal participants under the chairmanship of the writer, Tracy Vought, of White and Case handling legal matters and André Weismann, Berlin representative of Lee Higginson & Co., maintaining the contact with the German authorities and with Fritz Dreyse, vice president of the

Reichsbank. The technical discussions were held with Karl Blessing, one of the Reichsbank directors, but the last word in all matters pertaining to the credit rested with Dr. Schacht.

A by-product of the deteriorating outlook for this credit were the offers by astute intermediaries to the note holders (as well as to the holders of the 25 million dollars of Deutsche Bank 6 percent notes of 1929, due in 1932, and the 20 million dollars of 5 1/2 percent Commerz & Privat Bank notes due in 1937) to purchase their notes at a considerable discount. There were still owners of dollars in Germany and elsewhere on the Continent willing to take a gamble and prepared, if the worst came to the worst, to resell the notes to the Reichsbank for marks at an attractive price. Another proposition involved acceptance of repayment in marks, and the use of these marks to buy German coal and export it to Italy or to the Scandinavian countries for sale there in dollars; this transaction would be feasible only if a substantial allowance were made to the ultimate purchasers of the coal. Another suggestion submitted at that time was the financing of the construction of a 25 million dollar gas pipeline in the Argentine Republic for the account of a German manufacturer, for which the contracting Argentine government unit had guaranteed payment in seven to eight years. The American note holder was to purchase the pipe from the German tube manufacturer, paying for it in marks, and after the construction of the pipeline was to receive payment from the Argentine contractors in hard currency, either dollars or pound sterling. Finally Schacht had hopes that the Export-Import Bank, with the resumption of diplomatic relations between the United States and Soviet Russia, might grant a dollar credit to the latter from which Germany, because of her close trade relations with her eastern neighbor, might benefit indirectly.

The desire of some of the participants in the credit to realize on at least a portion of their holdings was recognized in the new agreement concluded on April 3, 1934, which gave the syndicate members the following option: once a month the Gold Discount Bank would offer to buy at the current rate for registered marks as substantial a share as possible of the marks accumulated in the amortization fund in accordance with the original contract. United States holders would be entitled to share pro rata in such sales. The marks would be credited to the German Government at the current rate of 2.505 marks for each dollar which was the new German parity of the

United States dollar after the latter's devaluation. The participant willing to sell would, of course, stand to lose on the market price of the registered mark. For the German Government the payment to the members of the United States group in devalued dollars meant a saving of 32 million dollars. The other European members of the group, who were not bound by the American gold clause legislation, were entitled to payment in gold dollars of the former standard of value. As early as April 8, 1933, the German Government had signed separate agreements with the British, Dutch, and Swedish groups providing, in the case of the British participants, for example that

> for every dollar [i.e., for every dollar expressed to be payable in gold coin of the United States of America of or equal to the standard of weight and fineness existing on October 11, 1930] there will be paid a sum in sterling equal to the price of 23.22 grains of fine gold calculated at the price of gold prevailing in London two business days before the due date.

On May 10, 1934, the German Government credit was extended for another year. The original amount of 125 million dollars had by now been reduced $28,302,000, while the German portion of 25 million had been segregated for repayment in *Reichsmarks*. Of the remaining $71,698,000, the American group held $57,768,000, or 80.57 percent.

As an illustration of the growing restiveness of some of the United States note holders and of their desire to part with the notes at any cost, one Chicago firm of brokers reported in July, 1934, that they had sold a block of one million dollars of notes at 40 cents on the dollar. It was surmised that the certificates had been purchased by Dutch affiliates of German banks or corporations acting for the account of their parent companies. In some instances, as an incentive to the buyer, the United States holder was reputed to have agreed to place the dollars obtained through the sale at the disposal of an approved German bank for the financing of self-liquidating exports, but only for one period of ninety days, without privilege of renewal. Knowing the eagerness of certain United States holders to liquidate their notes at almost any price, European middlemen flashed all sorts of fantastic offers over the wires. One agent suggested the exchange of notes against the common stock of a Venezuela railroad owned by one important German bank. Another broker recommended the acquisition of large blocks of German bank shares, while a third intermediary even offered some of the palatial bank buildings in Berlin, Frankfort, and other cities where the financial magnates plied their trade. It must be admitted that all these proposals were more or less in conformity with the spirit of the clause in the contract with the German Government according to which the Minister of Finance, through the Reichsbank and the Gold Discount Bank, undertook to make opportunities available to the participants in the credit for the use of the *Reichsmark* accretions in the amortization fund.

The unrest among the American holders was accentuated still more when neutral visitors reported that since the Hitler Government had assumed power it spent no less than eleven billion marks of which no one had been able to trace the origin and the German authorities had not found it prudent to divulge the source. The official budget, it was affirmed, failed to include certain heavy public expenditures. Moreover, the steadily mounting premium charged by Lloyds for insurance against the risk of war within five years reflected clearly the fear of the aggressive internal and external policies of the Nazi regime.

Nevertheless, it could not be denied that up to this time the German Government credit had on the whole enjoyed a relatively favorable position. Interest was being settled in dollars; the Dawes and Young Loan coupons, on the contrary, were paid only to the extent of 30 percent in dollars, the owner having to accept marks for the balance, a fact that was mirrored in the New York Stock Exchange quotations for those two loans of 41 3/4 and 31 percent of par. It was obvious that Dr. Schacht was partial to the short-term government credit, which had been arranged by him personally at a period when the country was in great need of foreign financial support.

The month of April, 1935, again found the representative of the note holders back in Berlin in connection with the prolongation of the credit for a further year. So far, owing to the opposition of some standstill creditors, the right coveted by the note holders that they, too, should be allowed to call for part payment in registered marks had been denied to them. Only 65 percent of the members represented by the American standstill committee were holders of government notes; the other 35 percent were opposed to adding to the volume of registered marks that might be offered in the international exchange marts, and in the end the latter carried the day. A year later, however, the committee recognized in principle the right of the holders of government notes to their liquidation by some reasonable allotment of registered marks.

In April, 1936, an important member of the United States syndicate obtained authorization from both the committee and Dr. Schacht for converting its holdings into marks. Although such a unilateral action as that of the particular bank threatened the solidarity of the whole group, the transaction was ultimately ratified. It was learned later that a bank in Holland had similarly succeeded in using its notes in connection with the purchase of a ten-year obligation of the North German Lloyd, for which, however, it had been obliged to pay a premium of 40 percent. A Chicago bank, too, decided to take its punishment and sold part of its participation at 33 cents on the dollar. By the end of 1936 it was estimated that the aggregate of the notes still held in the United States had fallen to 37 million.

In May, 1937, the credit was extended for another year with the proviso that the participants could request liquidation of 10 percent of their notes in registered marks. Although the latter were then quoted at the onerous discount of 52 percent the committee did not feel able to oppose the amendment in view of the insistent pressure from the syndicate members.

During the spring of 1937 a special subcommittee was appointed by the syndicate and the standstill committee to regulate the sale of registered marks, travel marks, and amortization fund marks, so as to prevent undue pressure on the market through simultaneous offerings by both standstill and Lee Higginson syndicate creditors.

In October, 1937, the continued weakening of German external credit was reflected in the slump of the Dawes loan on the New York Stock Exchange to 35 and of the Young bonds to 31 3/4. Realizing the precarious position of the German short-term government credit the Reichsbank delegates suggested to the standstill meeting that took place at that time in Berlin that a further grant of 10 percent in registered marks be accorded to the "Leehig" creditors. This received the approval of the various creditor committees. Technically the distribution was effected by means of negotiable certificates entitling the beneficiary to call for his quota share of the 10 percent accruing to the United States *tranche*. Those holders who did not wish to convert their notes into marks sold their "rights" to those who were anxious to dispose of a larger amount of notes than their own holdings entitled them to. The participation certificates bore the following legend:

> This certificate represents a participation held by a member of the American group and any right to demand repayment in Reichsmark on account of the principal of the notes for sale or use as Registered Marks is subject to the decision of the Special American Control Committee regulating the volume of such sales from time to time.

Repayment rights could be transferred from one national group to another, and the certificates were traded in Amsterdam and London; their value fluctuated between 7 and 9 percent.

The last but one renewal of the German Government credit agreement took place in April, 1939, and extended the expiry date to May 10, 1940. By the close of 1939 the American group participation had been reduced to 29 1/2 million dollars. A final one-year extension fixed the expiration date May 10, 1941.

The outbreak of the Second World War caused grave fears among the remaining holders of the notes lest the debtor take advantage of the political situation to default on the payment of interest in dollars. Until then interest had been paid regularly each month as it fell due. In view of the possibility that the United States might be drawn into the conflict on the side of France and Great Britain, most of the remaining members of the original group in this country now redoubled their efforts to rid themselves of the remnant of their holdings. By the end of 1940 less than 10 million dollars of the notes were still held in the United States, by a handful of banks; the notes themselves were selling at a small fraction more than 30 cents on the dollar. The loan, practically speaking, was a thing of the past, and for the great majority of the United States banks originally involved in the German financial debacle there came to an unlamented close a distinct, but in some respects not very creditable, chapter in their foreign banking relations.

SUMMARY

After the collapse of the mark in the early twenties, United States banking relations were gradually resumed. As a result of the lack of adequate credit statistics, the subsequent German malpractices in the use of short-term credit were not discovered until the calling of loans led to a financial crisis, the closing of certain banks, and bank moratoria in 1931. Protracted efforts were made by the various foreign banking creditor committees to avoid a general breakdown of the German financial structure, including a variety of proposals for consolidating or funding or permitting gradual redemption. Many devious expedients were resorted to in order to reduce commitments; the wide assortment of blocked marks invented to soothe the creditors, the constant deterioration of German public finances, the redemption of German long-term bonds through market purchases at sizable losses to the United States and foreign holders, all bear testimony to the distressing straits in which the foreign creditors found themselves.

The placing in the United States of a short-term German Government credit in the autumn of 1930 soon placed the participating banks in an unpleasant predicament when Germany proved able to pay only the interest in hard currency. Periodical renewals of the credit became necessary, and most banks were compelled to have recourse to costly methods to liquidate the investment and recover part of the capital.

XI

OTHER AREAS OF WESTERN EUROPE

BELGIUM

THE IMPORTANCE of the Kingdom of Belgium as a colonial power and the dependence of its hard-working population on the sale abroad of its manufactured products were early factors in the establishment of active relationships between the country's enterprising financial institutions and United States banks—ties that have withstood the vicissitudes of two wars and several economic recessions.

In 1931, as a result of the world depression and the abandonment of the gold standard by Great Britain, the Belgian currency became overvalued, exports declined, and the financial situation deteriorated so rapidly that the condition of the principal banks alarmed both English and American financial leaders. Substantial credits had been extended to the leading Brussels and Antwerp institutions. Two in particular were so deeply involved with Belgian industry that fears were entertained for their solvency; their heavy investments were temporarily frozen, and it appeared that serious write-offs would be necessary. Ultimately the two banks were drastically reorganized, and their close ties with industry were severed. Salvage companies were formed under government auspices to assist these banks by taking over some of their doubtful assets; although the banks remained liable, these corporations assumed full responsibility for the banks' bad debts and turned government bonds over to them so as to place them again in a sound liquid position. Despite the precarious banking situation at this time, United States short-term credits were not withdrawn, and maturing loans were renewed until the crisis had passed.

For several years, under the guidance of the eminent successive governors of the National Bank of Belgium, Messrs. F. Hautain, Louis Franck, and George Theunis, Belgium adhered firmly to the gold standard, even though her vital export trade continued to suffer from the resulting decline in overseas demand.[1] However, the belga came to be the object of systematic attacks by foreign speculators, and timid capital accordingly moved increasingly out of the country. End of March, 1935, King Leopold called on Paul van Zealand, youthful Deputy Governor of the National Bank, to form a new government with the primary mission of devaluing the belga by 28 percent. Eighteen months later, Belgium adhered to the Tripartite Agreement[2] and prohibited private gold shipments abroad. In the fall of 1937, however, the currency again suffered sinking spells, and the national bank was forced to make frequent bullion shipments to the United States to cover its dollar sales. As it was imperative to have the proceeds of the gold immediately available for the support of the belga, the American consignees placed overdraft facilities at the disposal of the bank.

At that period, in order to protect themselves against a fall of the belga, some United States exporters, including moving picture companies that had branch organizations in Belgium, requested their New York banks to arrange for them overdrafts in Belgian currency, to be repaid in six or twelve months after the proceeds of the goods sold or the revenues from pictures exhibited in Belgium had become available. By prompt selling for dollars the borrowed belgas they were assured against potential losses in the event of a decline in the Belgian currency prior to the placing of their collections to their credit in the United States banks.

On May 9, 1940, when Belgium and Holland were invaded, a series of new problems arose for American banks that transacted business in the two countries, the banks being suddenly faced with practical and legal questions of great complexity. A number of dollar export letters of credit, issued for the account of Belgian and Dutch banks to finance shipments from the United States, were outstanding, but few of them could be used by United States exporters because of the interruption in shipping. There were also many future-

[1] It is not generally known that, in contrast to the uncompromising confidence of their Dutch neighbor in the integrity of the pound sterling, the directing heads of the National Bank of Belgium were foresighted enough to change their sterling deposits into gold before England abandoned the gold standard in 1931. Similarly, very early in 1933 the worldly-wise governor of the bank decided that bullion was preferable to dollars and withdrew the institution's substantial deposits from the New York private banks.

[2] See pp. 20 and 198.

exchange contracts pending with both Belgian and Dutch banks and merchants. Dollar balances in the respective accounts, however, were ample to cover any amounts due United States buyers or sellers of exchange in connection with the settlement of or default on the contracts by their foreign "counterparties."

Efforts were promptly made on this side of the Atlantic to arrange for the direct compensation of pending transactions between American buyers and sellers of belgas (and also Dutch florins). The legal aspect of the situation favored the buyers, since under the existing foreign-exchange rules the purchaser was relieved of his obligation should the seller be unable to make delivery on the due date; some of the buyers, on advice of counsel, notified the banks that they considered themselves released from their contracts, since the banks were unable to carry out their obligations as originally agreed upon. The banks made herculean efforts, after having obtained the required licenses from the Foreign Funds Control, to "wash out" as many contracts as possible in order thereby to reduce the total commitments that remained open.

For the second time in the history of the United States foreign-exchange market a most entangled situation developed to harass traders on both sides of the Atlantic. Most printed exchange contracts contained a clause freeing the seller from all responsibility in the event of inability to deliver because of acts of governments and the like. However, there was no agreement among United States banks as to their right, in the event of circumstances beyond the control of the seller, to compel the purchaser of exchange to take delivery at a subsequent date. Banks that were long of foreign exchange were anxious to hold the buyer until the sale could be effected, while those that were short were satisfied to have the buyer cancel the contract, in the hope that later, perhaps after the end of the war, they might cover their positions more favorably.

Apart from the difficulties encountered in connection with the settlement of these pending foreign-exchange transactions, the banks had to contend with many problems of a strictly legal nature, owing mainly to the numerous decrees and regulations of the governments-in-exile resident in London. Both the Belgian and the Dutch cabinets issued ordinances in effect blocking all assets of their nationals in the United States. The Belgian orders provided no machinery for unfreezing the accounts; the Dutch authorities, however, were prepared to consider the unblocking of certain Dutch properties under given conditions. Yet, whether such foreign legislation could be enforced in this country was not so much a question of the good will and willingness of the American banks as a juridical matter which could only be decided by the competent United States courts. The following incidents will illustrate the confusing situations in which some banks found themselves.

Under both the Belgian and the Dutch decrees it was possible for corporations organized under the laws of those countries to transfer their domicile to a neutral foreign country. This change of seat gave rise at once to conflicting claims on the part both of creditors still resident in the original country, now occupied by the enemy, and of creditors living or operating in the foreign territory to which the firm's activities had been transferred. The Belgian cabinet, established in London, canceled the signing authority of all the officers of corporations still operating in occupied Belgium. At the same moment, certain Belgian companies, evidently under German compulsion, gave notice to their United States banking connections that they were not to act on instructions received from anyone purporting to represent their corporations in the United States. Confronted with these conflicting claims the banks only too willingly sought shelter behind the official decrees blocking all accounts without exception.

Nevertheless, in a number of instances where satisfactory evidence was presented by the owners of Belgian firms that had become domiciled in the United States and where the necessary licenses had been granted by the United States Treasury, exceptions were made, and the applications for the withdrawal of funds or securities were favorably acted upon because of the special circumstances.

After the liberation, thanks to the Draconian measures firmly advocated and sternly applied by Camille Gutt, her energetic Minister of Finance, Belgium was the first European belligerent to reestablish her international credit. This was made possible by several factors. The Belgian gold and foreign-exchange reserves for the most part had always been deposited in London and New York, and so had never fallen into German hands. During the war they were considerably enhanced by the rising dollar and sterling income from the vastly increased exports from the Belgian Congo, not only gold, copper, tin, cobalt, manganese, and tungsten, but also precious radium and uranium moving in ever-growing volume from the rich Katanga district to the United States and England. The rapid recovery of the country was aided by the above-mentioned drastic measures initiated by the Belgian Government immediately after its return. The government called in the outstanding German-inflated currency, limited the withdrawals of balances from the banks after new money had been issued, and pegged the belga to the dollar and the pound sterling. By its assumption of strict control over the currency the government undertook to create a stable standard of value for its people and a medium of exchange commanding renewed respect by foreign traders. While Belgium undoubtedly was favored by circumstances, it is nevertheless true that the kingdom's rapid recovery was due to no small extent to the adoption of orthodox policies. These included in particular the reduction of the debasing surplus of the floating note issue, the energetic coping with wartime inflation through rigorous monetary measures, and finally the setting of a Belgian exchange rate that permitted the country's industries, after their reconstruction, speedily to resume large-scale production and made the belga the first rehabilitated currency to resume its place alongside the dollar, the Swiss franc, and the Swedish krona.

In May, 1950, Belgium and Luxembourg authorized banks and foreign exchange houses to trade freely in United States dollars, Swiss and French francs, Italian lire, and *Deutschmarks* in exchange for their own respective currencies. In international banking circles this easing of the exchange regulations was interpreted as a symptom of the return of confidence in Belgium and Luxembourg in the stability of their currencies.

SUMMARY. The Belgian financial situation has been marked in the past by recurrent periods of financial solidity and reaction. Following England's abandonment of the gold standard in 1931, it was learned that the heads of the National Bank of Belgium had prudently converted their sterling balances into gold, thus protecting their institution against a heavy loss, but the world depression eventually caught up with the country. Owing to excessive industrial holdings by the Belgian banks, a severe banking crisis developed, which necessitated a drastic reorganization of several leading banks. Speculative attacks on the currency progressively reduced the gold stock of the bank of issue, finally resulting in devaluation in 1935.

The invasion in 1940 presented United States banks with a series of legal problems. After the liberation the kingdom was able to recover rapidly its former industrial pre-eminence.

HOLLAND

The Netherlands is one of the earliest seats of international banking and foreign exchange, Amsterdam tracing its financial origin back to the Middle Ages. In the seventeenth century, indeed, drafts on Dutch merchants were the favored medium of settlement in the Far Eastern and colonial trade. The leading Dutch banking institutions have always enjoyed a high standing, deriving their strength and prosperity not only from the substantial commerce with the Dutch colonies but also from the considerable inflow of capital attracted by the stability of the guilder and the soundness of the public finances of the kingdom. During the twenties the guilder acceptance credits of Amsterdam banks were next in importance to dollar and pound sterling bankers' bills in the financing of continental exports and imports.

Like Switzerland, Holland faithfully defended the metallic standard for five years after Great Britain was forced off gold. Finally, in September, 1936, in the face of serious trade losses to its neighbors and the heavy outflow of gold and capital that followed the devaluation of the Swiss franc, the cabinet placed an embargo on the export of gold and let the guilder find its own level. Simultaneously, an exchange stabilization fund was established which supported the currency at about 20 percent below the former par. The Netherlands Bank transferred 100 million guilders of gold to the fund out of its reserves and was prepared to supply a further 300 million in the form of Treasury Bills, but this did not prove necessary. Despite the heavy price that the Netherlands Bank had paid for its fidelity to the gold standard when England left gold in 1931, the stabilization fund kept large balances in London, where also a sizable part of the gold reserve was deposited. Later, because of the practice of operating in dollars derived from bullion shipments to the United States, Dutch official and private assets in New York gradually assumed substantial proportions.[3]

[3] However, in November, 1949, according to a New York *Times* despatch, the Netherlands Bank purchased 128 million guilders of gold with dollars, explaining that "although the bank does not believe in an early rise in the price of gold, it does not feel

The movement of European capital to the Western Hemisphere, following the advance of Hitlerism and Fascism in central and southern Europe, caused heavy withdrawals of funds from the Low Countries, where much German and Austrian money had found shelter. In March, 1939, shortly before the German invasion of Czechoslovakia a group of prominent industrialists transferred large amounts to the United States for investment in industrial stocks, to be held in custody for the account of a holding company that they had formed. Because of the important international affiliations of the individuals who had directed this move, their action was interpreted as indicating grave misgivings on their part about the political outlook in Europe. At that time so much frightened money had already found its way across the Atlantic that this transaction would have passed unnoticed had it not been for the amount involved and for the special information that it was believed to be available to the businessmen in question.

Another event of even greater significance heralded the approaching storm: on August 11, 1939, the foreign banking world received the startling announcement of the bankruptcy of the important banking firm of Mendelssohn & Co., of Amsterdam, an old and highly respected house, offshoot of a Berlin private issuing concern of the same name. Following the failure of the firm, its astute, but somewhat bluff head, who had been representative of the Reichsbank in Holland during the First World War, ended a most spectacular and meteoric career by committing suicide in his villa near Paris. Although a French Premier had been best man at his wedding, by a strange fortuity it was the failure of a French Government loan headed by the Mendelssohn syndicate that was the immediate cause of the collapse of his firm and of his untimely death.

Some of the questions that troubled American banks after the fall of Holland, in May, 1940, have already been mentioned in the preceding section of this chapter; others will now be noted. In 1941, in a test suit brought by a Dutch depositor against a New York bank, Supreme Court Justice Walter ruled that notices received from occupied territory pertaining to Netherlands assets held in the United States could not be deemed "claims," for this would make it possible for the German invaders to block Dutch deposits abroad. The

justified—following the policy of other European banks of issue—in running the risk of holding more dollars than necessary."

court denied the application of the defendant bank that the German administrators be afforded an opportunity to be heard on the complaint of the plaintiff resident of the United States.

The afore-mentioned American deposits of cash and securities belonging to Dutch nationals were so important that the Netherlands Government-in-Exile followed with particular care all questions relating to their investment and ultimate disposal, although, according to a decision of the New York State Court of Appeals, until the end of the war title to deposits belonging to Dutch nationals was vested in the Netherlands Government-in-Exile solely in its capacity of trustee.

Early in 1942, just prior to the Japanese attack on Java, United States banks received cable instructions to transfer all balances standing to the credit of banks in the Netherlands East Indies to the account of the Netherlands Purchasing Commission, which was functioning in New York under the direction of the Dutch Government-in-Exile. Shortly afterward, in view of the threatened occupation of the island by Japan, the Dutch colonial government, through the Javasche Bank, its central bank of issue, took urgent measures to protect the dollar deposits of the local banks and business community from being frozen by the United States Government, the Netherlands Purchasing Commission, which then was under the able management of E. C. Zimmermann, former Trade Commissioner in the Netherlands East Indies, assuming full control of all balances, securities, and other assets. Remembering their experience in the spring of 1940, when the Germans overran the homeland, the Netherlands cabinet this time was on its guard.

The Netherlands Government-in-Exile was represented in the United States during the greater part of the war by Johannes van den Broeck, Minister of Finance. Prior to his appointment to the cabinet, he had organized the Tin Processing Corporation (which later operated the Texas City tin smelter for the United States Government) and had also acted as chairman of the Netherlands Purchasing Commission in New York. He worked out the far-reaching plans to reduce the greatly German-inflated note circulation of the Netherlands Bank that were to be effectuated after the liberation of Holland. The man who was so unfortunate as to be president of the Netherlands Bank when the Germans invaded his country, the mild-mannered and cordial L. J. A. Trip, was forced to resign when he refused to co-operate unreservedly with the German financial authorities.

In the fall of 1944, after the landing of an Allied air-borne army in Holland, a banking syndicate composed of fourteen United States banks granted a three-year loan of 100 million dollars to the Dutch Government. The loan, secured by gold held by the Federal Reserve Bank of New York, was the first private postwar credit to be extended to a foreign government. Leading participants were the Chase National Bank of the City of New York, the National City Bank of New York, and the Guaranty Trust Company of New York. The gold was first held for account of the Netherlands Bank, but title later passed to the Dutch Government, the latter having the privilege of prepaying the loan, in whole or in part, on thirty days' notice.

Under the terms negotiated between the United States banks and the Government of the Kingdom of The Netherlands, the latter had the right either to contract cash loans for the full amount of the credit or to open bankers' commercial letters of credit for the payment of merchandise or products purchased in the United States. After a complete accord had been reached concerning the detailed conditions governing the loan and certain formalities required by Dutch law had been complied with, the agreement was signed on February 8, 1945, by Alexander Loudon, ambassador of the Netherlands, acting for the Dutch Government, and by the representatives of the participating banks. In international banking circles the transaction was hailed as a notable advance toward the ultimate restoration of private banking relations with Europe.

Before the war Dutch investors had been generous buyers of and experienced investors in American stocks and bonds. Although a considerable part of these holdings were requisitioned and sold during and after the war, it was a significant symptom of the country's gradual return to normalcy that beginning January, 1950, trading in Dutch certificates of the Netherlands investment trusts representing title to American stocks was resumed on a restricted basis. Moreover, like other Atlantic Pact countries, in the summer of 1950 the Netherlands, through its Minister for Economic Affairs, emphasized its readiness to afford overseas investors liberal treatment in the form of exemption from certain dividend restrictions, facilities for the repatriation of principal and income in the investors' own currencies, and the waiving of limits of the amount of capital that may be owned by foreigners in Dutch enterprises. Yet in the spring of 1951, because of the decline in trade with Germany and Indonesia, in order to repair the deficit in the balance of payments drastic measures were deemed necessary to control the extension of credit by the local financial institutions.

SUMMARY. Holland's courageous defense of the convertibility of the guilder and her constant support of the gold standard ended by involving the Netherlands Bank in serious losses in 1931. However, it was only after severe pressure on the currency and a persistent flight of capital abroad leading to substantial exports of gold that the country in 1936 followed the lead of Switzerland and abandoned gold as a measure of value. A contributing factor was the considerable losses sustained by its commercial banks through their disproportionately large credits and investments in Germany. The kingdom, because of the high regard in which it was held, was one of the first postwar recipients of a substantial American credit—in this case extended by a syndicate of United States banks, which received gold deposited in the Federal Reserve Bank of New York as temporary security.

SWITZERLAND

The sturdy and prosperous republic of Switzerland has become one of the principal creditor nations of the world. Ever since the First World War Switzerland has offered a convenient shelter for nervous capital from central Europe. The deposits of the large Swiss banks grew by leaps and bounds during the interwar years, and since the home market did not offer a sufficiently broad outlet for their rising liquid funds the banks proceeded to loan substantial amounts not only to Germany, Austria, and Hungary but also to Italy and the Balkans.

The confidence in the stability of the Swiss currency and in the soundness of the banks in Zurich, Basle, Geneva, and Lausanne was temporarily shaken in 1931, when many of their debtors in the adjacent countries were forced to invoke moratoria or "standstill" agreements, as already outlined in connection with Germany. The freezing of the considerable acceptance and cash credits extended by the leading Swiss financial institutions could not help but impair temporarily the confidence that these banks enjoyed both at home and abroad. One middle-sized bank, the Banque Populaire Suisse, had to be reorganized with the support of the Swiss Government. The three leading banks—the Crédit Suisse, the Swiss Bank Corporation, and the Union Bank of Switzerland—however, withstood the strain, and their excellent reputation was only slightly affected during this trying period.

Firm adherence to the gold standard has always been one of the outstanding traditions of the Swiss National Bank.[4] Nevertheless, in order to protect the country's foreign trade and its important tourist industry, the national bank some years thereafter found itself compelled to devalue the Swiss franc by about 30 percent to bring local prices to a more competitive level with those of its European rivals. The faith of foreigners in the currency was far from lessened thereby, and the newly created stabilization fund immediately afterward had to intervene vigorously in the foreign-exchange markets to prevent too pronounced a rise of the Swiss franc and too large an inflow of gold from abroad.

The effect of the Second World War on Swiss exchange has been described in Chapter I. Not only were there heavy transfers of funds out of Switzerland to countries more distant from the scene of hostilities, but in addition the Swiss exchange authorities were forced to use up an appreciable portion of their foreign-exchange reserves to pay for the heightened imports rendered necessary by the threat of interruption of shipping and railroad communications. The concurrent freezing of Swiss assets in the United States added to the country's monetary problems.

Owing to the prevailing exchange and trade restrictions, which often presented unbridgeable obstacles to importers and exporters, the normal operations of the Swiss banks were severely handicapped. Mention has been made elsewhere of the differentiation instituted early in 1941 between Swiss commercial and noncommercial francs, the rate for commercial francs being applied to remittances for the payment of trade obligations, the support of families, and charities. Meanwhile, the United States prohibited capital transfers to Switzerland—the repatriation of dollar deposits in the United States or of

[4] On a visit to that bank during the critical September, 1931, days, the present writer remembers keenly how he had to fight his way through a long queue of people at the main entrance of the building—waiting to exchange their notes for gold—only to be placidly assured by the genial Dr. Bachmann, then president of the bank, and Mr. Weber, at that time in charge of the foreign banking and exchange division, that the run would cease as soon as the news spread that the bank was prepared to satisfy all demands as quickly as the tellers could count and pass out the coveted gold pieces.

the proceeds of securities or other assets sold in this country—as constituting a withdrawal of blocked funds from United States custody.

By 1944 the bank notes of the various belligerents, including dollars, were being sold at heavy discounts in the Swiss exchange markets, as compared with the rates for ordinary cable transfers or drafts. The reason for the difference was that the former could not be shipped freely abroad and converted into credits or checks payable in Swiss francs; another reason was that in the use of the bank notes extreme caution and secrecy were often necessary, since in many cases the notes were apparently smuggled over the border before being placed in the hands of the Swiss money-changers for quick and discreet distribution.

A calculation made at that time of the quotations prevailing in the Swiss free market for foreign bank notes may be of some historical interest, reflecting as they do the abnormal conditions that existed in the exchange marts at a period when the war fortunes of the Allies seemed to be at a low ebb.

RATES FOR PAPER MONEY QUOTED IN ZURICH IN NOVEMBER, 1943

Pound sterling notes	$2.24
United States dollar notes	
Large denominations	0.77
Small denominations	0.71
Dutch guilders	0.05
Reichsmarks	0.028
Belgian francs	0.011
French francs	0.0065
Lire	0.004

These notes were purchased either for speculation or for hoarding, the discount being greatest for countries whose nationals were most pessimistic about the ultimate purchasing power of their money. Remembering the collapse of the mark and the Austrian crown in the twenties, the holders of the currencies with heavy discounts were willing to convert some of their savings into safer moneys at any price they could get. Some of the more venturesome souls in Switzerland who bought the foreign notes hoped to use them to travel during their vacations and live, as the saying goes on the Continent, like "God in France." Others, wise in the vagaries of foreign exchange, would first proceed to a Swiss border city and sell their sterling or dollars for Swiss francs; then they would exchange the latter for lire or French francs, and crossing over to Italy or France, they would start on a furious buying and spending spree prior to returning to their homelands. The demand for Swiss exchange persisted throughout the war. Since a free gold market was available, foreigners from hard-hit countries competed for the yellow metal or deposited their resources in Switzerland, trusting in the sound national policies of this friendly oasis in the midst of inflation and rigorous fiscal and trade restrictions and controls.

Meanwhile, however, the decline in Swiss foreign commerce, the difficulties that hampered the trade in foreign securities that had always been an important activity of the Swiss banks, the practical disappearance of the banks' once so prosperous foreign-exchange arbitrage, the decrease in normal banking and credit transactions as a result of the clearings and bilateral compensation agreements initiated by Germany, and finally the disastrous effects of the war on Switzerland's debtors brought about a new banking crisis in 1945. Two large banks, the Banque Fédérale and the Banque Commerciale de Bâle, were deeply affected.

The Swiss, sober and serious by tradition, have always prided themselves on protecting the interests of their foreign depositors and on respecting the confidential relationship existing between their banks and their foreign customers. This time-honored policy was seriously tested during and after the Second World War. The Allied nations suspected that their enemies had taken advantage of the Swiss laws to secrete substantial funds outside of their own borders in order to set up a hidden reserve against defeat and a clandestine fund for future underground activities. Prolonged negotiations in Berne and Washington failed to effect a reconciliation of the divergent views concerning the unblocking of noncertified Swiss assets in the United States. As a compromise, the United States Government offered the Swiss authorities the privilege of permitting Swiss citizens to withdraw their own balances from United States depositaries, provided the Swiss National Bank through its accredited representative certified that the sums so obtained were actually the property of Swiss nationals. While the Swiss Government delegates agreed to freeze German assets in Switzerland and to forbid the further importation and exportation of, as well as trading in, foreign bank notes, they firmly declined to disclose the names of the real owners of assets carried in Swiss accounts on the books of United States banks. It was also, of course, well known that besides German assets considerable holdings of French and, to a minor extent, Belgian, Dutch, and British funds had long found refuge in neutral Switzerland before the outbreak of the war. The total value of alien property in Swiss custody was currently estimated to exceed 300 million dollars. The Swiss negotiators firmly asserted that agreement to the United States proposal would mean breaking faith with owners who had entrusted the Swiss banks with their savings in full reliance on the traditional Swiss policy of not divulging the identity of alien customers under any circumstances.

As a result of these experiences, insistent demands have been voiced in some quarters that the rights of neutral custodians of enemy property be clearly defined so that in case of another war potential aggressors might be forewarned as to the fate awaiting the investments of their citizens wherever found. If such a covenant were adhered to by all nations, including those that have been neutral during the last war, it might settle finally the duties and obligations of commercial banks everywhere with regard to private capital held by them for alien account and do away with the conflicting national laws that have been the cause of so much controversy in the past.

In May, 1950, the Swiss people rejected a proposal of the Swiss Government to amend the constitution abolishing the legal obligation of the Swiss National Bank to redeem its bank notes in gold. Gold coin sales had been suspended since September, 1947. Resumption of the sale is ardently advocated by Swiss exporters and banks in order to render Swiss products more competitive in the world market especially as the Swiss franc, unlike many other leading currencies, had not been devalued in the autumn of 1949. Under the Swiss law the national paper currency will again become redeemable in gold at the end of 1952.

SUMMARY. Switzerland has long been the favorite depositary for foreign capital, especially since the advent of Hitlerism and Communism. The excellent reputation for sound management of the Swiss commercial banks was temporarily eclipsed by the considerable loans and credits that several of them contracted in central and eastern Europe, which were frozen and finally in part called for heavy write-offs. The Second World War led to heavy withdrawals of deposits and a shifting of funds to regions more distant from the field of combat. "Free" Swiss francs went to a high premium owing to the blocking of Swiss accounts in the United States, and there was at times serious controversy because of the refusal of the Swiss Government to reveal enemy ownership of assets held in this country for Swiss account.

ITALY

Five years after he assumed power, Mussolini, in December, 1927, finally stabilized the lira at 19 to the dollar, a devaluation, however, that was insufficient to permit Italian industry to compete again with its foreign rivals. In so doing Mussolini, as came out later, sought to overshadow France; having, at least on the surface, balanced the budget, the Duce was ambitious to raise Italian credit abroad to the level it had enjoyed prior to the First World War.

During the succeeding years, despite the general abandonment of the gold standard in the early thirties, it was the established policy of the Fascist Government to maintain the lira unchanged in foreign markets. However, as the world depression caused foreign emigrants of Italian birth to withdraw some of the funds previously deposited with Italian financial institutions, and as foreign bankers and economists became more and more skeptical about the government financial statistics, the gold reserves of the Bank of Italy began to decline and at the same time the faith of many Italians in the stability of the currency. By 1931 the Fascist Government faced the repugnant necessity of having to reorganize certain commercial banks whose resources had become tied up in immobile industrial loans and investments. The Instituto Mobiliare Italiano was created with capital subscribed by savings banks, the Bank of Italy, and other semi-governmental corporations, to take over 3 1/2 billion lire of industrial bank holdings. The commercial banks apparently suffered no loss in the end, and their current liabilities were thereafter covered by cash and quick assets. However, while regaining their liquidity, they lost their independence.

On December 8, 1934, the Ministry of Finance found itself compelled to issue a decree requiring the reporting to the National Foreign Exchange Institute of all holdings of foreign currency and foreign bonds. The holders were to be prepared to sell all such assets to the government against payment in lire at the current exchange rate. A few months later, in April, 1935, even more severe restrictions became necessary: henceforth, only the Big Five banks, supplemented later by the Banca Nazionale del Lavoro, would be authorized to deal in exchange, other banks, mainly those with foreign stockholders, receiving only a limited license. Thereafter, specific permission from the Bank of Italy was required before a commercial letter of credit could be issued for use abroad.

These stringent regulations were no doubt prompted by the revival of a bootleg market for domestic lire, which were being sold abroad at a 10 percent discount. Under the new rules a foreign exporter wishing to sell goods to Italy had now to ascertain first whether a quota had been fixed for the particular type of merchandise or whether its importation was prohibited; if the quota for these specific goods was not yet exhausted, he had to pay the customs duties in advance. Furthermore, the collecting bank in Italy was permitted to deliver the shipping documents to the drawee only against a deposit in lire approximately equivalent to the foreign currency due according to the seller's invoice. The total delay until the foreign exchange purchase was authorized by the central administrative office at the Bank of Italy was as a rule at least three to four weeks. If the bank refused to sell the exchange, the lire paid by the buyer, while not blocked, could be used only for such internal purposes as the purchase of domestic Italian securities, traveling expenses in Italy, and transfers to local residents, but in no case for the acquisition and export of Italian goods.

At this time a black market developed in Paris for Italian bank notes, which fetched about 117 francs per 100 lire. The property of foreigners in Italy, however, continued to be at their free disposal, and owners not resident in Italy were allowed to convert into their own currencies lire dividends received on their Italian stock holdings. On the other hand, the New York agencies of Italian banks could sell only lire that were intended for genuine emigrant remittances.

Early in 1936 a royal decree ordered Italian citizens to turn over to the government, in exchange for nine-year Treasury bonds in lire, all foreign securities, gold, and foreign balances owned by them. This immediately caused American banks to speculate as to whether the Italian authorities planned to contract dollar loans in the United

States, secured by foreign securities commandeered from their owners in Italy. If this proved to be the case, and if later on another regime should come into power, could these original holders then sue the foreign lenders if the latter had been obliged meanwhile to sell the collateral to recover the amounts of their loans? Would the courts hold that the law was unconstitutional and that the bona fide owners had acted under duress? However, Italian counsel advised that American banks making loans in good faith on securities registered in the name of Italian borrowers or in bearer form would have a valid pledge under Italian law.

An even more puzzling aspect of the problem was the question also raised at that time whether such loans were permitted under the Johnson and the Neutrality acts. The former, passed in 1925, placed a ban on loans to foreign governments in default of their obligations to the United States Government, incurred during the First World War, stating that

> hereafter it shall be unlawful within the United States, or any place subject to the jurisdiction of the United States, for any person to purchase or sell the bonds, securities or other obligations of any foreign government or political sub-division thereof, or any organization or association acting for or on behalf of a foreign government or political sub-division thereof, issued after the passage of this Act, or to make any loan to such government, political sub-division, organization or association, except a renewal or adjustment of existing indebtedness while such government, political sub-division, organization or association, is in default in the payment of the obligations, or any part thereof to the government of the United States.

The Neutrality Act provided in Section 1 (*a*) that

> Whenever the President shall have issued his proclamation as provided for in Section 1 of this Act, it shall thereafter, during the period of the war, be unlawful for any person within the United States to purchase, sell or exchange bonds, securities or other obligations of the government of any belligerent country, or any political subdivision thereof, or any person acting for, or on behalf of such government, issued after the date of such proclamation, or to make any loan or extend any credit to any such government or person; provided that if the President shall find that such action will serve to protect the commercial or other interests of the United States or its nationals, he may, in his discretion, and to such extent and under such regulation as he may prescribe, except from the operation of this Section ordinary commercial credits and short-time obligations in aid of legal transactions and of a character customarily used in normal peacetime commercial transactions.

All the important Italian banks had by now been declared public bodies, and their stock was no longer owned by the public, but by either the Reconstruction Institute or other governmental agencies. The Johnson Act did not bar the Export-Import Bank from extending an Italian credit,[5] but under the Neutrality Act authorization by the President would be necessary, since the Italian nationalization decree seemed to indicate that the Italian Big Five were "persons acting for" their government, even if only indirectly. The Reconstruction Institute then owned about 98 percent of the shares of the Banca Commerciale Italiana, 73 percent of the stock of the Credito Italiano, and 90 percent of that of the Banco di Roma; in addition, according to Finance Minister Conte Paolo Thaon de Revel, the Italian Government's subsidies to tottering banks and industrial enterprises since 1919 had aggregated more than the entire cost of the East African campaign. Moreover, when the President, on February 29, 1936, proclaimed that a state of war existed between Italy and Ethiopia, it became questionable whether even strictly commercial transactions with quasi-governmental Italian banks were permissible under the Neutrality Act.

When, in June, 1936, the Neutrality Proclamation against Italy was revoked, the question of the future policy of American banks with regard to Italian credits became once more acute. It was true that the Italian Government had so far faithfully honored its foreign obligations, including the payment of interest and dividends in dollars or foreign exchange. The gold reserves of the Bank of Italy had been considerably depleted during the Ethiopian venture, but the note issue was still sufficiently backed by metallic reserves. Furthermore, the Italian short-term debts were moderate, owing to the fact that most of these obligations had been paid off at the outbreak of hostilities in an attempt to bolster the credit of the country and make a favorable impression in foreign banking circles. Clearly it was now only a matter of time before the League of Nations' sanctions would be lifted and Italy would be able once more to resume the orderly tenor of her international commerce. The securities held in custody by New York, London, and Zurich banks for the account of the government's National Foreign Exchange Institute were conservatively estimated at 50 million dollars. A loan secured by some of these hold-

[5] The Export-Import Bank, as a government agency, was not regarded as a "person" under the Johnson Act.

ings was sought in order to provide funds for the purchase and shipment of American commodities and raw materials so urgently needed to replenish the depleted Italian stocks. However, apparently the loan was not consummated.

The resumption of credit relations between Italian and United States banks was keenly desired by the United States cotton trade. In normal times Italy had imported an average of 600,000 bales of raw cotton per year. In spite of the increasing use of rayon, it was expected that Italy would continue to look to the United States for the major part of her requirements, albeit Egypt and Brazil had proved to be equally satisfactory sources.

At the end of the so-called Ethiopian "Colonial Expedition," substantial amounts of American blocked lire balances were gradually released by the Italian exchange board, the motion picture companies and certain American manufacturers doing business in Italy being the main beneficiaries. Some of the released balances were used for the purchase of Italian products, and some were sold to emigrants and others for charitable and family-support funds. The lire were made available only for special purposes, and were traded in, with the tacit approval of the Rome Central Exchange Office, under the name *Vecchio* lire. United States owners who were reluctant to engage in merchandise transactions were thus enabled to turn their balances over to some commission house anxious to resume its former contacts with its Italian connections; however, before making a contract with the American importer, it had to assure itself that the *Vecchio* lire would be acceptable to the Italian seller, who had to obtain a permit from his home authorities.

When the Italian Government, on October 5, 1936, devalued the lire by approximately 40 percent, new regulations prohibited the use of *Vecchio* lire for exports. Evidently it was expected that with a currency more in line with prevailing world exchange conditions, Italy would be in an improved position to attract tourists and compete in international trade. Fantastic hopes centered on the development and exploitation of the resources of the newly conquered Ethiopian possession. The need for a more favorable foreign financial atmosphere no doubt also dictated the November, 1936, decree abolishing all remaining restrictions on the transfer of foreign funds to or from Italy provided such transfers were made through Italian banks; these regulations, however, covered only exchange operations in connection with the opening of new lire or security accounts created with the proceeds of freshly provided foreign exchange.

One day after the October, 1936, devaluation, the author had interviews with Conte Paolo Thaon de Revel, Minister of Finance, and Felice Guarneri, Under Secretary of State, and with Mussolini himself, who was anxious to obtain an opinion as to the impression that the devaluation was likely to create in United States financial circles. I told him that if his latest move should really prevent the spread of inflation, it would undoubtedly be welcomed and applauded at home. As he listened intently, his face lit up, and with a bang on his desk he said first in Italian and then in English: "I shall succeed!" The Duce asked a number of questions on conditions in the United States and, probably by design, sought to leave the impression that he was a simple citizen trying to attend to a difficult job in a serious businesslike manner.

Favorably impressed by the more constructive attitude of the Italian Government, the Export-Import Bank agreed in January, 1937, to grant the Italian banks a credit of 4 million dollars to finance the sale and shipment of 50,000 bales of cotton to North Italian spinners. By a rather complicated procedure, the bank guaranteed 75 percent of the invoices, the United States shipper 15 percent, and the Italian banks 10 percent. The credit was to run for 6 months, with an option for the Italian banks to renew it for 3 months more; the rate of interest was 3 1/2 percent, and the National Foreign Exchange Institute gave assurance that exchange would be forthcoming at the ultimate maturity of the credit. Most of the operation consisted in the opening of dollar letters of credit by the Italian banks for the account of the buyers, the credits being available through renewable 90-day sight drafts on the participating American banks. The latter retained the usual acceptance commission of 1 percent per annum, while the remainder of the 3 1/2 percent went to compensate the Export-Import Bank for its guarantee.

The extension of cotton credits to Italy was by no means an innovation. For many years the leading Swiss banks had granted credit facilities covering the spinning of cotton to the northern Italian mills, many of which were owned by Swiss citizens who were members of the official Italian Cotton Institute. Eventually these credit arrangements were expanded to cover other first-class Italian industries as well. For some of this business Italian banks were invited to share the risk and profit by working on joint account. Credits of this type, which generally ran nine months, enabled the mills to work up the cotton into cloth or manufactured goods and sell it abroad, thus obtaining the required foreign exchange for the repayment of the credit. The Swiss banks had a double guaranty, since the Italian Cotton Institute's authorization of the importation of the raw material and the exchange institute's permit for the ultimate transfer of the foreign exchange were both necessary before the purchase could be completed.

Next to the processing of cotton, raw silk was one of the most important items in Italy's balance of international payments. The kingdom accounted for about 85 percent of Europe's total production in the middle thirties, and Italian silk ranked first as to quality in the United States market. Foreign sales had been practically interrupted throughout the Ethiopian war, but after the hostilities had ceased the Rome authorities once more pushed with all their accustomed energy the sale of this valuable product. Through March, 1937, raw silk prices in New York had averaged about $1.70 per pound, a bale of 133 pounds consequently being worth about $226. If production could be raised to 75,000 bales, in accordance with the official program, this would bring in a total of 17 million dollars or its equivalent in other "hard" currencies, the Duce being accordingly reported as having in mind an ambitious project for a continued rise of local production. The United States was especially concerned with these prospects. New York silk importers with close affiliations abroad had made advances during the Ethiopian war to the Fascist industry, to be covered by shipments once the war was over. The raw silk importers were among the most valued customers of the banks' foreign departments, most of their purchases, not only in Italy but in China as well, being financed by dollar letters of credit.

With the approach of 1938 the credit situation in Italy became more strained. In contrast to their former conservative practice, the Italian banks began to increase and prolong their use of the United States credit lines, and even applied for larger facilities. Moreover, a 10 percent capital levy, imposed on all Italians to cover the heavy budget deficit, was disturbing. The British press openly criticized the extensive credits that English banks had outstanding in Italy. Nevertheless, the Export-Import Bank informed the United States banks that its credits for the financing of cotton shipments to Italy would be renewed if necessary for a further six months from their impending maturity.

In April, 1938, the signing of a pact between Great Britain and the Mussolini government appeared to foreshadow a period of relative diplomatic calm. Notwithstanding, an American banker who visited Italy at that time found the population restless and apprehensive over the dire happenings in Austria, where the Duce had been unable to prevent the Nazis from occupying the country and overthrowing the Schuschnigg government.

Despite the precarious situation in Central Europe, the Anglo-Italian agreement resulted temporarily in better sentiment for Italian bills, which were again in demand in the London discount market. A contributing factor was the expectation that Italy would be allowed to repossess herself of 17 million pounds in gold that had been on deposit with the Bank of England ever since the Italian-Ethiopian trouble and that Governor Montagu Norman, presumably under pressure from the British Government, had refused to turn back to the Bank of Italy. It was rumored that an arrangement concerning the return of the bullion, which at the prevailing world market price had risen in value to 30 million pounds sterling, was an integral part of the discussions then pending on the Italian foreign debt situation as a whole.

In June, 1938, there was some talk in Washington about the advisability of arranging a credit to Italy through the Export-Import Bank for the financing of the sale and shipment of United States grain. Such a credit, it was represented, not only would facilitate the disposal of the huge grain crop then being harvested, but also would impress favorably the politically powerful Italian-American group of voters, who were urging such a move in order to satisfy the pressing demands for wheat and cereals coming to them from the mother country. However, in the end, because of the Italian intervention in Spain and the resulting Neutrality Proclamation of the President, the matter was dropped.

Meanwhile, in London, notwithstanding the signing of the agreement with Italy, there had been no real loosening in the attitude of the City toward new Italian loans. Although the views of the English banks with regard to credits on the Continent did not as a rule determine the attitude of the American banks, nevertheless, their policies were always carefully scrutinized, because of the greater nearness and their longer experience with European conditions and developments. Now it appeared that British finance had again adopted a cautious course respecting the renewals of Italian credits owing to misgivings as to the Axis plans, the more so since the Spanish venture was a heavy drain on Italian foreign exchange. It was not surprising, therefore, that when the Munich crisis arrived, most English and some United States credit lines to Italian banks had been either suspended or canceled.

That conditions were continuing to deteriorate was evidenced by the fact that by September, 1938, Italian payments to British exporters were five months in arrears and a balance of 95 million lire due British shippers was awaiting conversion into pounds. Certain United States banks, perhaps partly because they were not so close to the picture, showed less anxiety during the Munich crisis. Naturally their conduct was warmly commended by the Italian authorities, who showed their gratitude by favoring them with such business as the Italian banks thought would be welcome.

The nervousness of the Italians themselves was reflected by the increased shipments of Italian bank notes to New York banks via Paris and Zurich, the American banks being instructed to deliver the lire notes to local money brokers against payment of the equivalent in dollars. When it became evident that these notes were being smuggled out of Italy and that there was doubt as to their origin, the United States banks instructed their correspondents abroad to abstain from sending further consignments.

As the outlook darkened, American corporations with affiliates or branches in Italy brought increased pressure upon their banks in the United States to help liquidate the lire holdings derived from the royalties and dividends of the Italian companies.

In the spring of 1940, after the invasion of Denmark, Norway, and later Belgium and Holland, the threatening foreign situation caused the Export-Import Bank to suspend the use by the Italian banks of the unavailed portion of its credits "until further notice." Certain United States commercial banks in turn informed their Italian correspondents that because of the serious international situation they would have to ask for satisfactory collateral as a guarantee for all credits to be opened thereafter. The Italian banks showed their disappointment at this action, the London joint stock banks sharing in this expression of displeasure, since they had formally withdrawn their outstanding lines.

The lire market was increasingly affected by the international crisis. Instead of 5.05 cents—the official quotation—some dealers offered lire at about 3 cents, although these lire could be used only for noncommercial payments such as benevolent remittances, investment in real estate, and the purchase of domestic Italian securities.

By June, 1940, another symptom of the aggravation of the European situation manifested itself in the form of steady and heavy withdrawals of Italian deposits from the United States; apparently the owners had been warned to be prepared for certain contingencies. American balances in Italy were, of course, reduced at the same time to the lowest levels compatible with minimum working requirements. Customers for whose account United States banks carried lire with their correspondents in Italy were cautioned that these deposits were being held henceforth at their entire risk. By early October, when Italians asked for advances against securities held in custody by United States banks, the last vestige of doubt vanished as to the significance of these financial preparations.

However, remittances to Italy could still be effected during most of 1941. The so-called *Misto* lira came into being, a mixture of two thirds free lire or dollars and one third *Vecchio* lire derived from blocked United States balances, which could thus be gradually withdrawn and disposed of, albeit at an increasingly heavy loss. After Pearl Harbor, in accordance with the provisions of this country's Trading with the Enemy Act, relations with Italy, of course, were severed.

In September, 1943, after the conquest of Sicily, the Allied Military Authorities announced the reopening of banks throughout the island. American bank officers in the United States Army were designated to assist in the reopenings, and in supervising the banks' initial operations. The Germans, they reported, had ransacked most of the financial institutions, dynamited the vaults, and stolen millions of lire in cash. However, the banks in Naples had apparently escaped the attention of the marauders and subsequently functioned normally, invigorated by the substantial funds brought in and deposited by the British and United States armies.

For a certain period American transactions were handled through a blocked dollar account carried by the New York correspondents of the Banco di Sicilia,[6] but it was intimated that United States banks would before long again be permitted to handle remittances to Italy. On October 17, 1944, the United States Treasury gave official notice to the United States banks that the restrictions under the Trading with the Enemy Act against commercial and business communications with liberated Italy had been lifted, although licenses for private transactions were not yet being granted, and the freezing regulations were remaining in effect with respect to Italian property in the United States. These regulations were finally removed in August, 1947.

Since the end of the war, helped by abundant crops and generous support of the Economic Cooperation Administration, the Italian economic situation has remarkably improved and aided by the Holy Year inflow of foreign funds, the country's dollar reserves are reported to have once more reached the billion dollar level.

SUMMARY. An outstanding financial development in the interwar period was the reorganization in 1931 of several leading Italian banks, which had too lavishly immobilized their resources in industrial loans and investments fostered by the Fascist Government. In part, this situation was also caused by the stabilization of the lira at too high a level for its internal purchasing power. Later, as foreign-exchange difficulties became acute, exchange restrictions, the forced conversion of foreign assets into lire, and the creation of various "second-rate" lire for foreign consumption were resorted to, until in 1936 official devaluation brought temporary relief. Foreign banks, however, still had to contend with continued delays in the payment of collections, which were aggravated when United States neutrality and the accompanying restrictions were proclaimed on the occasion of the Ethiopian expedition. Further perplexities resulted from the nationalization of the Italian banks. With the approach of the Second World War the United States banks became increasingly reluctant to extend new or renew old credits. Finally, after Pearl Harbor all relations were severed. Since the re-establishment of peace prewar relations have been resumed on almost the former active basis.

[6] For an interesting account of liberation finances the reader is referred to the book by Frank A. Southard, Jr., on *The Finances of European Liberation.*

SPAIN

The financial history of Spain has been traced back to the Middle Ages. In 1489 King Ferdinand and Queen Isabella are reported to have contracted loans at 10 percent interest; some of the proceeds may have been used to equip the small fleet navigated by Christopher Columbus. Pre-eminently agricultural, the successor of the Kingdom of Castile has not, however, played a significant role in international banking since the decline of its once enormous Western Empire. Nevertheless, during the nineteenth century Spanish credit stood high and the country's external rentes and the shares of the Rio Tinto copper mine were a favorable form of investment for European capitalists, while the securities of the Spanish railroads quoted on the Paris Bourse were actively traded in and were a preferred object of arbitrage between the Madrid and the French stock exchanges. Because of the heavy demand for Spanish products during the First World War, the peseta went to a premium of almost 50 percent: while its par was 19 cents, it fetched 28 cents in the autumn of 1918, the dollar being thus offered in the foreign-exchange markets at about a 32 percent discount. As will appear later, Spanish neutrality was again during the Second World War to redound to her distinct if temporary financial advantage.

With the United States, Spain, prior to her civil war, enjoyed active trade and business contacts. Through the government Banco Exterior and the principal Madrid banks, credits were opened for the payment of the large quantities of oil purchased by the Spanish Government. Dollars were created by Spanish bills drawn against olive oil, oranges, wines, and liquors exported to the United States. In those days the Spanish Government and the Bank of Spain, jealous of their credit, refused to provide guarantees in gold even though the foreign banks were willing to have the collateral held by the Bank of Spain in its own vaults. In fact, the statistics showed that notwithstanding exchange difficulties the gold holdings that formed part of the reserves of the bank did not decline perceptibly over a considerable period of years.

When the civil war broke out, on July 18, 1936, the republican government declared a moratorium on all bank payments in excess of small amounts. The United States Government issued a neutrality proclamation on May 1, 1937, which under the Neutrality Act forbade exports to Spain except on a "cash and carry" basis. The foreign exchange markets of New York and London were consequently soon confronted with difficulties in connection with the execution of pending contracts for future delivery. A tentative compilation made in both cities showed that London foreign-exchange dealers owed United States buyers on balance between 3 and 4 million pesetas, which the American banks had in turn sold to their commercial customers. Because of the uncertain outcome of the internal conflict, it was decided to extend temporarily all maturing contracts for an initial period of 30 days. Later, when conditions still rendered compliance with pending contracts impracticable, the settlement date was further delayed until such time as the Spanish moratorium should be lifted and payments could again be legally effected. Anxious to avoid the confusion and complications that had marked the adjustment of ruble transactions back in 1917, both the United States and British banks thereupon formed committees to insure united action for the preservation of their rights and interests.

By October, 1937, trading began again to take place in the New York market, although owing to the continuance of the civil war both the Nationalist and the Loyalist pesetas were quoted at a substantial discount. One important Spanish bank offered to make payments in free pesetas against credit in free dollars or pound sterling. Some of the American banks seized the opportunity to cover their overdrafts and matured acceptances, which had been charged to their pesetas accounts in the Madrid and Barcelona banks. Impatient buyers of pesetas who wanted to take delivery of merchandise purchased in Spain now started to press the banks in New York and other cities to make prompt delivery of the Spanish exchange that they had contracted to pay to the Spanish sellers of the goods. The banks, in turn, through the American committee, which was presided over by the late Ralph Dawson, of the Guaranty Trust Company, one of the most esteemed members of the foreign banking community, made urgent representations in London, albeit without much immediate success. Finally, after several months' delay, the situation was straightened out, although one of the commercial buyers threatened to sue the sellers for the loss incurred by him through the failure of the respective banks to make good on their contracts at the due dates. Behind the controversies was the fact that apparently some British and Dutch banks had sold pesetas short, and by delaying delivery up to the last moment counted on being able to cover their sales at a lower price after the expected complete collapse of the Spanish currency.

In this connection it should be noted that the Spanish exchange authorities were hardly helpful in assisting the foreign buyers of olive oil and other Spanish produce. United States meat packers, for instance, had balances blocked in Madrid banks, and notwithstanding pressing representations, the exchange control heads refused to allow payment with funds frozen in the Spanish banks. Barter also was frowned upon, and altogether the picture in regard to the mobilizing of blocked assets remained obscure for a considerable period. In the absence of a trade treaty and despite an adverse trade balance with this country, Spanish officials insisted upon payment in free dollars for the shipment of all essential products out of the Iberian peninsula. Since the beginning of the nationalist uprising Spanish banks, although desirous of preserving the good will of their foreign customers, were prevented from using the substantial amounts deposited with them by local importers as a temporary guarantee pending the release of dollars for the settlement of the invoices and drafts of United States shippers. The activities of the central exchange office had been indefinitely suspended. By December, 1937, a London banking house offered pesetas, payable in Franco Spain, for ship disbursements, war correspondents' expenses, and benevolent remittances, at 9.03 cents at a time when the rate for payments in Loyalist Spain was 4.90 cents per peseta.

After the fall of Barcelona, early in 1939, the Franco Government initiated conversations with American cotton firms, and as a result some minor sales were effected. Shipments had to be on a cash basis so long as the Presidential neutrality proclamation remained in effect. This precluded even deals in pesetas, which could have been used in the future for sale in the form of travelers' cheques. In the midsummer of 1939 the Franco Government was officially recognized by the United States, thus opening the way for a resumption of more normal banking intercourse. Reports came from London that acceptances of Spanish banks had again been offered in Lombard Street, the bills in certain instances being endorsed by Swiss banks. Soon thereafter the Export-Import Bank offered to United States banks participations in a credit of approximately 11 million dollars representing 80 percent of the c.i.f. value of cotton to be shipped from American ports to Spain. Two leading Spanish banks, the Banco Español de Credito and the Banco Hispano Americano, were to accept drafts drawn on them by the United States shippers which were to run between twelve and twenty-seven months. Upon acceptance of the drafts, the American participating banks were authorized by the Export-Import Bank, under its full guarantee for payment at maturity, to make advances to the shippers for the face amount of the drafts. The shippers assumed 20 percent of the risk.

With the outbreak of the Second World War the Spanish financial situation took a decided turn for the better. The important purchases made by the Allies, partly as a reward for the Caudillo's neutrality, permitted the country to repair gradually the losses suffered during the three years of fratricidal fighting. By the second half of 1942 Spanish bank deposits in the United States had almost doubled. The fear of a further devaluation of the peseta, which had caused a wild rise on the Madrid stock exchange, now made room for a more placid evaluation of the economic future of the country, and Spanish hoarders started to unload both commodities and industrial and shipping shares.

The preclusive buying by the United States of strategic raw materials such as tungsten was placed in the hands of the United States Commercial Company, this government agency also handling the export of nitrate, cotton oil, and other commodities. Letters of credit for account of the Spanish buyers were opened by the principal Madrid banks, while the exchange was centralized in the Spanish Foreign Exchange Institute (Istituto Español de Moneda Extranjera). Early in 1944 negotiations that were under way for additional banking facilities by private United States banks came to a temporary halt when the State Department announced that no more shipments of oil to Spain would be permitted until assurances as to their ultimate destination had been received from the Spanish Government. All credits opened by the United States banks were subject to confirmation that no Axis interest was involved in any shipments financed by them and that the exports had been licensed by the United States Government. For awhile documents were sent to Madrid by diplomatic mail so as to allow a change in instructions in the event of unforeseen difficulties arising during transit. Under Spanish exchange regulations the Spanish commercial banks were permitted to carry only nominal balances abroad, the bulk of the foreign exchange reserves being at all times centralized at the Spanish Foreign Exchange Institute.

With the end of the war, followed by the discontinuation of preclusive buying, Spain faced again the problem of balancing her foreign-exchange position in the absence of foreign short- and long-time credit. At last, in November, 1950, the Economic Cooperation Administration announced that the Export-Import Bank, in accordance with Congressional Authorization in the General Appropriations Act of 1951, had been requested to receive applications for individual loans up to an aggregate amount of $62,500,000 under the guarantee of the Spanish Government. The cold war and the world's rearmament efforts have again pushed Spain's mineral wealth in the forefront of diplomatic strategy special attention being paid to the nation's supplies of the critically valuable tungsten ore.

SUMMARY. The outbreak of the civil war in 1936 had disrupting effects on the pending foreign-exchange contracts to be settled in Spain. The delays experienced by United States exporters in obtaining payment for their shipments in agreed-upon currencies and the unraveling of outstanding purchases and sales of pesetas were particularly disturbing. The Franco victory brought somewhat more normal relations, especially when a cotton credit was granted by the Export-Import Bank. An impressive amelioration of the exchange situation occurred during the Second World War as a result of preclusive buying by the United States and other belligerent countries.

SCANDINAVIA

Before the Second World War the three Scandinavian kingdoms —Norway, Denmark, and Sweden—were favored and prosperous countries whose public finances were models of wise and prudent administration. Their external bonds commanded a ready market not only on the European stock exchanges but also among well-informed United States investors.

The war had serious effects on their economies, although the largest of the three countries succeeded in keeping out of the struggle. With the invasion of Denmark and Norway by the Nazis, in April, 1940, the merchant ships of the two countries were promptly placed on the prohibited list by both France and England. American shippers consequently encountered great difficulties in obtaining keenly needed cargo space for northern Europe, which proved a serious handicap to the carrying out of open sales contracts and caused numerous offers for resale of the merchandise originally manufactured or purchased on European orders. Restrictions were also placed by Britain on shipments to Soviet Russia via the Pacific, because here, too, many of the carriers were owned by Norwegian shipping interests.

On April 10, 1940, the President issued a Proclamation, and simultaneously the Secretary of the Treasury promulgated regulations prohibiting the payment or receipt of funds for Norwegian and Danish account without license from one of the Federal Reserve Banks acting as agents of the newly created Foreign Funds Control. The interdiction applied also to Norwegian and Danish subjects domiciled in the United States. This was the first instance when the United States Government took steps to protect the property of citizens and residents of foreign countries invaded by an enemy. The handling of the numerous pending transactions, the interruption of communications, the barring of all foreign-exchange dealings, and the absence of quotations for Norwegian and Danish kroner all combined to create innumerable problems and practical difficulties for those banks and business concerns that had current relations with merchants and banking institutions in the two occupied countries.

Shortly before the German attack, the Export-Import Bank had guaranteed credits placed at the disposal of Norway and Sweden. Neither of these credits, however, had been made use of as yet, and by tacit accord they were now considered void. On the other hand, a credit of one million dollars granted in May, 1940, by that bank to the Kingdom of Iceland, available by five-year promissory notes, was permitted to stand.

Long before the end of the war, the Norwegian Government-in-Exile engaged in preparing plans for the speedy rehabilitation of the country after its liberation, especially for the swift restoration of the state's financial and currency conditions. To cope with the existing inflation it was above all necessary to remove the excessive note circulation. The purchasing power of the krone would have to be re-established and a new exchange rate fixed that would command confidence abroad.

Relying on the ability of the Norwegian people to put their house in order, a strong American banking syndicate, six weeks before V-E

Day, extended a sizable credit to the valiant nation, which was thus the first belligerent to re-enter the United States market. The credit, which amounted to 16 million dollars and was arranged by the competent agent of the Bank of Norway, Hallvard Hillestad, acting under the orders of the governor of the bank, N. Rygg, was shared by eleven New York banks, the National City Bank acting as head of the group. Under the agreement, which was signed on March 28, 1945, the credit was to go into effect within one year, provided the participants were assured of the political and economic security of the Bank of Norway and the Norwegian Government. The revolving credit was available by means of commercial letters of credit. It was unsecured, resting solely upon the standing and guarantee of the country's bank of issue.

Denmark, although spared extensive destruction owing to the absence of large-scale bombing of its territory, suffered economically from five years of occupation by a ruthless enemy. By the end of the war the greater part of its formerly prosperous merchant marine was gone—sunk or taken over by the Germans. By 1945 the floating debt and the note issue of the national bank had increased sixfold. To reduce the excessive circulation, special measures became necessary, such as the forced exchange of all bank notes and the registration of bank balances and other Danish property. In addition, in order to bring the debt within more rational proportions, a capital levy and broad refunding operations were undertaken. Soon after the armistice the Export-Import Bank offered a loan of 20 million dollars, and Sweden and Britain also placed credit facilities at the disposal of the Danish Government. The unblocking of Danish accounts for current transactions was particularly welcomed by Danish businessmen and banks as facilitating the importation of most urgently needed raw materials and commodities. Altogether, the cost of the war to the small kingdom is estimated to have reached 7 billion kroner, while the national bank had been robbed almost completely of its gold and foreign-exchange holdings. On the other hand, private foreign assets, including expected refunds for merchant vessels taken over by England and the United States during the war, were believed to represent between 60 million and 70 million dollars (between about 300 million to 340 million kroner).

Sweden's capital, Stockholm, has been an important financial center for generations. Ever since the latter part of the nineteenth century the Swedish banks have enjoyed high prestige because of their conservative management and superior business standards. Next to Amsterdam and Hamburg, the Stockholm banking community ranks among the oldest in Europe.

The First World War brought neutral Sweden an unexpected windfall. The enormous purchases of the belligerents resulted in an advance of the krona beyond the value of its gold content. In order to stop the excessive inflow of bullion, the Swedish parliament took the unprecedented step of passing a law releasing the Bank of Sweden, the bank of issue, from its obligation to accept gold as legal tender. In 1925, even in advance of Great Britain, Sweden restored full convertibility into gold. However, in 1931, within a few weeks after England's divorce from the gold standard, Sweden, in turn, was forced to follow Britain's example.

Like the prewar German and French banks, the Swedish financial institutions not only provided credits for short-term trade requirements but also satisfied generously the working capital needs of the Kingdom's steadily expanding industries. In one famous instance, this policy was pushed so far that it endangered the solvency of one of the leading banks and embarrassed the central bank, which had granted liberal rediscount privileges to the establishment in question. Indeed, the crash of the match empire of Ivar Kreuger was the cause of one of the most severe financial catastrophes, which struck not only Sweden but also swept over all the international financial centers of the world.

The first warning in the United States came on Saturday morning, March 12, 1932, when sinister rumors began to be circulated in the financial district of downtown New York that Sweden's greatest industrial tycoon was in difficulties. Several days previous it had been noticed that the Kreuger stocks and bonds were declining without any sign of the usual banking support to stop the mysterious weakness. As the stock exchange opened on that tragic Saturday, the brokers charged with making the market for the Kreuger securities were overwhelmed by frantic selling orders to be executed at whatever prices buyers would pay. In the early afternoon the Dow Jones ticker announced that Kreuger had committed suicide in Paris. In Stockholm, as soon as the news of the dramatic event was received, the Bourse was closed. The death of the man who until then had been identified in the public mind with all that seemed most substantial and progressive in Swedish industrial life created a profound sensation. In the streets of New York special editions of the evening papers spread the news of the fatal end of the tall austere-looking man who had often been an honored visitor in the United States.

The bankruptcy of the Kreuger ventures came as a violent shock to the United States banks that had extended credits to the various corporations controlled by the Scandinavian magnate. The event was to have its repercussions even on such a prosperous and ably conducted concern as the powerful Swedish Match Company, which for several years was forced to suspend payments on its foreign-exchange obligations. Although convinced that the enterprise was entirely solvent and its difficulties merely temporary, the New York banks, in order to protect their interests, formed a small committee to maintain liaison with the company, the author serving as its chairman. Many meetings were held with Fred Ljungberg and Assar T. N. Gabrielsson, both managing directors of the company. These experienced and astute businessmen, together with the company's personable chairman, Bjoern G. Prytz, finally succeeded in again placing it on a sound operating basis. Gradually the corporation's dollar credits were paid off, and despite the delay in the final settlement, due to conflicting claims presented by various bondholder committees, the banks did not suffer any loss. In December, 1936, four and a half years after the collapse of Kreuger's world-wide enterprises, the last payment was made by the Swedish Match Company on account of its United States' obligations. To its credit it should be stated that the creditors collected not only 100 cents on the dollar but also the full interest due them.

Inevitably the Second World War had adverse effects on the Swedish economy. Like her neighbors Norway and Denmark, Sweden derived a large part of her foreign exchange from the revenue of her merchant ships; a considerable number of them were lost during the struggle, while her foreign trade was severely curtailed. On the other hand, the higher freight rates on that part of her ocean-going tonnage which could be chartered to the Allies resulted in a larger net income from this particular source and a corresponding increase in the gold and foreign currency assets of the Bank of Sweden.

Notwithstanding the temporary setback suffered by the krona after the suicide of Ivar Kreuger, the Swedish currency up to and during the war was counted among the "hard" moneys, which were resorted to by those who were zealously seeking a dependable hiding-place for their savings and cash reserves.

Since the end of the war Swedish gold and exchange possessions have dwindled astonishingly. The drain has been ascribed to the too hasty upward revaluation of the krona and to the shock of the Western world when Sweden concluded an apparently disadvantageous trade treaty with the Soviets. The resignation in December, 1947, of the respected governor of the central bank, Ivar R. Rooth, who had headed the Bank of Sweden since 1929, was undoubtedly due to his opposition to some of the financial and economic policies of the Socialist government. In April, 1951, he was elected to the post of Managing Director of the International Monetary Fund, succeeding Camille Gutt after the latter's resignation.

SUMMARY. The invasion of Denmark and Norway in 1940 resulted in blocking legislation by the United States and raised many problems for United States banks, as did the later effects of the war and the rehabilitation plans after liberation.

In the interwar period Sweden experienced a violent recession consequent upon the downfall of Ivar Kreuger's mammoth industrial undertakings and the deep involvement of a leading commercial banking institution. During the Second World War confidence in the banks and in the krona, considered a "hard" currency, revived, and much scared capital found its way to Stockholm. However, a reaction set in after the end of hostilities.

XII

EASTERN EUROPE

AUSTRIA

On Monday, May 11, 1931, the international banking world was confounded by the news that the Austrian Credit Anstalt, the largest and most powerful bank in the country, was in serious trouble. The institution belonged to what was known as the Rothschild group; Louis von Rothschild was chairman of its board of directors, and Ludwig von Neurath its general manager. The financial community was aghast when the dramatic tidings spread over all Europe and the Western Hemisphere.

That conditions in Austria were precarious had been apprehended ever since the autumn of 1929, when the Austrian Government had been forced to intervene to save another leading bank, the Boden-kredit Anstalt, from suspending payment. At that time, the Austrian Credit Anstalt had been compelled *nolens volens* to take over the affairs of its neighboring institution, and thus had added more frozen investments to its own partly immobilized industrial assets. According to reports circulating in Switzerland in May, 1931, the Austrian National Bank was now forced to grant the Credit Anstalt substantial help by rediscounting accounts receivable of the various Austrian industries to which the tottering institution had extended excessive capital loans. To avert the calamity that the fall of the most prominent Austrian commercial bank would mean to the country's economy and in a last-minute effort to stop the runs that had extended to other institutions and also to arrest the flight of capital abroad, the Austrian bank of issue enlisted the help of a group of other central banks headed by the Bank for International Settlements, a total credit of $14,070,000 being thus provided by the banks of issue of eleven different countries.

Wild reports circulated as to the immediate cause of the difficulties of a bank that not only occupied a commanding position in Central Europe but whose influence through the years had stretched out over the Balkans, Turkey, and Asia Minor. It was hinted that as early as 1930 France, dissatisfied with the conclusion at that time of an Austro-German customs union, had quietly started to reduce her loans in Austria. However, the other nations—England, Switzerland, Holland, and the United States—had continued their considerable short-term credits, which had been granted not only to the Credit Anstalt but also to most of the other important banks and banking houses in Vienna.

A last-minute endeavor by the directors of the Credit Anstalt to obtain help from the Paris house of Rothschild, and through it from the Bank of France, was said to have failed because of the crashing of the plane that carried the written appeal for assistance; as a result the message to the Paris house inadvertently became known to the French financial authorities. It was generally believed that this fatal accident may have brought to the French banks the definite confirmation of their own doubts as to the ability of the Austrian institution to carry on and to find a solution for what it was still hoped was, perhaps, only a temporary embarrassment.

In June the situation became more critical. There were unverified rumors of other imminent banking troubles involving even the old and respected Austrian National Bank. In the meantime accountants had been delegated to Vienna by the British creditors to make a report on the condition of the Credit Anstalt, based on a conservative inventory of its assets and a complete statement of all its foreign liabilities.

Following the precedent created in connection with the German credits, a special committee was formed by the United States banks to deal with the serious situation in which the creditors of the Credit Anstalt found themselves after its downfall. In line with similar committees established in Europe the American committee decided that the foreign creditors were most likely to recover part of their loans if the bank were kept alive and reorganized under new management supplied by the creditors themselves. In the United States the Guaranty Trust Company was designated as headquarters for the American committee. A. J. van Hengel, the jovial young manager of the Rotterdamsche Bankvereeniging, was promptly appointed senior executive officer of the Credit Anstalt; he promised at a dinner in his honor in New York to do his best to clean up the "Augean stables," as he put it. It was he who later prepared the way for the merger of the three principal Austrian banks. Notwithstanding his valiant efforts, however, the creditors suffered heavy losses, while he himself, perhaps as a result of his tireless exertions on behalf of the foreign banks, passed away prematurely soon after his return from his mission.

Two months after the Credit Anstalt incident, the Mercur Bank, a smaller Viennese institution, was also forced to close its doors. From that moment almost every week brought news of some further financial disturbance in some corner of the Continent.

The debacle of the Credit Anstalt had started a flight of capital from the country and given the signal for the hurried withdrawal of foreign credits. As the Austrian banks were unable to obtain renewals of maturing credits it soon became evident that a general standstill agreement was the only way out. The subcommittee for German standstill credits, headed by Abbot Goodhue and composed at that time of Robert Loree, Joseph T. Cosby, William Mitchell, and the writer, was commissioned to look also after the Austrian banking problem. Eighteen American banks, a considerably smaller number than the contingent that participated in the German credits, had commitments in Austria aggregating about 30 million dollars. On August 25, 1931, a provisional agreement along much the same lines as the German agreement, was signed by the various parties. The terms, however, were somewhat more liberal, for the Austrian delegates—more amenable than their German neighbors—consented to make an immediate payment on account of principal of 20 percent on outstanding cash loans and 15 percent on acceptance credits.

The spade work in connection with the Austrian *pourparlers* was done by the British banks, whose engagements were larger than those of the other creditor countries. The London creditors delegated John Beaumont Pease, later known as Lord Wardington, of Lloyds Bank, and Sir Harry Goschen, of Goschen Cunliffe & Co., as their negotiators. The Austrian committee consisted of keen-witted Alexander Weiner, senior partner of Ephrussi & Co. and chairman of the Board of the Wiener Bankverein, and Victor Brauneis, general manager of the Austrian National Bank. G. W. J. Bruins, the Dutch bank commissioner appointed by the League of Nations to guide Austrian economic reconstruction during the critical postwar years, took an important part in bringing about the adoption of the general principles laid down in the agreement, which in fact was known as the Bruins plan.

However, the temporary relief granted to the Austrian debtors could not prevent the gradual deterioration of the economic conditions in the Austrian republic. The Austrian schilling declined steadily and was offered in Germany at 40 percent discount. By November, 1931, the gold and foreign exchange reserves of the Austrian National Bank had decreased more than 60 percent. The dollar commanded a premium of 30 percent, as against Austrian exchange, and stock prices boomed on the Vienna Bourse, reflecting the growing fear of inflation. The bank of issue, to preserve its declining bullion and foreign currency reserves, proceeded to ration strictly the sale of foreign exchange. It also forced foreign exporters to leave on deposit in Austria the schillings paid to them by the Austrian importers of foreign merchandise. The subsequent delay in securing foreign currencies to settle merchandise debts exposed the exporter to heavy losses. It was inevitable under these conditions that recourse should be had to barter, a system of which Germany was soon to make the cornerstone of her economic policies.

Notwithstanding these various handicaps, between August, 1931, and the beginning of 1932, in pleasant contrast to the Germans, the Austrian banks succeeded in reducing their foreign short-term debts by an average of 30 percent. Yet, six months later the tide turned again, and in the fall of 1932 an aggravation of the situation brought another British delegation to Vienna to take up the questions arising from the expiration of the standstill agreement. Dudley Ward, of the British Overseas Bank, and Holland-Martin, of Martin's Bank, Ltd., took over the task of investigating conditions on the spot. Governor Kienbeck, of the Austrian National Bank, seemed eager to obtain a prolongation of the agreement as to both the short-term and the Credit Anstalt debts. One member of the Austrian bank committee expressed the view that the foreign creditors were too exacting. Ultimately, however, a renewal agreement emerged.

The foreign creditors pointed out at that time that Austrian intermediaries were engaged in buying Austrian coupons in the black market abroad at 25 percent discount and paying for them in hard currencies. Evidently, some owners of dollars in Vienna were able to make available the required foreign exchange, even while Austria claimed that she needed time to recover some of her lost foreign moneys before she could make payments on her frozen foreign credits.

Finally, the forbearance of the foreign banks was rewarded. By the end of 1933 the British committee obtained important concessions in connection with the extension of the standstill agreement to January, 1935. In the meantime the United States credits had been reduced to about 8 million dollars. In the early part of 1934 the committee consisted of Caesar Berteau, then vice president of the Marine Midland Trust Company, L. I. Estrin, of the Irving Trust Company, Lincoln Johnson, of the Manufacturers Trust Company, and the writer as acting chairman of the committee.

By November, 1934, it appeared that still more dollar credits had become extinct through private settlement between the debtors and their United States creditors. Moreover, general economic and financial conditions in the republic showed a decided improvement. There seemed to be no valid reason why normal relations should not be restored between Austrian and United States banks. The committee's task was ended, and the Austrian standstill came to an informal close. While the Credit Anstalt accords had to remain alive, the termination of the general banking moratorium was welcomed by the United States press as an omen of better times for Central Europe. Austria, the first country to experience financial trouble, was thus the first to move out of the shadow.

HUNGARY

Hardly five years after the termination of the League of Nations' control Hungary found herself again in deep financial distress. Because of the close commercial and financial interdependence of Germany, Austria, and Hungary, the declaration of the banking moratorium in Berlin in July, 1931, and the preceding embarrassment of the Austrian Credit Anstalt, the Budapest banks were bound to find themselves in the same credit straits as their Western neighbors. During the ensuing critical period the Hungarian Government, in order to avoid a suspension of payments, secured a loan of six million pounds sterling from the French, Dutch, Swiss, and United States central banks, secured by eighteen-month Treasury bills and the pledge of the excess revenues that had served as guarantee of the League of Nations loan of 1924.

As the financial crisis unfolded, Governor Montagu Norman, of the Bank of England, who always kept his finger on the pulse of Europe, advised Governor Harrison, of the Federal Reserve Bank of New York, that the Hungarian National Bank, because of the precipitate efflux of capital and the threat of a large-scale cancellation of foreign short-term credits, was in no position to face a further heavy slump in its gold and exchange reserves. The English banks had already formed a creditors' committee, and New York immediately followed London's example. The committee, with the co-operation of James Gannon, vice president of the Chase National Bank, who represented the American creditors, drafted a tentative agreement based more or less on the German and Austrian arrangements. The veteran banker, Philipp Weiss, of the Hungarian Commercial Bank of Budapest, acted as spokesman for the debtor banks. The accords finally perfected provided that collateral in the form of Hungarian commercial bills should be deposited with the Central Corporation of Banking Companies in Budapest for the benefit of the foreign creditors; otherwise the terms agreed upon resembled those incorporated in the German credit compact. The committee representing the American creditors was composed of R. F. Loree, J. T. Cosby, Clarence Hunter, L. I. Estrin, and the writer, with F. A. Goodhue acting as chairman.

Many meetings were held at the Federal Reserve Bank of New York with Governor Harrison and his associates, Deputy Governors Edwin Kenzel, Jay E. Crane, and Allan Sproul, in order to bring into line all the New York banks having credits outstanding in Hungary, and to convince them that it was in the general interest to forestall in Hungary such a collapse as had overtaken some of the Austrian and German banks. Finally, it was decided to ask Albert Wiggin, who was then in Europe wrestling with the German debtors, to take on the Hungarian problem as well. In the meantime the Budapest banks had formed a special committee to maintain contact with the foreign creditors. Governor Leopold D. Barany acted for the Hungarian National Bank, Baron M. Madarassy Beck, who later, after the occupation of Hungary by the Nazis, in 1944, committed suicide, for the Hungarian Discount & Exchange Bank, and Messrs. Ullman and Makai, for the Hungarian General Credit Bank. The Pester Hungarian Commercial Bank, owing to the foresight and conservative management of its directors, Oliver Jacoby and Emil Stein (another subsequent victim of the Hitler regime), was in a position to honor all its foreign obligations without having to take advantage of the standstill.

By December, 1931, the Hungarian National Bank's reserves had declined so far that a moratorium had to be declared on the long-term foreign bonds, while credit to local borrowers was severely rationed. Depositors became nervous and withdrew their balances from the private banks. Rumors circulated that the British-Hungarian Bank was in a precarious condition. Nevertheless, the Hungarian Ministry of Finance, despite its financial difficulties, granted priority to the foreign holders of the League of Nations' loan by providing for the payment of interest and sinking fund on these particular bonds. Upon learning of this, the American committee at once instructed its London representatives, Gannon and Chanler (of the Bank of Manhattan), to break off the negotiations then pending for a standstill renewal. Some of the New York banks, indeed, went so far as to attach credit balances in local institutions.

However, satisfactory explanations were ultimately given, and a new agreement was signed in June, 1932. The Hungarians were keen traders, using every trifling concession by any of their foreign creditors to claim the same favor from all the others. These tactics were made the easier by the fact that special committees had been appointed to defend the interests of the various classes of creditors. An English advisory committee, for instance, appeared for the holders of Hungarian Treasury bills sold in London, being represented by Sidney Parkes, of Lloyds Bank, Francis Goldsmith, of the National Discount Company, P. M. Spence, secretary of the Royal Insurance Company, Ltd., and G. Tyser, partner of Lazard Brothers.

A number of the credits granted by United States banks were for various reasons excluded from the benefits of the standstill conventions and made the subject of special arrangements between creditors and debtors. An example of this was a loan to the Farmers National Mortgage Institute of Budapest, secured by first mortgages on farms and by an unconditional guarantee of the Hungarian Government.

In September, 1932, the Hungarians formed a special clearing corporation to enable foreign creditors to finance Hungarian exports to other countries and use part of the proceeds to liquidate their claims, the plan being known, by the name of its author, as the Berkovits plan. Under this plan the creditor disposed of his pengoes at a loss of as much as 22 1/2 percent, since the Hungarian exporter could compete abroad only if granted a substantial bonus.

In October, 1932, Percy H. Johnston, president of the Chemical Bank and Trust Company and former president of the Chamber of

Commerce of the State of New York, reported on returning from a trip to Europe that he was convinced a foreign controller should represent all foreign creditors in Hungary. Dr. Teleszky, chairman of the Hungarian Bankers Committee, also thought that the Hungarian Credit Bank, considering its formidable foreign indebtedness, should be managed by a delegate appointed by the foreign creditors as in the case of the Credit Anstalt.

Nicholas Roosevelt, former Minister to Hungary and widely read writer on foreign questions, expressed similar views on his return to the United States in June, 1933. In particular, he was pessimistic as to the ability of Hungary to create an export surplus large enough to cover the interest and sinking fund on her public and private debts.

In the standstill agreement signed in 1934 foreign creditors were granted the right to demand repayment of 5 percent in pengoes from all debtors except state and municipally owned enterprises. A number of suggestions, originating mostly with Hungarian intermediaries, were submitted to the foreign creditors, having for their aim the use of blocked pengoes belonging to creditors and their conversion into exportable goods whose yield in foreign exchange would in part be turned over to the creditor. All these plans—the wool plan, the jute and burlap plan, the "additional exports" plan—were considered by the American committee, but only a few banks were inclined to give them a trial. In London some creditors joined a Central Pengoe Fund which was to finance exports from Hungary paid for with the blocked currency received in repayment of frozen credits. Some European individuals offered to purchase, and in some cases succeeded in buying at a substantial discount, the claims of American banks against Hungarian debtors; it was assumed that these transactions had the tacit approval of the Hungarian authorities, as otherwise no one mindful of the risk involved would have dared to be a party to such a hazardous undertaking. The fixing of interest rates gave rise to disputes at every meeting with the debtors, the foreign creditors being determined to maintain the terms unchanged. During the discussions with the Hungarians, the American committee worked closely with the British Joint Committee of Short-term Creditors and its general secretary, R. J. Stopford, who later, during the Second World War, was to act as Financial Secretary at the British Embassy in Washington. Stopford possessed an unusual grasp of the complex aspects of standstill matters, and showed a very real sympathy with the efforts of the banks to unravel the perplexing situations confronting them.

In the latter part of 1935 Hungary sold some 60 million pengoes worth of grain to Italy, which was then engaged in the Abyssinian conflict. The proceeds of the sales were blocked in Italy and could be mobilized only by the money spent by Hungarians vacationing on the Italian Riviera. Another scheme to employ pengoes received from Hungarian debtors—which, however, was discarded—involved the making of movies in Hungary by the English film magnate Korda.

In March, 1935, Harvey D. Gibson accepted the chairmanship of the American committee. From then on the London contacts were entrusted to Daniel B. Grant, vice president of the Guaranty Trust Company, and Gluckstadt, representative of the New York Trust Company. In June, 1935, the standstill was renewed for another year. During this period H. J. Bruce, League of Nations Commissioner-General for Hungary, with Royal Tyler as his adviser, was stationed in Budapest to supervise Hungarian finances.

On July 6, 1936, the standstill with the United States creditors was extended for one more year. By September 30 the total amount of the still outstanding Hungarian credits had declined to about 10 million dollars. In contrast to their Austrian neighbors, the majority of the Hungarian debtors did not show a co-operative spirit. For a time they paid interest in dollars as provided in the first few agreements, but later they forced the creditors to accept pengoes, which, sold at the prevailing 60 percent discount, netted the creditors only about 1.60 percent per annum. The Hungarian amortization of the principal did not exceed 3 percent, and also was effected in depreciated pengoes. At the standstill meeting in December, 1935, the American, English, French, and Swiss creditors jointly asked whether, because of the good grain crop and the improved export conditions, the debtors could not make a further reduction of the principal of their short-term debt, but were unable to obtain any action, the debtors pleading inability.

The banking situation generally, it must be admitted, continued to be dominated by the precarious condition of the Hungarian General Credit Bank, which operated with the support of the government. Without incurring the onus of direct default, the Hungarians, like many other central European debtors, attempted at this time through various subterfuges to free themselves of their foreign obligations by compromising with their creditors at a heavy loss to the latter; one leading Budapest bank was known to have settled with its American creditors at 55 cents on the dollar, although whether with or without the consent of the central bank was not disclosed.

The late Maurice Lewandowski, then managing director of the Comptoir National d'Escompte de Paris and one of the most kindly members of the French banking fraternity, expressed the opinion to the author in September, 1936, that the Hungarian debtors were taking unfair advantage of the foreign banks. It was much better, he said, for the foreign creditors to bide their time than to let themselves be stampeded into accepting ridiculously low offers of repayment. He was convinced that the Hungarian economic prospects had been wilfully misrepresented abroad. Similar views were voiced by Frantz Ichon, manager of the Credit Lyonnais, who asserted that the Hungarians had been spoiled by the leniency shown by some United States banks; this, by corrupting their formerly strict business ethics, had encouraged them to indulge in the same practices with all their foreign creditors.

The Federal Reserve Bank of New York, as it had done from the day of the first meeting on August 10, 1931, continued through its official staff to take a sympathetic interest in the committee's efforts to wind up the frozen Hungarian debts without excessive loss to the American creditors. Meanwhile, ailing Edwin Kenzel had retired from the bank, and Werner Knoke and genial Edward O. Douglas, who had taken a benevolent interest in the progress of the American bank acceptance from its inception, took his place. Ewen MacVeagh advised the committee on legal matters.

In early 1938 a pointed hint as to what might be expected in southeastern Europe was given to New York bankers by Lucian T. Zell, formerly one of the European representatives of Lee Higginson & Co. Zell called attention to the tremendous emigration of capital that had been taking place, not only from Hungary but also from Czechoslovakia and the Balkan countries generally. He attributed this flight in part to the recent internal changes in Rumania, which had resulted in the closing of many Jewish private banking firms and business houses, but he added that many commercial enterprises elsewhere in this part of the Continent were for sale and that naturally the exodus of some of the ablest merchants and industrialists was bound to have disastrous repercussions on the financial and economic conditions in the whole of central Europe. Subsequent events showed that the fears of this observer were only too well founded.

The committee at one period found itself in opposition to the late Leon Fraser, then president of the Bank for International Settlements. The Hungarian National Bank had contracted a short-term credit from the Basle institution. When it applied for a three-year extension, Leon Fraser insisted, as a condition for a renewal, that the Bank for International Settlements' credit enjoy a *pari passu* position with the standstill creditors as to payment of interest and amortization. The Hungarian Minister of Finance, with whom the negotiations were conducted, was Bela de Imredy, former governor of the National Bank of Hungary and subsequently Prime Minister during the Second World War. Because of his ardent fascist ideals, he lined up his country on the side of Hitler Germany; as a result, he was accused of high treason after the war and ended his adventurous career before a firing squad.

One of the last functions of the American committee was the conversations in October, 1940, with Eugene Havas, then Financial Agent of Hungary, in Washington. Havas, who before he became financial adviser to the Hungarian legation had been Budapest correspondent of the London *Economist,* had been commissioned by the Hungarian banks to resume the discussions for a possible prolongation of the standstill arrangements. The committee members had several meetings with him, but his views—which undoubtedly were those of his superiors—and those of the United States banks, were so divergent that the attempt at a new understanding came to naught. By this time, moreover, the danger of a further spreading of the war and the occupation of a great part of the Continent by the victorious German armies had persuaded most of the remaining creditors in the United States to unload the balance of their holdings at any cost. The few banks that were unwavering in the belief that ultimately, after the re-establishment of peace and the return of normal conditions in Europe, their patience and trust would be rewarded with repayment of their defaulted loans, were to be sadly deceived.

SUMMARY. The case studies of Austria and Hungaria expose weaknesses in financial practices in the twenties and thirties essentially like those in Germany. The failure of the Austrian Credit Anstalt revealed glaringly the bad judgment and mismanagement which led to its ultimate ruin. At the root of the trials of the foreign creditors lay the mistaken policy of many local banks in Vienna and Budapest of employing the proceeds of short-term foreign credits in long-term nonliquid investments in national industries. The inability to pay off these credits in foreign currency made painstaking efforts necessary on the part of the various creditor groups, with a result slightly more satisfying in Austria than in Hungary.

CZECHOSLOVAKIA

The relations of United States banks with Czechoslovakia have always been close. After the First World War the young republic, aided by foreign credits, had the distinction of being among the first countries in central Europe to stabilize its currency. From the Austrian Empire it had inherited highly developed industries, whose products were in wide demand both in Europe and the Western Hemisphere. Skoda, Bata, Petschek, and Weinmann were names of Bohemian industrialists that were household words throughout the Continent, where Czech armaments, shoes, coal, paper, glass, and chemicals enjoyed the highest reputation.

Freed from Austrian domination, the Prague banks, many of which nevertheless retained their former trained management, briskly expanded their foreign connections. They made abundant use of the liberal credit facilities placed at their disposal abroad, and in return they furnished collateral in the form of government or municipal bonds. To promote trade with the Anglo-Saxon world and to cater to natives who had settled and prospered in the United States, the Anglo-Czechoslovakian and Prague Credit Bank opened its own agencies in London and New York, where it assigned some of its ablest bilingual officers. Desirous of fostering the exchange of goods between the two republics, the Export-Import Bank allotted modest credits to certain Prague banks for the financing of the export of cotton and other commodities.

The new country's course, however, was not free from difficulties. Twice in the thirties, in 1934 and in 1936, when the crown became overvalued after England abandoned gold, the small country found it necessary to adjust its monetary standard by writing its currency down by an aggregate 16 percent.

After the seizure of Austria in March, 1938, the American banks that had loans outstanding in Czechoslovakia became uneasy and scrutinized their commitments with the Prague banks with redoubled attention, asking in certain cases for additional guarantees. These were furnished promptly by the leading Czech financial institutions; the men in charge of the latter understood only too well the reasons for the requests, and showed no apparent resentment.

The successive sundering of valuable slices of Czech territory by Germany, Poland, and Hungary necessitated increasing financial restrictions within the harassed state. Crowns owned by former residents abroad were blocked and were quoted at a heavy discount in outside markets. However, to allay the displeasure of the United States, English, and Swiss holders of frozen balances, Governor Englis and Director Malik, of the Narodny Banka Ceskoslovenska, authorized the use of blocked crowns for the payment of exports, a decision that was welcomed by foreign owners of Prague balances as well as by importers of Czechoslovakian goods.

When, in March, 1939, Hitler's forces took over the country, the foreign department officers of American banks watched with concern all withdrawals from Czechoslovakian accounts in the United States. However, no extraordinary movements were noticed, the balances and deposits remaining practically dormant. Vladimir Hurban, the Czechoslovak Minister to the United States, who in the eyes of the State Department was still the official representative of his country, earnestly advised the United States banks to effect no payments whatsoever for the account of the national bank. In London, too, the Bank of England asked the local banks to make no payments or any deliveries of securities unless they were the property of British citizens or of British residents in Czechoslovakia.

Banks everywhere were now for the first time confronted with a problem that was to plague them ever more frequently after the outbreak of the Second World War. The banks were acting as fiduciaries of deposits and other assets of Czech banks, business houses and private individuals. What would be their legal responsibility if they declined to honor claims presented by bona fide depositors or creditors of Czech banks or by certain partners of Czech commercial firms, or by Czech officials, or by Czech Government authorities, such as the Minister in Washington, or by an administrator appointed by the German usurpers? After prolonged conferences with counsel for the various New York banks, it was decided that the banks should operate the accounts in the normal way, as before, but that they should nevertheless exercise due diligence in the event that others than the original depositors attempted to make withdrawals or if it should become evident that the accounts were being depleted for the benefit of German nationals.

After the occupation of the country the Bank of England felt itself compelled under instructions of the Bank for International Settlements to credit the account of the Reichsbank with a large amount of pounds sterling in balances and gold held by it until then for account of the Czechoslovak National Bank.[1] According to Lechner's *As We Saw It in Prague*, 2d ed., the sum in question was 4 million pounds.

In May, 1943, the tall and austere Minister of Finance of the Czechoslovakian Government-in-Exile, Ladislav Feierabend, conferred with some New York banks in order to explore the possibility of placing a loan in the United States market after his government's return to Prague and the re-establishment of normal conditions in the republic. Oxford-educated, a former prominent industrialist and president of the Prague Produce Exchange, Dr. Feierabend possessed a thorough knowledge of world conditions and had a clear conception of what was required in the postwar era if his own country and the Continent as a whole were again to become economically and financially independent.

The more recent history of foreign banking in Czechoslovakia, following the occupation of Prague by the Soviet army in April, 1945, and the subsequent seizure of control of the Czech Government and parliament by the Communists, does not come within the purview of the present narrative.

SUMMARY. Before 1939 United States financial and trade relations with the aggressive bankers and merchants of Czechoslovakia had been intimate and extensive. However, after the return of the government-in-exile of President Eduard Benes, commercial intercourse between the republic and the Soviet Union and her satellites assumed larger proportions under the influence of the strong left-wing parties and was based increasingly on barter with its eastern

1 In his instructive book *Money in a Maelstrom* J. W. Beyen, former president of the Bank for International Settlements, now executive director of the International Monetary Fund and the International Bank for Reconstruction and Development, presents the reasons that actuated these decisions (pp. 137–39).

neighbors. Following the Communist coup in March, 1948, financial contact with western finance came to a virtual standstill because of the hostile attitude adopted by the country's new government toward foreign creditors and investors.

FINLAND

In the past, because of the ethnic structure of its population and its century-long close connection with Sweden, this stanch small democracy was ordinarily associated with the Scandinavian countries. During the interwar years Finland enjoyed a period of stable development and economic prosperity, the trade of its banking establishments and industries being ardently sought after by London and United States financial institutions.

Before the Second World War one third of the national income of the country was derived from exports and shipping. Timber, plywood, paper, and pulp products were (and still are) the mainsprings of Finland's international trade. Large combines maintained direct relations with United States importers of mechanical wood pulp for newsprint, and other combines exported the chemical wood pulp required by the manufacturers of high-grade paper. The Finnish trade associations which handled Finland's exports had ample cash reserves prior to the Russo-Finnish war in 1939, and only on rare occasions applied for mail credit during transit of the shipping documents and bills drawn on American buyers. In such cases, where 60-day acceptance credits were extended by United States banks, the documents were freely released to the New York agents of the Finnish producers against trust receipt. In the case of the Finnish Wood Pulp Union, all members were jointly and severally responsible for each member's debts, a fact that added a valuable guaranty to all their foreign banking commitments.

When, in November, 1939, Finland was attacked by Soviet Russia, the Export-Import Bank, in order to evidence the sympathy of the United States people for the small republic and in token of the fact that the country had always faithfully paid the interest on its debt, proffered its own guarantee for a banking credit of 7 million dollars to the Finnish-American Trading Corporation, repayable semiannually over the ensuing five years. The participating New York banks had the option of calling the credit upon ten days' notice to the guarantor. Because of the war, the payment of some of the installments was later reduced or deferred, new notes being substituted for those for which the maturity had to be prolonged.

During the years prior to Finland's war with the Soviets, the governor of the Bank of Finland, Rysto Ryto, was a frequent visitor to the United States. A student of banking and finance and speaking English fluently, he enjoyed a high reputation in European banking circles. He became Prime Minister in 1939 and President of Finland at the end of 1940. Resigning in 1944, he was sentenced in 1945 to ten years of hard labor on essentially political charges that he had led his country into war against Russia at the side of Germany. In May, 1949, because of failing health, he was pardoned by President Paasikivi.

Notwithstanding the loss of about one eighth of her territory during the war with the Soviets, the heavy war reparations having depleted her former substantial merchant fleet, the small republic has succeeded within the short space of five years to recover much of the ground lost in her trade with Europe and the rest of the world.

SUMMARY. The background of Finnish prosperity is its timber and wood pulp production, which enjoy a wide market in Europe and the United States. The central bank and commercial institutions have always been ably managed. The Russo-Finnish war and the Second World War, however, have inflicted deep wounds on the economy of the small republic.

POLAND

The contacts of United States commercial banks with Poland have never been as close as have those of the City of London, where before the First World War Polish textile mills, and wood and paper, chemical, and metal industries always found the merchant banking houses and overseas banks ready to extend short-term cash and acceptance credits. However, after 1927, following the flotation of a sizable loan in the New York market and the appointment of the former Assistant Secretary of the Treasury, Charles S. Dewey, as financial adviser to the Polish Government, the relations with United States finance became stronger.

During the early thirties, the Polish Government conscious of the growing pre-eminence of the New York market, delegated Janusz Zoltovsky, an energetic young financial attaché, to its Washington embassy to cultivate closely the country's relations with the leading

New York banks and issuing houses. His efforts were somewhat handicapped by the fact that certain Polish bonds placed on the American market were in default of their interest. The banks which acted as transfer and paying agents for the issues in question, when approached to finance shipments to Poland, were obliged to decline handling the credits because of a possible conflict of interest which might expose them to attachments, by holders of the bonds, of any funds that they might receive in connection with the payment of their own advances at their maturities. The banks recalled a similar problem that had arisen some years before with respect to certain unpaid German notes, when it had been asked whether the banks as creditors were entitled to priority in the event of cover reaching them from the debtors.

Other transactions, such as the financing of cotton shipments to the Polish port of Gdynia and their storage there pending payment by the buyers, were handled for several years to the entire satisfaction of the interested United States banks. The first such credit was arranged in May, 1937, by the Export-Import Bank for the benefit of Polish mills. It covered the cost of 50,000 bales, or about 3 million dollars, unconditionally guaranteed by the Bank of Poland, and was granted for six months with privilege of one 90-day renewal. The advance covered 75 percent of the invoice value; 15 percent was borne by the United States shipper, while 10 percent was for account of the buyer's local bank and was secured by collateral held by its American correspondent. In exceptional cases the Export-Import Bank assumed the full risk of 100 percent, the Polish bank providing a promissory note covering the c.i.f. value of the shipment.

Other commercial credits granted before the last war to Warsaw banks were against dock receipts for easily marketable raw materials and metals, for which there was a constant demand in Poland. Until 1935 the country was generally regarded as an unofficial member of the gold bloc, but thereafter its foreign-exchange situation deteriorated, and American exporters often were obliged to accept zlotys in payment of their invoices. On occasion, in order to convert the zlotys into hard currencies, such as Swiss francs or dollars, complex barter deals were devised. One skillful four-cornered arrangement was conceived by an American owner of blocked zlotys with the cooperation of banks in the United States and Poland, a United States film company also being a party. The latter agreed to purchase films made in Warsaw by a Polish producer and pay for them in dollars upon delivery of the shipping documents in the United States. As the production progressed, the Polish producer received installments in zlotys owned by the American, who received the equivalent in dollars at the agreed discount after the arrival of the finished films in New York. Everybody was content—the Polish producer, the American movie distributor, the owner of the zlotys, and the participating New York and Warsaw banking institutions.

Shortly after the invasion and occupation of Poland, in September, 1939, substantial remittances were made by United States relief societies and the Red Cross to Polish refugees in Rumania, Hungary, and that part of Poland occupied by the German armies. The Polish Savings Bank, in New York, sold these remittances through its various agencies, using for the payments abroad the services of the United States banks that were able to offer the best rates for the conversion of the dollars collected in the United States into the foreign moneys needed by the Polish refugees.

In January, 1942, arrangements were completed with the State Department under which the accounts of the Polish bank of issue on the books of its United States correspondents could be operated over the signatures of certain Polish officials, in accordance with Section *b* of the Federal Reserve Act, as revised on April 7, 1941. This amendment provided that upon certification by the Secretary of State to an American bank the Secretary should recognize the right of the ambassador or minister or other designated foreign government official to operate the account of the central bank of the country involved.

By June, 1943, despite the onerous occupation of the country by Germany and Soviet Russia, all Polish credits guaranteed by the Export-Import Bank had been fully paid off.

SUMMARY. After the First World War American-Polish banking and trade relations became more active and important, partly under the impulse given by the United States Financial Adviser Charles H. Dewey. Foreign credit was required mainly for the financing of purchases of cotton and copper. Later, the foreign exchange situation worsened, and large amounts of blocked zlotys, quoted at a heavy discount in foreign markets, proved disposable only through barter.

UNION OF SOVIET SOCIALIST REPUBLICS

Under the czars the financial relations of the Russian Empire were closest with Berlin and Paris, and to a lesser degree with London, Amsterdam, and New York. But by far the greatest part of the large Russian loans for the construction of railroads, for armaments, and for the general economic development of the country was sold to French investors. Encouraged by the lavishly subsidized French press, they absorbed eagerly the billions of Russian Government bonds offered them by European banking syndicates and distributed in every hamlet by the thousands of branch offices of the Crédit Lyonnais, Société Générale, and Comptoir National.

One American bank, the National City Bank of New York, had followed the example of the Crédit Lyonnais, and had opened its own branch in St. Petersburg, then the financial center of Russia. The Bolshevik Government took it over in 1918 and confiscated the deposits.

Following United States recognition of Soviet Russia, negotiations were initiated by the Roosevelt administration, in 1934, with Maxim Litvinov representing the Soviet Government for a settlement of the czarist debts but these came to naught. However, many years before the exchange of ambassadors and the re-establishment of normal diplomatic relations the Soviet Union had realized the need for a resumption of trade contacts with the United States. The first agent delegated to America to explore the possibilities appears to have been Victor P. Nogin, member of the Supreme Soviet Council. The red-bearded six-footer, though speaking English haltingly, made a favorable impression. Another early visitor was Comrade Fishman, vice president of the Russian Foreign Trade Bank, who came as representative of the Russian Textile Syndicate in connection with the purchase of American raw cotton. He was succeeded by E. W. Belitzky, a short retiring individual who was well versed in the cotton and textile business. After a few years, like many others of his countrymen who came to this country on commercial errands, he returned to the Soviet Union and disappeared from sight.

The first banking relations were established in New York by the Amtorg Trading Corporation, which was founded in 1924, its name being a contraction of the Russian phrase *Amerikanskaia Torgovlia,* or American trade. It became almost the exclusive purchasing and sales agency in the United States for account of the Commissariat of Foreign Trade in Moscow, headed by Anastas I. Mikoyan, later a Soviet Deputy Vice Premier.

Notwithstanding the refusal of the United States Government, prior to 1934, to permit the importation of Soviet gold, and despite the lack of judicial status of a nation whose government was not recognized by the United States Government, the State Bank of Moscow, in the early twenties, appointed two New York banks as its correspondents. This, however, did not solve the Soviets' problems. The financial requirements for the imports needed by Russia were constantly rising. Credit facilities, on the other hand, were extended only against first-class collateral, which could not be offered while the extension of short-term commercial credits by exporters to Amtorg was still in its infancy. Meanwhile, the proceeds of the furs, hides, caviar, manganese ore, and other commodities sold in the United States were insufficient to cover the steadily growing needs for dollars to pay for the heavy machinery, equipment, cotton, chemicals, and so forth purchased here. Only the International General Electric Company was willing at this time to consider a long-term credit for the sale of electric-power machinery. However, in 1933, to finance the sale of 60,000 bales of cotton a loan of 45 million dollars was granted by the Reconstruction Finance Corporation. Consequently, in the early years of Amtorg's existence it dealt with American manufacturers on a cash basis, the funds needed being generally created by the transfer of dollars or sale of sterling balances carried in London.

Until the ban on Soviet gold was lifted following diplomatic recognition in November, 1933, gold was sent instead to England. At times, while the shipments were en route and the documents evidencing title were in transit, the State Bank of the USSR succeeded in securing cash advances from the London banks to which the gold was consigned. Since the steamers on which shipment was made were Soviet-owned, the bills of lading were signed by the captains who cabled the banks the dates of departure of the vessels. During politically troubled times it happened that advances were sometimes requested and obtained even though the borrowing Soviet agency had more than ample funds in London, or later in New York. The only possible explanation was that the owners of the bullion preferred to have it formally pledged to an English or United States bank in order that in the event that a third party attempted to seize it or to place an embargo on it, the Soviet bank could then assert that the gold was hypothecated and that the consignee abroad had a rightful first lien that it would and could defend. It was rather costly protection, for the interest on check accounts in London rarely exceeded 1/2 percent, and no interest was credited for dollar sight balances, while the rate for the temporary cash advance was in the neighborhood of 2 3/4 percent.

In England, Lloyds Bank was a pioneer in according credit to the Soviet agencies. Later, other English and American banks with branches in London shared in the business. Finally the Moscow Narodny Bank opened its own office in the City. At first the export of timber to the United Kingdom, the most important buyer, furnished the chief opportunities for London banks to finance Russian shipments consigned to English ports. Various brokerage firms were instrumental in selling the wood in the British market, since for many years after the revolution, many English buyers declined to re-enter the market, inasmuch as a clear title to the timber offered for sale could not be established. The credits required for timber were longer, as a rule, than those known at that period in American banking practice: the lumber was stored in Archangel pending shipment; the freighters that carried the cargo to the English ports were rather slow; and after arrival it was often necessary to keep the wood in storage for many months until the purchasers were ready to take delivery.

At first, this business was done on a restricted scale, but gradually the volume was increased as the methods of the Soviet Timber Trust inspired more confidence. In addition, the commission and interest rates were attractive. Nevertheless, as competition developed, the banks in London had to offer concessions in order to retain the business. The banks would have preferred all of the insurance to be underwritten by British companies, but were compelled to accept the policy of a Soviet-controlled insurance company established in London for a considerable part of the risk. For timber stacked in Russia the margin was as a rule 30 percent above the current market price, and the interest 4 percent. During some seasons the amounts borrowed were large, a credit of 2 million pounds having on one occasion to be distributed among a number of banks.

While in the early years the Soviet representatives in the United States were prepared to pay higher prices provided the seller of the goods was willing to grant time for payment, and while they were disposed to be generous with the banks from whom they required temporary credit facilities, they were too good traders not to take advantage of every opportunity to insist upon better terms. As time went on they became so experienced and shrewd that in their dealings with both manufacturers and banks they fought for every cent of the cost and expense all along the line.

At the outset the USSR was compelled to finance its purchases by means of short- and medium-term acceptances of its foreign-trade agencies. These bills were offered for discount not only in New York but also in London and the German markets. Anxious to husband their gold reserves, the Soviet buying agencies tried whenever possible to pay foreign manufacturers in the form of these acceptances. Some of them ran as much as two, three, or four years. The seller, of course, raised his prices to include not only the discount at which he would have to dispose of the paper in the black market but also, if he assumed the risk of endorsing part of it, a more or less large margin to protect himself against loss in the event of a default of the acceptor. During the years following the revolution, the intermediaries were forced to sell these bills in Europe at usuriously high interest rates. The seller generally endorsed the paper "without recourse," the purchaser consequently having to stand the loss if the bills were not paid at maturity. Even before signing the sales contract with the Soviet buyers the seller tried to protect himself by making a tentative agreement with the broker for the sale of the bills "as, if, and when." The rates of discount at which these acceptances circulated varied, reaching at times as high as 30 or 40 percent. Many buyers bought them as a speculation and made enormous profits. Eventually, as the Soviet credit standing improved, the rates declined. Until then, however, the New York brokers who had a practical monopoly of the sale of Amtorg acceptances did a most remunerative business. In addition they acted as unofficial public relations counsel for Amtorg; thus the late Boris Said, who previously had been connected with the Standard Oil Company, and Isaac J. Sherman, one of the first agents for Amtorg, took the lead in "selling" the Soviet organizations in the downtown New York financial district.

In contrast to the United States and England, Germany, which had long had close trade ties with the Russian neighbor, fostered and on occasion subsidized sales to the USSR on long term either by assuming guarantee (*delcredere*) for the ultimate payment to the extent of sometimes up to 60 percent of the invoice or granting time loans in marks available for the settlement of merchandise purchases. Incidentally, some of the German short-term borrowing from the Western creditor countries undoubtedly facilitated the granting of long-term credits to Russia by German industries and banks.

The foreign trade commissariat in Moscow advisedly sent to the United States men who realized that the success of their mission depended on their ability to create confidence in Soviet business ethics and in the integrity of their dealings with United States merchants and bankers. For these reasons it was not too difficult in the early years to deal with the Amtorg heads, who appeared imbued with the desire to prove by discharging their obligations as agreed upon that trust could be placed in Soviet business methods. True, contracts were approached with infinite circumspection, and were concluded only after what seemed an unnecessary amount of red tape. However, once signed, they were executed, although Soviet representatives were tediously meticulous in their inspection of purchases and too precise about signing required inspection certificates. They insisted emphatically upon the strict observance of every condition that had been agreed upon, but payments were generally believed to have been promptly effected, up to the beginning of the Second World War.[2]

Of the many men who represented Soviet commercial affairs in the United States, the names of a few come particularly to mind: Alex Gumberg, who preceded Fishman as agent of the textile syndicate, a short, burly man who boasted of his connections in influential American political circles; Saul G. Bron, tall, a shrewd negotiator, one of the first presidents of Amtorg; Peter Bogdanov, former head of the Supreme Economic Council, who adopted the title of chairman of the Board, genial but withal stubbornly defending his side of every argument; Ivan V. Boyeff, who when not smiling could have easily impersonated a judge under the Spanish Inquisition, and stocky, determined Mikhail Gousev, whose sudden departure for

2 According to newspaper reports in December, 1950, a United States industrial corporation was granted an award of a substantial amount in a breach of contract suit against Amtorg Trading Corporation in connection with contracts entered into in May, 1947, while another action for repudiation of an agreement made in April, 1946, was pending before the Supreme Court of the State of New York.

home was the subject of much curious speculation after the end of the Second World War. All these men were surrounded by a host of subordinates with various titles, some of whom even although occupying minor positions in the administration of the Amtorg Trading Company were believed to wield great party influence.

One of the most important high personalities in Soviet American relations was the former Commissar for Foreign Affairs, Maxim Litvinov, ambassador in Washington from November, 1941, to August, 1943. Rather short, corpulent, with a high forehead and a crown of gray hair around the bald top of his massive head, Litvinov with his twinkling eyes looked more like a prosperous retired merchant than a leader of the red proletariat. He was a quiet advocate of closer trade relations between the two countries and constantly stressed the need for a less one-sided exchange of goods and products between the two countries.

His predecessors were men of a different type. Troyanovsky, looking out through his pince-nez, gave an impression of a man of the moderate faction, a quiet professor rather than a violent demagogue. Oumansky, on the other hand, appeared to belong to the left wing, protagonist of the more radical theories of the Soviet doctrine. Yet, the extreme ideologies that these men might hold seemed to be banished backstage, and they tried to outrival the "decadent capitalists" when, as on the occasion of the annual receptions at the elegant Russian Embassy in Washington, celebrating the October, 1917, revolution, their distinguished guests climbed the broad staircase at the top of which the Soviet ambassador at the side of his beautifully gowned wife received the long line of high officials of the State Department, members of the Cabinet, the diplomatic corps, and other prominent people. In the embassy salons the guests crowded around immense buffets loaded with victuals of all kinds, smoked sturgeon, goose, salads, and the various hors d'œuvres for which Russian cuisine is renowned, while stewards in courtly liveries passed around trays of champagne and vodka. On one such occasion I found myself standing with the late Eugene A. Black, Sr., governor of the Federal Reserve Board, who, noticing that I declined to touch the white Russian liquor, reproved smilingly with "Why do you disdain the only good things that nowadays come to us out of Russia—caviar and vodka?"

The growing importance of the Soviet Union as a factor in United

States foreign commerce was recognized by the United States Department of Commerce when it established a special division to assist American manufacturers and business firms in the development of their trade relations with the USSR. The late Ernest C. Ropes was chief of the division, and through his intimate knowledge of the country and his mastery of the Russian language, assembled information on Russian economic and financial conditions that was of much value to those seeking to do business in Russia. While at first he was rather skeptical of the success of the Soviet experiment, he later became persuaded that the communistic ideology might not be too incompatible with the creation of an economy that would offer valuable trading opportunities. The engaging, gray-haired official watched industriously the fate of the orders placed by Soviet organizations in the United States and in particular the statistics that he laboriously collected in the course of interviews with businessmen and bankers made possible an accurate picture of the extent of American commitments with the Soviets as regards both open contracts and credits due United States suppliers and manufacturers.

The New York banks that were known to be correspondents of the State Bank of the USSR and depositaries of Amtorg received frequent inquiries from industrial concerns and business houses all over the country about the credit-worthiness of the Soviet purchasing agencies and their reputation as to the carrying out of contracts. The terms of settlement proposed by the Russians varied widely. In some instances, however, the American sellers were willing to accept payment of 10 percent of the invoice after arrival at destination of the machinery or other articles of equipment, in effect gambling on the 10 percent as representing part of their profit. The more cautious manufacturers held out for a banker's irrevocable letter of credit, under which at least the raw-material and labor costs were paid to them in cash before they forwarded the orders to their plants.

The original mistrust of the Russians on the part of American industry and business was due in part to the policies initially proclaimed by the leaders of the Bolshevik party. Their program included a so-called "moneyless" economy. The paper ruble wholly lost its value during the civil war, and a new proletarian ruble, the chervonetz, was created after 1923, with a nominal exchange value of about 50 cents—the old parity of the czarist ruble. Soon, however, the Soviet ruble, despite official support and rigid exchange control, came to be sold at a discount abroad, and the government accordingly interdicted its export and even more strictly prohibited its importation. After the devaluation of the dollar in 1933 the exchange parity rose to more than 80 cents, but this rate proved impossible to maintain. Two years later the ruble was devalued, and the official rate became about 20 cents, the black market quotation, however, being 2 to 2 1/2 cents. There was a special rate for diplomats and newspapermen, who could legally exchange their dollars at 8 cents to the ruble.

Realizing that the instability of the currency scarcely bolstered Soviet credit abroad and that the only way to obtain foreign exchange for reconstruction was by increasing its gold shipments, the Soviet rulers were reported to have pushed the country's production of the yellow metal with the utmost energy. At one time the Russian plants were unable to refine all the ores that were mined, and the overflow, in the form of ores, precipitates, melted slimes, chlorides, electrolytic slimes, and gold residues, were therefore sold to the large United States refining and smelting companies on the Atlantic Coast, shipment being usually made from Black Sea ports and Leningrad via the Panama Canal to Tacoma. The smelters were willing to advance a large percentage of the potential proceeds upon delivery of the respective shipping documents; insurance was taken out with first-class American and British underwriters, the vessels carrying the cargo being as a rule not Soviet-owned.

Another important source of foreign exchange for the Soviet Union was the sale of manganese ore by the Soyuzpromimport, of Moscow, to leading United States steel companies. Here, too, the major portion of the invoice value was payable upon presentation of the shipping documents, and the balance upon the outturn after the unloading of the cargo.

During the Spanish civil war, in 1936–1937, the Loyalist Government was rumored to have entrusted Soviet Russia with the custody of considerable quantities of gold confiscated from Franco sympathizers. This was not confirmed, but it was observed that at this time a constant stream of bullion shipments was reaching London from Russia. Although the gold bars that were turned over to the Bank of England consisted of authentic Russian bars bearing the Russian mint impress, it was significant that the gold was pledged while en route and that loans were contracted upon its security so as to confer a first lien to the London consignees.

During this period the United States newspapers carried numerous articles on the subject of these gold shipments, the authors conjecturing as to the real motives back of the mysterious transactions. The press reports regarding the volume of the Russian gold reserves and annual production were mostly guesswork and were believed to have been vastly exaggerated. One writer, indeed, stated that the Soviet-controlled gold store amounted to seven billion dollars, although in banking circles at that time two billion dollars was believed nearer the truth. It was also asserted by some that, by disposing of a part of their gold, the Soviet exchange experts thought to anticipate a possible reduction of the gold price by Washington.

The British Contraband Control, initiated immediately after the declaration of war in 1939, forced the Soviet Union to make far-reaching changes in their shipping dispositions. Certain cargoes were promptly diverted to Mexico, and quite an important tonnage of copper was offered by an undisclosed seller in the New York market for resale. Inquiries were received by banks in the New York financial district as to a possible outlet for large quantities of motor benzoil stored in a Southern port. On the other hand, inability to obtain export licenses from the British authorities made it impossible for United States interests to take delivery of certain articles covered by letters of credit opened for account of Soviet purchasing agencies. In some cases these credits were available upon presentation of performance bonds that had been taken out by prudent sellers for 25 or 50 percent of the value of the order, and in others on presentation of railroad bills of lading, which placed the onus of obtaining export licenses and cargo space on the buyer. Many of these letters of credit had to be canceled with the approval of the parties concerned when the impossibility of carrying out the contracts became so clear that no good purpose was to be served by keeping them in force.

With the passage of Public Law 31 by Congress, early in 1941, a most perplexing situation arose for the banks that were carrying accounts of banks of issue located in invaded countries. Under this law the Federal Reserve Banks or member banks carrying accounts of such banks of issue or of the foreign governments of occupied states could make payments from such accounts under instructions from the ambassadors or ministers of the countries concerned, provided that they were approved by the State Department as duly accredited representatives of their countries. The banks had welcomed this law as affording them protection not hitherto enjoyed under American law. They had not expected, however, that they might be faced with a serious predicament should they, at the same time, also receive written or cabled instructions from the foreign banks of issue, duly authenticated by cable ciphers or binding signatures, making disposition of their credit balances under conditions which, on the basis of many years' practice, they would have to consider as perfectly legitimate. Fortunately, the banks were required under the Treasury regulations to obtain licenses for payments out of blocked accounts. When these licenses were not forthcoming, the banks' foreign departments had a satisfactory excuse for ignoring the foreign banks' orders. The result was that thereafter only the officials specifically certified by the Secretary of State could withdraw United States dollar deposits of the foreign banks of issue located in enemy-occupied countries.[8] Fortuitously, this and other litigious questions were resolved automatically by Hitler's attack on Soviet Russia in June, 1941.

Shortly before the Nazi assault, reports had circulated in Wall Street that the freezing of Soviet accounts was not unlikely. The Soviet Government, according to the reports, had defaulted on the payment of its sterling obligations contracted in connection with the purchase of the Lena Goldfields concession, and it was intimated that the reason for this action was not any inability to pay, but rather that government's displeasure with the seizure by the British Government of vessels belonging to the three Baltic states—Latvia, Lithuania, and Estonia—which had recently been incorporated into the USSR.

The whole question became relatively academic with the lining up of the Soviets on the side of the Allies. Soon gold shipments from Vladivostock to San Francisco began to make their appearance, and the Reconstruction Finance Corporation, the Defense Supplies Corporation, the Lend-Lease Administration, and the Treasury Stabilization Fund prepared to assist in the financing of Soviet military re-

[8] It is significant that eight years later New York banks faced similar claims when the Communist regime of China claimed balances carried in various financial institutions by the Bank of China. In this case, however, the banks operating in the State of New York leaned on a state statute authorizing them to reject orders canceling the authority of any persons accredited with depositaries, except upon court order or the furnishing of a satisfactory bond or surety.

quirements in this country. At the end of 1941 a United States Government loan for 100 million dollars was arranged against future shipments of Russian commodities to the United States, while the Federal Reserve Bank of New York granted the State Bank of the USSR substantial advances against gold in transit to the West Coast.

A Soviet Government Purchasing Commission was set up in February, 1942, which included K. I. Lukashov, chairman of Amtorg, and other officers of that organization. In the Lend-Lease Administration, Reeve Schley, long president of the American-Russian Chamber of Commerce, was appointed Assistant Coordinator in charge of operations with Russia, a position for which he was highly qualified because of his banking background and his intimate knowledge of Russia.

Since the end of the war, owing to the decline in United States trade with the Soviet Union in the absence of the hoped-for American large-scale credits and to the closely related deterioration in political relations, the business activities of the Amtorg Trading Corporation and consequently also the banking operations initiated by it have been reduced to small proportions.

SUMMARY. Before the First World War banking and trade relations with the czarist empire had largely followed the conventional pattern, Paris, London, Berlin, and Amsterdam sharing mainly the extensive public and private financing required for the building of railways and public utilities as well as the banking operations connected with the export of Russian grain, oil, and other raw materials. After the October revolution the early representatives of Soviet agencies in the United States were especially concerned to re-establish Russian credit. Special financing methods were used to provide funds in New York and London to pay for machinery and manufactured goods purchased here, and a market was created for medium- and long-term Soviet trade acceptances. The invasion of the Baltic republics and Poland in 1939 and the postwar developments raised a set of intricate problems for United States banks and merchants as regards their intercourse with the Union of Socialist Republics.

XIII

CHINA AND THE EAST

CHINA

SINCE the far-off days when, in 1784, the first American clipper landed in Canton and brought back to New England ports spices, teas, and silks, the trade with the Chinese Empire and later with the Chinese Republic has yielded growing rewards to United States enterprise. In the early twenties of the present century the increasing importance of United States commercial and financial interests in the Far East prompted the formation of several banking corporations especially dedicated to the promotion of United States banking in the leading Chinese ports and business centers. For the reasons mentioned in Chapter I these first ventures, with one exception, came to grief. Although the conditions under which they started their operations in that part of the world were not unpropitious, after a few years of hard effort they had to be liquidated or absorbed; however, their backers saw to it that creditors were not harmed and that American prestige did not suffer.

The branches of United States banks which during those years were opened in Shanghai, Hong Kong, and Tientsin took a leaf out of the book of painful experiences of their contemporaries. They followed conservative policies and cautiously felt their way before branching out into the field of local credit extension. By adapting their business practices to the differing local usages they gradually succeeded in earning the confidence of the mercantile community, native and foreign, and in establishing themselves firmly alongside the other foreign institutions—British, French, Belgian, Dutch, Italian, German, Russian, and Japanese—which under the protection of extraterritorial rights had already taken root in Chinese soil.

Until 1935 China was the largest and most populated country wholly on a silver standard. Transactions were handled and settlements made in a number of currencies: Shanghai dollars, Shanghai taels, Hong Kong dollars, Japanese yen, Philippine pesos, and other monetary units. In addition to routine banking, such as the opening of accounts in various currencies, the cashing of drafts received by the natives from members of their families in the United States and the financing of exports from and imports into China, loans were made on gold bars and silver metal, while exchange arbitrage was cultivated on a large scale between Shanghai, Hong Kong, New York, San Francisco, London, and Bombay.

In those days Shanghai was the center of the world's silver trade. At the Shanghai Mint silver bars were melted into sycee ("shoes," namely, ingots of about 50 taels' weight each) or into silver dollars (taels); sycee were the currency used between banks, while taels were the usual medium for ordinary commercial payments; both constituted the backing of the paper circulation. In the banks' exchange trading divisions, both in the Far East and in New York, foreign cable quotations were converted into local moneys, intricate calculating machines reducing the complicated mathematical problems by the mere mechanical tapping of keys and one or two turns of a lever. The importance of the Shanghai market in those days can be measured by the fact that in the late twenties two thousand gold-bar speculators had their headquarters in that port.

Next to Shanghai, New York and London were the most active silver trading markets. The sale of drafts payable in Hong Kong, to the Chinese living in the United States was one of the interesting auxiliary functions of some of the foreign exchange divisions at the New York head offices. Through a Chinese employee attached to the department, this business was daily solicited in New York's Chinatown. There in the morning he received the orders from the restaurant keeper and the laundryman and in the afternoon of the same day delivered the drafts against payment in cash. The Chinese living elsewhere throughout the country were served through the banks in Boston, Philadelphia, Chicago, San Francisco, and other large cities to which daily quotations were sent by wire and mail, while banks in Canada, Mexico, and Cuba were similarly equipped to sell Hong Kong exchange to the local Chinese population. These Hong Kong dollars were the favorite medium through which Chinese residents everywhere abroad supported their relatives at home, or in which they invested their savings against the day of their return to the land of their birth. The amounts sent to the old country, especially before certain Chinese holidays, reached six-figure proportions. To watch the Chinese gather at certain hours at the shop near the Bowery where one of the Chinese bank clerks made his headquarters and turn over to him the worn dollar bills that they wanted to exchange for Hong Kong drafts was a picturesque sight and a strange experience indeed. It was a distinct advantage to have this trade handled by a Chinese national understanding and speaking several dialects of Chinese and acquainted with the idiosyncracies of his people. The Chinese had implicit faith in the honesty of their countryman, who, unknown to them, was heavily bonded by the bank he represented.

For the banks the business in the Chinese remittances during this period meant a yearly turnover of more than 100 million U.S. dollars. In addition to the profit on the exchange, the sellers earned about 40 days' interest on the money, for it took about six weeks before the drafts could be presented for payment in Hong Kong. Some holders even refrained from sending them home and carried them for long periods on their persons or concealed them in their homes. These drafts of great United States banks were their most precious possessions; in their ignorance, they believed that by not cashing them they would be protected against the violent fluctuations of the Chinese dollar.

How did the banks provide the funds for the payment of the drafts abroad? The answer to this question throws an interesting light on the workings of foreign exchange and on the maze of currencies through which the dealers in the Far Eastern branches of foreign banks had to grope. As the supply of Hong Kong dollars in New York was limited, silver bars were bought in the United States, England, Mexico, Canada, and Peru, and shipped to Shanghai, where they were sold in return for Shanghai taels. The latter were then converted in Hong Kong into local Hong Kong dollars to pay the drafts sold four or six weeks earlier to Chinese in the United States. Hong Kong dollars were also obtained at times by selling United States dollars, pounds, or yen in the Hong Kong exchange market itself.

Besides the Shanghai market, in earlier days the Canton Mint and the city of Bombay were outlets for the white metal. Although since 1926, acting on the recommendation of a Royal Commission, the Indian Government had sold a large part of its silver reserve, Indian speculators continued to trade in the metal on a large scale. When silver was sold in Bombay, the rupee proceeds were disposed of in New York or London, the principal markets for Indian exchange. In the

United States, Boston, New York, and Philadelphia importers of jute and burlap were generally buyers of rupees, while oil and automobile companies were sellers. When local demand exceeded supply, traders as a last resort could sell sterling in Bombay or Calcutta in order to obtain rupee balances.

The market in Japanese yen was quite lively at times. Daily quotations were exchanged with Bombay, London, Hong Kong, Shanghai, and San Francisco, and compared with the rates in Kobe or Tokyo. Like all other foreign currencies, yen were bought in the cheapest and sold in the highest market or turned over to those merchants whose bids left a reasonable margin of profit.

In the Chinese branches it was necessary to have a responsible native to act as contact man with native customers. Few foreigners have a sufficient command of the Chinese language and its numerous dialects not to have to rely to a considerable degree on the integrity of an interpreter. Accordingly, each branch office had a Chinese compradore, combining in his person the functions of cashier and manager of the native employees, who were generally recruited by him. The bookkeeper, or "schroff," was under his orders, and he guaranteed the former's conduct, as well as that of all the native clerks. Speaking English, the compradore was in effect a liaison officer. He was personally responsible for business introduced by him or his employees, and in consideration of his guaranty or endorsement of any loan or business handled by him, received a commission, a fixed yearly minimum being generally granted to him. Selected from the local Chinese business community because of his standing, connections, and knowledge of banking and exchange, he was entrusted with a certain amount of cash to serve as capital in his daily operations.

The compradore thus filled a position of trust such as is not known in Western business practice. In a way, he was a banker within the bank. The Chinese carried their accounts with him. They issued checks on him, and he acted as their financial adviser. Often he would buy and sell exchange for them and give them his own contract. This, of course, offered him a temptation to speculate on the rise or fall of the currency he was to sell or buy, with the result that, in the event of severe fluctuations he might be unable to make good on his contracts. In such cases the danger was great that he would draw upon his employer's funds to cover his losses. In some concerns the compradore had the right to engage in private commercial trading of his own if it did not conflict with that of his employers; in this event, too, if he had reverses, he might be enticed to borrow as a last resource from the funds of which he was the trusted holder. Both the foreign banks and the leading business concerns thus in some instances discovered shortages in their compradores' accounts, generally after the defaulter had made away into the interior where it was often impossible to bring him to justice. In such cases, the guarantee fund, or the bond furnished by the compradore or his financial backer often proved inadequate to cover the entire loss. On the whole, however, Chinese honesty deserved its ancient repute, and the instances where the confidence placed in a compradore was betrayed were the exception rather than the rule. After the Second World War some banks abandoned the old compradore system and appointed educated Chinese of good local standing as junior officers in special charge of the native clientele.

For obvious reasons the United States banks in China tried to keep closely informed not only on the financial standing of their customers but also on the government finances, and prior to 1935 on the metallic cover behind the various bank-note issues circulating in the republic. The government notes were supposed to be secured by a 25 percent silver reserve, but it was not easy to ascertain the exact amount of metal held on this account at any particular moment. Official statistics were not published. Only the purchases of silver, traceable to government orders, sometimes gave an indication as to whether the official holdings had diminished and the reserves were likely to have declined. Such operations might also point to an imminent movement in the price of silver and therefore were watched with special interest by dealers everywhere.

Beginning in 1934, owing to the magnitude of the United States Treasury purchases, the rise of silver in the world markets started to depress profoundly the commodity price level in the silver-using countries in the Far East. By November, 1935, because of the constant drain on her reserves and the deflationary effect on her economy, China was forced to abandon the silver standard. The government ordered the nationalization of silver coins and bars and adopted a managed currency. The notes of the four government banks were made sole legal tender. In order to maintain the market value of the new inconvertible paper money a stabilization fund was created, managed by the Central Bank of China, the Bank of China, and the Bank of Communications. The fapi (which replaced the old yuan) was pegged at about 29 cents and 1 shilling 2 pence.

In 1936 and 1937 new issues of short-term government notes were offered to investors—the promissory notes of the Purchasing Committee of the Chinese Ministry of Railways, payable in Chinese currency. They had a maturity of twelve months and were guaranteed by a banking syndicate headed by the Central Trust of China, whose function it was to handle government business that because of its nature was outside the province of the Central Bank of China. The proceeds of the notes served to pay for materials needed for the completion of certain railway construction projects.

In the summer of 1937 the Export-Import Bank financed 50 percent of the cost of locomotives bought by a Shanghai commission house for account of the Chinese Government from a prominent American industrial corporation, which agreed to extend credit for the remainder of the order.

Among the lines of trade most keenly catered to by American banks in China was that of the fur buyers established in the principal Chinese ports. The purchases were financed by means of "authorities to purchase," opened by the head offices and other banks in the United States for account of United States importers of furs. Many of the "A/P's" contained the so-called "red-letter clause," which conveyed to the banking branches in China authority to open packing credits in favor of local fur merchants and buyers. The proceeds of the drafts issued under these credits served to pay for the furs and their processing until they were in condition to be delivered to the ocean vessels in return for bills of lading, insurance policies, and so forth, as provided in the "A/P." Upon receipt of the ocean documents together with invoices and drafts on the banks that had issued the "A/P," the local banks retained the amounts advanced under packing credits, including interest and charges, and paid the balance, if any, to the local beneficiaries. This form of financing, peculiar to the Far East, carried certain risks with it, and therefore the collateral was frequently inspected at the go-downs (warehouses) where the furs were stored or handled, for the benefit of the lending bank.

For many years Chinese investors and speculators counted among the active and shrewd operators in Wall Street. They purchased stocks and commodities on a large scale. Some of their holdings were carried on margin by various stock-exchange firms or served as security for loans from American branches and foreign banks in China. In turn the brokerage houses that carried the Chinese traders obtained loans from their New York banks. More or less substantial margins were required, according to the standing of the customer and the nature of the collateral. The foreign-exchange sales and purchases incident to these transactions were handled through foreign-exchange brokers in Shanghai and Hong Kong, or through the banks themselves.

The considerable volume of this business produced at certain periods large dollar deposits, which the Chinese banks sometimes lent to local borrowers in competition with the foreign institutions. The fluctuations in the Chinese bank accounts on the books of the New York banks reflected on occasion the state of Chinese internal or external politics. A threat of inflation would cause a sudden exodus of capital to the West, even the foreign-currency deposits in the Chinese offices of the American banks immediately showing a considerable rise. Natives frightened by a prospect of invasion, would hasten to place their savings in the local custody of foreign banks rather than in the Chinese banks, in the erroneous belief that there they would be better protected against enemy seizure.

In normal times American banks derived a large volume of trade from the financing of imports into China of raw cotton, scrap iron, machinery, airplanes, and so forth. Contrariwise, exports of silk, laces, embroideries, tea, skins, bristles, dried eggs, and tung oil were the objects of drafts on United States buyers or of the negotiation of bills at sight or 60 or 90 days' sight drawn on the American banks that had issued the credits for account of the United States purchasers.

Toward the middle of July, 1937, the situation in North China, then the principal seat of operations of the Japanese invader, grew alarming, as the enemy army expanded its operations southward. The government banks in Shanghai began to take precautions by shipping part of their silver and their confidential documents to Hong Kong. As conditions became worse, fears arose that the Chinese Government, instead of maintaining its gold and foreign exchange holdings as cover for the note issues, might be compelled to use them as a war chest irrespective of the detrimental effect on the national currency.

The apprehensions were only too warranted. On July 30 the Japanese took control of Tientsin, and on August 23 they landed in Shanghai, as the Chinese defenders retreated into the International Settlement. The Western markets were even more disturbed by the fear that Japan might blockade the entire Chinese coast and search all foreign vessels plying in Chinese waters. A possible ramification of the Chino-Japanese conflict, it was conjectured, might lead to international complications fraught with real danger for the peace of the other nations. On the other hand, from the economic angle the quota of the total world trade with the two contestants represented such a relatively small percentage of the international movement of merchandise that the threatened interruption of commerce with that part of the globe could be viewed with a certain complacency.

The Federal Reserve Board was alive to the problem that these events might create for United States banks established in foreign countries. Anticipating the subsequent grave developments, it issued on August 14, 1937, a new regulation, pursuant to the provisions of Section 25(a) of the Federal Reserve Act, as amended, authorizing the manager of any branch or agency of any bank or corporation established in any foreign country to suspend the operations of the branch "whenever a disturbed condition exists in the place or country which endangers the lives of its employees or the property of such branch."

On August 14, 1940, the United States banks received further protection by the terms of Regulation M issued by the Board of Governors of the Federal Reserve System. This regulation amplified and enlarged that of August 14, 1937, by empowering the officer in charge of a foreign branch to suspend operations not only in the event of a disturbed condition in the place where his office was established but also "for any other reason beyond the control of the branch and which relates to such disturbed condition." In this regulation stress was placed, however, on the duty of the branch to render every possible service to the depositors.

Notwithstanding the alarming situation created by conditions in Shanghai, no fear developed of an immediate devaluation of the currency. Foreign exchange remained pegged, and the accounts in the local banks continued to be blocked. Early in September the foreign governments, through their embassies, requested the banks and commercial houses to evacuate the wives and children of their foreign staffs to Hong Kong or Manila. Duplicates of important documents and photostatic copies of valuable papers, together with abstracts of ledgers, were shipped to Hong Kong for safekeeping. The Chinese and some of the foreign banks moved temporarily to the French Concession. A bank holiday was declared, and there was a great lack of legal tender. To escape the bombs of the Chinese fliers who attacked the Japanese warships just a block away from the Shanghai business center, many wealthy Chinese civilians left the city. The situation for those who stayed was most perilous. As one newspaperman put it, the Americans who remained placed their trust in God, but they were thankful that the Marines, too, were present. Large sections of the city, especially in Chapei and in the Kiangwan centers, were destroyed. Cotton mills, tobacco factories, warehouses, gasoline tanks, and wharves were hit and went up in flames.

When the Chinese banks were forced to suspend business, an interesting innovation in banking practice was born. Regulations were issued to the effect that all Chinese bank checks, that is, those payable by native banks, and payment orders issued prior to August 14 might be deposited to the credit of new "Huihua" accounts. No cash withdrawals from these accounts were permitted, but the balances could be used for the payment of debts by Chinese nationals to Chinese banks.

During these trying days there was practically no movement of import or export cargo. Because of the heavy damage to property, rumors were current that one prominent British house with large investments in Shanghai real estate and extensive interests in all parts of the East had suffered extreme losses. The firm had always enjoyed a high standing, and as matters turned out, it safely weathered the critical situation in which through no fault of its own it had found itself.

As soon as conditions returned to comparatively normal the banks made strenuous efforts to locate the merchandise (covered by letters of credit or bills sent for collection) that because of the fighting had been discharged at various ports other than those to which it had been consigned. The merchants who had purchased the goods were, of course, unable to make deliveries to their local customers and therefore could not take up their foreign-exchange contracts with the banks. But notwithstanding the existing chaos, confidence remained that ultimately they would be able to take care of their outstanding commitments, and it was expected that only in isolated cases would extensions of accounts payable have to be granted.

During these troubled weeks it was once more demonstrated that the flight of capital cannot be controlled or thwarted by governmental ordinances and laws, for in the East, as in the West, shrewd individuals were able to find loopholes to circumvent even the most rigid regulations. The general uneasiness about the fate of the Chinese dollar that was reflected in the capital leakage was not attenuated when it was announced that the government departments and the principal Chinese banks would be moved further inland from Nanking to Chungking.

In January, 1938, the United States Treasury concluded an agreement with the Chinese Government for the acquisition by the United States of 50 million ounces of silver per month at 45 cents per ounce. Since the agreement was to run for six months, this represented a sale of 300 million ounces, worth 135 million dollars. It was expected that this would supply China with ample funds to continue the prosecution of the war. At the same time the Chinese Government appealed to all foreign communities of its nationals to subscribe to Chinese national defense loans. The resulting demands for Chinese exchange competed with the purchases made by the Chinese expatriates for support remittances to their families at home. In making these remittances, citizens of Chinese descent and Chinese immigrants generally patronized United States banks, even being willing to pay a slightly higher rate for their drafts, which in the opinion of the Chinese buyers represented a greater guaranty of ultimate payment, regardless of any present or future Chinese Government decrees.

The Central Bank of China maintained large deposits in both New York and London. It bought and sold foreign currencies for account of the official stabilization fund and acted as depositary of the Chinese Government and of the nation's gold and silver reserves. In April, 1938, according to one estimate, the silver metal stored for its account in various London banks amounted to 290 million ounces, with a value at that time of 124 million dollars. In March, 1938, to husband the country's exchange hoard and prevent local speculators from illegally accumulating foreign currencies, the central bank began to exercise a stricter control over sales and purchases, allotting foreign cable transfers at the ratio of about 25 to 33 percent of the applications received from banks and merchants. However, there existed also an independent open market where the law of demand and supply continued to have its sway.

In addition to the Central Bank of China, the country boasted three other government banks: the previously mentioned Bank of China and the Bank of Communications, and the Farmers Bank of China. These institutions did not always follow uniform policies. In the late thirties they were still reputed to be more or less under the control of the powerful brother-in-law of Chiang Kai-shek, H. H. Kung, then Minister of Finance. One member of the official staff of the Bank of China was the resourceful Tsuy Pei, who had the reputation of being one of the ablest foreign-exchange experts of his country.

In June, 1938, the substantial payments that the central bank had to effect abroad to defray the government's military purchases began to be a heavy drain on its foreign-exchange holdings. The Shanghai dollar weakened. Although the central bank had reduced its allotments at the official rate to 15 percent of bona fide demands, Chinese dollars were now offered in the free market at 31 percent discount. The decline in the free market was perplexing, as it was constantly asserted that the Hongkong and Shanghai Banking Corporation, either acting as intermediary for the Chinese Government banks or operating independently with a guarantee of the British Government, had actively intervened in support of the exchange. The British had a considerable stake in the situation: the British investments in China before the outbreak of the hostilities were estimated at approximately 300 million pounds. On the other hand, in December, 1938, United States property jeopardized in China was valued at 200 million dollars by the late Julean Arnold, Commercial Attaché to China, to whom American foreign traders owe a deep debt.[1]

In the meantime, the Japanese conquerors, under the aegis of their provisional government, established a Federated Reserve Bank of Peiping, which was authorized to issue its own currency. Nanking fell, and huge quantities of legal tender notes were shipped by their frantic owners to Shanghai to be converted there into foreign money, while the local tobacco and oil companies also were heavy buyers of

[1] Arnold lived in the East for more than a generation. His reports on China were textbooks for those engaged in business and banking in that country.

dollars. The operations of the stabilization fund were surrounded by secrecy; like the Hong Kong fund, it was the object of frequent criticisms because of its policy of distributing exchange.

The remarkable capacity of Chinese traders for quickly reversing their positions was again exemplified when the news reached Shanghai of the German invasion of Czechoslovakia. There was a sudden rush to sell dollars and sterling and to buy in their place the national currency that had been slighted before. But this change of mood was of short duration. In October the advance of the Japanese army astride the Canton-Hankow railway was the occasion of renewed attempts to withdraw funds from the banks in Hong Kong.

Odd stratagems were resorted to in an effort to hide real estate holdings from the eyes of the Japanese. Wealthy Chinese asked for loans from British and American banks, guaranteed by mortgages on their properties: title deeds registered in the names of local realty companies were to be conveyed by trust agreement to the lending banks. However, the applicants were informed that in the event of Japanese interference the banks would not be able to call for intervention by their governments to protect the assets of Chinese borrowers.

By October, 1938, the silver stocks of the Chinese Government had diminished considerably. The Chinese Ministry of Finance was reported to be studying ways of commandeering the foreign balances and security holdings of Chinese banks and nationals, but it was not believed that the United States and British governments would assist in forcing the surrender of the important deposits held abroad for Chinese private account. By November, Hong Kong was practically isolated from the rest of China, and business in the colony was almost at a standstill. In spite of the strong sterling reserves built up by the administration of the colony, fears grew that it might be difficult to maintain the exchange rate for Hong Kong dollars.

In Tientsin the Japanese now operated through the Federated Reserve Bank of North China. Its notes, on a par with the yen, were made exchangeable on a basis of equality with the notes of the Chinese Government banks. The Japanese counted on the new issue driving out the old currency; their scheme was to encourage the exchange and then, with the Chinese legal tender notes so obtained, to buy foreign exchange wherever it could be secured. The Federated Reserve Bank currency was irredeemable even against yen. For this reason Chinese currency at first commanded a premium of 3 1/2 percent, which later declined to 3/4 percent. Japanese notes circulated in Tientsin in large volume. At the local branch of the Yokohama Specie Bank they could readily be exchanged for Federated notes, but the bank would not give yen in return for Federated notes presented at its windows. Yen notes were quoted at 5 percent premium. Meanwhile, trade in Tientsin was severely curtailed. In the past the city's main exports had been furs, skins, horsehair bristles, and wool. Now the Japanese governor of Manchukuo prohibited the export of these articles. Further obstacles were placed in the way of foreign exporters by refusing export licenses unless the transaction was financed by the Yokohama Specie Bank at its own rate. This forced the foreign banks in Tientsin to raise the cash margins when opening credits or making loans pending shipment abroad. They feared, moreover, that the Japanese might put an embargo on all dealings in foreign exchange and that they might make allotments to foreign banks only at the official rates. The complex local currency situation is best illustrated by the fact that in the foreign concessions in Tientsin shops refused to accept any other than Chinese national currency, while the Japanese stores took only Federated or yen notes. The natives consequently hoarded Chinese yuan, with particular preference for the larger denominations, which could be more easily secreted.

In self-defense the Tientsin branches of United States banks required their customers to sign waivers specifying that the local currency balances carried on their books would be payable only in notes of the Bank of China and the Bank of Communications stamped "Tientsin," and moreover that at the discretion of the managers the accounts could be closed by mailing cashier's checks for the balance, such checks also being marked "payable in notes of the Bank of China and Bank of Communications stamped 'Tientsin.' "

In Shanghai, too, in February, 1939, some of the foreign banks asked their depositors to sign a form letter confirming that the bank would not be held liable in case of events beyond its control. In other words, the only obligation now assumed by the banks in accepting deposits in Chinese currency was to repay them on demand in such notes as should then be legal tender at the place of deposit. This reservation was of particular importance to banks whose head offices were located in the United States, since it undertook legally to defeat in advance any such claims for damages as had been presented after the end of the First World War against a New York bank whose branches in Russia had been closed at the time of the Bolshevik revolution.

In the spring of 1939 the British Government extended a loan to China of 10 million pounds sterling for the construction of a 500-kilometer railway to the Burmese border. At about the same time the Chinese Ministry of Finance was forced to announce the suspension of interest and amortization payments on the government's foreign loans because of the seizure by the Japanese of the customs and salt revenues.

In the meantime, owing to the public distrust, Federated Reserve Bank notes had dropped to a discount of 10 percent against the fapi (Chungking dollar). Although the Chinese bank notes were irredeemable, confidence in them was not shaken, while people coming into possession of Federated notes lost no time changing them at the exchange shops, even though at a considerable sacrifice. In the British and French concessions the foreign banks carried separate accounts for each currency and sold foreign exchange only if paid for in Chinese notes.

To elude the export control maintained by the Japanese a special trading method was initiated by local merchants, consisting of linking exports with imports. Under the Japanese regulations all export documents had to be accompanied by a letter from the foreign bank financing the shipment, in which the bank undertook to hand over the exchange proceeds at the equivalent of 1 shilling 2 pence per Chinese dollar to the Yokohama Specie Bank for account of the Federated Bank. The Japanese bank agreed to sell back the exchange at the same rate in direct proportion to the quantity of foreign currencies received by it. Private arrangements now were made between exporters and importers whereby the latter agreed to refund to the exporters the difference in exchange between the official rate of 1 shilling 2 pence and the free market rate of about 8 pence (or the equivalent in United States dollars), which the importers would have to pay if they had to cover their exchange need at the official source. With the aid of the allowance of the importers, exporters were enabled to ship controlled articles ostensibly at the official rate of exchange, but by this method they recovered the loss resulting from the higher cost of the goods when invoiced at the fixed exchange rate, as well as the profit from the shipment. It was a kind of barter resembling in some ways the Schachtian device to hide the depreciation of the Reichsmark under the Nazis. The Tientsin importer did not lose in the bargain, for he secured a better rate of exchange than the one he would have been obliged to pay had he purchased the foreign currency for forward delivery to be settled upon arrival of the goods from abroad.

At the end of 1938 the Universal Trading Corporation was founded in New York by K. P. Chen, former general manager of the Shanghai Commercial and Savings Bank and member of the silver delegation that came to the United States in 1936, and Hsi Te Mou, general manager of the Central Bank of China. This corporation, which was formed under United States laws, was to handle Chinese purchases of American machinery and raw materials and the sale of tungsten, tung oil, tin, and other products of the republic. The Export-Import Bank granted the new enterprise a credit of 25 million dollars. The company's capital was moderate, and the entire stock was owned by the Chinese Government. Archie Lochhead, former technical assistant to Secretary of the Treasury Morgenthau and manager of the United States Stabilization Fund, became president, and S. D. Ren, previously an official of the Postal Savings Bank, in Shanghai, was elected vice president. The operations of the organization soon expanded to such an extent that in addition to further credits from the Export-Import Bank the facilities of private financial institutions had to be enlisted. The Fooh Hsing Corporation, another Chinese Government trading concern, exercised in China the same functions as the Universal Trading Corporation, while to the China Defense Supplies Corporation, in Washington, headed by T. V. Soong, were entrusted the large Chinese Government orders for army supplies, and so forth.

In April, 1939, the Japanese, ever alert to invent new financial weapons, formed a commercial bank in Shanghai, the Hua Hsing Bank, with a paid-up capital of 50 million Chinese yuan and the right to issue bank notes convertible into foreign currency. The Japanese authorities called on the local branches of foreign banks to accept these notes. Both the State Department and the United States banks regarded these steps as preliminary to the attempted extension of Japanese control over the finances and the commerce of the whole Yangtse region. Accordingly, although the new bank's fosterfathers emphasized that the Hua Hsing notes would constitute the best hedge against a collapse of the Chinese national currency the foreign banks adopted an attitude of passive resistance. The discount on the notes of the Federated banks in Tientsin, Peiping, and Shanghai at this time was rightly attributed by the Japanese to the nonco-operation of the foreign exchange banks and local merchants. In Shanghai the value of the yen dropped to a record low, with 100 yen offered for 88 Chinese dollars. Contributing to the yen oversupply were the funds imported by Japanese immigrants and the circulation of military scrip in the occupied area of China.

As the war progressed, the revenues of the Chinese Government declined, and the four government banks were compelled to absorb more and more internal bonds to finance the struggle against the invader. Increasingly the government had recourse to the printing press, the rising inflation obliging the Central Bank of China to let contracts in England and the United States for huge quantities of bank notes of steadily mounting denominations. As a result the note issues rose by leaps and bounds. The cost of living advanced as the Chinese currency dropped from 16 1/8 cents to 12 3/4 in June, 1939, reaching a record low in July of 6 cents. The British Stabilization Fund which operated in Hong Kong through a local committee stopped selling foreign exchange. The fall of the currency was a crushing blow for the Chinese wage earners and savers, although foreign employers authorized high cost-of-living allowances to alleviate the situation of the native staffs.

Notwithstanding the unfortunate conditions within China, when war broke out in Europe Chinese holders of sterling started to sell their London balances, convinced that at this juncture dollars were a safer investment. In the offices of the United States banks in Shanghai the declaration of war had a rather unexpected effect. It started such a rush of new depositors that at certain hours signs had to be put up to discourage the opening of new accounts, since the cashiers' departments were unable to catch up with all the deposits that piled up behind the tellers' windows. This sudden avalanche of business demonstrated once more that the Chinese cannot be matched when it comes to switching funds from one monetary center to another after every unexpected change in the direction of the wind.

As 1939 drew to its close, the Japanese armies controlled the main communication lines covering an expanse of 400,000 square miles (10 percent of the total area of the country), embracing roughly 75 percent of the Chinese republic's estimated economic resources. The year 1940 opened with even greater uncertainties than did its predecessor. The perpetual needs of foreign funds for the payment of war material, together with speculative demands, caused a constant leakage of the exchange at the disposal of the Central Bank of China for the stabilization operations. The quotas continued to be lowered in order to stretch the available foreign assets over as long a period as possible. The situation was especially acute at the end of each month, when merchants and operators found it necessary to request that their purchases maturing at the end of the month be carried over (in the Chinese vernacular "change over") to the next month. Probably at the instigation of the exchange control, it was announced in June that thereafter change-overs would not be handled for arbitrage houses or for speculators; only interbank transactions and legitimate commercial contracts would be prolonged from then on.

In the past, the change-over had been an important source of earnings for the foreign banks. For instance, whenever futures in dollars or sterling commanded a premium that gave a satisfactory return, they employed part of their Chinese currency deposits in purchasing dollars or sterling for immediate delivery and selling the same amount for settlement one month later. The only risk had to do with the solvency of the buyers of the future contracts, but these were selected with care. At times, in addition to the slight profit on exchange, some moderate interest was earned on the funds deposited abroad.

As the general situation kept deteriorating, the Chinese native banks were increasingly concerned about the fate of their real estate holdings in the international settlements. They approached some foreign banks confidentially as to whether they would be inclined to take over their properties. However, the probable complications outweighed the desire to be helpful even to institutions with whom their relations were of a close and intimate character.

In March, 1940, it was rumored that a new central bank would be established by the Japanese-controlled administration of Wang Ching-wei and that a printing establishment in the French concession of Shanghai was already engaged in turning out notes for the future bank of issue. When this news reached the Shanghai market, the price of gold bars went skyrocketing.

As time went on it became apparent that the risks of doing business in the Far East were growing in both number and degree and that the local bank branches were likely to be faced soon with the most serious contingencies. The officers in charge were therefore cautioned to be extremely prudent in placing new commitments on their books. Although some of the local managers still hoped for an easing of the tension, they were prevailed upon to take certain internal measures so as to be prepared for any emergency. No new accounts were accepted, and all important records were made in duplicate, the duplicates being mailed by different routes to the head offices.

The violent upsets in Europe had their repercussions even in these distant parts of the world. Chinese depositors withdrew their balances from the Belgian bank, and some of the more timid natives even closed their accounts in British and French institutions. Temporarily the Shanghai and Tientsin dollars gained strength as a result of the reverses suffered by the Allies. Perhaps the Chinese national currency was not so bad after all.

Early in October further restrictive instructions were sent to American foreign branches. Except those fully secured by cash or United States securities or those with first-class foreign banks and commercial houses, outstanding future exchange contracts were to be promptly reduced, and all unsecured commitments with Japanese concerns were to be eliminated. The danger of war between the United States and Japan now induced the alarmed Chinese to sell United States dollars and return once more to the fold of the home currency. Those who maintained foreign currency accounts in the branches of American banks were given drafts on New York or London in accordance with the legend printed in their passbooks that payment would be effected in this manner. Some hoarding of Chinese currency was reported, but soon the more informed natives realized that their money was safer in the vaults of a bank than in their stockings or under their mattresses. Wealthy Chinese purchased commodities or raw materials if they could be secured. But here, too, the danger of confiscation by the enemy haunted their search for protection.

Since the beginning of 1940 the Chinese dollar had depreciated by more than 22 percent in relation to sterling and by about 30 percent vis-à-vis the United States dollar. The attrition was steady and discouraging. The Nanking puppet government's central bank opened for business on January 6, 1941, its purpose, according to Japanese press dispatches quoted by the New York *Herald Tribune* on December 21, 1940, being to "wage financial war against the Chungking Government's currency." The Chungking dollars were to be withdrawn by the new bank in exchange for its own notes at par.

At this point, because of the multiplicity of moneys then current in various parts of China, it may be well to recapitulate the different currencies that circulated in free and occupied China at this particular period: (1) The old Chinese national or standard (CS$) currency known as yuan (or fapi) represented by the notes of the four government banks; in 1942 the note-issue monopoly was transferred to the Central Bank of China; (2) Chungking dollar notes; (3) Federated Reserve Bank Tientsin notes; (4) Federated Reserve Bank Peiping notes; (5) notes of the Hua Hsing Commercial Bank, Shanghai; (6) Japanese yen; (7) Japanese military scrip in yen; (8) hidden Shanghai taels (silver coins) no longer legal tender since 1935, but which may still have passed from hand to hand in the interior of the country, where the peasants clung to the metallic media whether demonetized or not.

The issues of Japanese notes raised a puzzling problem for American banks which sold drafts on Hong Kong and Shanghai payable in Chinese dollars. Should they mark on the face of the drafts that they were "payable in currency of the Chungking National Government," or would it be better to affix a legend to the effect that the bearer was entitled to "Shanghai (or Hong Kong) dollars of legal tender at the time of sale"? Reference is made later to the claims made by holders of uncashed drafts at the end of the war.

Disturbed by the somber outlook and only too aware of the wishes of the top managements in the United States, the bank officers in charge on the spot were between Scylla and Charybdis: if they stopped accepting business, the other foreign banks would pick up the trade of customers whom they had cherished for years and with whom they were anxious to continue to deal; if they did not conform to the instructions from their head offices, they exposed themselves to serious criticism should war break out and losses be sustained because of their having deliberately disregarded the definite advice of their superiors. Their situation was indeed most difficult. The British banks abided by their old maxim, "Business as usual!" Perhaps, as in the early thirties in connection with Central European credits, United States banks would again be blamed by British critics for having run to shelter at the first sign of danger.

By early 1941 international credit as it existed in prewar years had to all intents and purposes almost disappeared. In Europe barter transactions were the order of the day. Most governments had entered into bilateral trade agreements involving the direct exchange of goods. Under pressure of war the classical method of settling debts by means of gold shipments and international loans had generally been abandoned. The dollar, linked to gold through the official buying rate of the United States Treasury of $35.00 per ounce, had become the leading monetary unit. The "cash and carry" provisions of the Neutrality Act and the disinclination of exporters to accept orders unless paid in "hard" currencies—both contributed to the stagnation of private Far Eastern commerce other than orders from the belligerent and neutral governments. Moreover, the possibility that the United States might freeze Japanese and Chinese accounts was bound to create alarm and reluctance to enter into new contracts. Anticipating such a decision the United States banks in Shanghai were directed by their head offices to require all depositors having United States dollar balances of $5,000 or more to transfer their accounts to the respective main offices in New York, thus assuring that the relations with these customers would be clearly governed by United States laws and regulations. Further precautionary measures consisted in the immediate dispatch home of most negotiable assets, such as travelers' letters of credit, United States currency, bullion, and foreign bearer securities. Finally the branch managers were instructed to encourage the withdrawal of large Chinese-currency deposits so as to reduce the amount of cash held in the local vaults.

The last-named measure had a particular bearing on the Hong Kong offices, which carried their reserves in the form of notes of the two British banks, the Hongkong and Shanghai Banking Corporation and the Chartered Bank of India, Australia and China, Ltd. Ultimately, following an expedient devised in France under similar conditions, affidavits were prepared and countersigned by the two issuing banks showing the serial numbers of the larger denominations of bank notes held in special vaults of the branches, in order that in case of a bombing attack and actual loss of the currency through fire or any other catastrophe except confiscation by the enemy, the foreign banks would have authentic data upon which to base their claims for the replacement of the destroyed notes.

While it was impossible to make 100 percent fool-proof plans for every possible contingency, at any rate it was later possible, owing to the foresight of everybody concerned and by reason of the steady flow of duplicate records, as well as the deposit of vouchers, statements, and books in safe keeping with friendly neutrals, to reconstruct at the head offices the most valuable branch ledgers, pending the moment when after victory was won the work of straightening out the affairs of the foreign agencies could be effectively undertaken.

In the early part of 1941, upon the directive of President Roosevelt, the United States Treasury delegated Laughlin Currie, one of the President's administrative assistants and an economist of wide experience, to study on the spot the nature and extent of the Chinese inflation, and also to confer on other subjects with the high government personages in Chungking. In order to assist China the United States Stabilization Fund already had acquired substantial sums of Chinese currency. In May another credit of 50 million dollars was placed at the disposal of China for the maintenance of the Chinese dollar. At the same time, an Anglo-American-Chinese stabilization board was formed under the auspices of the United States Treasury and the British Government, with K. P. Chen, former chairman of the Universal Trading Corporation, as one of the Chinese directors. The board was to function in Hong Kong, Shanghai, and Chungking; its main task was to fix with the co-operation of the Central Bank of China, the official buying and selling rates for dollars and sterling against fapi and to supervise the operations of all buyers and sellers of foreign exchange, both Chinese and foreign. Washington appointed the late Manuel A. Fox, of the United States Treasury, as the American member of the board. The British Treasury contributed 5 million pounds, and the Chinese banks supplied 20 million dollars.

During the spring of 1941 a representative of the United States Treasury visited the New York banks engaged in Far Eastern business to ascertain what effect the freezing of Far Eastern accounts—should it be decided upon—would have on the Chinese branches of United States banks. To him it was pointed out that even if American branches should be permitted to operate under special licenses there was danger that the blocking of Chinese accounts would be misunderstood by the natives and that United States prestige would probably suffer. It would not be easy to explain to Chinese customers why they should no longer have free access to their dollar balances, especially since for more than a generation they had been accustomed freely to convert one currency into the other. Of course, it went without saying that if the accounts were finally blocked, the government regulations would be faithfully and vigorously enforced whatever the effect on the banks' fortunes.

On July 24, 1941, the United States Treasury took the contemplated action by blocking all Japanese and Chinese accounts. Chinese assets were included, it was carefully stressed in the public announcement, only to prevent any future transfers of Chinese funds to Japanese interests. Regardless of the complaints of individuals on whom temporary hardships were inflicted, the branch offices in China and the main offices in the United States set energetically to work to apply the new rulings. Their task fortunately was soon eased when the Treasury, realizing the need for exceptions in meritorious instances and in order to avoid unjust treatment, readily issued scores of general licenses tending to simplify and reduce the administrative work of the banks.

At first the operations of the Anglo-American-Chinese exchange stabilization board gave rise to inevitable confusion. Fourteen Chinese and foreign banks were directed to operate at the official rate fixed by the board (in August, 1941, 5 11/32 U.S. cents to the Chinese dollar). However, this rate was about 10 percent higher than the open market rate, and smart Chinese owners of United States dollars would accordingly refrain from selling them to British and United States banks, since they could obtain 10 percent more Chinese dollars by patronizing the free market. Furthermore, the other local foreign banks (French, Italian, German, and Japanese) were not bound by the regulations of the board, and the American branches naturally deplored the necessity of abandoning an important portion of their foreign-exchange business—their "bread and butter"—to their competitors.

Because of growing delays in the mails and other threatening possibilities, the Chinese branches of United States banks were now instructed to henceforth confine their negotiations of drafts issued under commercial letters of credit to those opened by banks that had specifically agreed in writing, with regard both to outstanding letters of credit and those to be issued in future, that upon simple advice of the head office of the negotiating branch to the effect that the drafts and documents had been honored abroad, they would pay the face amount of such drafts without any warranty that the drafts and the documents would actually arrive and be delivered later in accordance with the terms of the letter of credit. This precaution had to be taken because of fear that Japanese censors and postal clerks were tampering with the mails.

Immediately upon the freezing of the Chinese accounts the United States Treasury issued a general license permitting United States banks in China to finance imports and exports and business related thereto. The balances of the branches were not blocked, but payments for Chinese nationals were subject to special license. After our entry into the war redoubled measures were taken to prevent the handling of shipments where Axis nationals were involved, where the cargo was to sail on a Japanese vessel, or where transshipment of the merchandise was likely to be effected in Japanese ports.

In September the Anglo-American-Chinese stabilization board issued a ruling providing for the fixing of definite quotas of foreign-exchange to be supplied monthly for specified major import commodities that were exempted from the prohibited list. Reasonable amounts of foreign currency were made available for minor items such as personal insurance. The banks were asked to agree to deal only at official rates and to abstain from trading in the open market, directly or indirectly, while no forward contracts were to be entered into. These measures reflected the suspicion that Japanese banks were slyly operating in the free market, where by corralling dollars and sterling they could, through clandestine attacks on the Chinese currency, nullify the support given by the United States and Great Britain and thus undermine the morale of the Chinese people. The board designated the United States banks as depositaries. The latter were requested to hold in special compartments of their vaults the large quantities of Chinese paper money received in connection with the board's sales of exchange. All sales were subject to the approval of the board.

Because of the considerable work involved, the task assumed by the American banks of receiving and storing the tremendous number of small Chinese bank notes proved in the long run extremely arduous. However, the board released them from any responsibility other than that of taking care of the clerical work connected with the reception and safekeeping of the notes. Later, tribute for this service was paid by Daniel Bell, Under Secretary of the Treasury, who stated that the co-operation of the United States banks with the Treasury and the stabilization board was of distinct help during the trying months in the fall of 1941.

As the problems with which the board had to struggle were more complicated than at first expected, the Treasury Department asked Merle Cochran, technical assistant to Secretary Morgenthau, and the British Treasury delegated Sir Otto Niemeyer to join the board at Hong Kong. The former took with him a confidential memorandum prepared by the two United States banks, outlining the steps that in their opinion should be taken to improve the Chinese exchange situation.

At this time the bank branches in the Far East ran into another unexpected difficulty. Some United States importers of Chinese goods obtained restraining orders from United States courts to prevent the banks that had issued letters of credit for their account, from paying the drafts drawn in China under these letters of credit, on the ground that the merchandise covered by the drafts, and in some cases the bills of lading that should accompany them, had not arrived in the United States. The banks holding the drafts started action to set aside the restraining orders, but without success, although counsel for the banks pointed out to the judge the great damage inflicted on the prestige abroad of American banks' letters of credit. However, these were isolated cases. The great majority of traders respected their signatures, and their banks paid the drafts upon presentation, provided the usual guarantees were furnished to them in the absence of full sets of shipping documents or for other discrepancies.[2]

In spite of the operations of the stabilization board the price level in Shanghai rose without halt. In October bar gold climbed within two weeks from 7,000 to 20,000 Shanghai dollars. In Tientsin the fapi

[2] Proposals for the revision of the international code of Uniform Customs and Practice for commercial documentary credits fixed by the Seventh Congress of the International Chamber of Commerce have been submitted to the Committee on Banking Technique and Practice of the Chamber by Wilbert Ward, vice president of the National City Bank of New York and head of the Legal Committee of the Bankers Association for Foreign Trade. If accepted, they should go far toward clarifying the conditions under which letters of credit are honored by commercial banks everywhere and at the same time prove an effective aid to exporters and importers throughout the world.

broke to a new low of 2 7/8 cents, as against the board's official rate of 5 1/2 cents.

As noted earlier in this chapter, one of the principal problems raised by the Sino-Japanese war was the large amount of drafts on Hong Kong that were not cashed by their Chinese holders. The banks feared that if Japanese troops should occupy Hong Kong they would confiscate all cash held by the United States banks including that set aside for the payment of these drafts. During the first part of November General License 75 was therefore issued by the United States Treasury directing that thereafter remittances by any person through any American bank to any person in any part of China could only be effected if the dollars were deposited with the Bank of China in New York for account of the stabilization board for China, whose control had now been extended to all of China.

When advices were received in New York pointing to the possibility of a sudden attack on Shanghai, the branches there were instructed not to negotiate any further drafts under commercial letters of credit except where the United States importer had deposited with the head office the required cash, to be unconditionally applied to the payment of any bills negotiated under his authority in China. Simultaneously, in the hope that it would invite sizable withdrawals, one United States bank published a notice in the Shanghai press indicating that it would no longer assume responsibility for deposits held by it in the event of developments beyond its control.

Under its new regulations the Chinese Government prohibited further imports from the United States unless the Chinese importer had paid for the merchandise in United States dollars purchased from the stabilization board. On the other hand, Chinese exports to the United States were authorized only after the United States Collector of Customs of the port of entry had seen a consular invoice, stamped by the United States consul at the port of export, certifying that the United States dollar proceeds from the shipments had been sold to the stabilization board. In the United States, corresponding regulations were contained in the Treasury's General License 58, as amended, which required the United States exporter to file a statement with the customs officials that exchange had been covered by the Chinese importer with an authorized bank in China.

On December 8, 1941, the day after Pearl Harbor, the Japanese occupied the International Settlement of Shanghai. Cable and mail intercourse ceased. The Japanese army at once took possession of the British and American banks. Fortunately the situation, as it affected the branches, had been long anticipated. As has been noted, protective measures had been taken and commitments had been considerably reduced. At the head offices it was frankly recognized that certain losses would probably be incurred, but sufficient liquid resources were available to permit prompt and full settlement of all legitimate claims. On the whole, outstanding loans were adequately secured. Furthermore, so far as could be judged from a distance of eleven thousand miles, the occupying power would probably find it in its own interest to conduct the liquidation of the United States banks in a businesslike and honest way so as to protect both the depositors and the creditors. In addition, the head-office executives felt justified in assuming that after the end of the war, if losses had been sustained by reason of the seizure of the banks' property, the aggressor would be held to strict accountability. Nor were there any grounds for apology on their part; considering the important place that the United States had attained in the Far East, the banks could not in fairness have shunned whatever risks were inherent in the situation.

At the moment, however, the main preoccupation of the parent offices was the fate of their staffs. For a number of days no news was received. Then cables came through neutral channels that the personnel was well and safe. Meanwhile, Shanghai and Tientsin were completely shut off from the rest of the world apart from those countries under the domination of Japan. The first business problem in the minds of the New York officials in charge of the Far Eastern branches was the fate awaiting the exchange contracts pending at the time of the seizure of the branches. Would it be possible to extend them from month to month until such time as they could be liquidated in a normal way? Would the foreign offices be authorized by those now in charge to require the sellers to furnish security for the ultimate execution of contracts for the purchase and delivery of U.S. dollars and sterling in the event of the inevitable further depreciation of the Shanghai dollar?

Their next concern had to do with the drafts and shipping documents in transit from the Far East. The principal efforts of the head offices, accordingly were concentrated upon obtaining possession of these valuable remittances. Besides those forwarded by the Chinese branches, banks in the Philippines, Java, Borneo, Singapore, and the other Malayan islands now either under attack or in danger of invasion had negotiated drafts under American letters of credit covering urgently needed products, such as rubber, chemicals, and other products that had been purchased by United States Government agencies for use by the armed forces in the prosecution of the war. In this connection, some United States banks, when the political horizon began to darken, had taken the precaution to call on their correspondents in the Far East to send full cable reports as to the amounts of any drafts negotiated by them, the nature and volume of the merchandise shipped, the names of the vessels carrying the cargoes, and the dates on which they had left port. Moreover, fearful that the boats carrying the shipping documents might be torpedoed or captured, they had asked that triplicate documents be sent to certain addresses in countries remote from the potential war area in order that, should both original and duplicate documents go astray, they would still have one set of bills of lading which could be presented to the United States importer, the steamship owners, and in case of need, the insurance underwriters to sustain claims for any losses. Thanks to these prudent measures, harmful and costly delays were obviated, and the foreign departments concerned were thus able to render an unusual and valuable service to their customers at a most crucial time.

As to the merchandise bought in the United States by Chinese importers under the "authorities to purchase" issued by the Chinese and Japanese branches, these were by then mostly covered by cash or satisfactory American collateral. However, special divisions of experienced clerks had to be formed at the head offices to follow the fate of the goods that were afloat or in transit on their way to the Far East. Many of the ships could still be ordered into friendly or neutral ports. Some of the boats, with the generous co-operation of the shipping companies, were deviated from their regular course and their cargoes were discharged in Manila, Ceylon, India, Australia, and South America. There it was stored in warehouses, only to be impounded later, in some instances, by the local governments. Unless the foreign branch offices had received full payment in advance from the buyers, the foreign departments at the head offices had to exercise their own judgment as to whether to sell the goods or to run the risk that their value might be eaten up by accrued storage charges, war risk, fire, and theft insurance premiums, and finally brokerage fees and selling commissions. However, whenever possible, the officers in charge preferred not to incur the risk of giving directions for the handling of shipments when no orders had previously been received from the buyer. This policy was particularly indicated when there was danger that the government of the country where the merchandise had been landed might commandeer the goods and hold itself responsible for the proceeds. Banks do not cherish responsibilities of this nature. Still, owing to the demand created by the war, almost all the merchandise that was involved had risen in price, and in general the owners were content with and approved the action taken by the banks. Since in the main business had long been restricted to first-class names, the banks were justified in relying on the fair-mindedness of their customers not to make any unreasonable postwar claims. Subsequent events proved that this assumption was indeed an entirely legitimate one.

Goods that had not as yet left the United States were stored in independent warehouses, or else arrangements were made with the manufacturers to keep the merchandise on their own premises as long as space was available. However, in April, 1942, the United States Treasury issued instructions that all merchandise held by the banks for Far Eastern account and then located on docks and piers and in warehouses on the West Coast be promptly removed under directive licenses to be issued forthwith, since the government was in urgent need of the storage facilities. These directive licenses authorized the sale of the merchandise and the placing of the proceeds to the credit of a "whom it may concern" escrow account.

After the occupation of Hong Kong the operations of the stabilization board there were suspended, and the members moved from Hong Kong to Chungking in order to conduct the control from there. In April the press announced that out of the 500 million dollar lend-lease allotment promised to China, 200 million had been paid by the Treasury to the Federal Reserve Bank of New York for account of the Chinese Government.

In February, 1942, it was learned through neutral sources that several Japanese banks—among them the Sumitomo Bank, the Bank of Taiwan, and the Bank of Chosen—had been appointed by the Japanese as liquidators of the branches of the two United States banks. Another message received by the State Department related that the staffs of the two banks in Hong Kong were allowed to go to their places of business during the day, but were obliged to live in a third-class Chinese hotel and forced to subsist on inadequate Chinese food. From an anonymous letter it was learned that the liquidators of the banks had permitted Chinese and so-called "kind nationals" to withdraw limited amounts from their accounts, a maximum of $300 per month.

Early in July, 1942, a meeting was held in New York at which all the United States banks operating in China discussed the attitude to be adopted with regard to demands made by buyers of Chinese dollar drafts payable in Hong Kong and Shanghai. The holders claimed that upon return of the drafts to the issuing banks they were entitled to refund of their equivalent in United States dollars calculated at the currently prevailing rate of exchange for Shanghai currency. The representatives of the banks declared unanimously that while sympathizing with the plight of the bearers of their drafts, they could not for the time being agree to repurchase them for reasons of "force majeure." They stated that the cashing of these checks, payable in the territory now under Japanese control, would establish a precedent for other areas in enemy hands and that furthermore they would be taking a long position in Hong Kong or Shanghai dollars, which was obviously something that under prevailing circumstances, owing to the risk of loss involved, they could not be expected to do.

Slightly earlier, in June, 1942, the National City Bank and the Chase National Bank finally heard from the State Department that some members of their Hong Kong staffs were sailing on the S.S. *Asama Maru* for Lourenco Marques, where they were exchanged for Japanese diplomats and merchants interned in the United States. Returning from there on the *S.S. Gripsholm,* they landed in New York during the last week of August. The liberated officials reported that they had destroyed cipher keys and confidential documents before the arrival of the Japanese. They had even succeeded in concealing some valuable office records and bringing them home to the United States. They stated that the branches' safe deposit boxes had been opened in the presence of Japanese representatives; the contents had been turned over to the owners, apart from gold bars and foreign money for which receipts were given. Departing Americans had been allowed to empty their personal boxes, and gold had been purchased from them at $45.00 per ounce. Contrary to what happened in the Philippine Islands, no currency was destroyed in Hong Kong prior to the seizure of the port.

Up to the time when the Americans were permitted to leave for home, the liquidation of the branches apparently proceeded in a fairly orderly manner. The only serious quarrel some of the banks had with the Japanese administrators was over the creation of a "liquidation pool" at the Hong Kong branch of the Yokohama Specie Bank. The foreign banks were called on to pay their cash balances into this common pool, out of which the Japanese proposed to pay identical cash dividends to the depositors of the British and United States banks. Those banks whose cash reserves were larger than those of their neighbors lodged a strong protest against this arbitrary method, since it seemed unjust that their depositors should be penalized because some banks had been more generous in investing their resources in mortgage and other long-term loans. However, their protestations were ignored. The possibility that the United States banks, owing to this unfair procedure, might be liable at the end of the war for deposits that their own ample cash surpluses would have permitted them to redeem without delay was disregarded.

According to the views of the returning officers, moderate losses were likely to be suffered by reason of the possibility that some shipments, financed under "A/P's," might never reach their destination. Moreover, the documents and drafts pertaining to such shipments might be lost, too, especially those mailed on the S.S. *Harrison,* which apparently was sunk at the outbreak of the war. Others were undoubtedly pilfered by the Japanese in the Hong Kong and Manila post-offices, when these cities were captured. It may be mentioned in passing that some of the documents brought home were in the form of Recordak photostatic micronegatives, which could easily be enlarged.

According to one returning United States Government official, the liquidation of the American banks in Tientsin also was conducted on a normal basis up to the time he left the city. However, losses of up to 15 percent were caused to the branches owing to the manner in which the Japanese administrators obliged the banks to pay depositors with accounts in Chungking dollars. The Japanese insisted that the managers turn over to them their Chungking dollar cash reserves, buying them at an abnormally low rate (25 Federated Reserve Bank dollars, that is, Japanese controlled currency, for

100 Chungking dollars). On the other hand, they compelled the banks to pay their Chungking dollar depositors 40 Federated dollars for 100 Chungking dollars. The main offices in the United States, with regard to all such and similar transactions, went on record as refusing to accept responsibility on the ground that these were acts performed without their consent under compulsion of the enemy.

The Hongkong and Shanghai Banking Corporation was the first foreign bank to apply for and receive a license for the operation of a branch in Chungking under the new Chinese banking law. Although the United States banks were invited to do likewise, they abstained from following the example of the British bank and until the end of the war were represented at the capital by their officers, who made regular visits to Chungking.

In March, 1943, a cable received via neutral sources apprised the New York banks that their Shanghai staffs, which had not been molested until then, had also been interned in and around Shanghai. In September, 1943, the Japanese agreed to exchange some of these internees against a second group of their own nationals. The exchange took place on October 15 at Mormugao, in Goa, Portuguese India. The repatriates arrived in New York on December 1.

From the stories of the returning men it was possible to piece together an account of what happened in the two years that had elapsed since the interruption of communication with the branch offices, in December, 1941. Their impression was that at that time the Chinese Government still had ample dollar reserves at its disposal. The latter appeared to have been accumulated from sales of silver stocks, remittances to Free China by nationals resident in the United States, lend-lease funds, and also to no small extent the heavy expenditures of American and British forces stationed in various parts of the country.

One encouraging intelligence brought back by the staff was the news that, from all that could be learned the Japanese liquidators had paid off deposits and discharged other liabilities, so that it appeared as if the affairs of the various offices were being wound up in a reasonably businesslike manner. Obviously, it was impossible to hazard an estimate of what claims might ultimately be asserted. However, the employees expressed the opinion—later confirmed by events—that open future exchange contracts would be settled at the end of the war without any serious defaults on the part of the sellers of dollars and sterling, the only transactions about which there existed some concern as to the final outcome.

Early in 1944 it was stated by Chungking officials in conversation with a visiting American banker that in the effort to stop the wild currency inflation which was sweeping over the country and to build up renewed confidence among the peasants, as much as 200 million dollars in gold had been shipped from the United States to China to be used for government purchases and the support of the note issue. In another conversation a high member of the Chinese cabinet expressed his keen satisfaction with the co-operation China had been receiving from United States banks during such a difficult period of her history. The traveler in question was favorably impressed by the fact that in the provinces of China the note issues of the central government had come to have a broader circulation than in former days, when the individual paper currencies of the provincial governments themselves were the preponderant circulating media.

The amount of exchange acquired monthly from the Allied military forces was at that time estimated at about 25 million dollars. As the central bank bought these dollars at the official rate, maintained far below the one quoted in the black markets outside Free China, in a sense these United States sales represented a special financial subsidy accorded Free China. Remittances to diplomatic and administrative personnel and to missionaries, and transfers for family support, were granted a rate slightly more favorable than the official quotation.

Throughout this period, despite the apparent discrimination in the new Chinese banking law and the regulations governing the operation of the branches of foreign banks, the former branch staffs continued to look ardently forward to the end of the hostilities when they hoped that the United States banks would be encouraged to come back and to resume their former excellent relationships with the local business communities.

On September 2, 1945, V–J Day, the Japanese signed their surrender aboard the battleship *Missouri*. At last the score of United States bank officials still interned in China recovered their freedom. But no one at that moment, even among the best informed, could foresee the sinister forces already at work within this ancient people, which within the space of a few years were to snatch from its hands the fruits of its long and valiant struggle. In fact, in retrospect, the difficulties experienced during the war were small compared with the trials to which those Americans in charge of the branches in China were exposed after the Communist armies came into control of Tientsin and Shanghai, bringing the operations of the United States banks to a standstill and obstructing the repatriation of certain members of the foreign staffs.

On December 16, 1950, the United States Government froze Chinese Communist assets in United States territory the Federal Reserve Bank of New York being designated as fiscal agent for the Foreign Assets Control Division of the Treasury. In turn, on December 28 the Peiping regime issued an order blocking all United States public and private deposits within the territory of the People's Republic and placing an embargo on the transfer or disposal of United States property. The regulations of the United States Treasury Department prohibiting payments and transactions in which nationals of Communist China had a direct or indirect interest resulted in so substantial a reduction of business in the Crown Colony of Hong Kong that the Chase Bank, overseas affiliate of the Chase National Bank of New York, decided to liquidate the affairs of its Hong Kong branch.

SUMMARY. China was an early field for United States banking initiative, with the Chinese and Hong Kong branches marked by striking organizational features and local usages. The United States silver policy drove China ultimately off the metallic standard and forced her, after a vain attempt to protect her silver stocks, to adopt a managed paper currency and create several stabilization funds. The occupation by the Japanese of Tientsin, and later of Shanghai and Hong Kong, had disastrous effects on the banks' business. After Pearl Harbor all United States citizens were gradually interned, the branch administrations at the home offices experiencing harassing problems both during the struggle and after reopening of the branches following liberation. However, after the occupation of Tientsin and Shanghai by the Communist forces, the members of the American staffs who had returned to their posts encountered difficulties of quite another and much more tragic order being ultimately forced to wind up the affairs of their banks while the less fortunate ones were being detained as hostages pending the settlement of arbitrary claims against their institutions.

JAPAN

Until 1941 the Japanese commercial banks and leading business concerns were rather constant borrowers and credit seekers in the United States and England. Most of the banking facilities extended to them were on a secured basis. Partly in order to be able to manipulate the movements of their currency and to maintain it at a level advantageous for their growing export trade, the leading Japanese financial institutions carried important reserves in London and New York in the form of acceptable first-class collateral (British or United Government bonds, rubber, tin, silk, cotton, and other commodities) against which when necessary they could promptly secure cash advances in dollars or sterling, adequately margined and repayable on demand. Only in rare instances did the Japanese banks apply for loans against Japanese external or City of Yokohama bonds; in such cases the margin offered sometimes exceeded 100 percent of the market value on the New York or London stock exchanges.

Because of the nature of the easily marketable commodities held as guaranty for their outstanding loans and acceptances, the United States banks did not display any anxiety when the Japanese invaded Mongolia in the spring of 1936, however severely they criticized and deplored this arbitrary invasion of a friendly nation. A few weeks later, when Count Kodama, then president of the Yokohama Specie Bank, visited America, he expressed warm appreciation of the confidence shown by his bank's correspondents in the United States. He complained that this friendly attitude contrasted with the action taken by certain banks in Europe, which for the first time in the history of his institution had either reduced their credit lines or declined temporarily to increase existing facilities.

In order to add to their balances in the United States, the Japanese banks from time to time shipped gold to San Francisco, and on occasion contracted overdrafts secured by bullion in transit. This practice was especially noticed about the time the Japanese forces attacked Shanghai, in August, 1937, the gold shipments being insured by the Tokyo Marine and Fire Insurance Company, which reinsured as much as 90 percent with London underwriters. Later, when the situation in the Far East became more tense, some banks objected to the shipments being made on Japanese boats and insisted on American or British steamers carrying the bullion, and United

States or British insurance policies being furnished by the shippers. At that period the United States banks were particularly concerned over the risk, which could not be underwritten, of Japanese vessels being ordered to return to their home ports because of some sudden aggravation in the external situation. Altogether, between 1937 and 1939 Japan was reported to have shipped 580 million dollars' worth of gold to this country to pay for her purchases of equipment and raw materials.

Although the Chinese war was belittled by Japanese military leaders, who described it as a mere "incident," the potential repercussions of a prolonged conflict on Japan's balance of trade and ultimately on her government finances began to cause concern in the Western financial world. It was asked whether the probable reduction of exports and the increased demand for war supplies would not within a short time deplete considerably the empire's gold reserves and whether the government would not be forced sooner or later to have recourse to inflation. True, the yen had thus far been pegged, and so long as the Bank of Japan was able to cover any deficit in foreign-exchange by gold exports there was no immediate cause for apprehension. Still, the various foreign departments began to scrutinize with greater care the exercising of the trust receipt privilege by the trading outfits established in the United States. On these great financial and industrial trading combines—Mitsui, Sumitomo, Mitsubishi, that is, the *Zaibatsu*—the United States banks were confident that under no condition would the Japanese Government allow a shadow to fall so long as it could help it. In Japanese eyes these firms, like Caesar's wife, had to be above suspicion, the Japanese authorities realizing that any doubt as to their standing would destroy the national credit all over the globe. Even during the First World War Japanese firms had punctually honored their obligations; hence, no one doubted that as in the past the Japanese Minister of Finance would exert every effort to transfer to the United States the exchange needed by his countrymen to take care of their current banking and commercial liabilities. The "Land of the Rising Sun" could not afford to lose face.

Nevertheless, during the remainder of 1937 the situation continued strained, and some requests for loans against Japanese external bonds had to be declined. As if it suspected that some reservations existed in the minds of United States bankers the high financial command in Tokyo forwarded fresh cargoes of gold without asking for the usual temporary mail credits while the steamers were en route to the West Coast.

For some years the Japanese Treasury was ably represented in New York and Washington by T. Nijiyama. He was alert, well informed, and like most of his compatriots who were delegated to act as their nation's agents on this continent, affable in manner and conscious of the importance of cultivating friendly relations with local merchants and bank officials. He was a student of finance and was unusually versed in monetary and banking matters.

In the early months of 1938 some American cotton houses, at the suggestion of their agents in Japan, approached certain New York banks as to the possibility of arranging substantial loans to Japanese mills for the financing of their purchases of American raw cotton under the guarantee of the Japanese Government. Repayment was to be made in six months. However, in line with the existing attitude of the United States Government, word was sent to the intermediaries that for the time being the proposal could not be entertained. Nevertheless, some Southern firms continued to send consignments to their regular customers in Japan, the invoices being payable "cash on arrival."

By May, 1938, Far Eastern feeling regarding the Japanese financial situation was expressed by the considerable discount at which Japanese paper money could be bought in occupied China in the face of the firm official support of the yen exchange by the Tokyo Government. In September it was reported from Shanghai that the Bank of Japan had been granted authority over the whole foreign-exchange surplus of the Yokohama Specie Bank and the other foreign-exchange banks. For this reason, no doubt, the more enterprising cotton houses in Dallas and Houston felt confident that their buyers would obtain the necessary dollars when required by them. The margins of profit were extraordinarily attractive, and the American sellers felt therefore safe in pledging their own credit to the United States banks that agreed to finance these shipments during transit. It must be added that during the period under review the experience with these sales seems to have been entirely satisfactory.

In October of that year a New York banker investigating conditions on the spot vouchsafed the opinion that the Japanese economy was not likely to break down at any rate during 1939. Bullion on hand and newly mined gold were sufficient for the liquidation of all foreign liabilities, while domestically the paper currency was being accepted unquestionably even without the backing of a metallic reserve. Yet, by now imports were restricted to absolute necessities. Japan had succeeded in monopolizing 40 percent of all Chinese trade and in North China the proportion was nearer 70 to 80 percent, the Japanese military having put an embargo on the export from the occupied areas of cotton, wool, sheepskins, and iron, which were all diverted to Japan. The army also apparently hoped to seize control of raw materials in other parts of China in some form or another, and thus assume the exclusive control of the substantial foreign-exchange realized from the sale of Chinese tung oil, tungsten, bristles, furs, and egg yolks.

Another banking official visiting Japan in the early months of 1940 gained a different impression. To him Japan appeared a depressed nation. Then the country was short of all essentials, and restrictions were in effect on gasoline, coal, and power consumption. Even a foreigner with the desired hard currency found it almost impossible to buy many necessities. In the opinion of local American residents, Japan's condition was dangerous, but externally she should be able to meet her obligations for another year or two. By now, the foreign banks which were, as shown earlier, striving to hold their own in North China as well as in Japan, were no longer able to compete with the Yokohama Specie Bank, which had a practical monopoly of exchange and especially of bills created from exports. More and more rigid restrictions took business away from the branches of United States and British institutions. Earnestly and methodically, the Japanese authorities did their best to eliminate all trading by foreign corporations. About eighteen months before Pearl Harbor the traveler mentioned above learned that the Japanese officers, politicians, and newspapers talked more or less openly about the golden opportunities beckoning the nation in the South Seas, the Dutch East Indies, French Indo-China, the Malayan Islands, and even Australia.

When, on September 27, 1940, Japan joined Germany in a ten-year military pact, the impact on the banking relations between United States and Japanese financial establishments was immediate. The latter were notified that thereafter no credits would be extended except those guaranteed by cash or United States Government bonds. The American offices in the Far East received similar instructions, followed by the recommendation that they start lightening their pending future-exchange contracts in order to be prepared in the event of untoward political developments. It was hoped that these moves would prove conclusively to influential Japanese business and financial leaders that it would be highly detrimental to their enterprises to antagonize the last great neutral power and to incur the enmity of the country where for so many years their various undertakings had enjoyed generous hospitality and liberal treatment at the hand of the banking and business community.

The last line of the story of the prewar Japanese-American financial relations was written in February, 1942, when, at the request of Elliott V. Bell, Superintendent of Banks of the State of New York, the net deposits in New York banks belonging to enemy concerns were paid over to various trust companies designated by him. Before making these payments, the commercial banks that held collateral against loans, sold it under the general Treasury license, which permitted the purchase and sale of securities for account of blocked nationals. To the required degree the proceeds were used for the payment of such debit balances of the Japanese banks and business houses as remained. The epitaph to the history of Japanese commercial expansion on this continent was contained in a New York *Times* dispatch by its Tokyo correspondent Burton Crane, dated July 7, 1947. Under the headline MITSUI AND MITSUBISHI FULLY LIQUIDATED it read in part: "Japan's two largest trading companies—at one time perhaps the world's largest—have been ordered dissolved . . ."

In line with the official United States policy toward Japan since the armistice, however, United States banks have reopened or have opened their branches in the chief Japanese trading centers, where they not only are serving the occupation forces but also are making an important contribution to Japanese recovery.

SUMMARY. In the decade prior to 1940 the branches of Japanese banks and business enterprises established on the West and East coasts of the United States significantly expanded their varied trading activities. As conditions in Japan grew more acute during the crucial period preceding Japan's attack on Pearl Harbor, the United States offices in the Far East took timely precautions against possible emergencies. The liquidation of Japanese concerns in the United States after December 7, 1941, ended Japanese-American commercial and financial contacts. In line with the official United States policy toward Japan since the armistice, however, United States banks have again established offices in the principal Japanese business centers.

INDIA

Until England went off gold in 1931, except during the First World War and some years thereafter, India was on the gold standard. From 1899 on, the rupee was legal tender, being anchored to the pound sterling at the ratio of 15 rupees to one gold sovereign. To create the London exchange required in substantial amounts for the payment of interest on its British debt the Dominion sold British and foreign importers of grain, jute, and other products, India Council Bills payable on demand, or T.T.'s (telegraphic transfers), the rupee equivalent of which could be collected in Bombay, Karachi, Calcutta, and other commercial centers. Most of the circulating media consisted of silver rupees. In 1926, after a detailed investigation of monetary conditions in the country, the Royal Indian Commission recommended that it reduce its silver reserves and substitute gold in their place. Accordingly, India's periodical sales of her holdings of the white metal became a regular feature in the world's silver markets. In order to offset the effects of this large hoard that overhung international silver transactions, the delegates assembled at the World Economic Conference in London, in 1933, passed a resolution calling on the Indian Government to reduce its sales of silver during the next four years to 35 million ounces per year. The Indian representatives acquiesced the more readily as the large purchases of the United States Treasury guaranteed India a broad outlet for the remaining holdings at most acceptable prices.[3]

Because of the country's importance as a buyer and seller of bullion it offered attractive opportunities for profitable operations to Western traders in foreign-exchange. As early as 1927 one leading New York trust company started an active arbitrage business in silver between New York, Bombay, and London, with quite encouraging results. A representative office was opened in Bombay for the purpose of cultivating relations with the local banks and leading business houses, for United States importers were important buyers of many Indian products, such as burlap, jute, goat skins, tea, carpet wool, and

[3] The effect on India of the silver policy of the United States in the early thirties is discussed in Chapter V.

so forth, while our exporters supplied automobiles, electrical equipment, leaf tobacco, raw cotton, and pharmaceutical preparations. Another United States bank established fully equipped branches in Calcutta and Bombay. However, early in 1941, exchange and bullion trading with the United States had to be broken off because of the official restrictions required by the war.

Owing to India's former close ties with Great Britain, English banking has always occupied a predominant position in the Dominion. The share capital of many Indian banks was owned by British citizens, and their head offices were located in the City of London. Besides the United States banks, the Comptoir National d'Escompte de Paris maintained an old and prosperous branch in Bombay, and with a Portuguese bank, two Dutch institutions, and three Japanese offices, formed the foreign banking contingent. None of them, however, succeeded in making a real dent in the preponderance of the large English institutions, whose close ties with India antedated by many decades the arrival of the foreign banks. Nevertheless, the country was an interesting field for United States banks. The wealthy Indian princes—the maharajas—and the rich native merchants had important deposits in New York as well as in London, and they, together with prominent Indian bankers and industrialists visiting the United States, strongly urged the promotion of more active financial contacts between the two countries.

In 1937, through enterprising local brokerage firms as intermediaries, Indian capitalists and speculators began to operate on a large scale on the stock exchanges of New York and Montreal. Loans to finance their operations were contracted with foreign banks in Bombay, as well as with New York financial institutions.

With the outbreak of the Second World War American business efforts in India were suspended temporarily, because of the lack of dollars on the part of the buyers, interferences with shipping, and the urgency of concentrating on war production. Indian businessmen deplored the action of United States interests in what they considered too precipitately withdrawing from the country, and did not conceal their disappointment, having expected a greater show of faith in the future of India. This feeling, however, was not universal by any means. As early as 1943 a well-known Indian industrialist and economic expert expressed the conviction that after the conclusion of peace tempting opportunities for United States trade would be offered to those willing to evidence their confidence in Indian ability to prosper under a free and independent national administration.

The war had a notable effect on India. As to other parts of the globe, it brought her a great wave of commercial and industrial activity, stimulated by a constant flow of orders from the United Kingdom and the United States. From them resulted a greater measure of economic stability. Owing to the generous supply of Allied war orders, by August 1, 1944, India had practically no foreign indebtedness, but instead had a credit balance in London of about 1 billion pounds. For the first time in her history, India had become a creditor country.

For the local banks, both native and foreign, the financing of the increased production of goods for war purposes meant rising earnings. Because of the stringency of imports from abroad, a large expansion of deposits took place. Owing to the steadily growing issue of bank notes that was rendered necessary by the accumulation of blocked sterling, a great abundance of idle money followed which looked in vain for employment. During the resulting inflation new native banks were formed that were not always well sponsored. For this reason the Reserve Bank of India, the central bank which stands at the summit of the national banking organization, secured the enactment of legislation prohibiting the issue of any but fully paid-up bank stock in the future.

During the war Indian large-scale industrialization, which for many years had been fostered under the leadership of the far-seeing heads of Tata Sons & Co., Ltd., spread to the cities of Karachi and Calcutta. The Tata firm had long been a national institution. It controlled the largest steel works, the Tata Iron & Steel Co., Ltd. From an early date its directors' sympathies were with the Indian national cause. The steel company had its own office in New York to look after the combine's purchases in the United States of machinery, metals, and supplies and to act as agent for the numerous affiliates.

At the Bretton Woods Conference, in July, 1944, A. D. Shroff, the wise and learned director of finances of the Tata group, who was one of the Indian delegates, pleaded in vain for assistance from the proposed Monetary Fund in connection with the unfreezing of some of India's blocked sterling balances so that dollar funds could be made available for his country's purchases in the United States.

Along similar lines, Sir Chanmukham Chetty, head of the Indian

Purchasing Mission in the United States, and Hardit Singh Malik, Indian Trade Commissioner, earnestly voiced the opinion that India would welcome the co-operation of United States finance and the tender of assistance by United States banks at the end of the war when their country was sure to enter upon a new and auspicious phase of its history. Malik, a somewhat corpulent man, of stately appearance and carriage, attracted much attention whenever he visited the New York financial district, as he made it a point always to wear his national garb, with a picturesque turban that covered his tanned and heavily bearded face. A flier during the First World War, he had distinguished himself by many daring exploits, for which the Allied governments had conferred their highest decorations upon him. He was a crack shot and an expert golfer, all of which, in addition to his wide knowledge of his country's financial and economic resources, made him a welcome guest in United States banking and social circles.

The present desire of the political, industrial, and financial leaders of the young republic for more active and closer commercial and financial co-operation with the United States promises to be realized with the interested and tangible support of the International Bank for Reconstruction and Development. Private investment, too, has been encouraged by the more friendly attitude in official circles promising American capital the same favorable treatment as that granted local investors.

AUSTRALIA AND NEW ZEALAND

Prior to the Second World War the relations of the Australian and New Zealand commercial banks with the United States were active and close. Important dollar balances were carried with New York and out-of-town banks. Commercial letters of credit covering the export of United States goods to Australasia were issued payable as a rule in sterling. In these cases sight drafts for the amounts of the invoices were drawn by the American beneficiaries on the London correspondents or branches of the Australian and New Zealand banks. The latter designated one or two United States institutions where the sterling drafts, accompanied by the prescribed shipping documents and the letter of credit, could be negotiated "at the bank's buying rate for sight drafts on London"—an adaptation of the "colonial clause" appearing on English bills payable in Australia. The amount of the drafts was endorsed on the back of the letter of credit unless it was exhausted, in which case the bank negotiating the last draft drawn under it was authorized to retain it. In those exceptional cases where letters of credit were made payable in dollars, drafts created under their authority were charged to the dollar accounts of the Australian banks.

In Australia, in the summer of 1941, the growing needs for dollar credits in connection with purchases of tinplate and other materials needed for national defense suggested the advantage of pooling all dollar credit facilities available to the nine leading Australian banks in the hands of the bank of issue, the Commonwealth Bank of Australia, as a clearing house through which all applications for dollar credits would thereafter be distributed. Later, it was decided that it would be advisable for Australian financial needs to be incorporated into and at least in part covered by the lend-lease arrangements, and the plan to centralize the credit lines with the Commonwealth Bank accordingly did not go into effect. Evidently the British Treasury had in mind the high premium to which Australian exchange had risen during and after the First World War.

After America had joined the Allies the Australian and New Zealand banks vied in their service to the United States forces, army, navy, and air, and the United States diplomatic personnel and Government officials stationed in encampments, at naval bases, and in the capitals of the two dominions. From such information as came to the United States, it appeared that like the British banks, whose policies during the war were largely under the control of the British Treasury and the Bank of England, the Australian commercial institutions were broadly guided during this period by the wishes of the Commonwealth Government acting through the Commonwealth Bank, which exercised the functions of a central bank. Australian resources were mobilized through that bank's offices, and it was responsible for meeting the heavy payments due in the United Kingdom and the United States.

From the aspect of orthodox banking practice this departure was not welcomed by certain Australian commercial banks, although they admitted that in order to win the war they had to sacrifice some of their individual independence. As regards their dollar liabilities, the Australian banks were dependent, for the duration of the war, upon allotments by the British Exchange Control, which monopolized all the dollar and hard currency resources and revenues of the sterling bloc. The intervention and support of the mother country offered a salutary warranty to those foreign banks which viewed with some concern the appearance at that time of a pronouncedly socialistic bent in some parts of the dominions and which, in the absence of this guaranty, would have found it incumbent to subject any outstanding credits to a more stringent analysis.

While, as a result of the Second World War and the recent rise in wool prices, both Australia and New Zealand once more enjoy a high degree of prosperity, they suffer nevertheless from an acute dollar shortage. There has been talk of a possible upward revaluation of the Australian pound in order to bring about a reduction in the cost of imported merchandise and a lowering of the cost of living which has materially risen during the war-induced price inflation.

SUMMARY. The common vested interest in silver, which for generations was the chief circulating medium and the favorite object of private hoarding in India, early directed the attention of United States banks to that country. Although the United Kingdom occupied a preponderant position in Indian banking, United States representation in the principal business centers nevertheless was welcomed.

The relationships of Australian and New Zealand financial institutions with the United Kingdom inevitably have always been closer than their connections with United States banks, which were of more recent date. During the Second World War much fine service was performed by all the banks for the Americans stationed on the Australian continent. Because of the war and the demand for their staple products, especially wool, both dominions are enjoying a high degree of prosperity.

PART FOUR

ORGANIZATION OF THE FOREIGN ACTIVITIES OF UNITED STATES BANKS

XIV
THE FOREIGN BANKING WORKSHOP

GENERAL

FROM THE PREVIOUS CHAPTERS the reader will have obtained a bird's-eye view of some of the contributions made by United States foreign banking in the past two score years to the opening of new outlets abroad for American enterprise, and in general to the expansion of the country's international trade and influence in distant parts of the world. Against this background we shall now inquire more closely into the functions and organization of the foreign departments of United States banks.

The foreign departments are the channels through which the settlement of most overseas transactions usually takes place. If it is true that a nation's balance of payments mirrors its total financial activities with the rest of the globe, the volume of operations passing over the ledgers of the foreign departments of the country's banks should be in some measure a reflection of the nation's total foreign turnover. For this reason it may be said of them even more, perhaps, than of the British Empire that the sun never sets on their spheres of activity.

Necessarily, the overseas connections of United States financial institutions engaged in the foreign field today span the surface of the globe. In the present age the five continents are so closely knit together that a development in a distant corner of the earth may have profound repercussions within the walls of our great banks. It is essential, therefore, that the foreign departments be immediately and accurately informed of every important event that may have a bearing on their variegated dealings in remote lands. Through branch offices and correspondents in all centers of production, shipping, and finance, by means of thousands of cable messages and telephone conversations, significant tidings that might affect their or their customers' affairs are promptly relayed across the oceans. Charged with the responsibility of watching over the foreign loans of the banks, the officials of these departments often encounter the unexpected and at times considerable excitement. Especially is this so when their labors have to be carried on amid economic crises, financial panics, or wars.

The most challenging aspect of foreign banking is that it not only involves currencies, money, and credit but also calls for a constant study of the changing world situation in commerce, politics, geography, and national ideologies and ethics. In one way or another it is affected by all these factors. Those persons who have witnessed the reckoning that came after the First World War, with its collapse of prices and epidemic of bankruptcies, do not need a warning that conditions governing business in remote continents are never long static and unchanging. Indeed, constant flux, movement, and mutation are integral parts of international banking. Consequently, the time is rare indeed when foreign departments are not influenced directly or indirectly by some unexpected event at home or abroad. Both economic and political currents are likely to have baffling effects on the department's outstanding loans and credits. Even under normal conditions overseas banking is full of pitfalls. Customs, laws, and usages observed in the United States may be banned elsewhere. To deal with such questions foreign departments must be continuously in touch with trustworthy sources of information abroad in order that an up-to-date record of internal rules and regulations in different foreign countries may always be available to the staff and the banks' clients. More than ever before United States merchants are interested in receiving the latest advices on trade practices and trends in foreign markets. Not only is full knowledge of economic conditions in other countries of vital importance to businessmen but the latter require also complete and current information respecting the credit standing of individual foreign firms and corporations. It is for this reason, among many others, that the network of foreign offices maintained by leading banks in the United States and radiating through her insular possessions, Europe, Latin America, and the Far East is of such great value to the local foreign trade community. These offices, moreover, are equipped to bring to exporters and importers various other useful data, such as the best shipping routes, methods of packing preferred by foreign buyers, tariff schedules, warehouse facilities, and so forth. At these branch offices, too, business references can be established in order that overseas merchants may be able to inform themselves easily on the financial standing of American firms desirous of making purchasing or selling arrangements with them.

For these reasons well-organized foreign departments are resorted to by customers when initiating or implementing foreign business. Either of their own free will or upon the banks' invitation they will review with the departmental officers their buying and selling programs on which the international situation may have an important bearing. Conversely, foreign industrialists and merchants—directly or through their local banks—will consult United States banks as to the prospects for the sale of their products in the Western Hemisphere. Some of these inquiries are inspired by the periodical reviews edited by the statistical and research divisions of the leading metropolitan banks. Indeed, the scholarly information on business and financial conditions in the United States imparted by these publications has proved an excellent investment in both international and domestic good will. Of special interest to local, as well as to foreign, commercial houses, the foreign departments of some American banks from time to time prepare and distribute tabulations of the import and exchange rates and regulations of the principal countries of the world. These circulars contain answers to current questions on such matters as the need for import permits, the sources from which foreign exchange must be obtained, the local selling terms for dollars, the extent of exchange restrictions, export quotas, and so forth. Other institutions furnish to their customers summaries of the great mass of reports and statistical data that reach them with each transatlantic mail, on financial and trade conditions in many foreign countries.

The prodigious development of United States foreign commerce during the last quarter-century may be ascribed in no small degree to the co-operation between foreign traders and the foreign departments of United States banks. While it is true that this country is less dependent on overseas sources of supply than are many other nations, nevertheless there is no denying that with less extensive international trade the United States would enjoy a less high standard of living. Without the foreign markets which have been created and fostered with the intensive collaboration of United States finance to absorb our large surpluses of agricultural, mineral, and manufactured products, our domestic prosperity would be far less the envy of the world.

The foreign banking profession of the United States, as mentioned in Chapter I, was born soon after the beginning of the present century. The work now confided to hundreds of employees had its inception in the first demands for money to be sent abroad to the families in "the old country." A single teller behind the vertical bars of his window then handled all the "foreign" business for which there was a call. This was still true even later, when it expanded into the sale of travelers' checks and foreign money orders. Then, gradually, a few private banking houses established direct connections in London, Paris, Amsterdam, and other cities, in order to be in a position to offer to privileged customers, mainly in the grain and cotton trade, facilities for the use of 90-day acceptance credits granted by their correspondents abroad. At this time, in the early part of the nineteenth century, probably 90 percent of the world's trade, it was estimated, was being financed by means of sterling credits opened by English merchant banking firms.[1] The captains of almost all Russian freighters carried letters of credit payable at the London office of Baring Brothers. The United States was still a debtor nation, and her own foreign investments were negligible. It was undoubtedly for this reason that in those days a well-known banker-author—writing before 1914—called the United States "a dependency of the sterling bill."

Elsewhere in this volume the conditions have been described under which, after the First World War, the dollar bill gradually assumed its due place in international finance, and how in the course of time, with the efficient help of the discount market, a growing share of the foreign commerce of this country and many others in Latin America, Europe, and the Orient was paid for by means of United States bank acceptances. An amendment to the Federal Reserve Act—Section 25(a)—authorized by Congress on December 24, 1919, permitted the organization of special banking corporations for the purpose of financing foreign trade, bearing the name of the author of the act, Senator Walter Edge. Commercial banking in the United States now became aware that it had a constructive opportunity to promote United States foreign business expansion. The present generation has witnessed the gradual invasion of the foreign field by many large and small banks throughout the country.

1 According to H. K. Brooks, *Foreign Exchange Text Book,* first published by him in 1906.

As the years rolled by, some of the foreign departments grew from modest beginnings to be important units of the main banks. Conscious of the need of being prepared for an unprecedented evolution of United States international activities, the overseas sections made it a point to adjust themselves continually to the growing demand for their services. Through an intelligent process of adaptation, the extension of the facilities offered kept pace with the broadening and expansion of the operations of our exporters and importers. The larger industrial corporations and commercial concerns were able to have their own foreign offices or agencies, but the middle-sized firms and companies, without direct representation abroad, would, perhaps, have hesitated to venture into the new and still strange field without the practical encouragement and assistance tendered by their banks. Today, of course, the average merchant rarely requires outside advice as to the best ways of promoting the sale of his wares in Latin America, Europe, and elsewhere; in matters connected with his particular line of business he now can safely rely on his own knowledge and ingenuity.

Nevertheless, experience has proved that it is wise for foreign department officials, especially where the credit relationships are extensive, to study the particular problems and understand the specific nature of their clients' affairs. By evidencing their interest in their customers' progress and by spontaneously communicating facts and news pertinent to their business, the officers render the relationship more intimate, and customers will feel at liberty to take the bank into their confidence with regard to any difficult problems with which they may be faced. Especially at times of financial or economic depression or individual reverses there is no better way to cement the connection and earn the lasting good will of the customer than by exercising patience and extending a helping hand until the storm has passed.

It may accordingly be concluded that in the long run the progress of a foreign department depends to an important extent on the esteem and reputation it enjoys in the ranks of the foreign trade fraternity. Its services nowadays are rendered under conditions that have become extremely competitive. However, in practice it has been demonstrated that even more than by the rates that the department applies and the commissions it charges, its facilities are appraised on the basis of the efficiency and versatility of its officers and staff. In fact, the prestige of the entire institution is often heightened by the favorable estimation in which its foreign organization is held both locally and abroad.

In a considerable measure the growth and expansion of any foreign department depends on the character of the commercial clientele of the main bank and the size of its foreign trade interest. During its early years especially, its head will lean a great deal upon the sympathetic aid of the domestic divisions of the parent institution. The officers in charge of the latter's territorial sections can contribute much to its growth by calling the attention of clients and the public at large to the facilities of the foreign department and its excellent connections in the important centers of the globe. The manager of a newly created foreign department will owe much to the friendly support extended to him not only by the senior executives and directors of the bank but also by the bank's other departments, the trust officers, and the men in charge of the local branch offices. Foreign department staffs, perhaps deservedly, have the reputation of being hard-driving teams, and because they sometimes occupy a special niche in the general organization, the other divisions of the bank occasionally regard them as pampered by the top management and their members as too aspiring. Nevertheless, it can be said without exaggeration that over the years foreign departments have proved to be valuable business promoters for the other sections and domestic branches of the institution as well.

What services is a foreign department equipped to offer? The present-day department is the outgrowth of several decades of development. It may well be called a bank within a bank. In the foreign departments of the larger metropolitan banks more than two scores of integrated divisions are necessary to handle the routine work. To name only the most important: there are the loan and discount, commercial letter of credit, collection, foreign exchange trading, new business, personnel, auditing, statistical, and central liability divisions not to mention the Foreign Credit Department as well as the Foreign Branch Division, which in turn is subdivided into numerous territories. Transactions in these various divisions will generally run into hundreds of millions of dollars each day.

The operations of the various sections may be broken down into four main categories: (1) the handling of routine foreign banking transactions for American customers, including interior banks; (2)

loans and credits to United States merchants engaged in foreign commerce, including acceptance credits for the financing of imports and exports, goods in warehouse, and in transit within the United States; (3) banking services to foreign banks, firms, and individuals, including acceptance credits; (4) the buying and selling of foreign exchange for domestic and foreign account, exchange arbitrage, and gold and silver shipments.

To comment on the routine services such as the collection of foreign drafts, dividends, and coupons payable abroad, the purchase and sale of foreign currency, travel checks, and drafts on foreign banks, the purchase and sale of foreign securities, and so forth, would go beyond the scope of this chapter. We will rather address ourselves therefore to what constitutes the principal source of revenues for a foreign department—the opening of acceptance credits and the granting of short-term loans.

Under what circumstances are these facilities extended in foreign transactions? The answer is a matter both of facts and of judgment. As in domestic business, the extension of credit to a firm or corporation for use in mercantile operations overseas is governed not only by its assets or liabilities, important though these items are when weighing the financial responsibility of a debtor. The department also considers the borrower's character, the past record of the trade in which he is engaged, the value of his unpledged property, his profit and loss account over a period of years, and his reputation as to professional ability. In other words, in foreign as well as in domestic commerce, implicit faith cannot be placed solely in the security offered by the underlying merchandise, since changes are likely to take place in the market demand for the products to be shipped to or from overseas unless they have been sold in advance to responsible buyers or hedged in the future exchanges. The determining factor is, therefore, how the prospective debtor will meet his obligations to the bank should his purchasers, at home or abroad, be unable or unwilling to take delivery and make payment as stipulated. In such an eventuality, is his working capital adequate to provide cover for his maturing liability to the department? Moreover, in the event of an adverse turn in economic conditions will the customer be strong enough financially to survive possible heavy reverses?

It is the duty of the officers in charge to reduce the bank's risks to a minimum. Because of their specialized knowledge the foreign department staffs have on occasion found it wise to dissuade merchants from entering upon hazardous undertakings that might jeopardize their financial position and former excellent business record. From the lessons learned in other cases the officers are often in a position to point to contingent and unpredictable factors, such as detrimental currency conditions and impending political changes, that cannot be safeguarded or insured against. While the staffs cannot claim to be omniscient, when furnishing advice and expressing their views they must always be guided by what they believe to be the best interests of the client.

Within the sphere of foreign department activities the opening of acceptance credits plays an important role. Most of these credits finance the purchase and shipment of goods imported or exported by merchants of the United States. Banks abroad also utilize acceptance facilities by opening letters of credit available either at the head office in the United States or at the foreign branches (mainly in London and Paris), to pay for merchandise bought by foreign business concerns from manufacturers or distributors in the United States, South America, and other parts of the world. By granting the credit the accepting bank places its own warranty behind that of the buyer's assurance that he will pay for the goods shipped in accordance with the contract of sale. Thus, an acceptance by a responsible United States bank or an irrevocable letter of credit issued by it is in fact equivalent to a guarantee or insurance policy issued by a well-regarded underwriter in favor of the seller of the goods. Provided the merchandise is delivered at the time and place agreed upon and if the invoice is drawn up in conformity with the terms of the contract and is accompanied by the documents prescribed in the letter of credit, the bank covenants either to pay cash (if a sight credit) or to accept a 60- or 90-day draft issued by the seller, which can be easily converted into cash in the discount market. Nowadays elaborate printed agreements outline the detailed provisions under which sight and acceptance credits are extended by the foreign departments, which the customer by his signature agrees to be binding upon him.

Since the First World War the American bank acceptance—the dollar bill of exchange—has become one of the mainstays of the machinery by which overseas operations are financed in the foreign departments. In the early days the banks confined themselves to self-liquidating credits, so called because the proceeds of the merchandise covered by the credit was expected to be sufficient to discharge the debt of the customer. Later this underlying consideration began to be disregarded, especially when the customer possessed large cash reserves with which to pay the amount due at maturity irrespective of the arrival, or acceptance by the purchaser, of the merchandise that the acceptance was created to finance. While on the whole the experience with acceptances has been satisfactory, it must be admitted that during the twenties and thirties some of the credits of this type, both domestic and foreign, were the cause of grave concern and disappointment to those responsible for the foreign banking activities of United States institutions. Under those fortunately abnormal conditions renewals and extensions had to be granted to the debtors, partial payments had to be accepted in full settlement, and compromise arrangements such as the standstill agreements described in detail in Chapter X had to be entered into with Central European debtors. During those trying years foreign bankers both in the United States and in the creditor countries of Europe had occasion to recall unhappily that what originally had made acceptances such welcome instruments of short-term finance was the fact that they were irrevocably due at fixed dates and that lacking payment by the debtors the proceeds of the merchandise could serve to reimburse the accepting bank for the amount due it. For having too generously assumed the financial burdens of Europe after the First World War, the banks of the United States, England, Switzerland, Holland, France, and other countries were obliged, during the course of almost a decade, to commute and partly write off their overdue credits to defaulting Central European debtors.

The same general rules that are observed with respect to acceptance credits largely govern the policies of foreign departments with regard to unsecured or "straight" short-time cash loans and overdrafts. David Harum's definition of banking as "lending your money and getting it back" may be applied with even greater emphasis to foreign lending. After the fall of the German Republic and the seizure of power by Hitler in 1933, the general external situation and the threat of war, even more than the financial responsibility of the foreign borrower, had to be taken into account to an ever growing degree. Foreign bankers, during the era when totalitarianism came into the saddle in Central and Eastern Europe, were reminded of the warning uttered by the late Dwight Morrow (*Foreign Affairs,* January,

1927) to the effect that "if good faith can not be relied upon, it is better that the loan be not made."

To a greater extent than ever before it now became necessary to watch the size of the individual lines and the aggregate of all loans extended in each foreign country in order to avoid the dire consequences of a lack of co-ordinated lending by the different creditor countries and by the various banks within each country in the event of a general world conflagration. Events have proved that the United States foreign bankers of 1940 were wiser and more discerning in this respect than their predecessors a decade or two earlier.

Although absorbing a great deal of the attention of the foreign departments, the cash advances, secured by readily marketable staples such as grain, sugar, rubber, and tobacco, will not be treated here. However, the financing of raw cotton has in the past occupied such a significant place in the work of some foreign sections that it deserves at least a casual reference in this chapter. Loans on cotton in warehouse or in course of shipment to distributing points or to buyers in the United States and overseas have indeed been one of the most interesting and at the same time one of the most lucrative activities of some specialized foreign departments. These loans have been a useful outlet for the investment of liquid funds provided by foreign dollar deposits, while the security offered has been inviting if the cotton was sold to desirable buyers or hedged in the future markets and fully insured against all risks. The banks' relations with the cotton shippers were often instrumental in bringing about the establishment of valuable contacts with textile mills, whose acceptances formed an attractive short-term investment and whose open accounts and bills receivable, properly assigned, served as collateral for additional advances. During the active cotton season shippers were regularly sellers of foreign documentary bills at sight or 90 days' sight, drawn on banks in Liverpool, Manchester, and London in sterling, or payable in French francs, in guilders, marks, and so forth. On steamer sailing nights the bill collection divisions would have to work overtime to catch the transatlantic mails and avoid heavy losses of interest. Nonetheless this exchange was keenly sought after by the foreign exchange traders. Although the transactions involved a large volume of clerical work, they were profitable to the department, because foreign banks ardently competed for these remittances. In return for being favored with the bills the foreign banks were willing to reserve an equivalent share of their dollar collections and credits for those American institutions that entrusted them with the bulk of their documentary portfolio.

To give an idea of the scope of foreign department activities brief mention should be made at this point of the great variety of products financed by means of credits or transfer of funds. The statistics of the Department of Commerce reveal the range of the imports and exports, settlement for much of which is effected through the offices of the foreign departments. Thus United States industrial machinery is frequently paid for by letters of credit or money transfers ordered by foreign banks or purchasers. Grain and leaf tobacco are important commodities, for which settlement is made through the foreign departments in one form or another. Oil, both crude and refined, as well as iron and steel-mill products are prominently represented on the list of exports financed by foreign departments. The motion picture companies, too, have numerous occasions for the services of the banks with foreign organizations, and the conversion into United States dollars of their foreign revenues in a great variety of currencies calls at times for much intelligent intervention on the part of the departments. The chemical industry, with its markets all over the globe, is also a rewarding client of the foreign sections. On the other hand, although automobiles are a leading export article, for their financing the powerful motor industry, because of its own competently managed foreign divisions, no longer depends on the co-operation of United States banks to the extent it did in former years. A further measure of the range of export financing handled in the foreign departments can be found in the long list of metals and commodities, settlement for which is made in the letter of credit divisions; here, in the course of an average day, payments may be effected for such widely different shipments as copper, lumber, wood pulp, fertilizer, meat packing products, rosin, typewriters, and locomotives. On the other hand, in the import letter of credit division drafts with documents attached may be presented for payment covering hides and skins from South America, rubber from the Malayas, antimony mined in Mexico, cane sugar and chrome ore supplied by Cuba, nickel received from Canada, platinum from Colombia, furs from the USSR, silk from China and Japan, wool from Australia, and nitrate from Chile.

Because of their constant association with the import and export trade, foreign bankers follow closely the detailed reports of the Department of Commerce as to the trends of United States foreign traffic. Enough tribute cannot be paid to the large number of United States officials, consuls, commercial attachés, and trade commissioners who faithfully and continuously survey the foreign field in order to broaden the outlets for domestic goods. Their periodic reports on the ebb and flow of United States participation in world commerce are carefully studied and scrutinized. In addition, the manifests of the ships entering our ports are searchingly analyzed.

In order to develop foreign business and to make a bank a factor in overseas financing, the officers and men attached to the new business divisions have to be ever on the lookout for opportunities to expand existing contacts and to enlist the patronage of additional customers. They have to be alert at all times so that the managers may be apprised of any new channels through which the services of the bank may be profitably brought to the attention of prospects. Their main efforts are directed to houses of established standing that have adequate working capital at their disposal and have a record of successful operation. However, they follow with equal care the notices regarding new concerns whose backers promise to be interested prospects. From the very start of these new enterprises it is worth while to cultivate their officials diligently, so as to establish the bank in their good graces, should their affairs prosper. Among foreign departments there is eternal jockeying for such clients.

Friendly personal relations have always been a good foundation for the formation of valuable contacts on the foreign as on the domestic banking level. No occasion is missed to build up and assure the steady growth of the number of those who take advantage of the broad area in which the foreign department services can be utilized. Thus, the representatives of the New York foreign departments can be seen daily roaming through the shipping district in downtown Manhattan near the Whitehall building and the red edifice of the Produce Exchange, where steamship companies, grain merchants, and freight brokers have their headquarters; in the narrow streets bounded by Maiden Lane, Nassau Street, and lower Pine Street, where the insurance underwriters and brokers are located; near Gold Street in the "swamp," where leather and hide merchants ply their trade; and uptown between Fourth and Fifth avenues around 34th Street, where the silk trade is likely now and then to offer good leads to the inquisitive and aggressive ambassadors of the new business divisions. These present-day couriers must be vigilant and ready to explore every avenue that seems likely to meet better the needs of customers and prospects, lest their nimble-footed and ever bustling colleagues in competing banks offer to match or improve upon the terms quoted by their own institution.

It will be inferred from what has been said so far that at no time can even the largest and best-known foreign department rest on its oars. There must be a resolute and sustained effort to deserve the favor of the foreign trading community. In foreign banking, perhaps even more than in the domestic end of the business, good public relations depend greatly on the continual pursuit of policies that create confidence in the judgment of the officers and in their ability to serve the genuine interests of the patrons of the bank.

No less ardent than the striving for domestic accounts is the struggle for the good will of foreign banks, firms, and individuals, and for the highly coveted deposits of the banks of issue and their governments. The work of the officers concerned with this special field is indeed rewarding when, as a result of long solicitation, a desirable account is at last opened on the books of the bank; frustrating when, after years of patient nursing, a valued relationship is severed because of an unfortunate clerical mistake or simply the underbidding on the part of a determined rival. It follows that foreign departments must never feel snug. If they do not wish to lose out to some ambitious competitor they must at all times and under all circumstances furnish the highest quality of service both at home and overseas.

The common denominator in all foreign departments is the wish to attract large dollar deposits from foreign countries. In bygone years, when interest was allowed on demand deposits, an enterprising competitor could secure accounts merely by quoting a higher rate than that allowed by the regular United States banking correspondent. During the middle twenties, too, when the European agents of United States banks practically stumbled over each other in the attempt to bestow short-term credits on continental borrowers, both commissions and interest rates frequently were cut in order to secure some eagerly desired account. Instances were not lacking in which contacts of long standing were suddenly broken off because another bank offered an unusual and tempting concession in the form of a larger line of credit. On other occasions, formerly cordial relations were interrupted because of the reluctant refusal on the part of the United States correspondent bank to add to existing loaning facilities that it considered ample. In such a case, even though a competitor did not volunteer to grant the desired increase, the account would be transferred to him merely because the *amour-propre* of the foreign customer had been unavoidably hurt. The intense emulation among foreign departments, legitimate enough on the whole, was also responsible on occasion for the tendency to shower upon visiting foreign bankers the most profuse hospitality, although it should in fairness be mentioned that, when delegates of United States banks traveled overseas, they were also the object of often breathtaking attentions and generous treatment of one kind or another.

The magnitude of the problems with which foreign departments had to cope during the interwar period assumed almost overwhelming proportions after the outbreak of the Second World War. All belligerents and most neutral nations placed not only rigid restraints on exports and imports but also severe exchange restrictions on the movement of foreign funds. Because of the legal aspects of many of the questions that arose in connection with international transactions of all kinds, foreign departments were obliged to rely even more than ordinarily on the guidance of their legal counsel. During this period, too, the letter of credit business for foreign accounts dwindled as commercial banks abroad had less call to open such credits. In most instances, foreign balances remained stationary, for a substantial portion of these funds were frozen. To a larger degree than during peacetime, domestic financing at this time consisted, as explained in a previous chapter, of credits opened and transfers effected for account of the different United States Government agencies and foreign purchasing missions. The shrinkage of European and Far Eastern business was compensated in some measure by the rising activity in relations with Latin American banks and business houses. The situation called for superior skill in adapting policies and operations to the changed conditions. Indeed, few sections of the American banks were obliged so frequently to adjust their affairs to the sensationally revolving events of the past ten years as were the foreign departments.

SUMMARY. Most of the development of international banking in the United States took place during and after the First World War. A wide variety of services is ordinarily rendered by foreign departments at home and in outlying parts of the globe, especially acceptance credits, import and export letters of credit, and short-term advances against commodities. Definite principles govern the extension of credit and other forms of assistance to foreign traders. The practical tasks of the banks' new business divisions are of special importance. An acute series of problems was brought by the Second World War to the banks' foreign sections. As a general matter, these departments have made a very significant contribution to the growth and reputation of American financial institutions.

THE FOREIGN EXCHANGE DIVISION

It is in the foreign exchange division that the cash settlement of most foreign transactions takes place. Here dollars are bartered for the moneys of other countries. Trading in foreign exchange has a long history. The word "money" itself has been traced back to remote antiquity. Mythology attributes the origin of the word to a legend that about 270 B.C. the legions of Rome, hard-pressed in a battle with Pyrrhus, King of Epirus, prayed to the Goddess Juno, daughter of Saturn and consort of Jupiter, to come to their assistance. Through her intervention, so the story goes, the enemy was repulsed, and the grateful Romans gave to her the appellation *moneta*—the giver of good counsel. Later the first metallic coins were minted in the temple of Juno Moneta and from that time on were popularly called *moneta.*[2]

Many centuries were to pass before the first "letters of payment" —the ancestors of the bills of exchange of modern times—were introduced by Italian merchant princes at the public fairs of Genoa and Florence and, later, Lyons and Antwerp. But it was not until the dawn of the nineteenth century that interest in monetary matters and foreign exchange really became worldwide.

Within the limited compass of this chapter the many vicissitudes that have marked the history of the foreign exchanges since that time cannot be adequately described. Only to a few outstanding developments which since the beginning of the present century have had a decisive bearing on the activities of the foreign exchange divisions of United States banks can brief reference be here made.

During the halcyon era before 1914 the fluctuations in the international exchange markets were almost stereotyped in character. Confidence in the stability of the principal currencies reigned supreme in

[2] Source: Sédillot, *Le Drame des Monnaies.*

all the leading financial centers. From day to day, the exchanges reflected faithfully the normal movements of funds from one country to another. The rates varied mainly with the seasonal ebb and flow of demand and supply and the movements of merchandise and capital from one center to another. Fluctuations were circumscribed by the upper and lower gold points—the respective quotations at which it would become profitable to import or export gold. Through the operation of the international gold standard, up to the First World War, all the principal currencies were closely tied to one another. For the exchange dealers in those distant days the summer and autumn months, when tourist travel and the marketing of crops were at their peak, were the busiest period of the year. On the other hand, the inflow and outflow of credits and loans, and the remittance of funds for the provisioning of deposit accounts abroad or for employment in those countries where interest rates were attractive, presented year-round opportunities for active trading by foreign exchange divisions. At a time when it was still relatively riskless to engage in money arbitrage, the call-money rates in foreign capitals such as London, Paris, Amsterdam, and Berlin—the "contango" interest charged forward buyers of stocks for their monthly term settlement—were keenly watched by foreign exchange traders. Similarly the private discount rates quoted for commercial and bankers' bills payable in pounds, guilders, or francs were eagerly scrutinized.

Prior to 1914 the banks of Berlin, Vienna, Budapest, Warsaw, Petrograd (then still St. Petersburg), and Moscow discounted in Paris and London their so-called "domiciled" bills, that is, acceptances of their local merchants and industries, or of the banks themselves, payable in francs or sterling at the offices of French or British banks. These Eastern European banks also contracted loans for periods of three to six months with banks in London, Paris, and Amsterdam, where money was cheaper than in their own still capital-hungry countries. As collateral they furnished suitable portions of their portfolios of internal commercial bills payable in their local currency. These transactions were known as "pensions"—the French equivalent of boarding-house—so called probably because the paper was put out "at board." For financial houses and corporations in Paris and London (the Rothschilds, and the railroad and insurance companies) disposing of large temporary liquid funds, these resale arrangements were a convenient method of investing funds for brief periods in what until 1914 appeared to be sound bona fide commercial bills, which moreover generally carried the endorsements of several foreign banks as well as a local banking firm acting as intermediary. To safeguard the proprieties and to avoid disclosing to the drawees that the paper had been pledged abroad, the endorsements were not affixed directly on the bills but on a rider ("allonge") which was pasted to the original drafts but could be easily removed before presentation at maturity.

The rise and fall of the official discount rates of the Bank of England, the Bank of France, and other continental banks of issue were events of capital significance. Repercussions were felt not only on the money markets but also on the stock and commodity exchanges as they might be aiming either at attracting foreign funds, or, on the contrary, at discouraging the outflow of domestic capital and at stopping the exodus of bullion. In normal times these factors exercised a decisive effect on exchange rates. At a time when political equilibrium existed in the world and no foreign exchange restrictions had to be taken into account, an appreciable difference in interest rates in the various countries would induce traders to remit funds to the point where the return was most remunerative, provided of course that the working capital available to the foreign exchange division for operations abroad had not already been wholly absorbed by previous transactions. Elsewhere mention has been made of the 90 and 180-day sight credits in foreign currencies placed at the disposal of banking houses in New York by their London, Paris, and Amsterdam correspondents. Foreign exchange naturally played a far from negligible role in these transactions. Often in the fall, when the crops moved overseas in substantial volume, sterling, guilders and other continental exchanges were under pressure from the heavy offers then appearing in the markets. For this reason the banks could afford, without too serious a risk of loss, to stay short of the sterling and other exchanges required to cover the "finance bills" at their maturity abroad. If, by some untoward incident, exchange moved against the bank before cover had been secured, the loss was limited since the rate for the needed foreign currency could not rise much above the gold point and any damage was therefore restricted to the cost of shipping gold abroad to meet the maturing obligations.

After the First World War conditions changed. Most European nations experienced difficulties in maintaining the free convertibility of their moneys into gold. One after the other, monetary systems became disorganized. Under the leadership of the United States the creditor countries attempted vainly to support the tottering gold standard by stabilization credits extended both by the Federal Reserve Banks and by syndicates of private financial institutions. In addition the League of Nations took a series of active steps to assist in the reorganization of the finances of certain countries (Austria, Bulgaria, Danzig, Estonia, and Greece).[3]

In earlier chapters the debacle of the German, Austrian, and Russian currencies in the twenties has been set forth, as has also the flight of capital from Central Europe, and intermittently from France and Italy as well. Waves of gold shipments to the safe shores of the New World began to succeed each other without pause. In order to bring some relief to the sorely pressed foreign banks of issue the Federal Reserve Bank of New York purchased foreign bills endorsed by United States commercial banks and repayable in dollars. In addition, it opened accounts with certain foreign central banks. Yet, except for short intervals, no lasting equilibrium could be attained. Surges of optimism and discouragement best describe the attitude of the exchange markets during that uncertain period. After the resumption of gold payments by Sweden and England in 1925, and later by Belgium, Holland, Switzerland, and others, banks in the creditor countries—England, Holland, France, Switzerland, and the United States—decided, as described elsewhere, that it was now safe to extend short-term credits and long-time loans to Central Europe, Latin America, and other capital-poor nations. However, these transfusions of credit and capital, did not take sufficiently into account—as was recognized in retrospect—the transfer problem that was to be encountered later.

By one of the strange reversals of which international financial history is profuse in examples, the Wall Street boom in 1928–1929 lured capital again from Europe. Funds were "put out" in the New York call money market in order to take advantage of the abnormally high interest rates. The foreign exchange divisions of United States banks, which had previously profited from the stream of credit eastward across the Atlantic, now thrived on the heavy transfers of funds in the opposite direction.

[3] See Margaret G. Myers, "The League Loans," *Political Science Quarterly*, LX (December, 1945), 492–526.

In March, 1933, the banking crisis and the reported monetary plans of the Roosevelt administration threatened to cause a reverse movement—a flight from the dollar. In one of his first executive orders, the President on March 10, 1933, prohibited the export of gold except by Treasury license and directed the banks not to "engage in any transaction in foreign exchange, except such as may be undertaken for legitimate and normal business requirements, for reasonable traveling and other personal requirements, and for the fulfillment of contracts entered into prior to March 6, 1933." This order was followed on March 12 by Circular No. 1176 of the Federal Reserve Bank of New York, under the terms of which dealers operating in foreign exchange within the Second Reserve District were instructed to "obtain from each person to whom they sell foreign exchange directly or indirectly a written declaration signed by each person describing the purpose for which the foreign exchange is purchased and certifying that the transaction in no way contravenes the Act of March 9, 1933, the Executive Order of March 10, 1933, or any regulation thereunder." Furthermore, each dealer was directed to file with the bank a written report showing his exchange position as of the close of business on March 3, 1933, and an additional statement showing "all foreign exchange contracts entered into by him prior to March 6, 1933, for the delivery of foreign exchange after that date," classified by currencies and maturities. Dealers were also required to submit to their banks daily reports regarding their current foreign exchange transactions and to notify them in writing concerning the fulfillment of each contract entered into prior to March 6.

When Hitler assumed power in Germany, capital in Central Europe once more took fright and moved out of the threatened areas toward more secure resting places. With the help of the fugitive wealth of Europe, substantial private assets were built up in the United States. During the same year of 1931 the abandonment of the gold standard by England had already shaken the confidence of investors and savers everywhere. Finally, when the United States Supreme Court sanctioned the invalidation of the gold clause the faith in the policies that had long been the mainstay of international capitalism suffered another even more severe jar.

The gold block formed in the summer of 1933 was short-lived, collapsing two years later. During this period began the era of import controls, exchange restrictions, bilateral trade agreements, and currency depreciation, as many European and Latin American countries found themselves compelled to resort increasingly to emergency measures in the effort to offset the pressure of falling prices on their exports and husband their dwindling foreign exchange reserves. For the exchange divisions these different measures were a source of constant concern, although most of the United States regulations and restrictions mentioned above were abolished in November, 1934.

By 1939, exchange controls in one form or another were in force in practically every country of the world. As early as 1934, the United States Department of Commerce reported that between 125 and 150 clearing and compensation agreements had been concluded between Europan and Latin American nations. The Nazis were masters in making of these various contrivances instruments for the hidden protection of German industry, the shackling of the German domestic economy, and the furthering of the totalitarian way of life. By strict controls they succeeded in limiting undesirable imports of luxuries, while at the same time obstructing the exodus of capital abroad.

In October, 1936, the Tripartite Agreement brought about a period of relative stability for some of the principal exchanges, providing for the reciprocal purchase of the currencies of the adhering countries. The dollars of the United States Stabilization Fund also for a time helped to stem the further depreciation of the French franc.

The outbreak of the Second World War at once disrupted the whole monetary sphere. France and Britain, and later other nations, placed the foreign assets of their citizens under government control. The free exchange markets ceased to exist, while all dealings in the currencies of the countries occupied by the enemy came to an end. Even trading in neutral moneys was subject to strict governmental regulations both in the United States and abroad. Often two exchange quotations existed side by side in certain European markets, one being the official and the other the open or black market price, a situation that still survives in some parts of the world.

After the beginning of hostilities, when the first scramble for sterling and continental exchanges to pay off American short-term liabilities had ended, foreigners sold United States securities and bought dollars to create the funds required for the purchase of war material and foodstuffs. The dollar became a scarce currency. Once more the United States played a major role in the financing of friendly belligerents, That after the end of the war the world dollar shortage became the paramount problem in international financial relations needs no emphasis here.

Owing to the unprecedented exchange situation large United States industrial and commercial concerns doing business abroad were unable to secure adequate cover in dollars for their exports and local trading activities in Europe and elsewhere. In order not to lose their position in foreign markets, some of them formed special divisions and private companies for the purpose of bartering United States machinery and other goods badly needed abroad for local foreign products such as tobacco, metals, minerals, fruit, and so forth. The countries whose exchanges were blocked were for their part willing to authorize the exportation of raw materials and commodities produced by their nationals in return for equipment and construction materials urgently needed for the rehabilitation of their shattered economies.

Four years after V–J Day the foreign exchange situation still remained confused in many countries. Some countries, such as Canada and Sweden, formally revalued their currencies—too precipitately as subsequent experience has shown. Other nations in spite of the September, 1949, devaluations, still had to contend with dollar-deficiency problems while the exchanges of some of the former enemy countries remained in a chaotic condition.

To summarize, the record of the past three decades shows: prior to 1914, comparative stability and tranquility; after the First World War, instability and unrest, briefly relieved by concerted efforts to promote monetary reconstruction through public and private financial aid; then, a second phase of disorganization of a number of currencies, again succeeded by an era of international co-operation in the effort to bring about free convertibility of the various national moneys; after a few years of comparative calm, another and more disastrous world struggle followed by a precarious peace and by communist-inspired fears of a deep economic depression spreading from this continent all over the capitalistic world. Such in brief is the shifting background against which the operations of the foreign exchange divisions of United States banks evolved during the past thirty-five years.

With this sketchy historical outline behind us we can now enter upon a more detailed description of the work of the foreign exchange divisions, for since the First World War the New York market has become a major factor in the settlement of international accounts. Almost three fourths of the world's commerce is estimated as being today conducted in United States dollars or pounds sterling. The foreign exchange divisions serve all those at home and abroad whose business calls for the conversion of dollars into foreign currencies or vice versa. Most of the transactions that call for the services of the banks' foreign exchange divisions are now "spot" or cash deals for immediate settlement; the future exchange market, which formerly occupied a prominent place in the divisions' turnover has in recent years, except when fear of inflation prompted buying of futures as a hedge, been relegated to a more modest position.

The following listing, made without regard to order of importance, may serve to give a broad outline of many of the transactions that daily pass over the position sheets of a bank's foreign exchange traders. There are indeed few services of the foreign department that, directly or indirectly, do not touch the foreign exchange division at some point or another. It is called upon to remit funds abroad for the importer who buys goods overseas and pays for them in foreign currencies, and to repatriate the proceeds of merchandise sold in foreign markets by United States exporters. It sells foreign travel money to the tourist and drafts to the immigrant who wants to send his savings to his family in a distant land. If the bank makes a loan to a borrower somewhere in a remote region, one of the division's traders will be asked to purchase the required foreign currency. If foreign holders of United States securities sell them in the New York market a division trader may have to cover them in the respective local money. Vice versa, if a foreign citizen buys United States stocks, bonds, or commodities he may request the division to convert his own local funds into dollars in order to cover the cost thereof. Similarly, if Americans buy foreign securities the division procures the required exchange, and if and when they sell foreign property the division will be asked to turn the yield into United States dollars. Orders are received from banks all over the globe for the purchase and sale of exchange. Foreigners may need dollars for the payment of dividends, interest, commissions, fees or the accumulation of sinking funds on bond issues. American companies may owe foreigners for royalties on patents. Publishers may have to pay authors abroad for their percentage earnings. Insurance companies and steamship owners use the services of the division to transfer premiums or freight income to their principals, as well as wages, tolls, and repair costs in foreign ports. The postal services, the cable and radio companies, United States corporations and firms with branches abroad, missionary or charitable societies, educational institutions all have occasion to use the offices of the exchange divisions. Inland banks throughout the country which maintain their own accounts with foreign correspondents will be buyers or sellers of exchange from time to time. Finally, the United States Treasury, the Federal Reserve Banks acting for the United States Stabilization Fund, and various United States Government agencies are at times important clients of the exchange divisions. Thus, daily there takes place an unending movement of capital abroad and to this country. Every visible and invisible item in the United States balance of payments—if it has to be settled in a foreign currency—may sooner or later give rise to foreign exchange transfers. It has been estimated that since the end of the war, and including the operations of the Marshall Fund and other governmental contributions to foreign nations, the United States has handled approximately 50 percent of the total exchanges in world trade.

The above enumeration of the wide variety of functions of the foreign exchange divisions is by no means exhaustive. As indicated before, the foreign exchange division has in normal times attended to the investment of some of the dollar deposits in the foreign department. While the balances carried in foreign currencies are strictly limited in accordance with the daily volume of sales and purchases, the division's traders will spontaneously move excessive deposits as soon as financial or political conditions appear to be deteriorating in the countries where balances are maintained. This is especially vital in the case of "swap" transactions entered into in order to take advantage of interest rates higher than those obtainable at home.

Scarcely any group is more concerned with the movements of foreign exchange than United States importers and exporters. Fluctuations of the currencies of the countries with which they deal have been among their most serious problems at certain periods within the memory of the present generation. The merchant when placing an order overseas must know fairly accurately what his cost will be, that is, how many dollars he will be called upon to pay for the goods purchased abroad, or how many United States dollars he is likely to collect for merchandise sold to a foreign buyer. For this reason the heads of the foreign exchange division are often confronted with questions about the future trend of one or another currency. By making intelligent use of the services of the bank the merchant is ordinarily able to protect himself against exchange losses. The division's traders will endeavor to eliminate or minimize such losses for him. Of course, a reliable future market is of the essence. With moneys no longer firmly anchored to gold, depreciation or appreciation can be insured against only by buying or selling foreign currency for forward delivery. The bank attempts to relieve the exporters and importers of the risks that these cannot safely assume. By supplying the merchant with the bank's own contract for the amounts required they place him in a position in which he will be able to effect or receive payment in the currency required to honor his own obligations—United States dollars.

In the thirties the United States Stabilization Fund was an important factor in the foreign exchange market. The original capital of the fund of 2 billion dollars was derived from the book profit of the Treasury in connection with the devaluation of the dollar early in 1934. Through the Federal Reserve Bank of New York the fund has bought and sold gold bullion and has acquired silver in all the world's markets. To effect these transactions, the fund—also through the Federal Reserve Bank of New York—has more or less regularly traded in all the principal currencies, the monthly amounts involved being at certain periods in excess of hundreds of millions of dollars. The net results of the fund's operations have been highly advantageous for the public purse. Profits on exchange, commissions for handling gold and silver, and interest on its investments in United States Government bonds have accounted for most of the earnings of the fund. Undoubtedly it served a worth-while purpose through its temporary contributions to the maintenance of free convertibility of certain currencies and to the pegging of others around an agreed level.

At this point it may be timely to refer briefly to the gold and silver arbitrage centered in the foreign exchange divisions. During the thirties, after England, France, Holland, Switzerland, and the other members of the gold block had successively gone off gold, only the United States, through the Exchange Stabilization Fund, was prepared to buy gold from central banks abroad, or sell it to them, at $35.00 an ounce, and consequently with the active help of the foreign departments of the commercial banks accumulated the world's largest gold hoard. Before this time, when it was still possible to deal in gold for individual account and when traders, to cover foreign sales of exchange, could ship bullion freely from one country to another, one of a good trader's indispensable attributes was his thorough familiarity with gold arbitrage. This involved dexterity and skill in converting quickly and accurately various weights and grades of fineness of gold, first into those that were valid under the mint laws of the other nations, and then into their respective currencies, allowing for the length of transit, the cost of freight, the loss of interest, and the charges at both ends. Most traders carried constantly with them small parity books, showing at a glance the cost of a unit of gold converted at various exchange rates into the units traded in at the other capitals; new editions of these books were not required so long as the currencies moved within the fixed gold points.

Contrary to popular belief, the profit on gold shipments, under normal conditions, was exceedingly small. Sometimes shipments were made if the margin was only 1/2 per mill. If, for one reason or another, the steamer on which gold was to be loaded was delayed in arriving or in reaching its destination or if it docked late on a Saturday afternoon when the banks were closed, the loss of interest might easily swallow up the modest profit that the trader had calculated his bank would derive from the transaction. In former days, gold arbitrage was often made for joint account. No commissions were charged by shipper and consignee except actual expenses and interest on the advance during transit. In some cases, when private discount rates were low enough to warrant it, the shipper would draw on the consignee or the consignee on the shipper and sell the demand draft or a 30, 60, or even 90-day acceptance, and the capital obtained—after the proceeds of the gold had been collected—either could be used for subsequent shipments or would be placed on call, or else would be invested in short bills on London, Paris, or Amsterdam if the exchanges favored such a purchase. In this country, perhaps as a heritage from the 1849 gold fever, bullion shipments have generally received much publicity and, for that reason, the heads of some of the commercial banks and the officers in charge of public relations and advertising have been known to encourage their foreign exchange traders to engage in gold shipments mainly for the sake of prestige. Since 1934, when the Treasury entered the field, this phase of banking no longer receives the public notice it rated when the world was still on the gold standard. It cannot be denied that formerly a certain fascination surrounded these shipments of the yellow metal from one country and one continent to another. However, the exchange men themselves seldom had the leisure to watch the securely strapped and sealed wooden boxes containing the precious cargo being taken into the strongrooms of the transatlantic boats, while armed guards of the insurance companies (in the case of exceptionally heavy consignments) watched over the treasure until steamer sailing, and after arrival at the foreign port.

At some critical moments in the past the attitude of certain countries in Europe with respect to the outflow of gold permitted foreign traders to draw interesting conclusions concerning the likelihood of impending trouble in the international sphere. Thus, in the early months of 1914, it was reported in Paris that the German banks made concerted efforts to attract gold even though the actual parity of the reichsmark in foreign markets did not seem, on the face of it, to justify the cost of importing bullion. On the other hand, although exports of gold from Hamburg were in other cases frowned upon, when French banks later applied for gold during the critical summer months of that year, the German banks, perhaps in order to deceive France as to German intentions, readily supplied the metal for export on French account.

In former years an unwarranted veil of mystery surrounded the work of the foreign exchange traders. During the life of the present generation, however, the public has learned a great deal about international currencies and monetary matters. The world has grown smaller. News travels faster. The desk of the foreign exchange manager is no longer separated, except physically, from those to whom he sends or from whom he receives orders. The radio and the teletype, supplementing rapid cable service, have reduced the time required to communicate with most financial centers to a matter of minutes. For this reason the margin between the rates quoted in the various markets had, except under unusual conditions, become so minimized prior to the last war that only the most skillful exchange operators were able to make even modest profits from old-fashioned three-cornered arbitrage.

Nevertheless, during certain periods, the foreign exchange division has been one of the busiest spots of the foreign department. Like the owners of any commodity the officers in charge direct the sale of their inventories—represented by all currencies for which a regular demand exists—and replace the sales or add to their stock by purchasing exchange offered to them. If they are successful, the day's operations show a profit. Most trades are made by word of mouth over the telephone, and millions of dollars of exchange thus change hands during the average working day. However, all contracts are subject to prompt written confirmation. It is good policy for the division to execute customers' orders at the most favorable price obtainable in the market at the time the order is received. Valuable accounts may be lost if the trader applies too high or too low a rate when carrying out a "best" order. It may even be good business in the long run to absorb a loss rather than forfeit the good will of an important concern. The officials responsible for the finances of commercial and industrial corporations and business houses must therefore be assiduously cultivated, and pleasant personal contacts with them must be maintained by the proffering of timely information on trends in the markets of the currencies in which they are primarily interested, since the fluctuation of a certain exchange may be a matter of great consequence to their concerns.

The earnings of the division are of course favorably affected by wide fluctuations in exchange rates and by large orders in which the division's traders are given broad latitude by the customer. But it must not be forgotten that the tides are not always favorable and that the traders occasionally run into squalls, while in any event in calm weather, when the risk is smaller, the earnings are inevitably reduced. The trader who makes it a point, whenever possible, to cover his positions at the close of the day, will as a rule fare better in the end than his rival who, in the hope of "making a killing" the next morning, cannot bring himself to even his accounts. The history of foreign exchange has not been free from instances in which even brilliant individuals have lost their sharp sense of values, and years of hard-earned profits have been wiped out by a single error of judgment or unforeseen event. The operations of traders are therefore facilitated by the presence in the foreign branches of the bank of experienced officials whose information and views are trustworthy and of whose co-operation advantage can be taken to adjust, favorably, positions entered into by the home office.

During the earlier stages of United States foreign banking, exchange brokers played a conspicuous role in the New York market, and for many years most business was handled through them. The men dedicated to this high-speed and sometimes nerve-racking profession had private telephone wires leading into the trading room of every important bank. During the First World War the broker charged by J. P. Morgan & Co. with the pegging of the pound sterling and the French franc occupied for a time a dominant position in the exchange market. However, after the war, when the Allied exchanges were again left to their own devices, the star of this influential broker set like that of other luminaries on the foreign exchange horizon whose names for a while were bywords in the international financial centers.

The number of brokers declined gradually during the ensuing years, but in 1937 there still existed some two score firms.[4] Of these a few specialized in the Far Eastern exchanges and silver, others devoted themselves to selling grain and cotton documentary bills, the brokers for the latter being established in the principal Southern markets—Dallas, Houston, Galveston, and Memphis. Few, if any, foreign exchange men are left who remember the early days when brokers called in person at the various banks to offer bills or solicit orders. Who, for example, recalls the genteel representative of a leading oil company who visited the foreign department managers in the twenties to obtain their bids, good for several hours, for the different currencies of which his company was at times the most important seller; and who remembers the afternoons when the same greyhaired deputy called the by then apprehensive exchange trader on the telephone to inform him that his price had been accepted so that his division was now long of a substantial amount of Danish kroner or Spanish pesetas or some other currency which it would be impossible to sell except in the European exchange markets, which by then were closed for the day?

Foreign exchange divisions were among the first sections of the United States banks to feel the effects of the outbreak of the Second World War. The volume of trading was immediately reduced. Arbitrage was practically impossible, except on a small scale, with the few countries that escaped being drawn into the conflict. Moreover, exchange clearings and controls played havoc with the busi-

[4] Nowadays the Foreign Exchange Brokers Association represents and protects the interests of the members of the profession.

ness of the formerly most active clients. However, during the first critical months after the beginning of hostilities, it was nevertheless demonstrated that a wisely managed foreign exchange trading division has a legitimate place in the setup of every well-equipped foreign department. Most outstanding future contracts were liquidated without any appreciable delay except in the countries actually overrun by the enemy. Indeed, it is a significant fact that for many years no heavy losses were incurred in these divisions. When the conduct of the operations has been in able and cautious hands, when speculation has been proscribed and overnight positions strictly limited and controlled, trading divisions have been proved year in and year out to be valuable adjuncts of the foreign departments.

What background is necessary for the head of a foreign exchange division? What makes a top-notch exchange trader? Basic is a broad knowledge of financial conditions and developments in the principal international exchange markets. In addition to the swings in interest rates, the department head as well as the chief traders must pay attention to circumstances and occurrences that may affect the market in respect to certain currencies: excessive note issues; the fall of governments; defaults in the payment of government debts; the threat of devaluation; rumors of war; and flights of capital from various causes. Every development, internal or external, favorable or unfavorable, may have an immediate or remote effect on the trend of the exchanges.

In order to be accurately and speedily informed on all such factors the traders must be in constant communication with correspondent banks and branches in the various countries. They must be able to interpret intuitively the latest foreign and domestic news coming to the division; to array logically the advices received for the bearing that they may have on the trend of the exchanges, and then to decide upon the best course permitted by the circumstances. It follows that especially the manager must possess imagination and vision, so as to be capable of applying the lessons of years of diligent observation. The mind of the skilled exchange man must be trained to take without delay advantage of the fluctuations that arise during the average day, by buying in the market where quotations are temporarily depressed for one reason or another, and by selling where it is profitable to satisfy demand at higher prices. He must be quick in perceiving possibilities for a rapid "turn." There are occasions when, after having cautiously felt the pulse of the market, the trader may decide that it is relatively safe to operate on what is almost a premonition—in the foreign exchange trader's vernacular, on a "hunch." In such a case, after having taken into account all the imponderables, the trader may decide that the stakes are sufficiently high to warrant taking a chance. The best traders are those who have the flair for detecting the moment when a moderate risk is justified. The ranking members of the profession, in the course of many years of experience, have developed a keen perception of coming trouble and are able to sense when a reaction is just around the corner. They are accustomed to think under pressure and are prepared to form instantaneous conclusions. Therefore, when a crisis arises and an unexpected situation confronts them, they are not thrown off balance. Many unforeseen incidents have troubled their operations at one period or another. It is not a beginner's job to trace a safe course through the large body of present-day currencies and exchange regulations. The task calls for a keen mind and a superabundance of nervous energy.

Today, in some countries, exchange rates still fail to function according to the law of supply and demand, and even those traders with a shrewd sense for anticipating the gyrations of the exchanges find it perplexing to foresee the final solution to the problem of certain unredeemable postwar moneys. In the meantime, the wisest traders will continue to rely upon their experience and instinct, shifting their positions with events and looking the field over cautiously before every important move. More than ever before, the still confused conditions of the postwar world seem to place a premium on cool calculation and calm thinking, joined with prudent and judicious restraint.

SUMMARY. Since 1914, foreign exchange trading has undergone an extensive development. Particularly important are the factors that influence the foreign-exchange markets, the daily work of the traders, the bearing of outside events upon their decisions, their tools and sources of information, their attitude toward customers, the intricacies of gold arbitrage, and the role of the exchange brokers. An exchange trader must have many qualities and must avoid many snares. The work of the foreign-exchange division itself is of the broadest character, and offers an attractive future for persons with the proper qualifications.

XV

THE MEN BEHIND THE ORGANIZATION

THE EXECUTIVE OFFICE

THE NERVE CENTER of the foreign department is its executive office. Thence, within the powers assigned to him by the top authorities of the bank, the head of the department frames the policies and directs and supervises the overseas affairs of the institution, while under his guidance and control with the aid of experienced officers and division heads the daily business is transacted.

What qualities and aptitudes go to make up a foreign department executive, and what are the requirements for holding this important post in the foreign banking field? Those who have made international banking their lifework and who strive to be leaders in their profession have to be experienced in many lines of activities. As a rule, foreign department managers must have behind them long years of practical training in the field. During prolonged stays in many lands they acquire an intimate knowledge of the countries' economic and financial status and a thorough acquaintance with their business methods. By periodical visits they keep informed on changes and new developments. More than in former generations, the present-day international banker not only must possess a vast store of data on exchange and monetary conditions abroad but must also be conversant with the constantly varying customs and usages in trade.

To the foreign department official, merchants and manufacturers must be able to turn for up-to-date advice in connection with their pending or proposed deals overseas, especially as to the foreign exchange situation. Anything that happens in the monetary sphere may have profound repercussions on his clients' business and the department's own operations. Without the steady accumulation of reliable and timely reports on the latest happenings his views are therefore likely to be sterile and his counsel lacking ingenuity. Thus he needs to be familiar with every material fact bearing on overseas trade and finance. Notwithstanding the saying that a slight knowledge of the law is worse than no knowledge at all, he must also have at least a smattering of law, economics, and accountancy, not to mention foreign taxation and business practices. That he must have the technique of banking itself at his finger tips goes almost without saying.

Naturally an acquaintance with the history of banks in the leading foreign centers will add to the stature of the banker responsible for the destinies of a large foreign department during these postwar years, and from their recurrent setbacks and recoveries he will have learned many a useful lesson. Despite all this, he will at times be confronted with unexpected new problems calling for careful scrutiny and putting his sagacity and intuition to a severe test.

However, it is not sufficient to know the markets, money systems, and even the languages of foreign nations. In the era through which the world is passing the foreign banker must also have qualities of a more personal nature. He must be a realist. While attending to his immediate job, he must constantly survey the world scene. He must be a keen observer, endowed with perspicacity when he looks into the future. Finally the ideal foreign department head should also have adaptability, administrative skill commingled with courage, more than average energy, and unremitting willingness to work.

One of the essential requirements of a good foreign executive is ability to determine the credit-worthiness of an applicant for a line of credit. Although he will depend very much on the thorough investigation made by the credit department and on the recommendations of the officer in charge of the account, a well-trained department head must himself be able to analyze financial statements and to appraise the business record and personal competence of the men in charge of the customer's affairs. In the course of time he will acquire a broad knowledge of the origin and background of the principal merchants engaged in foreign commerce, and the significant data of their balance sheets will become so well fixed in his mind that no request for additional credit facilities will take him unawares.

Much of the work of the officers in charge of foreign departments is necessarily concerned with the cultivation and extension of the bank's connections at home and overseas. The officers must make it a special point to create personal ties and remain on good terms with those who are or may become customers not only of the foreign department but also of other divisions or branches of the institution. The human factor plays a major role in foreign as well as in domestic banking, and the success of the officers will therefore depend in great measure on their ability to earn and retain the good will of those firms and concerns whose foreign business the department wishes to handle.

What are the foreign department manager's specific functions in addition to those already mentioned? He watches over the department's domestic and overseas commitments, including those of the foreign branches under his supervision. Accordingly he decides upon all important loans and credits extended both by the head office and by the affiliates abroad. He directs the policies and sees to it that when necessary the brakes are applied. He keeps in touch with the chief operations of the commercial letter of credit and foreign exchange divisions. Above all he follows with particular care the inflow of new business, domestic and foreign. Everything of consequence that concerns the foreign department is brought to his attention and is judged by him from the angle of its effect on the progress and the fortunes of the department.

Within the limits of the responsibilities assigned him by the senior officers, he administers the foreign business of the institution. This comprehensive job is facilitated by daily meetings with his assistants and division heads, when pending matters, the renewal of loans, and the granting of new credit lines are examined. The detailed reports and the recommendations of the territorial officers are here reviewed and either approved, amended, or tabled. Should the total advance or credit under examination exceed the maximum that he has the power to authorize, the sanction of the higher decision-making executives or the bank's board of directors has to be obtained.

These staff meetings permit an exchange of views on current organization problems, and the advisability of expanding new business efforts, either locally, elsewhere in this country, or abroad. Suggestions are presented as to improvements in service or rule changes in the interest of more effective co-operation between the various divisions. During these meetings, as well as in his contacts with his associates, the efforts of the department chief are directed to keeping the work of the department running smoothly, detecting potential sources of trouble, and taking precautionary measures in due time. One of his major tasks at all times is to focus the attention of his colleagues and subordinates on the department's earnings and to streamline his organization so as to keep its overhead within a reasonable ratio to the department's anticipated yearly profit income.

From what has been explained it is apparent that the position is a highly exacting one. Eternal vigilance is of the essence in foreign as in domestic banking. The need for time to think and take stock is therefore ever present. However, it is not often that in the privacy of his office the department head can divorce himself from the demands of his routine duties and without interruption calmly plan and consider the vital issues with which he may be confronted. Only those who have sat awhile by the desk of the manager of a prominent foreign department can appreciate the multifarious questions of policy and organization that he is called upon to consider and solve in the course of a normal working day. Even though a competent secretary has regulated his agenda and assists in reducing his schedule where feasible, the daily routine of correspondence, meetings with the staff, conferences with the senior officers, telephone conversations, visitors, business luncheons and dinners, committees outside the bank, calls on important customers, and so forth, is at times overwhelming and frustrating.

As the volume of operations grows, it becomes imperative that much of the managerial responsibilities be divided among other officers so as to relieve the department head of burdensome minor details. Accordingly, today the routine conduct of current business is delegated to trusted assistants who, equipped by experience and practical knowledge, receive ample latitude for conducting the normal range of operations and making the required decisions. While still exercising the over-all supervision, the department head is nowadays consulted only about major credits and loans and matters of important administrative strategy. Under such circumstances it can no longer be said of the foreign department that it is "the lengthened shadow of one man."

One of the more stimulating tasks of the senior officer is selecting from among the younger members of his staff those who by temperament and background are fitted to help in building up and enhancing the reputation of the department as an efficient and trustworthy organization. After having gained a thorough knowledge of their character, intelligence, and personal ability, there is no more pleasant assignment for any department head than to recommend their appointment to positions where they will make increased and more distinct contributions to the success of his team. While exacting a high standard of responsibility from his associates, the department head will always endeavor to bring out their best capabilities, and at the same time will assiduously seek to evaluate justly their talents and their claims to advancement, happy when he can recognize and encourage exceptional initiative and outstanding work.

General de Gaulle is reported to have said to one of his aides: "You can expect only as much work from your juniors as you put in yourself!" This might have been addressed to the head of a foreign (or, indeed, of any) department. He must be able to put his shoulder to the wheel whenever there is a call for aid from any temporarily overburdened division. He must therefore be as expert in each kind of work as any member of his staff. Above all, he must know how to get along with all the staff members. Aware of the need for the willing co-operation and support of all employees he will constantly endeavor to enhance the general level of morale in the department.

The career of a foreign department executive is not devoid of occasional dramatic moments and crises. Almost anything of consequence that happens anywhere abroad may of course have a bearing on the department's affairs. Therefore the department head must be prepared for any emergency. Especially in these days of both financial instability and interdependence critical moments come when even the consciousness of past sound conduct may not spare the foreign department officials from anxiety and concern. It is at such critical times that the responsibility for protecting both the bank's and its customers' commitments becomes particularly weighty, and it is then the mettle of the department chief will be put to its acid test. Yet, an experienced skipper will not let a sudden storm affect his nerve; if at a critical juncture the officer in charge can be counted upon not to lose his equanimity he has one of the most essential qualities of a foreign executive. Calmness and the ability to alter policies with shifting circumstances are indispensable requirements in times of stress.

No man of course can claim infallibility, least of all the head of the foreign department. In spite of his best efforts and his most considered direction errors will be made, and the position therefore inevitably involves personal risks, however levelheaded and cautious a man may be. A name built up over a generation will count for little if disaster overtakes his operations. While he does not make the most momentous decisions alone and while his department is by no means a one-man show, he cannot escape accountability when mistakes are made. Even though the blunder be committed in spite of his definite orders, in willful disregard of the department's known policy, and without his knowledge, he still must shoulder the consequences.

There are times when countries in which heavy commitments are pending find themselves in the throes of political or economic upheavals. At such periods, when an atmosphere of doubt and gloom is likely to descend over the executive offices, the officer in charge must be ready to defend past actions and to urge calm consideration in the face of unduly pessimistic apprehensions. Under such circumstances the department head is fortunate who can point to a long record of successful conduct of the department's affairs and whose confidence in the ultimate surmounting of temporary setbacks has been tested in the crucible of life-long experience. Foreign department officers to be successful in their contest for business need a wide latitude for individual initiative and quick action. With due allowance for occasional failings and errors of judgment the satisfactory record over a great many years has on the whole justified beyond question the confidence reposed in and the broad powers entrusted to the heads of foreign departments by the senior officers and the boards of directors of our banks.

What then can be said about this career that will help the younger men to find themselves in foreign banking work? It is certainly true that those who acquire the special knowledge of this important branch of financial science and practice enjoy a special standing that is enhanced by the fact that it is commanded by relatively few members of the commercial banking fraternity. But it would be misleading to leave with aspiring beginners the impression that the roads of all brilliant foreign bankers automatically lead to Rome. Far from it, the rueful fact is that some of the outstanding men who in years gone by ranked high in the American foreign banking fraternity—experts whose opinions were eagerly sought after in all that pertained to international exchange and banking—suddenly vanished from the scene of their former triumphs. Their names mean little or nothing to the present generation of students of international finance.

To attain the top of the profession and reap the rewards which await those who reach the higher positions in foreign banking, one foremost requirement is to devote oneself heart and soul to the job, and to realize that the desired results can be attained only by everlasting study and application. While international banking may appeal to the imagination, it taxes the fortitude and patience of those engaged in it. The great effort that has to be exerted in order to become competent to assume heavy responsibilities is not to be minimized. Enthusiasm for the calling must therefore never cool down. The life of the foreign banker is laborious and at times harassing to the last degree. The strain of conducting an immense foreign business is often extremely wearing. Men with steady nerves and strong physical resources have been known to break down under the load. Nevertheless, with good teamwork, common counsel, and concerted planning and action, most difficulties in the path of the foreign department executives will ordinarily be overcome. Mistakes may be made in the press and urge of trying times, but with courage and coolheadedness and a little good fortune there are few situations to which an efficient and zealous foreign organization will not prove equal.

SUMMARY. The success of a foreign banking organization depends in no small degree on the caliber of its principal executives. Through them the top management executes the broad policies laid down or approved by the board of directors for operations and commitments in the international field. Manifold qualities are essential for leading positions in this line of work. The conditions to be observed in the extension of foreign credits are outlined, as are the details involved in day-to-day administration and the importance of selecting able and experienced associates. Finally, some ideas are advanced as to the risks and rewards attending a career in international banking.

THE DEPARTMENT STAFF

Well-staffed divisions, headed by capable officers and senior clerks, are responsible for carrying on the routine work of the foreign departments. Experience and able direction on the part of the top management are not enough; they must be supported by an efficient organization and by intelligent co-operation in the ranks.

In the foreign sections of the leading United States banks at home and in the overseas branches, thousands of carefully trained men and women perform the various routine functions such as the issuance and honoring of commercial letters of credit, foreign collections, credit investigation, the handling of foreign exchange, and the other multifarious activities to which reference has been made in previous chapters. Specialists are required for much of the technical work performed in the various divisions, which must be closely knit together, and to mold them into an effective machine is one of the principal tasks of the managers. The daily bulk of labor accomplished in the department is exceedingly large and in many instances both exacting and complex. While it must be conceded that drudgery is inherent in some of the work of the foreign department staffs, nevertheless their members in general must have not only a broader knowledge of banking routine than in some other departments but also greater initiative and ability for independent thinking. For this reason those who seek an opportunity to become acquainted with the international aspects of banking and to acquire at the same time a cosmopolitan education find attractive a career in the overseas sections or foreign branches of our metropolitan institutions. It is a calling that offers chances for growth to men who are above the average in their outlook, who seek a profession full of broad possibilities for advancement, and who, if called upon, do not mind spending years away from their native country.

Because of the major role now played by the United States in world finance, young men should feel encouraged, more than ever before, to embrace a calling where industry and ingenuity are likely to bring them to the fore more rapidly than in domestic fields of endeavor. The scientific education gained in a college or law school undoubtedly offers distinct advantages to those who are attracted to a career in foreign banking. Nevertheless they must be prepared to undergo prolonged periods of training at home and abroad if they wish to qualify for the higher positions.

There is no easy way to acquire the mental equipment of an international banker. Individual progress depends in a large degree on securing a mastery of the mechanics of foreign banking, including at least a rudimentary knowledge of economics and law. The assimilation of foreign languages, too, is a skill that has proved helpful. What are the other qualities that will advance a man in a foreign department? They are elementary in character. Eagerness to learn; willingness to work hard; preparedness to fit into any foreign surroundings to which one may be transferred; expectation of promotion through ability rather than by reason of seniority; and finally a ready response, when singled out to assume difficult assignments at home or abroad.

Of course, even though animated by the best of intentions, not every man is equal to the requirements of a lifework in international banking. Some are not adapted to the inexorable routine of much of the work that they will be expected to do, and their temperament and nature would accordingly find better outlets elsewhere. Such persons may fit well into some less demanding occupation, offering better opportunities for their particular talents.

Among the most useful members of the staff of a foreign department are those officers, heads of division, and senior clerks who direct the work of the hundreds of men and women employed in that section of the bank. The supervision of the staff is a full-time job in itself, and a most responsible one. Those engaged in it have to be most adroit in handling individuals, for a harmonious and smooth-working team is essential for every organization. For the department's officers to do their own work successfully, they must have the loyal assistance of those men and women on whom devolves most of the department's tedious inside toil. The ideal departmental setup is one in which the officers can at all times depend on the fine wholehearted co-operation of the staff in the recesses of the rear offices. To achieve this intimate combination of effort there must be close co-ordination between the front office and the working divisions. The officers in charge of personnel must see to it that there is no overlapping of functions and that the lines of authority and the various duties of the division heads are clearly demarcated. They must endeavor so to shape the organization that if any individual resigns or is promoted his position can be filled without interfering with the routine of the division. They must know how to make the best use of the experience and abilities of each member of the staff. The well-intentioned personnel head can do much to promote amity and avoid friction within the ranks. Pleasant personal relations, the ability to get on with the various members of the staff are prerequisites for those charged with the direction of the affairs in the various divisions. Especially when things go wrong, as happens in even the best-administered departments, it is the duty of the supervisors and all those in charge of office groups to bolster the morale and to instill patience and enthusiasm in the employees so that they remain interested in their share of the common work. No excuse is ever needed for expressing to them the bank's dependence upon them for efficient assistance, or for recognition of their services when progress is achieved. Then, when hectic times come, when world conditions threaten, when the pressure of business is great, the ready willingness of all members of the staff will be of inestimable help in coping with the intensified demands upon the department. No one who has witnessed the loyalty and the zeal that were displayed under the strain and rush and the complexity of conditions present during the Second World War will forget the debt owed to their steadfast and unswerving co-operation.

At periodic intervals, in every department the question arises as to which member of the staff should be advanced for demonstrated ability, as to the one among several aspirants who has the most valuable traits and qualities that make for future leadership. It is not an easy task to select the men who have shown exceptional aptitude and have the best personal characteristics. The top executives at these moments have to exercise independence of judgment. There is no denying that good fortune sometimes plays a certain part in promotion, but, on the whole, those will be picked out who have evidenced that they are satisfactorily equipped for holding higher positions. They will secure recognition because they have performed their past tasks better than others, because they have shown willingness to apply themselves to any work assigned to them, and because they have always measured up to their duties with marked ability.

The selection of the men to be recommended for preferment is a delicate task, and the prospect of disappointing some deserving associates casts a shadow over the end of the year when the annual promotions and salary advances are generally decided upon. Some individuals, despite a consistent record of devotion and service, may feel that they have not received their share of credit. It is then that the executive must find words of encouragement and know how to inspire renewed self-reliance and hope for the future.

It is true today, perhaps more than ever before, that the need for men possessing the specialized skills required in the foreign banking organizations is as great as it ever was. Nor can it be disputed that the possession of such special knowledge and the readiness for hard work and at times sacrifice are the main factors that count in the rise to the higher positions in the foreign departments and the overseas branches. To those who may be hesitating about embarking in the international banking profession let it be pointed out that most of the men who have been or are now in leading places have worked their way up from modest beginnings through their own endeavors, with no other assets than, in addition to native intelligence, an undefeatable spirit and unceasing readiness for whatever difficult task lay ahead. There is no glut of well-rounded competent men with the needed background and training. Notwithstanding the obstacles that have been cited, it is not an overstatement to say to those who contemplate a career in foreign banking that the office still seeks the man and that "still o'er the earth hastes opportunity."

SUMMARY. For the internal organization of foreign departments and the qualifications of its employees, special preparation is needed to cope with the practical and often unusually complex aspects of overseas banking. Particular stress is placed on the weighty duties assigned to junior officers, supervisory chiefs, and division heads, as well as the considerations guiding the heads of the department and of the bank in advancing the ablest and best equipped among the staff to higher positions both in the department at home and in the foreign offices.

XVI

DEVELOPING BUSINESS IN FOREIGN COUNTRIES

GENERAL

A CAREER IN FOREIGN BANKING calls, on the part of the heads of foreign departments and the territorial officers, for periodic visits to Europe, Latin America, the Far East, and other regions where their institution has branches or close correspondent relationships. It also offers to a selected number of employees and younger members of the staff the opportunity to roam the world and become acquainted with the people and customs of distant countries. The practice of having qualified junior assistants spend some time in foreign banks has become a recognized fixture in the personnel policies of the larger United States banks, for it has proved an excellent investment in practical training and the preparation of the candidates for future official duties at home or overseas.

The habit of regularly visiting the bank's correspondents in the various international centers has sprung from the observation that personal interviews are more instrumental in promoting the active development of business relations than reams of letters of offers of service, sent at recurring intervals. In foreign lands, even more than at home, the best way to please and win men is to mingle with them, and so, year in and year out, the representatives of United States banks can be seen wandering up and down the different continents, studying conditions on the spot, searching for opportunities for contacts and new associations, making it their business to meet every banker and merchant of importance, making rounds of calls, and thus trying to turn their trips to good account. Sometimes there are specific subjects on which they have been requested by customers to secure local information, or matters to be discussed that are of common concern to their own bank and the foreign institution or concern.

In Europe the most lengthy stops are usually in London, Paris, Brussels, Amsterdam, Zurich, Rome, and the Scandinavian capitals; before the Second World War, Berlin, Vienna, Prague, Budapest, and Warsaw were also included in the circuit. Wherever the American banker goes, he makes assiduous visits at the United States embassies and consular officials in order to be posted on local credit and business conditions and, if necessary, to ask for introductions to cabinet members or other government officials and agencies. Everywhere, the secret of gaining good will among local financial and mercantile circles consists not only in meeting them on their own ground but also in evincing interest in their and their nation's problems, and if the call is on a new firm whose custom is being solicited, in emphasizing the desire to be of assistance irrespective of the importance of any business contacts that may ensue.

Just as the American traveler is eager to obtain competent and reliable data regarding economic and internal conditions in the countries visited, it is more than ever true nowadays that the foreign bankers and merchants he interviews also are keenly desirous of receiving authentic news about the situation in the United States and regarding the views of financial and political leaders on the special matters that concern their people and their part of the world. It is therefore helpful if the visitor, through his own knowledge and background and with the aid of detailed and relevant reports from his bank, is able to give an enlightening account of the situation at home and can answer authoritatively the often numerous questions that he will be asked. The impression made by him and the breadth of information he is in a position to convey are immeasurably important for the cementing of old and the founding of valuable new contacts for his bank. For even more significant than the knowledge acquired on these trips—valuable as it may be—is the personal impression made by the bank's delegates, since more often than not the foreign questioner will form his opinion as to the home bank's qualifications and the kind of service it can render from his conversations with the foreign department's representatives and the members of the staff of the overseas branches.

In the course of such visits, differences that may have arisen or complaints about some oversight on the part of the bank are more easily ironed out, especially if the visiting official, because of his longstanding acquaintance, is under all circumstances a welcome caller.

In most cases he will gather a valuable crop of fresh impressions and instructive suggestions of a nature that will impart an added incentive to the efforts of the department at home in expanding its operations. Conversely, the intelligence sent to the head office may be of such a nature, as in 1931 and 1938, that the senior executives will decide to haul in the sails and contract the bank's outstanding loans in that part of the world. However repugnant such conservative counsel may be to the new-business-minded official or foreign agent, in the long run it will do him more credit than wishful but unwarranted optimism, perhaps colored by a long stay in the country or by a sense of loyalty to respected business or personal friends. In addition, in the present obscure condition of world affairs, the ability to appraise the good faith of statements made by interested informants is one of the priceless gifts with which the American banker and representative abroad should be abundantly equipped. He must beware not to let his judgment be influenced by lavish entertainment or by other demonstrations of high esteem with which foreigners are often apt to evidence their regard for distinguished visitors.

Whoever is entrusted with the important mission of being the envoy of his bank in foreign lands needs to realize that it is a complimentary but arduous assignment. The object is not, as a rule, to afford the traveler an opportunity for a pleasurable vacation. During his trip to his initial destination the conscientious bank delegate will review the voluminous material that has been prepared for his benefit by the territorial divisions of the bank's foreign department and the branch organization. From the time of his arrival until his return, the ships, trains, and airplanes which rush him from one capital to the other become his offices. In order to be able to ask relevant questions and make pertinent recommendations for the furtherance of relations with his institution and, in a broader sense, for the expansion of trade between the United States and the nation whose hospitality he will enjoy, he has to pore through reference and information books, whether in the privacy of his hotel room or while traveling rapidly to the next place on his itinerary. Rarely is there a day when he can relax. During the few hours when he has no appointments or social engagements he must think over the events of the day and endeavor to digest the whirl of observations he has made, so that he may prepare his missive to the home office and include a hurried but nonetheless comprehensive and clear outline of conditions and recommendations as to future policies.

Yet these business trips, however strenuous they may be, are of great personal advantage to the ones selected to undertake them. Most of those on whom the agent calls go out of their way to offer assistance and render the visit profitable. In one city after another debts of gratitude are incurred for courtesies shown and as, on the homeward boat, he puts the final touches to his reports to senior executives, the delegate is excusably apt to emphasize with pride the fact that he has been fortunate enough to secure some particularly desirable accounts in the course of his trip.

SUMMARY. In addition to the advantage of regularly discussing its current relations with banking correspondents and customers abroad, the desire to keep in permanent touch with conditions in the foreign areas where a bank operates or wishes to expand its activities accounts for the frequent and extensive trips abroad of American bankers. These visits, while stimulating and rewarding, are at the same time strenuous and call not only for the gift of observation and perspicacity but also for a well-equipped mind and a thorough knowledge of the domestic economic and financial situation.

THE OVERSEAS BRANCHES OF UNITED STATES BANKS

Strung out around the world, the offices of the prominent United States financial institutions are the outward manifestations of the process of foreign expansion that set in shortly after the First World War, determined by the dominant role United States capital and industry had played during the struggle. The movement received increased impetus when, in the thirties, the demand for dollar loans and credits rose in Europe, Latin America, and Asia.

As already mentioned in Chapters VIII and IX, the first branches of American commercial banks were opened in London and Paris around the beginning of the twentieth century. Later, as the financial outlook of the banks widened, the value of having on-the-spot representation in other centers became evident. Following the example of other nations—the British, Canadian, French, Dutch, German, Belgian, Swiss, and Italian—New York, Boston, and San Francisco banks established their own branches where apparently there was a legitimate demand for their services. Some banks, such as the National City Bank of New York and the Chase National Bank, organized special local or Edge Act corporations to act as their agents. Through stock ownership these corporations fulfilled to all intents and purposes the same functions as regular branch offices. Close relations with banks operating in foreign countries had already existed since the time the Farmers Loan and Trust Company and the International Banking Corporation became affiliated with the National City Bank. At a later period the American Express Company was for some years closely allied with the Chase National Bank. But whatever the shape of the association, the various branches of the institutions already named and those of the other banks that gradually entered the foreign field—the Guaranty Trust Company, the Empire Trust Company, the Bankers Trust Company, the Central Hanover Bank and Trust Company, The First National Bank of Boston, and the Bank of America—have consistently been a credit to United States enterprise and efficiency.

The foreign plants and factories of United States industrial corporations (automobile manufacturers, tire companies, meat packers, shipping lines, and so forth) and the branches of American export and import houses naturally count among the principal customers of the foreign offices of United States banks. Their deposits in local currency and in dollars, and the credits and loans required for their foreign operations, together with the routine banking services, such as collections, the providing of exchange, and so forth represent a substantial part of the branches' normal turnover. By dealing with banks of their own nationality United States merchants are assured of the careful defense of their interests. For example, when goods are entrusted to the care of the United States banks for warehousing and delivery to local buyers, the banks watch to see that they are properly protected and insured, and above all that the American firms' business is treated with the utmost discretion. As previously mentioned the banks' foreign offices are particularly useful for the procurement of up-to-date and trustworthy information on the financial and moral standing of local merchants. Thus the American depositors have permanent foreign listening posts. Moreover, generally the United States bank branches are in a favored position to advise American inquirers candidly as to the political situation and the outlook as to the public finances and the soundness of the currency of the country where they do or plan to do business.

Another service currently rendered by United States branch offices is to point out to their customers and to their head offices opportunities for promoting trade in American products and possibilities for the opening of new contacts with foreign enterprises. The days are gone when the banker could calmly sit in his office, certain that those who were desirous of doing business with him would find the way to his retreat. Nowadays American bank officers overseas must be constantly vigilant to discover new concerns anxious to enter the local market or to make sales arrangements in the United States. Hence there are no more vigorous defenders of the reputation of the products of United States farms, mines and industries than the officers of United States bank branches. Little is publicly known of their patient labors in the promotion of United States commerce irrespective of any direct benefit to their employers. This spirit of intelligent enterprise, in addition to bringing benefits to American merchants and manufacturers, indirectly also builds United States prestige in distant continents. Furthermore, at critical times the personal contacts of private United States bankers and their quiet defense of their government's international policies have been of distinct assistance in the cultivation of friendly relations with the countries to which they are assigned or to which they pay periodical visits. They have been eloquent advocates of amity between nations, and as individuals they have rendered many services in the cause of solidarity and better understanding among the peoples of the world.

Opinions are divided as to the relative advantage of branches as against relationships where United States and foreign banks act as each other's agents. Wherever the volume of trade between the United States and a foreign country is substantial enough, offices managed by competent Americans, assisted by local talent and operating according to American business methods, have in practice best answered the needs of United States foreign trade. Most United States merchants and corporation executives prefer to entrust the bulk of their local banking transactions to them, knowing that the protection of their American customers' interests is their paramount concern.

In many countries, nevertheless, the existing volume of commercial intercourse is too small to justify the opening of branches, or else other nations already on the ground control most of the desirable accounts. Under these circumstances American banks can best work through local institutions with whom they often entertain close reciprocal correspondent relationships. Some New York and out-of-town banks, rather than maintain an elaborate network of foreign branches whose permanent earning power is uncertain, prefer connections with first-class foreign banks. They use their correspondents' local contacts and intimate association with the leading local business circles, and at the same time they derive advantages from the natural tendency of some foreign bank managers to favor those United States banks which do not compete with them in their own territory.

An intermediate solution of the problem of foreign representation is to have offices in London, Paris, and other capitals manned with either an officer or an able local agent with banking experience. Such offices sometimes trade in foreign exchange, but they do not accept deposits, and they serve merely as a convenience for the bank and its customers and correspondents at home. Familiar with local usages and idiosyncracies and entertaining friendly relations with the prominent business houses and banks of their district, these offices co-operate with their parent institutions by cultivating its clients and soliciting the patronage of desirable new customers. When they share with these their nationality and citizenship, they are sometimes successful in gaining a foothold in those cases where local *amour-propre* plays a role in the distribution of business among various contestants.

One of the more absorbing functions of the branches in the great tourist centers such as London and Paris is catering to the requirements of traveling Americans. Congregating at the offices of the United States banks and the American Express Company, the visitors cash checks, withdraw funds under letters of credit, exchange dollars for local money, obtain traveling and shopping information, make boat, train, and plane reservations, collect mail, and so forth. Many travelers carry letters of introduction from either the head office or some banking correspondent in the United States. By various small services the branch managers strive to win the good will of visitors and thus contribute to the strengthening of their relations with the home office. During the Second World War particularly, the branches rendered extensive help to the armed forces, the members of the Red Cross, and other patriotic, religious, and welfare organizations.

In the early days, since in certain instances the foreign-branch organization at the head offices in the United States had to be rather hurriedly improvised, it lacked at first the necessary full co-ordination and methodical direction and supervision. Gradually the administrative control was systematized so that the local activities and outstanding commitments could be reviewed periodically in the course of personal interviews with the managers on the occasion of their regular home leaves and personal trips by the territorial officers. Moreover, in the course of such conferences with the principal officers special subjects that did not lend themselves to discussion by correspondence or radiotelephone could be brought up and the required action taken without delay.

The men in charge of the foreign branches have no easy assignment. Sometimes they have to spend a great part of their lives in far-off places, without the comfort and associations enjoyed by those working at home. They may be living in countries where competition is sharp and where their reception is frigid. Even banks of the same nationality have been known to tread on each other's toes. The officers directing the most important foreign branches, such as those in London, Paris, and so forth, play a conspicuous role in shaping their institution's conduct of operations in their territories. Often they represent the banks in negotiations of consequence. For this reason it is essential to have at the helm of the branch offices in the leading financial centers sound and experienced bankers who possess initiative, courage, and flexibility. As a rule most of the managers in the main banking strongholds are veterans whose long stay and personal reputation add strength to the banks' standing in the local communities. One of their duties is also to retain cordial relations with the bank of issue and the government authorities on whose good will the bank's local progress often depends. While the possession of a wide acquaintance among banking and business circles in an undoubted and most valuable asset in the advancement of the affairs of their own particular office, yet they never forget that the interests of the branches and those of the parent institution as a whole are irrevocably linked together and that both work for a common objective.

The assistants of the branch managers in foreign countries also must be endowed with certain special qualifications. They must be chosen for both their educational background and their thorough training in the technique of banking. Past study in economics will be found to be a valuable asset in the studying of local conditions and the preparation of soundly elaborated reports on trade and finance, such as are often called for by the executives at home for their own or their customers' benefit. It is perhaps for this reason that newspaper work on the financial section of the great daily publications has in several instances led right into the top ranks of domestic and foreign banking. Americans working in foreign agencies enjoy a distinct advantage if they have at least a rudimentary knowledge of the language of the country to which they are assigned. On the other hand, a comprehensive knowledge of the country's usages and customs can be acquired only after long residence and personal observation. In the effort to establish pleasant personal relations with local customers and the members of the branch personnel the newcomer will be obliged to do much diplomatic spade work. In short, one must be pliant and show a certain degree of adaptability in order to feel at home far away from the mother country.

One essential requirement for men stationed abroad is that they be cosmopolitan in their sympathies. While remaining good Americans, they must endeavor to understand the *amour-propre* and pride that are the marked traits of all nations. They must know how to get on with men of widely different standards of business conduct and must understand the likes and dislikes of people of different races and upbringing. Those who have the gift of adjusting themselves easily to strange surroundings and alien ways of life, who are not afraid of an itinerant existence, and who are filled with the spirit of adventure and exploration are naturals for positions in foreign banking organizations abroad. Almost until the Second World War, in many branches overseas Englishmen, Canadians, Scotsmen, and also some French, Dutch, and Swiss nationals, trained in international banking and speaking several languages, formed the backbone of the staff of many foreign branch offices. The Second World War has brought the youth of our country into closer contact with foreign civilizations, and with it has come a greater appreciation of the advantages accruing to young men from service outside the United States. Hence their minds have begun to turn with newly awakened interest toward the international sphere.

The years between 1939 and 1945 have not been easy for those in the service of American banks abroad. Under most difficult conditions they did a hard job well. Through the trying years of war they carried on, and not enough tribute can be paid to their courage under even the most arduous circumstances. Through invasion and civil disturbances they clung to their posts, and when faced with capture or internment those who could escaped and opened emergency offices elsewhere from which they sought to serve the interests confided to them, while endeavoring at the same time to co-operate with the friendly governments whose hospitality they had so long enjoyed. In the correspondence files of the United States banks there is hidden many a story of the dramatic sufferings of loyal officers and employees who in the face of the mounting threats to peace refused to leave their station and paid by years of internment for their devotion to their institutions and their allegiance to the peoples among whom they had lived.

SUMMARY. American banks were early led to establish branches and representative offices in practically every part of the world, and in certain respects found definite advantages in a chain of banking offices as compared with a correspondent bank system. The chief services of the branches, especially with regard to the promotion of United States commerce, are outlined in this section, followed by a survey of the branch organization, the qualifications of the managers, their relations with the head office, their important contribution to the growth of friendly feelings for America in their respective areas, and finally the proved value to their institutions of recruiting and training competent and loyal personnel.

PART FIVE

THE OUTLOOK AFTER THE SECOND WORLD WAR

XVII

THE FUTURE PATTERN OF UNITED STATES FOREIGN BANKING

THE DISTURBED STATE of the world after the end of the Second World War delayed the full resumption of the normal operations of United States commercial banks in many foreign countries. After their emergence from the enforced state of relative quiescence imposed by wartime restrictions and government intervention in trade and finance, the banks with foreign organizations at first concentrated their principal efforts upon the reassembling and strengthening of their overseas personnel and the gradual renewal of former business relations in allied and neutral countries interrupted by hostilities.

Subsequently, despite the fact that the problem of exchange stabilization remained unsolved, United States banks started cautiously, but with progressively growing determination, to resume the extension of short-term credit so essential for the furtherance of American trade with Europe and Latin America. After the ravages of the long struggle, foreign buyers more than ever before needed assistance in bridging the period of the shipment and marketing of merchandise acquired in the United States. American manufacturers and merchants similarly benefited from the initiative of the banks in supplying needed credit facilities in those countries where the buyers or their banks were in a position to furnish the necessary cover in foreign exchange at the maturity of the credits.

Because of the continuing lack of financial equilibrium the banks were forced to proceed with great circumspection. Nevertheless, important headway was made in a relatively short time. Rather sooner than had been expected, they regained their former position, especially in western Europe. This is vividly demonstrated by an examination of the figures of the total volume of American bankers' acceptances outstanding at three crucial dates, which give a rather encouraging account of the progress during the years that have elapsed since the conclusion of the armistice. By July 30, 1945, American bankers' bills had declined to $116,717,000 from $235,033,000 on August 31, 1939, the eve of the outbreak of the war. Yet, by January 31, 1951, they had recovered to $453,275,000, equal to 192 percent of their prewar level. As a matter of comparison it may be noted that the highest point ever reported was on December 31, 1929, when outstanding short-term acceptances of United States banks totaled $1,732,000,000; [1] however, at that time the Central European short-term credits were still at their peak.

It is also significant that acceptances furnished to finance imports and exports were substantially higher in 1950 than in 1939, as shown by the following table.

ACCEPTANCES OUTSTANDING ACCORDING TO NATURE OF CREDIT [a]

	August 31, 1939	*August 31, 1950*
Imports	$78,512,000	$237,634,000
Exports	40,179,000	87,297,000
Domestic shipments	8,301,000	11,864,000
Domestic Warehouse	31,481,000	14,062,000
Dollar Exchange	17,635,000	1,372,000
Goods stored in or shipped between foreign countries	58,925,000	21,410,000
Grand total	$235,033,000	$373,639,000

[a] Source: Federal Reserve Bank of New York, *Monthly Acceptance Survey*, August, 1950.

Has the acceptance failed to keep its vantage position as a result of the war and its aftermath? From the figures presented here it would appear that in spite of disturbed world conditions the American bank acceptance has not forfeited its appeal as a desirable instrument for the financing of United States domestic and foreign trade. On the contrary, it has succeeded in regaining more than all of the ground lost after the outbreak of the Second World War. During 1950 in particular acceptances and letters of credit to finance imports were employed in a growing measure their use being stimulated by the re-

[1] Source: F. C. Lexa, *Bankers' Acceptances*, St. Louis, Missouri, Mercantile-Commerce Bank & Trust Company, 1946. See also the excellent article on *Bankers' Acceptances* in the Monthly Review of the Federal Reserve Bank of New York, January, 1951, vol. 33, No. 1, p. 4.

quirements for increased production and the re-armament program.

In this respect it must not be forgotten that a moderate part of the acceptance business of the commercial banks has been handled for the account of the Export-Import Bank. That institution has carried a portion of the risk involved in those credits, which, because of the length of the commitment or for other reasons, could not be taken by the private commercial banks. After the end of the war the Export-Import Bank's relations with the latter were generally confined to the issuance of sight commercial letters of credit, cash loans, and straight advances under the guarantee of the bank in conformity with the institution's policy—stressed by all its successive presidents and chairmen—of not entering into competition with commercial banking. Its board of directors recognized that it was unrealistic for government agencies to assume the burden of financing normal short-term requirements for United States and foreign merchants. By undertaking the share of the risk that is outside the scope of private banking, however, the bank has contributed conspicuously to the spread of the range of action of the commercial banks, notably during and since the end of the hostilities. In such cases, where without the backing of the government institution they would have been obliged reluctantly to hold back, the commercial banks were enabled not only to render service to valued customers but also to make a broader use of the facilities of their organizations at home and abroad.

Besides granting sight and acceptance credits and loans of a commercial character after the war syndicates of United States banks provided rehabilitation credits for various European countries. In February, 1945, the Netherlands Government, as noted elsewhere, contracted a credit, secured by gold, of 100 million dollars while a month later the Norges Bank, the central bank of Norway, received an unsecured revolving line of credit of 16 million dollars. In October, 1949, several American banks participated in a three-year revolving credit arranged by Dillon, Read & Co. for the Government of South Africa, and at the end of the same month an agreement was signed by the Chase National Bank and the Guaranty Trust Company of New York for a loan of 75 million dollars to the French Government, repayable in three to five years, for which gold of the Bank of France was deposited as security with the Federal Reserve Bank of New York. The National City Bank, J. P. Morgan & Co., the First National Bank of New York and the French-American Banking Corporation participated in this credit. In the autumn of 1950 the French Government obtained another loan of 225 million dollars from a banking group headed by the Chase National Bank of the City of New York and J. P. Morgan & Co.

Although following the war most European countries suffered from pronounced dollar anemia, the net capital movement to the United States, with the exception of the years 1946 and 1947, has shown a significant increase as reflected by the accompanying table.

INTERNATIONAL CAPITAL TRANSACTIONS
OF THE UNITED STATES [a]
Increase in foreign banking funds in U.S.

From through	*Total* (*In millions of dollars*)
1938–Dec. (Jan. 4, 1939)	1,513.9
1939–Dec. (Jan. 3, 1940)	2,522.4
1940–Dec. (Jan. 1, 1941)	3,239.3
1941–Dec. 31	2,979.6
1942–Dec. 31	3,465.5
1943–Dec. 31	4,644.8
1944–Dec. 31	4,865.2
1945–Dec. 31	6,144.5
1946–Dec. 31	5,272.3
1947–Dec. 31	4,120.3
1948–Dec. 31	5,119.5
1949–Dec. 31	5,226.0
1950–July 31	5,831.1
Aug. 31p	6,091.0
Sept. 30p	6,616.5

[a] Source: Federal Reserve Board, *Bulletin*, December, 1950, p. 1688.

Not included in the latter figure are the foreign banking funds in the International Institutions amounting to 1,626.6 millions as of July 31, 1950. It should also be noted that between 1945 and 1949 the United States monetary gold holdings rose by almost 4.7 billion dollars,[2] on September 21, 1949, reaching 24.7 billion, although Treasury statistics showed that during the succeeding fifteen months they declined by 1.7 billion reflecting both United States aid to European countries and withdrawals by foreign nations for the purpose of bolstering their reserves.

[2] Source: Federal Reserve Bank of New York, *Monthly Review*, November, 1950.

The circumstances that in the thirties made the United States a favored repository of vagrant capital still militated after the end of the war against the precipitate repatriation of that capital, although certain portions of the blocked funds released by the Foreign Property Control may have been converted into permanent investments here and abroad. The considerable dollar balances accumulated during the war by the neutral nations did not on the whole lead immediately to a heavy outflow of deposits. Moreover, because of the rise in the United States price level, higher working balances had to be maintained here, while the large amounts spent under the lend-lease program and the Marshall Plan also resulted in a temporary concentration of liquid capital pending its disbursement through commercial channels.

This brings us to a consideration of the effect on private banking of the activities of governmental agencies, such as the International Monetary Fund, the International Bank for Reconstruction and Development, and the Economic Cooperation Administration. The announced object of the Fund is the elimination of exchange risks by promoting exchange stability and the discouraging of indiscriminate exchange restrictions, multiple currency practices, and bilateral trade agreements; at the same time it contrives to assist members to bridge temporary balance-of-payment difficulties. Until September, 1949, the Fund was not able to deal as constructively as had been hoped with the complex monetary aspects of the postwar situation.

While the International Monetary Fund seeks only to aid in meeting a short-time disequilibrium in a member's balance of payments, the International Bank for Reconstruction and Development aims at encouraging and promoting the international flow of long-term capital. To the extent that it renders long-term financial assistance for the purpose of developing the productive facilities and resources of its members, the commercial banks operating in member countries are indirectly benefited by any improvement in economic conditions brought about by its lending, and for that matter, and to no less a degree, the financial activities of the Fund. The latter, as of August 31, 1950, had made net purchases of foreign currencies amounting to 759.8 million U.S. dollars (pounds sterling, French francs, Indian rupees, Netherlands guilders, Brazilian cruzeiros, and Mexican pesos being the most important) [3] and according to the New York *Herald*

[3] Source: Federal Reserve Board, *Bulletin*, October, 1950, p. 1412.

Tribune of October 31, 1950, the International Bank, as of October 30, 1950, had made loans in the principal amount of $1,017,245,000. During that month Eugene R. Black, president of the institution, announced an important departure from the bank's earlier policy of granting loans only to governments or government agencies. Loans had been made in Turkey and Mexico to local banks for the purpose of facilitating the purchase of American equipment and supplies required by local industries and business enterprises for which private investment capital or banking credit, because of the non-self-liquidating nature of the loans, could not be obtained at sufficiently attractive terms.

The Economic Cooperation Administration has also played a significant part in the expansion of the postwar operations of United States banks. This is graphically illustrated by the fact that, up to September 28, 1950, sixty United States banks had issued under ECA guarantee letters of commitment totaling $4,123,034,094 enabling merchants in twenty countries of Europe, Asia, and Africa to pay for their purchases in the Western Hemisphere. However, these foreign credits did not as a rule give rise to the creation of bankers' acceptances. Procurement under ECA is mainly financed by sight letters of credit, which provide for payment in cash upon delivery of the required shipping documents at the counters of the issuing banks. Dollarwise, the credits backed—directly or indirectly—by ECA are understood to have represented at certain times a substantial part of all sight letters of credit outstanding for account of United States banks.

From what has been disclosed of the importance of government-guaranteed operations in postwar banking, it would be misleading to conclude that such operations have had a harmful effect on the spirit of private banking enterprise. It would be mistaken also to believe that hereafter the commercial banks are likely to rely too much on government protection and that rather than shoulder risks themselves, they may become excessively subservient to official support in connection with their credit and lending operations throughout the world. It is certainly true that, confronted with external economic and political ills of unfathomable portent, the banks have been faced with a serious dilemma: they have had to choose between doing a considerably reduced volume of independent business, undertaken at the risk and peril of their stockholders or keeping their costly foreign organization intact and occupied during the transition phase by means of close collaboration with the administrative branches of the United States Government. They possessed what in the premises was most urgently needed: experience, technical know-how, and valuable personal contacts in every corner of the globe. By giving the various government agencies the benefit of their advice and assistance the banks served both the national cause and their own individual interest. In this manner the lack of adequate opportunities for the commercial extension of credit abroad was compensated by the facilities granted to foreign buyers for account of the Economic Cooperation Administration and the Export-Import Bank.

In the light of the present-day world situation it does not appear that government intervention in international trade and finance is likely to be dispensed with for some considerable time to come. However, this need not cause any undue concern to private banking enterprise. The policy followed so far by the United States authorities involved would seem to indicate that the latter will continue to limit their functions to those occasions where the use of private capital and credit is precluded because of either the nature of the risk, the length of accommodation required, or doubts that the borrowers will be able to repay short-term credits or loans in the lender's currency at maturity. Undoubtedly this was the intention of Congress when in the act creating the Economic Cooperation Administration it directed that commercial channels of trade be used to the maximum extent in carrying out the ECA program. Moreover, the ECA's practice of using letters of commitment was designed to encourage the establishment of lines of credit by the commercial banks in order to enable suppliers to finance their sales under the ECA program.

What are, then, the lessons that may be gleaned from the experience of the four decades since American foreign banking first came of age, and what is the outlook for the future? Viewing in retrospect the succession of events and series of changes through which it has evolved during these momentous years, one may venture to assert that United States banks, despite the harsh conditions to which they were exposed during and after two world wars, have on the whole shown a remarkable resiliency even under admittedly adverse circumstances. Notwithstanding many obstacles, they have continued their activities purposefully and vigorously. At the end of every interruption due to hostilities or financial disorders they have started again, with such caution as has been dictated by the local situation, to expand their operations wherever this can be done legitimately and expediently. After the recent war progress was made on a conservative basis, and there was absent the ill-considered overreaching that marked the period immediately after the First World War. Recovery of the ground lost during the years 1939–1945 would have been even greater had not official restrictions of various kinds seriously interfered with the systematic resumption of international commerce and handicapped normal banking operations.

If one compares present-day developments and problems with those which perplexed and harassed the international financial world back in the early twenties and thirties, one is tempted to agree with the ancient author of the Ecclesiastes that "there is nothing new under the sun." In some directions undoubtedly far-reaching changes of an entirely novel character have taken place. Yet, in retrospect, the difference between the conditions existing after 1918 and 1931 and those following 1945 are chiefly their magnitude and breadth rather than their fundamental nature. As has been shown through the pages of this book the world of those earlier years already had to contend with many of the taxing questions with which the nations all over the globe have recently been beset—exchange dislocations, undervaluation and overvaluation of moneys, maldistribution of gold, inconvertibility of currencies, the transfer problem, inflation, devaluations to readjust exchange rates, and economic nationalism, with its long list of trade restrictions that have oppressed world commerce and finance practically ever since the First World War.

Thus American foreign bankers have gone through a long and at times dearly paid-for period of training. More particularly during and since the Second World War United States finance may be truly credited with having put on an eminently meritorious performance in meeting the heavy duties imposed upon it in connection with the rehabilitation of the sadly depleted economies of the former Allies and even some of the late enemy countries. Nevertheless, in certain foreign quarters whose views deserve consideration, the opinion seems to prevail that the United States still lacks the qualifications that would make it a real center of monetary stability. These critics believe that the New York market is not yet sufficiently equipped with institutions and personnel specialized in matters of foreign financing. They assert that London provides a more finished apparatus for international banking and that not only Belgium and Switzerland but also France and Italy are likely in the future to make a worth-while contribution to international monetary equilibrium. Admitting that with active and generous United States support these latter countries have made gratifying progress during recent years, it is by no means certain that the prominent position in world finance that has been attained by this country is to be lost hereafter owing to failure on its part to develop a properly qualified banking organization and the mature skill and technique required in the financing of overseas trade. Yet, coming, as the judgment did, from well-informed sources, it cannot be disregarded. It should rather serve as a challenge to the American foreign banking community to improve and add to its facilities unceasingly and to frame and conduct its policies at home and abroad so as to furnish ever-growing and convincing proof of its fitness and determination to continue to play a leading and fruitful role in international affairs.

In any appraisal of the part that it may be called upon to perform in the future, a number of contingencies, pregnant with profound repercussions on United States foreign trade and finance, deserve careful consideration. United States exporters and importers, as well as commercial bankers, have rejoiced in the important steps taken in September, 1949, in the direction of restoring the mechanism of the exchanges. The elements that have been at work to promote the establishment of greater security in commercial intercourse between countries had just cause to be encouraged by the timely action of the various governments in devaluing their currencies. Yet, even disregarding the possibility of a future clash between the capitalistic and communistic worlds, there are some crucial questions which cannot be overlooked in any conjecture as to the future course of American banking overseas.

(1) Will United States exports, so tremendously expanded during the years 1945–1949 as a result of generous gifts and grants under the European Recovery Program and the vast expenditures for reconstruction by ECA as well as the liberal loans of the Export-Import Bank, not suffer a serious reverse when at some time in the future some of these activities may be either terminated or curtailed?

(2) Will not the devaluation of a great number of currencies, by raising the prices of American goods for foreign buyers in terms of their own moneys, bring about a sharp decline in American sales for export abroad that ordinarily are financed by the commercial banks?

(3) Will the prospective deficit in the supply of dollars in the event of a slackening of our foreign support after the expiration of the European Recovery Program be offset, at least in part, by an increase in our imports of foreign goods such as will give rise to a more balanced trading relationship between our country and the rest of the world and to a more rational and less erratic earning of dollars by our foreign buyers?

(4) Although until recently this nation controlled more than three fifths of the world's gold supply, is it not within the realm of possibilities that if the future flow of partly unrequited exports should indeed be seriously curtailed in the course of the coming years, the stability and soundness of the dollar itself may in time be questioned unless the drift toward inflation can be more firmly held in check and the trend toward continued budgetary financing more vigorously resisted?

As this last chapter is written, the events of the summer of 1950 seem to suggest answers to some of these queries that are at least partly encouraging. Spurred by the Korean War and the growing needs for rearmament, this country has become a greater importer of goods and commodities from the rest of the world. By the force of circumstances rather than of deliberate planning, it has thus been led to assume the classical obligations of a creditor nation. As a result, those countries that have surplus supplies of critical materials required for war production and for increasing the national stockpiles are being enabled to earn more coveted dollars. Already, owing to rising dollar prices and the accelerated tempo of United States purchases, the currencies of the western European countries have been greatly strengthened. Through their devaluation, a certain degree of monetary stability has been achieved. Import quotas and restrictions between some individual nations have been mitigated. The Swiss and Belgian currencies have been made fully convertible, the French franc has been stabilized *de facto,* and the Canadian dollar has been permitted to find its own level. Encouraging steps have been made toward the gradual economic integration of Europe. Because of the recovery of Britain and the sterling area and the disappearance of the dollar deficit, the governments of the United States and the United Kingdom have agreed to the suspension of Marshall aid to the United Kingdom from January 1, 1951. The currencies of seventeen nations represented in the Marshall Plan are to become mutually convertible through the instrumentality of the European Payments Union, which was formed to facilitate the "automatic multilateral compensation of surpluses and deficits arising out of intra-European trade." Generally the dollar gap has been narrowed, and Europe is expected to make gradual progress in its efforts to achieve the desired complete equilibrium in its global balance of payments that will promise the restoration of free markets for both its goods and its currencies. The Point Four Program for the economic development of underdeveloped areas has been incorporated into law to supplement—in the words of Nelson A. Rockefeller, chairman of the Advisory Board on International Development—"the contributions United States investors have made to the countries where they have gone." Along similar lines seven British Commonwealth countries have under consideration a Colombo Plan for Cooperative Economic Development in South and Southeast Asia involving, with the hoped-for United States participation, expenditures of $5,230,000,000 over the next six years while three colonial powers—Britain, France and Belgium—have under consideration development programs to cost additional $2,000,000,000. Finally, according to the recommendations of the *Report to the President on Foreign Economic Policy,* known as the Gray report, Europe is to continue to receive aid for three or four years after the end of the Marshall Plan, although the emphasis may be placed thereafter on the production of armaments and the increased supply of needed raw materials.

The impact of all these factors on American foreign trade and banking has not yet had time to make itself fully felt. It is too early fittingly to assess the effect of the important changes that have taken place during the past eventful years and months upon the volume of international business likely to accrue to United States banks in the times ahead. Some salient facts, however, may be cited that will indisputably affect some of their operations hereafter. While the promotion of an adequate volume of United States exports through private channels of trade will continue to be the motivating force of this country's industries it is nevertheless notable that our exports, amounting to 12,437 million dollars in 1949, have declined to 10,275 million in 1950. Imports aggregating 6,626 million dollars in 1949 have risen in 1950 to 8839.8 million. As a consequence of the Korean crisis and the threatening world situation the increased imports of merchandise and services, government expenditures overseas, tourist, and private disbursements, and some investment of private United States capital abroad (the latter reduced because of the uncertain foreign outlook), the foreign gold and dollar reserves in the United States amounted to 19,081 million dollars as of December 31, 1950, as compared with 15,300 million at the end of December, 1949.[4]

In the early months of 1951, because of the fear of war and the declining purchasing power of many currencies including the dollar, a growing tendency to export capital through conversion of soft currencies into dollars and to hoard gold was reflected by an increased turnover of the yellow metal in the free markets of Europe, the Middle East, and India where South Africa, Soviet Russia, the Belgian Congo, and France were reported to take advantage of the premium quoted as against the fixed price paid by the International Monetary Fund.

What are the general conclusions to be drawn from the changes in trends and policies here cursorily described, so far as the future of United States foreign banking is concerned? Provided that a third world war can be avoided and that the inflationary threat caused by the rearmament program can be removed or mitigated, it may be safe to assume that the European, Latin American, and Asiatic nations will persist in their efforts to expand their exports by raising productivity and lowering costs. In this case the potential loss to United States traders and banks as a result of a reduction in United States sales abroad will be compensated, at least to some extent, by the increase in demand for commercial letters of credit, acceptance financing, and foreign remittance and exchange transactions on the part of importers in the United States and overseas, as well as for dollar loans required by both domestic and foreign borrowers for the payment of goods in course of production and marketing. Moreover, an as yet indeterminable part of any future lag in this country's exports may be counterbalanced, as far as the business of United States financial institutions is involved, by the realignment of and the enlarged trading between the various foreign-currency areas. Given a relaxation in international tension and a loosening of exchange and trade controls where these still exist, United States banks will be prepared, as in former normal times and under proper safeguards, to finance shipments resulting from international exchanges of merchandise. Besides, if world peace can be maintained and internal conditions are such as to in-

4 Source: Bank for International Settlements, *Twenty-First Annual Report,* Basle, June 11, 1951, p. 163.

spire confidence to private capital and business enterprise, the demand for United States financial support should receive a strong impulse through the coming decades as the productivity of newly developed areas of the globe is stimulated by the introduction of modern technical processes and machinery. With the restoration of the European economy well on its way and given reasonable assurance of the maintenance of peace, United States finance and trade interests will again be aroused as in the past to assume the risks of large-scale investments for the exploitation of mineral and waterpower resources and for the uncovering of the immense untapped natural wealth of many still virgin regions in Latin America, Africa, and Asia. Of course, pledges of fair treatment must be secured in the matter of repatriation of capital and other assets, the unfettered movement of commerce and credit must be assured by multilateral legislation and defensive treaties, and protection must be given against expropriation of property, and invested rights, and discriminatory trade agreements.

Although the longer view is obscured by the discouraging external outlook it may be confidently asserted that, as and when conditions will again favor the expansion of the financial and commercial action of this country throughout the earth, the nation's commercial banks will be prepared—deriving inspiration and encouragement from the lessons of the past—to devote their earnest efforts to add to the massive record of achievement which we have attempted to portray in this volume. Then, after the era of stress and strain of its adolescence, it may be hoped that the future evolution of United States foreign banking will unfold in a more serene atmosphere, and yet along progressively wider and auspicious paths.

SUMMARY

However crucial the tests that beset foreign departments during the last war, in some respects the difficulties encountered since then have been immeasurably greater. Yet, notwithstanding the still prevailing derangement in economic conditions in certain countries abroad, statistics show decided progress in many instances, notably in the field of American bankers' acceptance credits. Furthermore, the Export-Import Bank has continued to make extensive use of the facilities of United States commercial banks, and a number of short-term private rehabilitation loans have been arranged by United States banking syndicates for the benefit of European borrowers since the close of the Second World War. The Economic Cooperation Administration, too, has made use of the services of the commercial banks in connection with the purchases by foreign countries financed under the European Recovery Program. Despite the adverse circumstances, American foreign banking may be said, on the whole, to have made satisfactory progress, at the same time that it has been helping Europe's and the world's recovery from the war. Considerable can be learned from past experience. The chapter closes with an analysis of some of the factors that may hamper the future advance of United States foreign banking and of others that on the contrary may exert a favorable influence on its course.

BIBLIOGRAPHY

GENERAL WORKS

Anderson, B. M. Economy and the Public Welfare. New York, E. van Nostrand Co., Inc., 1949.
Angell, James W. Financial Foreign Policy of the United States. New York, Council on Foreign Relations, 1933.

Baster, A. S. J. The International Banks. London, P. S. King & Son, 1935.
Beckhart, Benjamin Haggott. The Discount Policy of the Federal Reserve System. New York, Henry Holt & Co., 1924.
—— The New York Money Market. New York, Columbia University Press, 1932, Vol. III.
Bernstein, E. M. Money and the Economic System. Chapel Hill, N.C., The University of North Carolina Press, 1935.
Beyen, J. W. Money in a Maelstrom. New York, The Macmillan Co., 1949.
Bradford, Frederick A. Money and Banking. New York, Longmans Green & Co., 1937.
Brown, Harry Gunnison. International Trade and Exchange. New York, The Macmillan Co., 1914.
Burgess W. Randolph. The Reserve Banks and the Money Market. New York, Harper & Brothers, 1927.

Cassel, Gustav. The Crisis of the World's Monetary System. Oxford, The Clarendon Press, 1932.
Crump, Norman. *The A B C of the Foreign Exchanges.* London, Macmillan & Co., Ltd., 1951.

Deutsch, Henry. Arbitrage. London, Effingham Wilson, 1910.
De Vegh, Imre. The Pound Sterling. New York, Scudder, Stevens & Clark, 1939.
Djoerup, Christian. Foreign Exchange Accounting. New York, Prentice Hall, Inc., 1926.
Dulles, Eleanor Lansing. The Dollar, the Franc and Inflation. New York, The Macmillan Co., 1933.
—— The Bank for International Settlements at Work. New York, The Macmillan Co., 1932.

Edie, Lionel D. Dollars. New Haven, Yale University Press, 1934.
Edwards, George W. International Trade Finance. New York, Henry Holt & Co., 1924.

Edwards, George W. Investing in Foreign Securities. New York, The Ronald Press Co., 1926.
—— Principles of Banking and Finance. New York, The Ronald Press Co., 1932.
Einzig, Paul. Bankers, Statesmen and Economists. London, Macmillan & Co., Ltd., 1935.
—— The Theory of Forward Exchanges. London, Macmillan & Co., Ltd., 1937.
—— World Finance, 1914–1935. New York, The Macmillan Co., 1935.
—— Foreign Balances. London, Macmillan & Co., Ltd., 1938.
Ellis, Howard S. Exchange Control in Europe. Cambridge, Harvard University Press, 1941.
Everest, Allan Seymour. Morgenthau; the New Deal and Silver. New York, The King's Crown Press, 1950.
Evitt, H. E. An Introduction to the Practice of Foreign Exchange. London, Sir Isaac Pitman & Sons, Ltd., 1932.

Feis, Herbert. Europe, the World's Banker, 1870–1914. New Haven, Yale University Press, 1930.
—— The Spanish Story. New York, Alfred A. Knopf, 1948.
Feuerlein, Willy, and Elizabeth Hannan. Dollars in Latin America. New York, Council on Foreign Relations, 1941.

Gonzales, V. Modern Foreign Exchange. New York, C. S. Hammond & Co., 1920.
Gordon, David L., and Royden Dangerfield. The Hidden Weapon: The Story of Economic Warfare. New York, Harper & Brothers, 1947.
Graham, Frank D. and Charles R. Whittlesey, Golden Avalanche. Princeton, Princeton University Press, 1939.
Gregory, T. E. Foreign Exchange before, during, and after the War. New York, Oxford University Press, 1921.
—— The Gold Standard and Its Future. New York, P. Dutton & Co., Inc., 1932.

Hall, Ray Orvid. International Transactions of the United States. New York, National Industrial Conference Board, 1936.
Harris, C. R. S. Germany's Foreign Indebtedness. London, Oxford University Press, 1935.
Heilperin, Michael A. International Monetary Economics. New York, Longmans Green & Co., 1939.

International Chamber of Commerce. International Economic Reconstruction. Paris, 1936. Vol. II.
International Chamber of Commerce and Carnegie Endowment Joint Committee. The Problem of Monetary Stabilization. Paris, International Chamber of Commerce, 1936.

Irving Trust Company. International Financial Stabilization. New York, 1946.

Johnson, Griffith G. The Treasury and Monetary Policy. Cambridge, Mass., Harvard University Press, 1939.

Kemmerer, Edwin Walter. Money. New York, The Macmillan Co., 1935.

—— Inflation and Revolution; Mexico's Experience, 1912–17. Princeton, Princeton University Press, 1940.

Keynes, John Maynard. Monetary Reform. New York, Harcourt, Brace & Co., 1924.

Kisch, C. H., and W. A. Elkin. Central Banks. London, Macmillan & Co., Ltd., 1928.

League of Nations. The Course and Phases of the World Economic Depression. Geneva, Secretariat, League of Nations, 1931.

—— Economic Stability in the Post-War World. Geneva, 1945. Part II.

Lechner, O. As We Saw It in Prague. 2d ed. London, George Allen & Unwin, Ltd., 1943.

Lester, Richard A. Monetary Experience, Early American and Recent Scandinavian. Princeton, Princeton University Press, 1939.

Lewis, Cleona. America's Stake in International Investments. Washington, D.C., The Brookings Institute, 1938.

McQueen, Charles A. Latin American Postwar Monetary Standards. New York, The Monetary Standard Inquiry, 1943.

Madden, John T. and Marcus Nadler. The International Money Markets. New York, Prentice-Hall, Inc., 1935.

Madden, John T. Marcus Nadler, and Harry C. Sauvain. America's Experience as a Creditor Nation. New York, Prentice-Hall, Inc., 1937.

Margraff, Anthony W. International Exchange. New York, International Exchange, 1912.

Morton, Walter A. British Finance, 1930–40. Madison, Wis., University of Wisconsin Press, 1943.

Moulton, Harold G. Financial Organization and the Economic System. New York, McGraw Hill Book Co., Inc., 1938.

Myers, Margaret G. Paris as a Financial Centre. London, P. S. King & Son, Ltd., 1936.

—— The League Loans. New York, Academy of Political Science, 1945.

Nadler, Marcus, and Jules I. Bogen. The Banking Crisis the End of an Epoch. New York, Dodd Mead & Co., 1933.

National Industrial Conference Board, Inc. The International Position of the United States. New York. 1929.

Paris, James Daniel. Monetary Policy of the United States, 1932–38. New York, Columbia University Press, 1938.

Patterson, E. L. Stewart. Canadian Banking. Toronto, The Ryerson Press, 1941.

Phelps, Clyde William. The Foreign Expansion of American Banks. New York, The Ronald Press Co., 1927.

Philippe, Raymond. Le Drame financier de 1924–28. Paris, Librairie Gallimard, 1931.

Princeton University, International Finance Section. Survey of United States International Finance, 1949. Princeton University Press, 1950.

Redelmeier, W. The Gold Standard. Toronto, The MacLean Publishing Co., Ltd., 1941.

Richards, Frank A. The Marketing of Cotton and the Financing of Cotton Merchants. New Brunswick, Rutgers University, 1948.

Rogers, James Harvey. America Weighs Her Gold. New Haven, Yale University Press, 1931.

Sédillot, René. Le Drame des monnaies. 2d ed. Paris. Librairie du Recueil Sirey, 1937.

Shaterian, William S. Export-Import Banking. New York, The Ronald Press Co., 1948.

Somary, Felix. Bankpolitik. Tuebingen, J. C. B. Mohr (Paul Siebeck), 1930.

Southard, Frank A., Jr. Foreign Exchange Practice and Policy. New York, McGraw Hill Book Co., Inc., 1940.

—— The Finances of European Liberation. New York, King's Crown Press, 1946.

Spalding, William F. Eastern Exchange, Currency and Finance. London, Sir Isaac Pitman & Son, Ltd., 1917.

Tate's Modern Cambist. 25th ed. by H. T. Easton. London, Effingham Wilson, 1912.

Thomas, S. Evelyn. The Principles and Arithmetic of Foreign Exchange. 6th ed. London, Macdonald & Evans, 1934.

United States Department of Commerce. The United States in the World Economy. Washington, D.C., Bureau of Foreign and Domestic Commerce, 1943. Economic Series No. 23.

United States Treasury Department. Census of Foreign-Owned Assets in the United States. Washington, D.C., 1945.

Van Zealand, Paul. Regards sur l'Europe. Brussels, Office de Publicité, 1932.

Waight, Leonard. The History and Mechanism of the Exchange Equalization Account. London, Cambridge University Press, 1939.

Ward, Wilbert. American Commercial Credits. New York, The Ronald Press Co., 1922.

Whitacker, Albert C. Foreign Exchange. New York, D. Appleton & Co. 1919.
Whittlesey, Charles R. International Monetary Issues. New York, The McGraw Hill Book Co., Inc., 1937.
Willis, H. Parker, and B. H. Beckhart. Foreign Banking Systems. New York, Henry Holt & Co., 1929.
Willis, H. Parker, and George W. Edwards. Banking and Business. New York, Harper & Brothers, 1925.
Willis, H. Parker, and William H. Steiner. Federal Reserve Banking Practice. New York, D. Appleton & Co., 1926.
Woodward, Donald B., and Marc A. Rose. A Primer of Money. New York, The McGraw Hill Book Co., Inc., 1935.

Young, John Parke. European Currency and Finance. Foreign Currency and Exchange Investigation, Washington, D.C., Government Printing Office, 1925.

SERIAL PUBLICATIONS

Bank for International Settlements, Basle. Annual reports.

Federal Reserve Bank of New York. Annual reports.
—— Monthly Review of Credit and Business Conditions.
Federal Reserve Board. Annual reports. Washington, D.C., Government Printing Office.
—— Bulletin (monthly). Washington, D.C., Board of Governors of the Federal Reserve System.

International Bank for Reconstruction and Development. Annual reports. Washington, D.C.
International Monetary Fund. Financial News Survey. Washington, D.C.

INDEX

Bei Fragen zur Produktsicherheit wenden Sie sich bitte an:
If you have any questions regarding product safety,
please contact:

Walter de Gruyter GmbH
Genthiner Straße 13
10785 Berlin
productsafety@degruyterbrill.com